I0161098

BIBLE IN
DIALOGUE
2

Studies in
Judaism and Christianity

Exploration of Issues in the Contemporary Dialogue Between Christians and Jews

Editors
Kevin A. Lynch, CSP
Michael McGarry, CSP
Mark-David Janus, CSP
Yehezkel Landau
Dr. Peter Pettit
Dr. Elena Procario-Foley
Dr. Ann Riggs

 A STIMULUS BOOK

Paul's Jewish Matrix

THOMAS G. CASEY - JUSTIN TAYLOR (eds.)

With an introductory essay by Karl P. Donfried

We would like to express in a special way our gratitude
to Herbert and Aldegonde Brenninkmeijer-Werhahn.
Their generous support has helped
bring this volume to fruition.

Cover: Serena Aureli

Layout: Lisanti sri - Roma

Piazza della Pilotta, 35 - 00187 Roma, Italy
www.gbpress.net - books@biblicum.com

Stimulus Book edition published in the United States in 2011 by Paulist Press
997 Macarthur Boulevard, Mahwah, New Jersey 07430
www.paulistpress.com

Library of Congress Control Number: 20111923239

ISBN: 978-0-8091-4740-3

Printed and bound in the United States of America

Table of Contents

Contributors 7

Editors' Foreword 9

Introductory Essay
Paul's Jewish Matrix:
The Scope and Nature of the Contributions
Karl P. Donfried 11

Chapter 1
Paul's Jewishness
E. P. Sanders 51

Chapter 2
Paul's Stance on the Torah Revisited: Gentile Addressees and the Jewish Setting
Serge Ruzer 75

Chapter 3
Paul, the Pharisee, and the Law
Antonio Pitta 99

Chapter 4
Paul and the *gezerah shawah*: A Judaic Method in the Service of Justification by Faith
Pasquale Basta 123

Chapter 5
The Heavenly Journey in Paul: Tradition of a Jewish Apocalyptic Literary Genre or Cultural Practice in a Hellenistic-Roman Context?
Adriana Destro and Mauro Pesce 167

Chapter 6
Paul, Moses, and the Veil: Paul's Perspective on Judaism in Light of 2 Corinthians 3
Emmanuel Nathan and Reimund Bieringer 201

Chapter 7
Paul, Deicide, and the Wrath of God: Towards a Hermeneutical Reading of 1 Thess 2:14–16
Didier Pollefeyt and David J. Bolton 229

Chapter 8
From Permission to Prohibition: Paul and the Early Church on Mixed Marriage
Shaye J. D. Cohen 259

Chapter 9
"Someone who considers something to be impure – for him it is impure" (Rom 14:14): Good Manners or Law?
Daniel R. Schwartz 293

Chapter 10
Paul and the Jewish Leaders at Rome: Acts 28:17–31
Justin Taylor 311

Chapter 11
Judaizing the Nations: The Ritual Demands of Paul's Gospel
Paula Fredriksen 327

Bibliography 355

Pasquale BASTA is Professor of Biblical Hermeneutics at the Pontifical Biblical Institute in Rome, and Professor of Scripture at the Seminary of Basilicata, Italy.

Reimund BIERINGER is Professor of New Testament Exegesis in the Faculty of Theology of the Katholieke Universiteit Leuven, Belgium.

David BOLTON is a doctoral candidate in Christian-Jewish relations at the Katholieke Universiteit Leuven, Belgium.

Shaye J. D. COHEN is the Littauer Professor of Hebrew Literature and Philosophy in the Department of Near Eastern Languages and Civilizations of Harvard University.

Adriana DESTRO is Professor of Cultural Anthropology at the University of Bologna, Italy.

Karl Paul DONFRIED is the Elizabeth A. Woodson Professor Emeritus of New Testament Studies at Smith College in Northampton, Massachusetts, USA.

Paula FREDRIKSEN is the William Goodwin Aurelio Chair Emerita of the Appreciation of Scripture at Boston University, USA.

Emmanuel NATHAN is a post-doctoral researcher at the Faculty of Theology in the Katholieke Universiteit Leuven, Belgium.

Mauro PESCE is Professor of the History of Christianity at the University of Bologna, Italy.

Antonio PITTA is Professor of New Testament at the Pontifical Lateran University, Rome, Italy.

Didier POLLEFEYT is Professor of Pastoral Theology in the Katholieke Universiteit Leuven, Belgium.

Serge RUZER is Professor in the Department of Comparative Religion at the Hebrew University, Jerusalem, Israel.

E. P. Sanders is Emeritus Professor of Religion at Duke University, North Carolina, USA.

Daniel R. Schwartz is Professor of Jewish History at the Hebrew University, Jerusalem, Israel.

Justin Taylor is Professor of New Testament and Christian Origins at the École Biblique, Jerusalem, Israel.

Editors' Foreword

Thomas G. Casey, SJ
Justin Taylor, SM

To mark the 'Year of St Paul' in 2009, the Cardinal Bea Centre for Judaic Studies of the Pontifical Gregorian University, in collaboration with the Pontifical Biblical Institute, the Centre for the Study of Christianity of the Hebrew University of Jerusalem, the Catholic University of Leuven and the Papal Basilica of St Paul Outside the Walls, organized an international symposium on the subject of 'Paul in his Jewish Matrix'. This was held in Rome from 20 to 22 May, 2009, and was attended by scholars from Italy, Israel, the United States and Belgium, both Jews and Christians. The present volume is a collection of most of the papers and lectures presented at the symposium.

A printed book can reproduce the texts of the various contributions. It cannot, however, convey the collegial and cordial atmosphere – not without a due element of critical attentiveness – that characterised these days in Rome. The out-of-town colleagues were hospitably housed and fed at the guesthouse 'Domus Internationalis Paulus VI', in the historic heart of the Eternal City. Most of the presentations were given at the Pontifical Biblical Institute or at the Pontifical Gregorian University, whose rectors, respectively Rev. Fr. José María Abrego De Lacy, SJ, and Rev. Fr. Gianfranco Ghirlanda, SJ, welcomed the participants. As well as prepared conference papers, the presentations also included a public lecture by Professor E.P. Sanders, on 'Paul's Jewishness', which heads the collection in this volume, and the annual Brenninkmeijer-Werhahn lecture given by Professor Emmanuel Tov, of the Hebrew University of Jerusalem and the Pontifical Gregorian University, on 'The Septuagint Between Judaism and Christianity', which is published elsewhere. On the final morning, the symposium was held – most appropriately – at the Papal

Basilica of St Paul Outside the Walls, traditional site of St Paul's burial. Participants were welcomed by His Em. Card. Andrea Cordero Lanza di Montezemolo, Archpriest of the Basilica and by Abbot Edmund Power, OSB, Abbot of the Benedictine Community that serves St Paul's. At the conclusion of the discussions, Cardinal Montezemolo gave the participants a personally guided tour of the church and its museum. Be it noted in passing that not only was the Cardinal the first Apostolic Nuncio to Israel, but that, during the Second World War, his father was executed in the Ardeatine caves near Rome along with Jewish and other non-Jewish Italians.

The subject of 'Paul in his Jewish Matrix' is obviously of the highest interest as well as raising a number of delicate issues regarding the origins of Christianity and Christian and Jewish identity, in particular the interplay of continuity and rupture between the apostle and the Judaism that formed him. It was a noteworthy feature of the symposium that Jews and Christians could discuss these matters not only with serenity but also with a surprisingly high level of agreement. We are grateful to the noted Pauline scholar Professor Karl P. Donfried for graciously undertaking to present and discuss the contents of this volume. Professor Donfried was not present at the Rome symposium. He is therefore able to take an external point of view in assessing its contribution to Pauline studies.

It remains for us as editors of the volume to thank all those who worked to make the gathering in Rome a success: in the first place Professor Joseph Sievers, at the time Director of the Cardinal Bea Centre, who took on the greater part of organizing and running the event, with the discrete and efficacious assistance of the Centre's Secretary, Ms. Flavia Galiani; also the symposium's hosts, the Pontifical Biblical Institute, the Pontifical Gregorian University and the Papal Basilica of St Paul Outside the Walls; the other academic institutions who contributed to the symposium, namely the Hebrew University of Jerusalem and the Catholic University of Leuven. Finally we wish to thank the contributors themselves, especially for their co-operation in hastening the publication of this volume.

PAUL'S JEWISH MATRIX
THE SCOPE AND NATURE OF THE CONTRIBUTIONS

Karl P. Donfried

The work of this conference on "Paul in His Jewish Matrix" is of extraordinary importance since it tackles a series of issues foundational for the proper understanding of Pauline thought. During the decades of the 1970s and 1980s forceful criticism was leveled at the failure to include Judaism as an essential component in the interpretation of Pauline theology or, when applied, that its application often represented a deficient and distorted perspective of first century Judaism. The resultant attempts at correction engendered an entire new set of questions, many to this day unanswered, including how Paul the Jew is to be understood given the internal diversification of Judaism and the often harsh polemical tensions within and between the various Torah schools.[1]

A wall that has made an analysis of the Jewish Paul a virtually impenetrable phenomenon includes the distorting and commonly used descriptors "Judaism" and "Christian/Christianity." On the hand it must be asked whether the term "Judaism," as it is frequently perceived, allows for an adequate view of both the diversity and polemics inherent in late Second Temple Judaism and, on the other hand, whether the categories "Christian/Christianity" do not automatically place the Jesus movement as a development external to the Judaisms[2] of the period. The importance of this last query takes on particular significance since Paul never uses the terminology "Christian/Christianity" and the entire New Testament only uses the terms "Christian/Christians" three times (Acts 11:26; 26:28; 1 Pet

---

[1] For a brief overview, see Karl P. Donfried, "Rethinking Paul: On the Way Toward a Revised Paradigm," *Biblica* 87 (2006): 582-594.

[2] A term to be further defined and discussed in this introductory essay; see below 40-42.

4:16). For contemporary scholars to give prominence to such uncommon New Testament language in discussing both Paul and Pauline thought retrojects characterizations from a much later period that frequently lead to blatant distortions. Paul refers to believers in Christ as "saints" (eg., Rom 1:7; 1 Cor 1:2) and he views himself as part of a larger, broader Jesus movement, thoroughly Jewish both in its roots and in its contours, that he never characterizes as either "Christian" or as "Christianity."

Given these late twentieth century developments as well as the resulting questions, we have reached a point in time when the issues inherent in the theme "Paul in His Jewish Matrix" have become exceptionally relevant. A more precise profile of Paul's Jewish matrix and his "Jewishness", as well as his intramural conflict with some of the Judaisms of his day, will require sustained focus and concentration. And it is precisely with that expectation and hope that we turn to the essays that follow.

1. E. P. SANDERS, *PAUL'S JEWISHNESS*

This essay by Ed Sanders, among the most distinguished interpreters of Judaism and Paul, seeks to define what it means to speak of "Paul's Jewishness."[3] The fact that Paul's thought is comprehensively Jewish is suggested by key dimensions of Judaism that he shares: 1. a "Jewish form of modified monotheism;"[4] 2. a Jewish understanding of time and history that was "highly eschatological;"[5] 3. a Jewish "vision of the world"[6] that served as the basis for Paul's mission; and, 4. an understanding of ethics that was distinctively Jewish. Although Paul's theology is deeply Jewish, he nevertheless distinguishes his own group from what he refers to as "Judaism" (*Ioudaïsmos*). Based on the use of the noun "Judaism"

---

3 E. P. Sanders, "*Paul's Jewishness*," 51-73.
4 Sanders, "*Paul's Jewishness*," 62.
5 Sanders, "*Paul's Jewishness*," 63.
6 Sanders, "*Paul's Jewishness*," 63.

in Gal 1:13-14, Sanders concludes that Paul does not use this term to refer to his "present in-group"[7] but rather to "his earlier life in Judaism" (Gal 1:13); rather, Paul refers to his group in a number of ways including the term "congregation" (Sander's preferred translation for [*ekklêsia*]; see 1 Thess 2:14; 1 Cor 10:32; 11:16) and the phrase *hoi pisteuontes* ("those who believe" 1 Thess 1:7; 2:10, 13; Rom 1:16).

Sanders continues that (a) "Paul's converts" are "'Christians,' people 'in Christ,' not 'Jews' or 'Israelites.'" The reference in 1 Cor 10:32 ("Give no offense to Jews, or to Greeks, or to the church of God") gives evidence to "the *social fact* that Paul inhabited a tri-partite world: there were Jews, pagans and those who belonged to Christ, some of whom had belonged to Judaism, and some to paganism."[8] Further (b), in order to sustain this line of argument Sanders urges that "there is no indication of Jewish converts within his own churches"[9] and, further, that there "is no hint that Paul's converts attended synagogues."[10] This being the case, Sanders concludes that there is no "evidence that Paul viewed his churches as the 'true Israel'...", a view argued by some on the basis of Gal 6:16 and Gal 3:16-29.[11] Sensing that his analysis may raise questions, Sanders wonders whether some "will think that this social and terminological distinction between Paul's group and Judaism means that I have just claimed that Paul stopped being Jewish. His self-identity is another issue entirely. He was Jewish and regarded himself as the Jewish apostle to Gentiles in the last days."[12] Further, the case is made that "we must note his strong conviction that he and other members of the body of Christ acquired a new identity. Paul was a Jew who had become one person with Christ. And, as he wrote, if anyone is in Christ, he is a 'new creation' (2 Cor 5:17). Nevertheless,

[7] Sanders, "*Paul's Jewishness*," 64.
[8] Sanders, "*Paul's Jewishness*," 66.
[9] Ibidem.
[10] Ibidem.
[11] Sanders, "*Paul's Jewishness*," 64-65, n. 21.
[12] Sanders, "*Paul's Jewishness*," 68.

being one person with Christ, part of a new creation, did not make Paul himself a non-Jew. Jesus was a Jew (Rom 9:5), and we cannot think that at any point Paul would have rejected his ethnic identity. He was a Jew who was in Christ, and his converts were Gentiles who were in Christ."[13] As a result the conclusion is reached that Paul "was Jewish as well as a new person in Christ, but his congregations did not constitute 'Judaism,' which was a separate entity."[14]

Especially significant for the current scholarly discussion is the affirmation that Paul "in his own mind...did not stop being Jewish"[15] even though other Jews might have disagreed. Given the importance of this assertion it is urgent to query whether the following conclusions reached by Sanders are consistent with and cohere with this proposition, including that:

1. "there is no indication of Jewish converts within his own churches"?[16] Should this be the case, how does one explain Paul's intention "to win Jews" in 1 Cor 9:20?

2. the Pauline followers of Christ were "not 'Jews' or 'Israelites"? If this is true how can one assert that "we cannot think that at any point Paul would have rejected his ethnic identity. He was a Jew who was in Christ..."?[17] Why could not such an assertion be made about the members of the Pauline churches who are Jews and also, like the Apostle, in Christ?

3. there "is no hint that Paul's converts attended synagogues"?[18] Is this a not too restrictive view of the synagogue in the Graeco-Roman world? Does not the evidence increasingly suggest that the synagogue was a community-gathering place not only for diaspora Jews but for Gentile as well?

---

[13] Sanders, "*Paul's Jewishness,*" 68.
[14] Sanders, "*Paul's Jewishness,*" 69.
[15] Sanders, "*Paul's Jewishness,*" 68, n 27.
[16] Sanders, "*Paul's Jewishness,*" 66.
[17] Sanders, "*Paul's Jewishness,*" 68.
[18] Sanders, "*Paul's Jewishness,*" 66.

4. Paul did not consider "his churches as the 'true Israel'..."[19] An examination of this conclusion will require an in depth discussion of Paul's intention when he uses the term "Israel of God" in Gal 6:16 as well as a detailed probing into Paul's mind when in Rom 11:13-24 he unequivocally declares that Gentile Christians were "grafted in... to share the rich root of the olive tree... (Rom 11:17). Essential to such an inquiry will be to determine the meaning of both the terms "root" and "olive tree" and what it means that as a result of such engrafting the Gentile believers are "holy" (ἅγιος; Rom 11:16).

Certain to stimulate further conversation is Sanders's proposal that Paul's use of biblical quotations suggests that he had memorized the Bible in Greek. Should this be the case it would explain why a good number of Paul's quotations are conflated, as well as the fact that the language of the Greek Bible influences such letters as Philemon, 1 Thessalonians, Philippians and 2 Cor 10-13 where there is no explicit quotation from Jewish Scripture but where its influence is evident as, for example, in Phil 2:15 where language such as "blemish" and "crooked and perverse generation" is taken from the Greek translation of Deut 32:5. Sanders is quick to add that such intimate knowledge of the Greek Bible does not in any way preclude that Paul either studied in Jerusalem or was conversant with the Bible in Hebrew.[20]

A further probing of this intriguing proposal will require consideration of the words found in 2 Tim 4:13, a text that describes Paul addressing his co-worker Timothy with these words: "When you come, bring the cloak that I left with Carpus at Troas, also the books (τὰ βιβλία) and above all the parchments (τὰς μεμβράνας)." The major issue in 2 Tim 4:13 is the meaning of the term "parchments" (τὰς μεμβράνας). In Latin, the term *membrana* became the term for parchment and is taken over into the Greek as μεμβράνα. But its usage in Greek seems clearly connected with the codex, the technical term for a leaf book. It is likely that the reference in 2 Tim 4:13

[19] Sanders, "*Paul's Jewishness*," 65, n 21.
[20] Sanders, "*Paul's Jewishness*," 61.

is specifically referring to "parchment notebooks" for which there is sufficient evidence that they were pocket anthologies intended for the convenience of the traveler. Sanders is correct when he mentions the impracticality of Paul carrying scrolls with him[21] and it is hard to imagine that when arguing in a synagogue that he would roll and unroll many feet of papyrus scrolls to find the relevant texts. One alternative to this cumbersome process is the suggestion that Paul had memorized the entire Greek Bible. Another would be that the *membrana* just mentioned would provide a vehicle that would allow Paul to collect the necessary reference texts that he would require for these discussions.[22] These parchment codices would, in addition to providing inexpensive and convenient compactness for the travelling missionary since both sides of the page could be used, serve as testimony books with easy to find proof texts, a phenomenon not to distant from the 4QFlorilegium (4Q174).

2. SERGE RUZER, *PAUL'S STANCE ON THE TORAH REVISITED: GENTILE ADDRESSEES AND THE JEWISH SETTING*

A major thesis of this essay is that dimensions of Paul's attitude toward the Torah that have been found to be problematic may well reflect tensions current within an intra-Jewish setting and thus already present in pre-Christian Judaism. Ruzer expresses a high degree of skepticism with regard to an interpretation which maintains that Paul's positive evaluation of the Law was intended for Jews alone, that the "denial of the salvific effectiveness of its commandments"[23] were exclusively directed at those Gentiles who joined the

[21] Sanders, "*Paul's Jewishness*," 54.

[22] For further details see "Paul as ΣΚΗΝΟΠΟΙΟΣ and the Use of the Codex in Early Christianity," in Karl P. Donfried, *Paul, Thessalonica and Early Christianity* (Edinburgh and Grand Rapids: T. & T. Clark and Eerdmans, 2002), 293-304.

[23] Serge Ruzer, "*Paul's Stance on the Torah Revisited: Gentile Addressees and the Jewish Setting*," 75-97, here 71.

Jesus movement, and, further, that Paul's intended audience was exclusively non-Jewish. Rather, the so-called "anti-Torah" assertions suggest a group of Jewish agitators within the broader Jesus movement who are subsequently identified as those "who are with James (Gal 1:19; 2:6-11, 12-14)."[24] Important here is Gal 2:15-16 ("We ourselves, who are Jews by birth and not gentile sinners, yet who know that a man is not justified by works of the Torah but through faith in Jesus Christ, even we have believed in Christ Jesus, in order to be justified by faith in Christ, and not by works of the Torah, because by works of the Torah shall no one be justified") which cannot be dismissed as "mere rhetoric"[25] and which also indicates that "the problematic efficacy of the Torah commandments as a means of attaining redemption was not foreign to the intra-Jewish religious discourse of Paul's days, both in the Hellenistic Diaspora and in the Land of Israel."[26] Certainly by the time of Paul, Jewish tradition reveals a more pessimistic position that questions "a person's ability to gradually build the edifice of righteousness by his/her own efforts."[27] In support of this later contention are a series of texts found in the Qumran literature that include 1QS 11:7-19 and 1QH 4:17-26. Among several themes found in these texts is that of a "cleansing by the Spirit," a subject that is also employed by Paul (Gal 5:15-26; Rom 7:14-8:11) as a way of demonstrating that "works of the law" are unable to result in the hoped transformation. Ruzer concludes that "the 'Pauline threat' to the contemporaneous formative Judaism was not in the extremely revolutionary character of his claims but in the fact that they were highlighting insights concerning the problematic aspects of Torah observance, inherent in the Torah-centered world itself."[28] Additionally, by focusing on selected

---

[24] Ruzer, "*Paul's Stance on the Torah Revisited*," 96.
[25] Ruzer, "*Paul's Stance on the Torah Revisited*," 84.
[26] Ibidem.
[27] Ruzer, "*Paul's Stance on the Torah Revisited*," 87-88.
[28] Ruzer, "*Paul's Stance on the Torah Revisited*," 97.

aspects of Torah interpretation in Paul, Ruzer reveals several contradictory currents in contemporary Pauline studies that lead to confusion rather than to clarity. Given this situation he properly suggests that we look closer at Torah interpretation in the Judaisms prior to and contemporary with Paul that might illuminate differing Pauline emphases. The references to the Dead Sea Scrolls cited in his essay do indeed show pertinent and applicable parallels to Pauline thought at several key points. Additionally, Ruzer's thesis about pre-existing tensions with regard to Torah interpretation within intra-Jewish settings can, furthermore, be supported by greater concentration on a variety of texts from the Qumran literature that demonstrate, on the one hand, the polemical tensions between the Yaḥad, the Sadducees and the Pharisees with regard to Torah interpretation, and, on the other, sharp tensions within the Qumran texts themselves. One thinks here of the strains between the 1QS and 1QH texts cited and 4QMMT. In 4QMMT C27 one reads מקצת מעשי התורה ("some deeds of the law") and in 4QMMT C 30-31 the emphasis falls on the correct practice of these deeds ("in your deed [בעשותך] you may be reckoned as righteous"). Particularly significant is the recognition that Paul's polemic against the "deeds of the Law" is frequently found within a broader apologetic context, as is the case in Rom 3:31 ("Do we then overthrow the law by this faith? By no means! On the contrary, we uphold the law") and Rom 7:12 ("So the law is holy, and the commandment is holy and just and good"). While the "deeds of the Law" are not the basis of righteousness – for Paul only Christ is – that does not deny a positive function for the Law, properly understood, in the life of those who are "in Christ."

3. Antonio Pitta, *Paul, the Pharisee and the Law*

Phil 3:5 ("according to the Law, a Pharisee") represents Paul's only use of the term Pharisee; beginning with this text Pitta explores the range of its meaning. Although Gal 1:13-17 is relevant to the discussion since it employs the phrase "the traditions of my fathers," it its important to recognize that the overlap between Ἰουδαϊσμος in Gal 1:12–14 and φαρισαῖος in Phil 3:5 should "avoid a simple merger of the two terms"[29] according to which every one of Paul's statements on the Jews is directed to the Pharisees. Perplexing, however, is the comment that because the Septuagint always employs the term Ἰουδαϊσμος in the singular that it is incorrect for contemporary scholars to refer to "Judaisms," especially since Pitta writes that it is indeed "difficult to identify common features among the various Jewish tendencies of the first century."[30] Do not those scholars who intentionally use the term "Judaisms" do so as a way to emphasize the diversity of Second Temple Judaism and to avoid the possible reductionist effect of the term of "Common Judaism," especially subsequent to the publication of the Dead Sea Scrolls?[31]

Referring both to the dearth of information about the Pharisees in ancient sources as well as the stinging criticisms of the Pharisees found in the Qumran Pesharim, Pitta laments that "unfortunately the only Pharisee whose writings we still have, even until today, remains Paul of Tarsus!"[32] Such an assertion, however, raises a series of urgent queries. (1) To what extent is the remarkably terse reference to "according to the Law, a Pharisee" in Gal 3:5 able to determine a broader identification with the Pharisees, especially given our tenuous knowledge of this Jewish group. Can Overman[33] be followed when he urges that Paul is speaking only about confidence with regard to the Jewish Law and not thereby claiming to have been a Pharisee? (2) Can it be persuasively demonstrated that the expression

---

29 Antonio Pitta, "*Paul, the Pharisee and the Law*," 99-122, here 103.

30 Pitta, "*Paul, the Pharisee and the Law*," 105.

31 See a further discussion of this term below, 40-42.

32 Pitta, "*Paul, the Pharisee and the Law*," 107.

33 J. A. Overman, "κατὰ νόμον Φαρισαῖος: A Short History of Paul's Pharisaism," in *Pauline Conversations in Context: Essays in Honor of Calvin J. Roetzel*, (ed. J. C. Anderson, P. Sellew, and C. Setzer; London and New York: Sheffield Academic Press, 2002), 180–193.

"tradition of the fathers" in Gal 1:14 and the process of transmission in the early communities of the Jesus movement "give witness to the presence and permanence of the Pharisaic model in the Pauline letters,"[34] or might Martyn be correct when he asserts that this phrase "is one of the typical expressions by which virtually any Jew of the time referred to the Law, the venerable tradition studied under the guidance of senior scholars"?[35] And, (3) finally it must also be asked whether a broader conceptual and thematic comparison between the Pharisees and the authors of the Dead Sea Scrolls might not be instructive. Elsewhere I have urged that Paul's overall place in the Judaisms of the day reveal considerably closer proximity to the writings of Qumran related to the Yaḥad (the self-identifying term of the community at Qumran) than to the rationalist tradition that the Pharisees inherited.[36] Briefly, then, the important observations that Pitta makes with regard to Paul, pharisaic Judaism, and the Mosaic Law will need to be more fully examined within the broad variety and diversity that marked Second Temple Judaism, a phenomenon illuminated dramatically by the texts from the Dead Sea.

4. PASQUALE BASTA, *PAUL AND THE GEZERAH SHAWAH: A JUDAIC METHOD IN THE SERVICE OF JUSTIFICATION BY FAITH*

Focusing particularly on Rom 4:3-8 and its relationship to justification, Basta asks why two Old Testament texts are consecutively cited and compared by Paul: Gen 15:6, "And Abraham believed the Lord; and the Lord reckoned it to him as righteousness," and Ps 32:1–2, "Happy are those whose transgression is forgiven, whose sin is covered. Happy are those to whom the LORD

---

[34] Pitta, "*Paul, the Pharisee and the Law*," 117.

[35] J. L. Martyn, *Galatians* (AB 33A; Garden City, N.Y.: Doubleday, 1997), 155.

[36] "Justification and Last Judgment in Paul - Twenty-Five Years Later," in Karl P. Donfried, *Paul, Thessalonica and Early Christianity*), 279-92.

imputes no iniquity." These texts, he proposes, represent a common Jewish principle of biblical interpretation, *gezerah shawah*, that specifically employs such consecutive, analogical quotations.

A major goal of Paul is to insist that justification results from faith, not works; yet for this intention Gen 15:6 is not adequate since the Old Testament would not agree that someone has been justified aside from the Law. In fact, Ps 105:31 and 1 Macc 2:52 both understand Gen 16:6 as signifying justification by works. The apostle needs to refute this position in light of the coming of Christ and the resultant necessity of rereading certain key passages in light of this event. Thus he needs another text that "allows him to separate the πιστεύειν from the ἔργα νόμου and the μισθός and so to move in an opposite direction to the Judaic interpretation of his time."[37] And that text is Ps 32:2 since it is the only one within a semantic range of over one hundred texts using λογίζομαι in which God does not count sin.

Basta is quick to add that "every accusation leveled against the apostle of distancing himself from the νόμος proves to be a mistaken understanding of his biblical hermeneutics."[38] What Paul, in fact, does is not to deny Gen 15:6; rather "he clarifies it, remembers it and reaffirms it, starting from the search for a more complete meaning than that offered by tradition, a meaning at the same time more open and accessible to the Gentiles."[39] So, then, the apostle "did not connect two disparate texts, but he remained perfectly within the methodological limits respected by those who do not annul the Law, but search for a more reliable foundation for it, from an exegetical point of view as well." [40]

---

[37] Paquale Basta, "*Paul and the gezerah shawah: A Judaic Method in the Service of Justification by Faith*," 123-165, here 153.
[38] Basta, "*Paul and the gezerah shawah*," 160.
[39] Ibidem.
[40] Basta, "*Paul and the gezerah shawah*," 161.

This essay will certainly lead to both greater sensitivity and deepened reflection with regard to Paul's exegetical methodology in general as well as to the more specific use of consecutive citations from the Old Testament in light of the Apostle's conviction that the Messiah has come. Given this insightful contribution one may still wish to ponder whether it is helpful to assert that when Paul and the New Testament use *gezerah shawah* they are employing a *rabbinical* exegetical method[41], especially since Basta recognizes that this approach also appears earlier and regularly in Qumran as well as in the rabbinical sources.[42]

5. Adriana Destro and Mauro Pesce, *The Heavenly Journey in Paul: Tradition of a Jewish Apocalyptic Literary Genre or Cultural Practice in a Hellenistic-Roman Context?*

With a specific focus on 2 Cor 12:1-4 the concern that is addressed in this essay is whether Paul's image of a heavenly journey is influenced by Graeco-Roman or Jewish models or, perhaps, by a confluence of both. Destro and Pesce's goal is not to determine a literary genre classification but rather to examine "the heavenly ascent in terms of a religious *form* and *practice* in all its experiential and social aspects."[43] And, indeed, this practice is unusually widespread in a variety of Christian and Gnostic texts, including Rev 4:1 and the Gospel of Thomas, as well as in a broad range of Jewish texts together with a surprising representation in selected texts found in the Dead Sea Scrolls. Rather than understanding the *topos* of the heavenly journey as a transmitted literary genre, this essay argues

---

[41] My emphasis.

[42] See further Elieser Slomovic, "Toward an Understanding of the Exegesis of the Dead Sea Scrolls," *RevQ* 7 (1969–1971): 3–15.

[43] Adriana Destro and Mauro Pesce, "*The Heavenly Journey in Paul: Tradition of a Jewish Apocalyptic Literary Genre or Cultural Practice in a Hellenistic-Roman Context?*" 167-200, here 169.

synchronically rather than diachronically, viz., for the strong influence of social contact with contemporary groups.

Turning attention to the theme of the "heavenly journey" in selected texts situated in Graeco-Roman culture, some interesting commonalities between these and 2 Cor 12 are noted. In Cicero's *Somnium Scipionis* a range of Scipio's psychosomatic experiences in the heavens are compared to 2 Cor 12:4: "(he) heard inexpressible words, that no man is permitted to pronounce."[44] Summarizing Plutarch's *The Demon of Socrates* it is concluded that the "journey always leads to the knowledge of an esoteric doctrine concerning the cosmic structure, man's nature and ultimate destiny."[45] As a result such an esoteric "doctrine may end up counterbalancing popular representation or traditional vision of the world, conferring authority on specific persons (who become specialists) and legitimizing their doctrine and functions."[46] The final comments in this section refer to Philo, "a figure steeped in Hellenic culture."[47] He demonstrates that the "heavenly journey" is a practice that had widely penetrated the religious environment of the period thus demonstrating that it was neither "eccentric nor marginal"[48] nor necessarily dependent on "the apocalyptic 'tradition' of the heavenly journey…."[49] The wide influence of this "heavenly journey" experience results from the fact that it is deeply embedded in the practice of Graeco-Roman religion and philosophy.

Following a discussion of Jewish and Graeco-Roman backgrounds, the focus shifts to the function of the "heavenly journey" theme in the writings of Paul. Since evidence of "visions and revelations" are found in many of the Apostle's letters, 2 Cor 12:1-4 is not to be understood as an extraordinary occurrence in his ministry and coheres well with the assertion made in 1 Cor 2:7 that "we speak

[44] Destro and Pesce, "*The Heavenly Journey in Paul*," 178.
[45] Destro and Pesce, "*The Heavenly Journey in Paul*," 179.
[46] Destro and Pesce, "*The Heavenly Journey in Paul*," 179.
[47] Destro and Pesce, "*The Heavenly Journey in Paul*," 181.
[48] Destro and Pesce, "*The Heavenly Journey in Paul*," 183.
[49] Destro and Pesce, "*The Heavenly Journey in Paul*," 184.

God's wisdom, secret and hidden, which God decreed before the ages...." Destro and Pesce then link this revelatory tendency in Pauline thought to the theme of mysticism and the specific theme of "in Christ." They write: "The formula "in Christ" is a condensation of all kind of religious attitudes, rituals and practices that allows the individual to be incorporated in Christ, to remain within him, and to be open to his power. The heavenly journey could be prepared or permitted by one of these practices."[50] These connections and associations are indeed suggestive and need to be explored more fully and comprehensively against a broader range of Pauline texts.

Revealing "a profound combination of Greco-Roman and Judaic elements..."[51] the purpose for employing the "heavenly journey" theme in 2 Cor 12:1-4 is both polemical and apologetic, i.e. against the opponents in Corinth and in defense of his apostolic ministry. Further, Paul's "recourse" to this theme "*sprang* from the fact that members of the Corinth *ekklêsia* practiced this type of religious experience, on account of their connection with a Greco-Roman form of religiosity, or from the likelihood that the Jewish adversaries themselves had boasted of such experiences. Whatever the case, the scenario is one of a religious form that was quite widespread among the various religious groups present in Corinth."[52] Subsequent discussion of this theme will also need to distinguish more fully between Paul's experience and his narrative expression of that experience.

6. EMMANUEL NATHAN AND REIMUND BIERINGER, *PAUL, MOSES, AND THE VEIL: PAUL'S PERSPECTIVE ON JUDAISM IN LIGHT OF 2 CORINTHIANS 3*

The first part of this essay, "On Paul's use of καταργέω *and* τέλος in 2 Cor 3:7, 11, 13 and 14," is by Emmanuel Nathan and

[50] Destro and Pesce, *"The Heavenly Journey in Paul,"* 192.

[51] Destro and Pesce, *"The Heavenly Journey in Paul,"* 190.

[52] Destro and Pesce, *"The Heavenly Journey in Paul,"* in this volume, p. 191; italics mine.

the second part, dealing with "The Glory and the Veil," is written by Reimund Bieringer. In order to clarify the exceptionally difficult and controversial text found in 2 Cor 3:7-18, Nathan and Bieringer enter into a detailed discussion of καταργέω, τέλος, κάλυμμα and δόξα, to a large extent in response to the Windisch's influential commentary of 1924.[53] With regard to καταργέω it is suggested, following a review of the complex exegetical decisions that are required, that, rather than "fading" as suggested by Windisch and for which there is no lexical evidence, καταργέω is best translated as "render ineffective," a phrase that fits all Pauline contexts. This decision does not, however, settle the question of the referent of τὸ καταργούμενον in 3:11. Is it the glory of Moses' face, the ministry of Moses, the Law, or the entire Mosaic covenant? Based on grammatical considerations Nathan opts for the ministry of Moses as being the most likely candidate, with τοῦ καταργουμένου in 3:13, a genitive singular neuter, in all likelihood referring to the glory on Moses' face because of the terminological parallelism with 3:7. Even more problematic in this same verse is whether the translation of τέλος should be "goal" or "cessation" with Nathan opting for the former.

Concerning the relationship of ἡ παλαιὰ διαθήκη to the last occurrence of καταργέω (καταργεῖται) in 3:14, two decisions are reached. First, as a result of the metonymic use of Moses ἡ παλαιὰ διαθήκη embraces the Mosaic covenant. Given Nathan's conclusion that κάλυμμα as the subject of καταργεῖται denotes the veil, it is the veil and not the covenant that is being abolished.[54] This is a clear repudiation of Windisch's position, viz., when he and his followers "assume that Moses was hid-

---

[53] Hans Windisch, *Der Zweite Korintherbrief* (Göttingen: Vandenhoeck & Ruprecht, 1924).

[54] Nathan and Bieringer, "*Paul, Moses, and the Veil: Paul's Perspective on Judaism in Light of 2 Corinthians 3*," 201-228, here 218.

ing a fading glory. It suggests for them that the real point of the figure is the obsolescence of the old covenant and the superiority of Christianity to Judaism, themes not readily pertinent to Paul's self-defence against the charges of other Christian apostles."[55] A similar repudiation of Windisch in this same context is also represented by the more recent work of Hafemann[56] and Blanton[57] who "are firmly situated within the new trend of Pauline scholarship that no longer sees 2 Cor 3:7-18 as offering a negative assessment of Judaism."[58] Yet at the same time Nathan offers a word of caution: "The sheer ambiguity of καταργέω and τέλος," together with locating their referents, intensifies the uncertainty of what exactly Paul means. "Even though Paul can, and should, be appreciated within his Jewish matrix, we believe that this ambiguity helped to contribute to the later understanding of the old covenant that is abolished."[59]

In second part of this essay dealing with "The Glory and the Veil," Bieringer argues that the main theological concept in 2 Cor 3:7-18 is δόξα, and concludes that in this context it intends to communicate "the nature of the deity in its manifestation."[60] It is further observed that the the "main interest of 3:7-11 is how this δόξα which was on the face of Moses is related to the διακονία

---

[55] Nathan and Bieringer, "*Paul, Moses, and the Veil: Paul's Perspective on Judaism in Light of 2 Corinthians 3*," 213.

[56] Scott J. Hafemann, *Paul, Moses, and the History of Israel: The Letter/Spirit Contrast and the Argument from Scripture in 2 Corinthians 3* (WUNT 81; Tübingen: Mohr [Siebeck], 1995), 257.

[57] Thomas R. Blanton, *Constructing a New Covenant: Discursive Strategies in the Damascus Document and Second Corinthians*, WUNT 233 (Tübingen: J.C.B. Mohr (Paul Siebeck), 2007) 220.

[58] Nathan and Bieringer, "*Paul, Moses, and the Veil: Paul's Perspective on Judaism in Light of 2 Corinthians 3*," 216.

[59] Nathan and Bieringer, "*Paul, Moses, and the Veil: Paul's Perspective on Judaism in Light of 2 Corinthians 3*," 218-219.

[60] Nathan and Bieringer, "*Paul, Moses, and the Veil: Paul's Perspective on Judaism in Light of 2 Corinthians 3*," 220.

of the Spirit and the διακονία of death respectively."[61] Important to realize is that δόξα is used to refer *both* to the ministry of the old as well as the new covenant and that *both* are filled with the "majesty and splendor of God."[62] Further, by introducing the theme of the veil in connection with the phrase παλαιὰ διαθήκη, Paul suggests neither the ineffectiveness nor end, but rather "the hiddenness of the 'old covenant.'"[63] The reference to ἐν Χριστῷ καταργεῖται in verse 14 suggests a hermeneutical key that allows Paul to *continue* read the "old covenant" from the new perspective of Christ.

Even though Paul in 2 Cor 3:7-18 does not speak about Judaism explicitly, the implications for the Jewish matrix of Paul's "post-Damascus view of Judaism"[64] become manifest especially insofar as the continuity between the old and the new covenant is considerably more evident in this text than has been hitherto recognized by many interpreters. And yet antithetical terminology is evident throughout, including a ministry of death contrasted with a ministry of Spirit as well as a ministry of condemnation in opposition to a ministry of justification. The possible misreading of such language not consistent with the emphases of the entire text carries with it dangerous potential and great care must be taken "not to actualize this potential."[65]

---

[61] Nathan and Bieringer, "*Paul, Moses, and the Veil: Paul's Perspective on Judaism in Light of 2 Corinthians 3*," 220.

[62] Nathan and Bieringer, "*Paul, Moses, and the Veil: Paul's Perspective on Judaism in Light of 2 Corinthians 3*," 223.

[63] Nathan and Bieringer, "*Paul, Moses, and the Veil: Paul's Perspective on Judaism in Light of 2 Corinthians 3*," 225.

[64] Nathan and Bieringer, "*Paul, Moses, and the Veil: Paul's Perspective on Judaism in Light of 2 Corinthians 3*," 227.

[65] Nathan and Bieringer, "*Paul, Moses, and the Veil: Paul's Perspective on Judaism in Light of 2 Corinthians 3*," 228.

7. DIDIER POLLEFEYT AND DAVID J. BOLTON, *PAUL, DEICIDE, AND THE WRATH OF GOD: TOWARDS A HERMENEUTICAL READING OF 1 THESS 2:14–16*

An overriding focus of this essay is captured in the opening citation from Leon Morris that these verses are "a denunciation of the Jews more severe than anything else in the Pauline writings"[66] and, as a result, to find a hermeneutical approach that will permit the acceptance of this "seemingly oppressive text"[67] develops into a dominant focus. In order to move toward this goal Pollefeyt and Bolton provide a overview of the problems as well as the proposed solutions related to this text, the primary of which is whether it was written by Paul or not. After considering the evidence, they decide in favor of the passage's authenticity.

Issues directly relevant to the primary concern of the conference include a range of observations and questions related to Paul's Jewish matrix including various issues related to the question of intra-Jewish polemics.[68] Is this text an example of such intra-Jewish polemics? In this connection it is asked whether the fact that Paul writes as a Jew deflates or defuses the polemical thrust of the text? "In light of the sheer extent of the critique and condemnation given against Jews, is it not possible to classify Paul here as a Jew acting anti-Jewishly? That is not to say, of course, that he is a self-hating Jew, but it is to say that he found little with which to identify in the mainstream or common Judaism of his day. In fact there is nothing in the passage itself that identifies Paul with οἱ Ἰουδαῖοι as his own people. He appears to speak of himself as an outsider and an accuser, rather 'than as a member of penitent Israel.' One could easily assume that this passage actually supports an early parting of the ways rather than disproves it.

---

[66] Didier Pollefeyt and David J. Bolton, "*Paul, Deicide, and the Wrath of God: Towards a Hermeneutical Reading of 1 Thess 2:14–16*," 229-257, here 230, n. 2.

[67] Pollefeyt and Bolton, "*Paul, Deicide, and the Wrath of God*," here 253, n. 83 (citing Bieringer).

[68] Pollefeyt and Bolton, "*Paul, Deicide, and the Wrath of God*," 243-247.

Paul, it would appear, has been able to distance himself from his own kind to such an extent that he is able to condemn them without a blush."[69] This comment raises an essential and critical issue: are Paul's acerbic assertions representations of an anti-Judaism or of intra-Jewish polemics? Pollefeyt and Bolton waver but eventually side with the former position. If that, in fact, is their position one must ask how one would classify the polemics found in the various Qumran texts: anti-Jewish or intra-Jewish? Would there be significant support to argue that these texts are anti-Jewish? Hardly, given the Qumran group's self-understanding that they are the true Judaism. In much the same way could it not be argued that Paul appropriates Judaism as the Israel of God (Gal 6:16) in light of the Messiah's arrival? If so, he is not "a Jew acting anti-Jewishly" any more than the author of the Pesher Nahum is when he denounces the Pharisees.

The oppressiveness of 1 Thess 2:14-16 for contemporary Christians, it is argued, calls for a "universal horizon of God's call" that transcends the "heat of his immediate contextual conflict."[70] and it is salvation (σωτηρία) that opens up the "widest eschatological horizon" of 1 Thess 2:14-16. Or, put another way, "God's salvation reaches beyond God's wrath."[71] The essay concludes with the assertion that in "our theological-hermeneutical perspective, we find that this passage's own ultimate horizon of σῴζω shoots beyond ἡ ὀργὴ εἰς τέλος, highlighting that God's covenantal faithfulness is greater than his wrath"[72] This may be a correct hermeneutical approach to this most difficult text, but one will have to raise the question whether or not it has been raised prematurely? As helpful as the entire overview of scholarly positions with regard to these verses

---

[69] Pollefeyt and Bolton, "*Paul, Deicide, and the Wrath of God*," 246.
[70] Pollefeyt and Bolton, "*Paul, Deicide, and the Wrath of God*," 254.
[71] Pollefeyt and Bolton, "*Paul, Deicide, and the Wrath of God*," 256.
[72] Ibidem.

are, very often positions are reviewed but exegetical conclusions not reached; methodologies of utmost significance are assessed yet others omitted, as, for example, the important work carried out in the area of rhetorical criticism.[73] Thus one must not only ask whether hermeneutical directions can be suggested in the absence of exegetical conclusions and, further, whether such directions need not only take into account selected themes in 1 Thessalonians and such as salvation and but must not take into account the theological emphases of the entire Pauline corpus?

8. SHAYE J. D. COHEN, *FROM PERMISSION TO PROHIBITION: PAUL AND THE EARLY CHURCH ON MIXED MARRIAGE*

Shaye Cohen's response to whether Paul, as Tertullian and others claim, prohibits marriage between believers and non-believers is negative based on his analysis of the relevant Pauline texts. The conclusion of Tertullian and post-Pauline Christianity is derived from essentially two texts: 1 Cor 6:15-19 with its reproof of porneia (commonly understood by contemporary scholars as illicit sexual relations) and 1 Cor 7:39 containing Paul's admonition that a believing widow can only remarry "in the Lord." With regard to the first text the evidence is wanting that porneia addresses the issued of mixed marriage and, further, such an interpretation would stand in tension with 1 Cor 7:14 where the Apostle explicitly states that the non-believing spouse is "sanctified" by the believing spouse. To argue that Paul prohibits mixed-marriage in the second text, 1 Cor 7:39, is made difficult by the uncertain meaning of the phrase "in the Lord."

The essay is enhanced by an analysis and discussion of other relevant Pauline texts as well. 1) When discussing **1 Cor 7:39-40** it is asserted, as already noted, that reference to marriage only "in the

---

[73] See here, for example, Karl P. Donfried and Johannes Beutler, *The Thessalonians Debate: Methodological Discord or Methodological Synthesis?* (Grand Rapids: Eerdmans, 2000).

Lord" is unclear.[74] However, as Kramer has observed, the twenty-nine references to ἐν κυρίῳ are distributed either in passages of exhortation or personal messages.[75] While not as explicitly theological as the phrase "in Christ," Paul's use of "in the Lord" as well as "in Christ" clearly reference God's saving redemption through the Messiah, Jesus Christ. Given such an orientation of the phrase "in the Lord" in 1 Cor 7:39 one will need to ask whether this text does not, in fact, clearly specify that a believing widow is only free marry to one who is "in Christ," i.e., a believer in Christ as she herself is? 2) It is concluded that Tertullian's reading of **1 Cor 6:15-17**, in which Paul uses the term porneia to refer to mixed marriages, is incorrect and in this analysis Cohen would gain the support of the vast majority of exegetes. Although porneia refers to illicit sexual relations there is no evidence that Paul has in mind marriage between a believer and unbeliever and 1 Cor 7:14 speaks directly against such a broader inclusion with in the category of porneia. 3) **2 Cor 6:14** is the focal point within the broader discussion of 2 Cor 6:14-7:1. The conclusion is reached that "if 2 Cor 6:14 prohibits mixed marriage, it does so implicitly, subtly, and indirectly—and perhaps not at all."[76] This observation may be correct. Yet it must be asked whether the similarity of the language and concepts found in 2 Cor 6:14-7:1 to that found in the writings of the Dead Sea Scrolls would not suggest that Paul does, in fact, have in mind the prohibition of mixed marriages, particularly if Paul is influenced by this or a similar tradition.[77] Not to be overlooked is that the Temple Scroll (11Q19 lvii.15-17; see also MMT B 75-82) explicitly prohibits all marriage between Jews and non-Jews. 4) In

---

[74] Shaye J. D. Cohen, *"From Permission to Prohibition: Paul and the Early Church on Mixed Marriage,"* 259-291, here 264 and 284.

[75] Werner Kramer, *Christ, Lord, Son of God* (SBT 50; Naperville, Ill.: Allenson; London: SCM, 1966), 177-78.

[76] Cohen, *"From Permission to Prohibition,"* 272.

[77] For a further discussion of this text and the Temple theme, see Karl P. Donfried, "Paul the Jew - But of What Sort?" in *Testimony and Interpretation: Early Christology in Its Judeo-Hellenistic Milieu* (Pokorny Festschrift; ed. J. Mrazek and J. Roskovec; Edinburg, T & T Clark, 2004), 11-27.

his discussion of **1 Cor 7:12-14** Cohen disagrees with Tertullian's interpretation that restricts its applicability only to mixed marriages prior to the conversion of one partner. The question is raised how such a prohibition remarriage can be brought into agreement with 1 Cor 7:39? It is suggested that just "as there is nothing in 1 Cor 7:39 to suggest that Paul is speaking only about widows once married to non-believers, there is nothing in 1 Cor 7:14 to suggest, let alone require, that Paul is speaking only of mixed marriage brought into being by the conversion of a spouse to Christianity."[78] However, must one not consider the time sequences of each passage more precisely before reaching such a conclusion? Such a consideration might reveal that 1 Cor 7:39 makes reference to a *future* marriage (whether or not the previous marriage was to a Christian or not seems irrelevant) whereas 1 Cor 7:14 to an *existing* marriage.

Cohen alerts us to the use of *hagios* in 1 Cor 7:14 and indicates that it does not have its usual meaning in Paul for whom it most often refers to the believer in Christ. In this verse "a minimum we can say [is] that the non-Christian spouse and the offspring are made sacred, to one degree or another, by one means or another, by virtue of their proximity to the Christian spouse and parent."[79] And, further, it is quite correct to observe that the "'holiness' of this relationship means that *porneia* is absent."[80] Given, however, Cohen's relatively brief references to "holiness" in Paul, a next stage in the conversation might well be a fuller exploration of *kadosha/kadosh* in the Dead Sea Scrolls where, given its dynamic character, all the dimensions of the Pauline usage as we know them are represented. The "acquisition of holiness," writes Hanna Harrington about Qumran, "becomes a never-ending dynamic activity since holiness can always be increased."[81] And as Jacobus

---

[78] Cohen, "*From Permission to Prohibition,*" 275.

[79] Cohen, *"From Permission to Prohibition,"* 279.

[80] Ibidem.

[81] Hannah K. Harrington, "Holiness and Law in the Dead Sea Scrolls Author(s)," *DSD* 8 (2002): 124-35, here 130.

Naude has written, holiness in the Dead Sea Scrolls indicates "a state of or transition to purity."[82]

Finally, given the emphasis on Paul as a Jew in many of the papers delivered at this conference it needs to be asked whether the following conclusion can be documented or properly derived from the Pauline letters. "Paul," writes Cohen, "believes that the old Jewish rules of table fellowship no longer obtain, and that believers may freely sup with unbelievers (1 Cor 10:27; cf. Gal 2:12–14). If Paul believes all this, surely he could believe too that the followers of Christ may freely marry non-believers. Perhaps he thought that mixed marriage was a fine way to spread the light of truth and the knowledge of Christ. The Jewish prohibition of mixed marriage was irrelevant to Paul...."[83] In order to evaluate the continuing validity of this Jewish proscription of marriage between unbelievers for Paul, must one not first distinguish more precisely between the elimination of boundaries between Jews and Gentiles in Christ and the interaction of such believers in Christ, whether of Jewish or Gentile background, and the world of paganism as, for example, through mixed-marriage?

9. DANIEL R. SCHWARTZ, *"SOMEONE WHO CONSIDERS SOMETHING TO BE IMPURE – FOR HIM IT IS IMPURE"* (ROM14:14): *GOOD MANNERS OR LAW?*

What exactly did Paul have in mind in writing Rom 14:14: "I know, and am persuaded in the Lord Jesus, that nothing is impure by itself, except for someone who considers something to be impure – for him it is impure" (as translated by Schwartz). How does one resolve the tension within this verse in which the Apostle both rejects the validity of dietary restrictions at the outset and then

[82] Jacobus A. Naude, "Holiness in the Dead Sea Scrolls," in *The Dead Sea Scrolls Fifty Years After Their Discovery* (vol. 2; ed. Peter W. Flint and J. VanderKam; Jersusalem: Israel Exploration Society, 2000), 171-219, here 198.

[83] Cohen, *"From Permission to Prohibition,"* 286.

affirms them at the end? Linking this with the final verse in the chapter, 14:23, ("But those who have doubts are condemned if they eat, because they do not act from faith; for whatever does not proceed from faith is sin"), Schwartz argues that if "Jews who think certain foods are impure nonetheless eat them they will be sinning. The only way for them not to sin when they eat that which they consider impure is to accept the faith that, for them as for Paul, will bring the "knowledge" that indeed nothing is impure."[84] Thus, it would be a significant misstep to force those who maintain that something impure "*is indeed impure*"[85] to violate their position. What will be argued throughout is that Paul in Rom 14:20-23 "forbids the strong to do anything that might bring the weak to want to do something that they, the weak, think is forbidden to them—even though Paul, and the strong, believe that in fact there is no basis for the prohibition."[86]

This interpretation of Rom 14:14 is supported by Rom 5:13 ("sin was indeed in the world before the law, but sin is not reckoned when there is no law") where sin only exists if one is aware of it. "In both cases," urges Schwartz, "it is the *logos*, not the *physis* of the matter, that constitutes the sin—and that which it constitutes really *are* sins. Just as much as they are real in chapter 5, for they serve to define Jesus' atoning function, so too are they real in chapter 14."[87] A development of this emphasis on *logos* rather than *physis* can be observed in the Diaspora where Jews in Rome, for example, were living as Jews in spite of and as a result of their circumstances. In "a place where being Roman was the default, they were Jews because they chose not to do like the Romans but, rather, to be Jews."[88] In such an environment the rules that bound Jews together was the result of a "volitional process."[89]

---

[84] Daniel R. Schwartz, "*Someone who considers something to be impure – for him it is impure" (Rom14:14): Good Manners or Law?"* 293-309, here 299.

[85] Schwartz, "*Someone who considers something to be impure*," 299.

[86] Schwartz, "*Someone who considers something to be impure*," 308.

[87] Schwartz, "*Someone who considers something to be impure*," 302.

[88] Schwartz, "*Someone who considers something to be impure*," 305.

[89] Ibidem.

As a result of these observations an important conclusion is reached with regard to the matrix of Judaism during the Pauline period, viz., that a type of non-priestly Judaism emerges "which tended in the same direction as the Diaspora: a view of law as divorced from nature and deriving, instead, from the will and decisions of the individual Jew. That is, a certain diasporization, which is an artificialization, seems to have characterized non-priestly Judaism in Judaea just as much as it characterized Judaism of the Hellenistic Diaspora."[90] This "artificialization" is further reflected and developed in a Judaism of "Pharisaic and proto-rabbinic orientation."[91]

Given this provocative analysis of Rom 14:14 as well as the Apostle's apparently positive relationship to a "Pharisaic and proto-rabbinic orientation," further discussion will have to analyze the methodological and exegetical rationale for placing Paul at this particular juncture given the very diverse spectrum of first century Judaism.

10. JUSTIN TAYLOR, *PAUL AND THE JEWISH LEADERS AT ROME: ACTS 28:17–31*

In an age in which the account of Paul in Acts is readily dismissed as unreliable, this essay takes up the important question concerning the relationship of the Apostle's attitude toward Judaism as described by Luke in Acts 28 with those of Paul in Romans 9-11. If, as many scholars hold, Acts 28 represents a condemnation of the Jewish people, then the question must be raised whether this is "the moment when Paul separates himself from his Jewish matrix?"[92]

There are other interpreters, however, who read Acts 28:17-31 differently. Israel, in contrast, is not condemned as a whole but is portrayed as divided. Taylor presents a range of arguments support-

---

[90] Schwartz, "*Someone who considers something to be impure,*" 305.

[91] Schwartz, "*Someone who considers something to be impure,*" 305-306.

[92] Justin Taylor, "*Paul and the Jewish Leaders at Rome: Acts 28:17-31,*" 311-326, here 312.

ing this position including the fact that Paul in Acts on several occasions announces that he is "turning to the Gentiles" and then, in fact, proceeds to speak in a synagogue. Further, prophetic declarations such as Isa 6:9-10 are understood to be admonitions to bring about conversion rather than absolute condemnations. The point that Paul is making, especially evident by his use of the term "kingdom of God," is that "both Jews and Gentiles will have a share in the world to come...."[93] It is this that the Apostle hopes the Jewish leaders in Rome will accept, a message that indeed coheres well with Romans 9-11 in general and Rom 11:2-5 in particular: "God has not rejected his people whom he foreknew" and therefore remains a "remnant, chosen by grace."

The final section of Taylor's analysis focuses on the theme of the future restoration of the Jewish people after the Exile referred to in Acts 28:28 with its echo of Isa 40:5 (LXX, "All flesh will see the salvation of God") and by Paul in Rom 11:23-27. Further, some exegetes have urged that Paul, especially in 1 Thess 4:13-18 and 1 Cor 15:22-28, "expected an earthly kingdom as a element in his eschatological scenario."[94] Given the apocalyptic horizon that formed part of the "Jewish matrix" of Paul it is indeed likely that he would have been acquainted with such eschatological concepts. The possibility that both 1 Thess 4:13-18 and 1 Cor 15:22-28 may refer to an earthly kingdom suggest that he is an "eschatological realist,"[95] a description that may be appropriate for the Paul of Acts as well. Further probing of these and related passages will need to ask whether or not these two Pauline texts are, in fact, able to bear the weight placed on them, viz., that Paul expected some form of earthly kingdom to be established at the time of the parousia. However this may be decided, the critical issue of locating Paul within the diversity of first century Judaism is once again placed squarely before us.

---

[93] Taylor, "*Paul and the Jewish Leaders at Rome,*" 320.
[94] Taylor, "*Paul and the Jewish Leaders at Rome,*" 324.
[95] Taylor, "*Paul and the Jewish Leaders at Rome,*" 326.

11. PAULA FREDRIKSEN, *JUDAIZING THE NATIONS: THE RITUAL DEMANDS OF PAUL'S GOSPEL*

Using Augustine as a starting point, this essay provocatively argues that the Bishop of Hippo understands quite correctly that the Temple in Jerusalem remains "at the heart of Paul's religious universe" and that "the first generation of what would eventually become the church, Jewish Christians, Paul emphatically included, continued to live according to their ancestral practices, while the apostles encouraged gentile Christians, without converting to Judaism, to Judaize."[96] Therefore, Fredriksen urges, the phrase "Law-free mission", among others, should be eliminated by those scholars seeking to understand the historical Paul.[97]

An observation of great significance, repeated throughout this essay, is that life in the Diaspora involves a far greater degree of interaction between Jews and pagans than is generally acknowledged. Not only were pagans benefactors of synagogues and Jewish activities but they also "sponsored Jewish philanthropic initiatives; they participated in Jewish prayer and study, and took part in Jewish fasts or feasts."[98] Pagans indeed tolerated the recognition of the Judean god but only if these *pagan* "god-fearers" continued to honor their ancestral customs as well as the gods of the Graeco-Roman culture.

Turning now to the contours of Paul's gospel, Fredriksen maintains that converting to Judaism does not mean becoming a Jew. Rather these converts, referenced in 1 Thess 1:9, are to live as eschatological pagans during "the brief wrinkle in time between the resurrection and the Parousia..." and Paul's pagans, in contrast to the pagan god-fearers are "to worship only Paul's god, the god of Israel, empowered to do so by that god's risen Son."[99] But her next step is likely to generate lively debate, particularly the

---

[96] Paula Fredriksen, "*Judaizing the Nations: The Ritual Demands of Paul's Gospel,*" 327-354, here 329.

[97] Fredriksen, "*Judaizing the Nations,*" 330.

[98] Fredriksen, "*Judaizing the Nations,*" 335.

[99] Fredriksen, "*Judaizing the Nations,*" 341.

assertion that "both in the older Jewish apocalyptic traditions and in their newer Christian refraction, the nations join *with* Israel, but they do not *join* Israel."[100] While this may be a correct portrayal with regard to some of the Jewish apocalyptic traditions, does it accurately describe Paul's understanding? Does not the image of grafting in Rom 11:13-24 suggest an image that is considerably more intimate than simply to "join with Israel...." Here as well it needs to be asked in what sense Paul refers to the former pagans in the churches in Galatia as the "Israel of God"?[101]

In a significant section dealing with purity issues a variety of provocative proposals are presented for which one will look forward to more detailed exegetical treatment. With reference to 1 Cor 5:7, for example, it is remarked that the paschal image "refers to Jewish time-keeping, not to a sacrificial death on the part of Christ."[102] Could it not be argued that Paul understands Jesus Christ as the one who died on the cross (1Cor 1:18) at Passover and is thus indeed the Passover lamb of the new messianic age? Having already passed through Passover by way of Jesus' death, the believers now live within a new paschal reality. Similarly, the discussion of ἁγιασμός needs to be broadened both exegetically within the Pauline letters as well as within the diversity of the Judaisms of the first-century. Also, a more detailed explanation of the assertion that the rituals of Jerusalem's temple "serve as his template" might prove as instructive as are Fredriksen's comments about Paul's representation of his own work "as priestly service."[103] In this context it would be helpful to consider to what degree the citations about the temple made by Paul in 1 Cor 3:16 and 2 Cor 6:16 reflect a substantially more transformed, transferred and purified view of the Temple as found in the writings of the Qumran community?

---

[100] Fredriksen, "*Judaizing the Nations*," 341.

[101] This theme is also discussed by Sanders, "*Paul's Jewishness*," 64. See also note 21 on that page.

[102] Fredriksen, "*Judaizing the Nations*," 346.

[103] Fredriksen, "*Judaizing the Nations*," 347.

With her keen sensitivity to fundamental issues in Pauline theology, Fredriksen queries the meaning of Rom 11:26: "And so all Israel will be saved…." Without doubt this topic is of central importance for comprehending Pauline theology at its deepest level. To distinguish oneself from Augustine's position that "'all Israel' that is to be saved must become *Christian* Israel, the 'Israel' of the church…" is it adequate to respond that "for Paul, 'Israel' always means his 'kinsmen according to the flesh – they are Israel' (Rom 9:4)" without further exegetical elaboration?[104] Similarly, although some significant directions are explored with regard to the question of how Paul conceptualizes "the incorporation of his pagans-in-Christ into Israel's redemption," it must be asked whether it is helpful or accurate to summarize the matter by claiming that "Paul demands that his pagans Judaize"?[105] Given Paul's negative usage of this term in Gal 2:14 (ἰουδαΐζειν) might it not have been more useful to have employed a less negative and controversial term? Fredriksen would, most likely, respond in the negative for it appears that the issues she wishes to raise are entrenched misunderstandings of Paul that need to be challenged and confronted. The conclusion to this essay reinforces this likelihood. "This insistance," it is urged, "that none other than the god of Israel be worshiped ultimately came from the first table of the Law. It was defining; it was non-negotiable; it was uniquely Jewish. For all of the reasons reviewed above, then, but most especially for this one, the last way we should describe Paul's gospel to the Gentiles is to say that it was 'Law-free.'"[106] Such a bold declaration properly focuses attention on Rom 3:31 ("Do we then overthrow the law by this faith? By no means! On the contrary, we uphold the law") and similar texts in Paul, but in what ways does it help clarify the intention of Rom 7:1 about "being discharged from the law" or the very problematic contention that "Christ is the end of the law" in Rom 10:4? It is hoped that provocative assertions such as these will lead to

---

[104] Fredriksen, "*Judaizing the Nations*," 351.
[105] Ibidem.
[106] Fredriksen, "*Judaizing the Nations*," 351.

exegetical reexaminations of critical and neuralgic dimensions of Pauline theology that will allow Paul's thought to be understood with far greater precision in the context of his Jewish matrix.

SUMMARIZING REFLECTIONS

A. Clarity In The Use Of Descriptive Terminology

A remarkable consensus emerges in this volume, viz., that Pauline thought can only be properly understood and analyzed when related closely and meticulously to its Jewish matrix. Paul's Jewishness is foundational for the Apostle's theology. This is a major breakthrough that if pursued will, without doubt, move Pauline studies forward in significant ways and directions. Next steps will need to focus more specifically on the precise meanings of the terms *Jewish* and *Jewishness* as applied to Paul, a term used frequently in papers given at the 2009 Rome conference. Further specificity and exactitude with reference to this and related terminology, such as the term Judaism, will be essential. With regard to all three terms, but with particular reference to the non-plural use of the term Judaism, one needs to ask whether they are presently adequate descriptors for the broad range of variegated and polemical tendencies within the late second Temple period? Does the term "Judaisms" perhaps more effectively express the religious diversity of this period in Jewish history, a period that includes both rationalist and prophetic movements, streams of interpretation and practice that do not necessarily cohere with one another?

Pitta has warned that one should not define Judaism in the Pauline period as essentially being equivalent to the Pharisaic school of Torah interpretation.[107] For some this is an assumption and for others a conclusion reached after considerable reflection. Based on Phil 3:5 ("according to the Law, a Pharisee") some have urged that

[107] Pitta, "*Paul, the Pharisee and the Law*," 103.

Paul was/had been a Pharisee and received significant theological impulses from this movement. Both Pitta and Schwarz, in the essays contained in this volume, are sympathetic to such an approach with the latter scholar referring to Paul's tendency toward a "Pharisaic and proto-rabbinic orientation."[108] Others, as we have noted, do not believe that Paul is particularly influenced by this stream of Judaism;[109] in Phil 3:5, they would maintain, Paul is only referring to confidence in the Jewish Law and does not claim to be a Pharisee. To speak of Judaism without reference to the contradictory streams within it at this time limits our ability to grasp the specific areas of influence upon the Apostle's thought and proclamation.

Greater concentration and focus must be given to the various movements within the Judaism of the late second Temple period, particularly the Qumran community (i.e., the *yaḥad*) and the Pharisees, as well as the tension between them. From the Damascus Document, one of the major texts found in Cave 4, we know that the Essene movement was spread throughout the land that we now know as Israel.[110] And it was not a small movement. Josephus tells us that during his time the Pharisees numbered 6,000 and the Essenes about 4,000.[111] Since 1947, we now have many original texts describing this community, thus shedding enormous light – sometimes directly and sometimes indirectly - on the entire shape of the Judaisms[112] of this period, including the Sadducees, the Pharisees, the Essenes and the early Jesus movement. The pioneering work of Shemaryahu Talmon may prove invaluable for an ultimate solution to these questions since he maintains that we witness in the texts of the Dead Sea Scrolls a confrontation between a prophetically inspired movement inclined toward apocalypticism and a rationalist stream that will ultimately develop into Rabbinic

---

[108] Schwartz, "*Someone who considers something to be impure*," 296.

[109] See note 33 above.

[110] For example, CD 7:6-9.

[111] Josephus, *Ant.* 18.18-22.

[112] The term "Judaisms" is used intentionally in order to indicate the diversity and non-monolithic character of Second Temple Judaism.

Judaism.[113] He observes, further, that "Rabbinic Judaism shelved prophetic inspiration and progressively developed a rationalist stance.... By contrast, the *yaḥad* embrace unreservedly the Bible's high appreciation of prophetic teaching and continue to subject the life of the individual and the community to the guidance of personalities who were possessed of the divine spirit... In this respect, the Covenanters and nascent Christianity are on the same wave length. The acceptance of inspiration as the paramount principle of individual and communal life informs also the followers of Jesus."[114] The words of Paul to the Corinthians echo such a perspective: "And we speak of these things in words not taught by human wisdom but taught by the Spirit, interpreting spiritual things to those who are spiritual" (1 Cor 2:13), and again, "And I think that I too have the Spirit of God" (1 Cor 7:40).

B. Paul And The Essenes: Essential Agreements

Even a rapid perusal of Paul's earliest letter, 1 Thessalonians, will suggest affinities with the *yaḥad*, the prophetic movement of the Community of the Renewed Covenant at Qumran and beyond. Some of the similarities between the two include:[115]

1. eschatological/apocalyptic similarities in their intense expectation of the final consummation of history;

---

[113] Shemaryahu Talmon, "The Community of the Renewed Covenant," in *The Community of the Renewed Covenant: The Notre Dame Symposium on the Dead Sea Scrolls* (Christianity and Judaism in Antiquity Series, 10; ed. Eugene Ulrich and James VanderKam; Notre Dame, Indiana: University of Notre Dame, 1994), 3-24, here 22.

[114] Talmon, *Community*, 20-21.

[115] For further details see Karl P. Donfried, "Paul and Qumran: The Possible Influence of סרך on 1 Thessalonians," in Donfried, *Paul, Thessalonica and Early Christianity*, 221-231; "The Assembly Of The Thessalonians: Reflections on the Ecclesiology of the Earliest Christian Letter," in Donfried, *Paul, Thessalonica and Early Christianity*, 139-162.

2. the election and calling of God, as when Paul writes to the Thessalonian church that "we know, brothers and sisters beloved by God, that he has chosen (ἐκλογή) you" (1:4);
3. holiness/sanctification, as in 1 Thess 4:3, "For this is the will of God, your sanctification" (literally, holiness [ἁγιασμός]);
4. the light/day//night/darkness contrasts and the use of the term "sons of light." In 1 Thess 5: 5 Paul writes: "for you are all sons of light and sons of the day; we are not of the night or of darkness." One of the major descriptors for the *yaḥad* is that they are "sons of light;"[116]
5. the wrath/salvation dualism. "For God has destined us not for wrath but for obtaining salvation…" are words found in 1 Thess 5:9;
6. the phrase "church of God" which has its direct parallel in the Qumran term קהל אל;[117]
7. ἄτακτος and the ethical order. It is now quite likely that the "idlers" or "loafers" of 1 Thess 5:14, the ἄτακτοι in Greek, should, on the basis of parallel texts related to the Dead Sea Scrolls, be translated as those "who are out of order," namely not following the סרך, the order of the community as described in 1 Thess 4:1-12. One of the major documents of the Qumran library is *The Community Rule* (1QS), the סרך היחד and it, too, contains admonitions and encouragements to properly follow its order.

Of course, more specific analyses revealing Paul's proximity and indebtedness to a prophetically inspired apocalyptic community similar to Qumran need to be carried out. By way of example, two such themes are reviewed briefly: ברית and biblical hermeneutics.

ברית

There is significant variance in the use of ברית between the conceptual frameworks of the Essene Community of Qumran and that of the Pharisees, with the Qumran community's understand-

[116] For example, 1QS 2:16; 1QM 1:1, 13; 13:16.
[117] See Donfried, "The Assembly," 405-407.

ing of ברית virtually absent from the latter. Talmon suggests that the Rabbis "did not develop the notion that in their days, and with their community, God had renewed his covenant of old with the people of Israel. In contrast to the pointed *communal* thrust of the Covenanter's concept of ברית and specifically ברית חדשה the noun ברית, *per se* and in diverse word combinations, connotes in the Rabbinic vocabulary exclusively the act of circumcision. On the strength of this rite, every male infant is *individually* accepted into ברית אברהם אבינו, God's ancient covenant with all Israel." This "specific technical connotation of ברית," he continues, "is not documented in *yaḥad* literature. On the other hand, the *communal* dimension of ברית which attaches to the concept of 'covenant renewal' in the Covenanters' theology, as reflected in the Foundation Documents, appears to be altogether absent from the Rabbinic world of thought."[118]

In light of this strikingly different usage between these two Torah schools, it is of considerable interest to note Paul's evident affinity for the *yaḥad's* use of ברית, particularly in the context of an ecclesial comparison of the καινὴ διαθήκη with the old in 2 Cor 3:6 and 3:14. For Paul there is correspondingly a communal thrust in the context of the new covenant. It is also remarkable that the only two communities that accentuate and interpret Jeremiah's ברית חדשה are the *yaḥad* and the early Jesus movement, especially as reflected in Paul.

Biblical Hermeneutics

In his comparison of the approaches to the Law represented by Qumran and the rabbis, Daniel Schwartz makes reference to "the rabbinic refusal to grant normative importance to contemporary (since Sinai!) divine revelation, as opposed to Qumran which took it for granted."[119] Such an assertion raises the entire issue of how

---

[118] Shemaryahu Talmon, "The Community," 14-15.

[119] Daniel Schwartz, "Law and Truth: On Qumran-Sadducean and Rabbinic views of the Law," in *The Dead Sea Scrolls: Forty Years of Research* (eds. Devorah Dimant and Uriel Rappaport; Leiden: E.J.Brill, 1992), 229-40, here 238.

biblical interpretation was practiced by the Qumran *yaḥad*, the Rabbis and the Jesus movement represented by Paul.

The *pesher* method of biblical interpretation used by the Qumran community has become well known as a result of the publication of the Dead Sea Scrolls. It is a contemporizing form of interpretation in which prophetic texts are understood as referring to present events in the life of the *yaḥad*. More specifically, in its use of biblical texts it divided the law into distinct categories, i.e., the revealed (*nigleh*) and hidden (*nistar*). The revealed law was known to all of Israel but the hidden was known only to the *yaḥad*. Representative of the former is 1QS 8:15-16: "This (path) is the study of the Law which He commanded by the hand of Moses, that they may do according to all that has been revealed (*nigleh*) from age to age, and as the Prophets have revealed by His Holy Spirit."[120] Thus, the "hidden laws were thus progressively revealed and changed with the times."[121] Both principles are also evident in 1QS 5:11-12: "For they are not reckoned in His Covenant. They have neither inquired nor sought after Him concerning His laws that they might know the hidden things [נסתרות] in which they have sinfully erred; and matters revealed [נגלות] they have treated with insolence."

A further result of the *yaḥad's* prophetic hermeneutic is sharp criticism of Pharisaic rationalist interpretation. They are referred to as *dorshe halaqot*, meaning literally "seekers after smooth things," but more properly understood as "interpreters of false laws."[122] In CD 4:19-20 they are called "builders of the wall…", a phrase remarkably similar to the mishnaic tractate Avot 1:1 where it is taught that one should "Build a fence around the Torah." Similarly, in 1QH 4:10-11 it is stated that "they planned evil [literally, "Belial"] against me to replace your Torah which You taught in my heart with smooth things

---

[120] Translation Geza Vermes, *The Complete Dead Sea Scrolls in English* (New York: Penguin, 1997).

[121] Lawrence H. Schiffman, *Reclaiming the Dead Sea Scrolls: The History of Judaism, the Background of Christianity, the Lost Library of Qumran* (Philadelphia and Jerusalem: The Jewish Publication Society, 1994), 248.

[122] Schiffman, *Reclaiming*, 250.

[i.e. false laws] (which they taught) to Your people."[123] For Schiffman, the Pharisees are accused of following "false laws, finding ways around the requirements of the law, and pronouncing false verdicts in legal cases – practices leading to the virtual annulment of Jewish law in the view of the sect. Indeed, the very existence of such laws constitutes an annulment of the Torah, because it replaces Torah laws with the laws of the Pharisees."[124] Tradition could not be authoritative "since all Israel had gone astray. The true way had only been rediscovered by the sect's teacher."[125]

It should come as no great surprise that the *yaḥad* and Paul cite biblical texts in ways not unrelated. Joseph Fitzmyer has made a careful comparison of the introductory formulas used by Paul to introduce the Old Testament with those used in the Dead Sea Scrolls.[126] He also makes references to the study by B. M. Metzger in which a comparison is made between the formulas used to cite "Old Testament" quotations in the Mishnah and the New Testament.[127] Fitzmyer concludes his meticulous evaluation with the conclusion that Paul's introductory formulas are far closer to the *yaḥad's* method than to the Pharisaic-rabbinic approach of the Mishnah. He then raises two perceptive queries with regard to the

---

[123] Translation and comment by Schiffman, *Reclaiming*, 251.

[124] Schiffman, *Reclaiming*, p. 251. Schiffman adds the following: "Yet the matter is even more complex. In early rabbinic literature, the term 'talmud' referred to the Pharisaic-rabbinic method of study that allows the deduction of laws from one another. It is precisely that method of study that the sectarians are excoriating in this text… Apparently, a substantial difference did exist between these two modes of interpretation. Although the method, known as 'talmud,' used by the Pharisees in this period certainly seemed to yield laws derived from biblical exegesis, the Pharisees did not regard such exegesis as divinely inspired." 252.

[125] Schiffman, *Reclaiming*, 254.

[126] Joseph A. Fitzmyer, "Paul's Jewish Background and the Deeds of the Law," in *According to Paul: Studies in the Theology of the Apostle* (New York: Paulist, 1993), 18-35, here 29-31. See also J. A. Fitzmyer, "The Use of Explicit Old Testament Quotations in Qumran Literature and in the New Testament," *NTS* 7 (1960-61): 297-333.

[127] Bruce M. Metzger, "The Formulas Introducing Quotations of Scripture in the NT and the Mishnah," *JBL* 70 (1951), 297-307.

mode of Pauline citation: "Can the mode have so radically changed from the pre-70 Palestinian custom to that of the Mishnaic in the course of some 150 years? Or is a different custom being followed?"[128]

In this connection one other comment is in order. In Otto Michel's important volume, *Paulus und seine Bibel*,[129] he concluded that no collections similar to Paul's *testimonia* lists or *florilegia* (e.g. Rom 3:10-18; 9:25-29; 15:9-12) could be found in the Jewish tradition.[130] The publication of 4Q Testimonia in 1956 raises in yet another way the intriguing relationship between Paul and the *yaḥad* of Qumran.

Before moving to our final section on Jewish Matrix and Graeco-Roman thought, let me add that I am confident that as additional studies are carried out along the lines suggested the fertile ideas and proposals raised in these conference essays will bear even more significant results. This would include the proposal that Paul's controversial attitude toward the Law may well reflect tensions that were already current with pre-Christian Judaism and that the use of the term "anti-Judaism" may reveal a far more intense "intra-Jewish" polemical situation than recognized given the wealth of new information provided by the Dead Sea Scrolls. And, then too, such fundamental categories as apocalyptic, *hagios*, Temple, the question of a "law-free mission" as well as the subject of exegetical methodology will have received not only a deeper anchoring but also a sharper profile. Additionally, by employing such categories as the realism of Qumran and the nominalism of the Rabbis one may gain a far more precise understanding of the similarities and dissimilarities between these two movements.

---

[128] Fitzmyer, "Paul's Jewish Background," 31.
[129] Otto Michel, *Paulus und seine Bibel* (BFCT 2.18; Gütersloh: Bertelsman, 1929).
[130] Michel, *Paulus und seine Bibel*. 43.

C. The Jewish Matrix And Graeco-Roman Thought

By stressing the Jewishness of Paul one must not deny the validity of the Graeco-Roman context for Paul's apostolic activity; it must be recognized that the Jewish Paul who is now "in Christ" interacts with the pagan culture in partnership with his churches and as one who himself proclaims a theology that is in fundamental conflict with the political theology of the Empire. A splendid example for the use of such political-religious language is 1 Thessalonians. It is difficult to reconstruct in detail the original Pauline message proclaimed in the city and all we can hope for are glimmers of it in the written correspondence. If 1 Thessalonians is at all representative of his original preaching then we certainly do find elements that could have been understood or misunderstood in a distinctly political sense. In 2:12 God, according to the Apostle, calls the Thessalonian Christians into his own βασιλεία; in 5:3 there is an unabashed attack on the *Pax et Securitas* program of the early Principate and in the verses just preceding this criticism one finds three terms heavily laden with political allusions: παρουσία, ἀπάντησις and κύριος. When used as court language παρουσία refers to the arrival of Caesar, a king or an official; ἀπάντησις refers to the citizens meeting a dignitary who is about to visit the city; the term κύριος, especially when used in the same context as the two preceding terms, also has undeniable political connotations. Paul's gospel of Jesus Christ as Lord is in fundamental opposition to the gospel of Caesar Augustus as Lord. It is for this reason that I have argued elsewhere that the deaths referred to in 1 Thessalonians 4 result from an ad hoc persecution are due to politico-religious conflict generated by Paul's preaching in that city.[131]

Paul interacted with pagan culture not only at the political level but also through a wide-range of social interactions, including the

---

[131] For further details see Karl P. Donfried, "The Cults of Thessalonica and the Thessalonian Correspondence," in Donfried, *Paul, Thessalonica and Early Christianity*, 21-48.; also, in the same volume, "1 Thessalonians, Acts and the Early Paul", 69-98.

Synagogue with its *pagan* "god-fearers" who were eventually attracted to Paul's proclamation of the Gospel of Jesus Christ. Renewed attention must be given to the dynamic interaction between cultures in the Roman cities of the period and the fact that the Synagogue stood closer to the center than to the periphery of such interchange. The essay by Destro and Pesce is in many ways paradigmatic precisely because the Diaspora Synagogue welcomed Gentiles and, with that, an entire range of thought and practice that could either be analogous to Pauline thought and practice or in considerable tension and conflict with it, including such themes as the heavenly journey with its "profound combination of Greco-Roman and Judaic elements...."[132] And it is in this context of cultural interpenetration that Cohen's concern for the issue of mixed-marriages takes on particular relevance.

The discerning and perceptive essays gathered together in this volume make evident that a comprehensive understanding of Pauline thought must include the following aspects of his entire and comprehensive matrix:

— an examination of the Pauline letters in their specific and contingent as well as their broader and coherent contexts;

— a careful and precise analysis of all relevant Jewish literature, including the Dead Sea Scrolls;

— the incorporation of all relevant archaeological, historical and literary evidence for the reconstruction of the political, cultural and religious matrix of the Graeco-Roman cities to which Paul's letters are addressed.

---

[132] Destro and Pesce, *"The Heavenly Journey in Paul,"* 190.

Chapter 1
Paul's Jewishness

E. P. Sanders

Two major facts about Paul are well known and not in dispute, thanks to the explicit autobiographical passages in his letters and the most obvious inferences to be drawn from reading those letters: he was a Jew who spoke and wrote in Greek. (Whether or not he knew other languages we do not know.) It is highly probable that he was "at home" in eastern Cilicia and Syria, which were the first areas of his missionary activities as an apostle of Jesus Christ (Gal 1:21). His activity in this area coheres with the statement in Acts that he was originally from Tarsus, in eastern Cilicia (Acts 22:3).

There has long been a question of how deeply Paul was influenced by Hellenistic or Greco-Roman culture. Historically, New Testament scholarship offers a wide range of possibilities: everything from the man who Hellenized Christianity[2] to a Jewish Rabbi whose vision in or near Damascus modified and expanded his thought, without changing his rabbinic characteristics.[3]

I am incompetent to assess the depth of Paul's Hellenism. Many other scholars have imbibed the spirit, tones, and nuances of Greco-

---

[1] Parts of this paper are a revision and expansion of some sections of an earlier essay: E. P. Sanders, "Paul between Judaism and Hellenism," in *St. Paul Among the Philosophers*, (ed. John D. Caputo & Linda Martin Alcoff Bloomington: Indiana University Press, 2009), 74–90.

[2] See e.g. Albert Schweitzer, *The Mysticism of Paul the Apostle* (ed. and trans. William Montgomery; London: A. & C. Black, 1956; repr.; 1st ed. 1931), 26–36. Schweitzer attributes this view especially to F.C. Baur and H.J. Holtzmann. See further Erwin R. Goodenough (with A.T. Kraabel), "Paul and the Hellenization of Christianity," in *Religions in Antiquity: Essays in Memory of Erwin Ramsdell Goodenough* (ed. Jacob Neusner; Leiden: E. J. Brill, 1968), 23–68.

[3] W. D. Davies, *Paul and Rabbinic Judaism: Some Rabbinic Elements in Pauline Theology* (Mifflintown, Pa.: Siglar Press, 1998). This publication includes the original text of 1948 and additional material from 1955, 1980, and 1998.

Roman discourse much more deeply than I have, and I must leave to them the task of defining the scope and depth of Paul's Hellenism. I am not opposed to their efforts: on the contrary, I urge them on.[4] I suspect that the level of specialization that our fields have now reached makes it almost impossible for any one person to do full justice to Paul's cultural setting, what we usually call his "background." I am rather pleased that I have avoided the task of trying to define his background and the influences on him, pursuing, rather, comparison and contrast between his letters and other material that I have studied.

What I shall try to do in this essay is to define some of the main aspects of Paul's Jewishness, and I want to focus on the largest categories that are accessible to us. The essay falls into three main parts. I start with education, which we shall explore by considering quotations; this in turn requires us to investigate memorization.

1. EDUCATION, QUOTATIONS, MEMORIZATION

A few months ago my brother-in-law told me that he had recently run across a word he did not know, "guerdon." It appeared to him to mean "something earned," and he asked if I knew it. Because my brain is old and slow it took several seconds, but I came up with a quotation, "ere the guerdon be gained, the reward of it all," which confirmed the meaning "something that is earned."

I knew the source: "Prospice" by Robert Browning. So I got the book and we read through the poem. Later that day, I became curious about how much of the poem I could recite, now that my memory had been jogged. It turned out to be about half of the whole—some lines here, some there.

---

[4] See, for example, Stanley Stowers, *A Rereading of Romans: Justice, Jews, & Gentiles* (New Haven: Yale University Press, 1994); Troels Engberg-Pedersen, *Paul and the Stoics* (Edinburgh: T&T Clark/Westminster John Knox, 2000); Dale Martin, *The Corinthian Body* (New Haven: Yale University Press, 1995).

I had never set myself the task of memorizing Browning's poem on facing death: that is the prospect to which the title refers. About fifty years earlier, I had read through the collected works of Browning once, and I had read the poems a few times, perhaps thrice; part of "Prospice" had lodged in my memory, to be called forth at the mention of an unusual word.

For the sake of contrast and comparison with Paul, I shall indulge myself in the sentimental recollection of my life as a memorizer of poetry. In my childhood in the vast and dusty plains of north central Texas, besides attending school, I had only three activities: reading my mother's college books, especially English literature; playing informal games of baseball; and playing informal games of American football. I had from 3:30 to 10:00 p.m., plus weekends and summers, to indulge my three pastimes. So I read and re-read a lot of English literature.

From about the age of seven to age fifteen I memorized my favorite bits—those that appealed to a boy who liked strong rhyme and rhythm, fast pace, action, blood and gore, and romantic sentimentality.

The Jewish participants in the conference on which this volume is based grew up in an academic environment that encouraged memorization. My life as memorizer was opposed to the educational philosophy of my time and place, which was that learning by rote was damaging because it (supposedly) ruined creativity: memorization was at best unnecessary; one should know only where to look things up. I personally resented this doctrine and imagined myself being forced to go through life with reference works strapped to my back, and so I carried on memorizing. From my untrained reading and repetition, I learned several things about memory. It can, on demand, supply lines containing specific words, such as "guerdon," and thus permit word studies; it will therefore produce texts that are related to one another in content or vocabulary; it can recall lengthy texts with no more than minor variation from the original; it will sometimes conflate similar texts. In my adulthood, for example, I discovered that my boyhood memory had conflated Mark Antony's two orations over the corpse of Caesar in Shakespeare's "Julius Caesar."

The educational philosophy of Paul's time was totally different from that of my day. In the ancient world, everyone knew that children memorize quite easily, and also that memorization in childhood and youth is much easier than carrying heavy scrolls around and rolling them backwards and forwards when in search of a favorite passage. Ancient education was based on reading aloud, repeating, and often memorizing, either deliberately or incidentally, from mere repetition. The elite young males of the Greco-Roman world memorized tons of Greek poetry, and the Romans also memorized a lot of Latin material.[5] One of the purposes of education was to allow a man to come up with an apt quotation in the law court, the *boulê*, or the Senate.

We do not know very much about Jewish education in Paul's day, either in Palestine or in the Diaspora. We may assume that students learned to read, to repeat, and thus to memorize. More importantly, we can use inferences from later Rabbinic sources to consider the quantity of material that students could memorize. Memorization of the Bible is almost self-evident to the reader of rabbinic literature, and it has been confirmed by experts who have studied the issue.[6] It would be impossible to conduct the discussions of the *Midrashim* by turning scrolls. Thus we may be absolutely certain that memorization of the Bible is within the mental capacity of an intelligent person during childhood and youth. I suppose that an unusual adult, such as Rabbi Akiva, could do the same.

We may construct a kind of syllogism: education inculcated and relied on memorization; memorization resulted in quotation; therefore quotation reveals education.

---

[5] See Henri Marrou, *A History of Education in Antiquity* (London: Sheed and Ward, 1956; repr. 1981), e.g. pp. 154, 166; Stanley F. Bonner, *Education in Ancient Rome from the Elder Cato to the Younger Pliny* (London: Methuen & Co., 1977), pp. 39, 111, 144, 307.

[6] Saul Lieberman, *Hellenism in Jewish Palestine: Studies in the Literary Transmission, Beliefs and Manners of Palestine in the I Century B.C.E.-IV Century C.E.* (New York: Jewish Theological Seminary of America, 5722/1962), p. 52.

Paul wrote that he exceeded most of his contemporaries in zeal for the traditions of his ancestors (Gal 1:14), which I take to mean that he was the smartest boy in the class and learned the most about the subjects that they studied. When we meet Paul in his letters, he was probably in his 40s or 50s, and his brain may not have been quite as quick as when he was 15, but he still had the facility to recall and quote what he had learned.

It seems to me that on the basis of his quotations we must assume that Paul memorized the Bible in Greek, or at least large portions of it. In the surviving letters he does not quote any other source, except for one adage—"Bad company ruins good morals" in 1 Cor 15:33—which immediately follows a quotation from Isaiah. I think that if Paul had memorized the right bits of Greek philosophy he would have come up with a quotation in 2 Cor 4:18, where he wrote that what is seen is transient but what cannot be seen is eternal. Even the works of his older contemporary, Philo, would have helped out there. Similarly it would have been easy for a scholar of Greek philosophy to use a quotation to support Phil 4:11, "I have learned to be *autarkês*," "self-sufficient." The word was applied to Socrates, and it was used in various schools of Greek philosophy, including Platonism and Stoicism.

Paul clearly was not entirely ignorant of Greek thought, but he seems not to have had at his fingertips apt quotations, which probably means that he had not memorized a lot of Greek literature during his life as a student—which presumably ended at about the age 15 or 16.[7]

---

[7] Elite Roman males took the *toga virilis* between the ages of 14 and 16 and were ready to begin learning how to govern the empire by entering military service. A few went on to advanced studies. The future Augustus was studying in Apollonia (Dalmatia) when the assassination of Gaius Julius Caesar called him back to Rome at age 17 or 18. This system continued until fairly recent times. For example, John Adams (born 1735) finished school at 15 and then spent four years at Harvard; John Lloyd Stephens (born in New Jersey in 1803) finished school at age 13, graduated from Columbia College at 17, and finished law school at 19. See, e.g., J. P. V. D. Balsdon, *Life and Leisure in Ancient Rome* (London: Phoenix Press, 2002 [1969], pp. 92–106, 233–235; *Oxford Classical*

Thus I have a simple proposal for basic aspect number one of Paul's Jewish matrix: as a boy and youth he studied the Greek Bible, which meant that he memorized it either in whole or in part. If not exclusively Jewish, his education was at least heavily Jewish.

Two aspects of Paul's use of quotations in argumentation stand out when considered in the light of memorization. One is that he could do "word studies," which would otherwise be very difficult. In Gal 3 he quotes the only two passages in the Septuagint that combine the roots for "faith" and "righteousness" (Gen 1:6; Hab 2:4). He also quotes the only passage in the Septuagint that combines the words "law" and "curse" (Deut 27:26). This is easily explicable if he had memorized Genesis, Deuteronomy, and Habakkuk. If he actually had to find every single use of these word combinations by turning scrolls, he and his assistants would have been at it for weeks if not months. The only reasonable explanation is memory. He did not wish to say in general that disobeying commandments brings a curse, but rather he wanted to connect "curse" with the word *nomos*, "law," and his memory produced the only instance in his scripture.

I think that memory is also responsible for the fact that a lot of Paul's quotations are conflated—like my quotation of Mark Antony's orations over the corpse of Caesar. Staying just with Gal 3, we note that Gal 3:8, "all the Gentiles will be blessed in you," conflates Gen. 12:3 with 18:18, while Gal 3:10 borrows from Deut 27:26 and 28:58. Once the memory has a key word, it will produce passages containing that word, and conflation is much more likely to be the result of memory than of turning the pages of a scroll and deliberately taking one word from one passage and

---

Dictionary, s.v. iuvenes; David McCullough, *John Adams* (New York: Simon & Schuster, 2001), pp. 34–35f. Victor Wolfgang von Hagen, "Introduction," in John Lloyd Stephens, *Incidents of Travel in Egypt, Arabia Petraea, and the Holy Land* (Norman Okla.: University of Oklahoma Press, 1970; repr. Dover, 1996). Stephens's work was originally published in 1837. Conceivably Paul was a student beyond the age of 16, but his principal period of study and memorization of literature would have ended by then.

a few words from another. Perhaps that is not so difficult if one conflates passages that are only a few chapters apart. But elsewhere Paul conflates Isaiah and Jeremiah, for example, which is much harder if one thinks of him as studiously rolling scrolls.

In Paul's usages of the LXX that are not signaled as quotations by the phrase "as it is written," and the like, there is also conflation, as we shall see immediately below. This is even more telling: his head was filled with the words of his scripture.

Paul *could* write and argue without quoting his scripture explicitly, and he may well have routinely preached to Gentiles without overtly referring to the Bible. In Philemon, 1 Thessalonians, Philippians, and 2 Cor 10–13, there is not a single explicit quotation from Jewish scripture: that is, no instance in which Paul wrote "as it is written," or a similar phrase. Together, these four parts of Paul's letters amount to about 20% of the entire seven-letter corpus.

Nevertheless, in all these cases except Philemon, the language of the Greek Bible is clearly evident at several places. I shall take only three examples: one from 1 Thessalonians, one from Philippians, and one from 2 Cor 10–13.

a. 1 Thess 4:8, which states that God gives his Spirit to people, called "you," is a combination of two verses from Ezekiel, 36:27 and 37:14.

b. The words "blemish" and "crooked and perverse generation" in Phil 2:15 are taken from Deut 32:5.[8]

c. "Let the one who boasts boast in the Lord" (2 Cor 10:17) is taken from 1 Kngdms. [1 Sam] 2:10[9] or Jer 9:22–23.[10]

The first of these examples contains conflation. It is also worth noting that the quotations in Philippians and 2 Corinthians

[8] The Hebrew and English of Deut 32:5 do not include the word "blemish," which appears in the Greek translation of Deuteronomy and in Paul's quotation of it.

[9] The verse that Paul partially quotes is in the Greek translation of the Bible but does not appear in Hebrew or English.

[10] The verse numbers are 22–3 in the Greek and Hebrew, 23–4 in the English translation.

agree with the Greek translation of the Bible where it differs from the Hebrew version (see notes 8 and 9).[11]

Thus, although Paul did not use formal quotations all of the time, he did not write very long without using at least a few phrases from his scripture. This fact argues very strongly in favor of substantial memorization. One of the things that we know about him with greatest certainty is that his brain was saturated with the words of his scripture.

It appears to me that New Testament scholars often think of Paul as having a considerable library, containing the 20 plus scrolls required to hold the Bible, as well as possessing a large study with several tables where the scrolls could be rolled out and compared. This is a view of Paul as the prototype of a modern professor. Reality was quite different. During many of his years he spent weeks or even months on the road. Did he have enough money to own the Biblical scrolls? Did he have enough asses to carry a large library through the Gates of Cilicia and across the Anatolian plateau? And when he was ready to set up a table for leatherwork, to produce tents, did he manage to rent a huge studio instead of a mere hole-in-the wall? His financial difficulties argue against such views and in favor of his carrying the Bible where it should be carried, in his brain.

Prior to the conference at which this paper was read, my experience in verbally proposing to various colleagues that Paul had memorized the Bible had been that Christian scholars regard the idea as somewhere on a line running from "highly improbable" to "totally impossible," while Jewish scholars assume that he had done so. To

[11] This issue is very complicated, since we know neither that the Greek Bible that Paul studied is the same as the Septuagint (LXX) as we now have it, nor that the Hebrew text of his day was the same as the Masoretic (Hebrew) text that is in use today. I assume, however, that there is some continuity in both cases. Paul so often agrees with the Septuagint (as reconstructed by modern scholars) against the Masoretic text that it is likely that his disagreements with the Masoretic text result from the fact that the Greek text as he learned it in his childhood and youth was close to the Septuagint as we know it. There are, to be sure, counter-examples, in which Paul's quotation is closer to the Masoretic text than to the LXX (e.g. the quotation of Job 41:3 in Rom 11:35).

some degree, this response continued at the conference. One of the Jewish scholars present, for example, asked which of the extra-Biblical traditions Paul had *also* memorized.[12] Christian scholars proposed, among other things, that even if he did not travel with scrolls he consulted them in synagogues or even in public libraries in each city. Moreover, after his call to be an apostle, but before he began his travels, he could have spent months in study, during which he composed Biblical arguments that would serve him well in his apostolic career.

To respond to such doubts, I shall itemize a few points:

1. To repeat, memorization of a text the size of the Hebrew Bible is well within the capacity of a human brain, especially a young person's brain, and more especially the brain of the young person who was the smartest in his class. If Rabbis could and still can do it, why should we doubt that Paul could and did?

2. We should accept that Paul learned the way his contemporaries did—by reading, repetition, and memorization.

3. We should accept that Paul used his learning the way his contemporaries did—by pulling apt quotations out of his memory at the right moment. If everyone knew that memorization in youth is easier than turning scrolls in adulthood, why should we insist that he did it the hard way? Or why have him, alone among ancient sages, return to his (supposed) library for study before answering a question or responding to an objection?

4. Our general conception of Paul's life and career should be, I think, that Paul was busy and that he was in a rush to complete his mission before the Lord returned. With regard to busyness: as noted above, he was on the road for a high percentage of the time. During

---

[12] Unfortunately, I could not answer this highly appropriate question, though Paul himself refers to learning "traditions" (Gal 1:14). The problem is that the traditions that we can securely attribute to pre-Pauline Pharisaism have to do with legal issues that he does not mention, such as *'ērûvîn* ("the fusion of Sabbath limits"), laying one's hand on the head of a sacrificial victim on a Festival Day (*yôm tôv*, for which see *m. Betsah*), and the number of tithes paid in each seven-year cycle. I have discussed these legal topics briefly in *Judaism: Practice and Belief, 63 BCE–66 CE* (London: SCM, 1992), 425–6, 147–50, 429.

his establishment of his churches he often supported himself by working with his hands, so as not to burden his converts (1 Thess 2:9, "we worked night and day"; 1 Cor 4:12, "we grow weary from the work of our own hands"; 1 Cor 9:6, he and Barnabas had to work for a living).[13] He also had to spend time converting Gentiles. Then there was the "daily pressure" to take care of his churches (2 Cor 11:28). He had to pastor his converts while present, write letters to provide support and advice from afar, and make emergency trips to try to quell rebellions against his authority or to prop up the wavering. He did not have the leisure quietly to sit and study when issues arose. He relied on his memory to provide biblical arguments when he needed them.

5. Some of Paul's biblical arguments could not have been prepared in advance. Galatians 3 is the simplest case, since during Paul's days in Arabia he could not have foreseen the Galatian controversy. Gal 3:10–12 would be almost impossible to write without memorization of substantial parts of three books of the Bible. If his memory was good enough there, why not elsewhere?

6. On the other hand, re-using an argument that he had developed as a youth or as a persecutor is quite possible. My own favorite case in favor of prior preparation is 1 Cor 10:7–10, which is easily comprehensible as part of a synagogue sermon.[14] The passage is both ingenious and complicated, and it would, I think, have merited praise from expert Jewish exegetes.

An unintended consequence of this discussion of Paul's quotations is that we need to consider the possibility of schools that

[13] Paul thought that he had the right of support from his churches (1 Cor 9:4–11), and in Corinth he accepted gifts from other churches (2 Cor 11:8), but apparently neither the Thessalonians nor the Corinthians supported him during his founding visits to those cities. 1 Cor 9:6 seems to reflect a *general* resentment of having to support himself. Possibly the special status of himself and Barnabas indicates that other apostles took their need to work to show that they were inferior.

[14] I proposed above that Paul's vice lists were derived from synagogue homilies, and elsewhere I suggested that Rom 2 is synagogal material. See *Paul, the Law, and the Jewish People* (Philadelphia: Fortress, 1983), 123–135.

emphasized learning the Hebrew Bible in Greek. One could speculate on the nature of such schools, but I shall not do so. The lack of quotations from the curriculum of the ordinary *gymnasion*, however, makes me doubt that Paul had attended a regular Hellenistic school, though I suppose that he might have disciplined his brain not to quote the Greek classics.[15] In any case, I think that we should consider the possibility of Diaspora schools that made the Bible the principal object of study. Someone—not I—might wish to suggest that Paul attended a Greek-speaking school in Jerusalem.[16]

I have two last points before leaving Paul's quotations: first, we do not need to think that Paul memorized the Bible by beginning with the first words of Genesis and learning every single word straight through the entire Biblical text. What Paul's quotations reveal, rather, is what Albert Baumgarten has called "an art of investigation and retrieval."[17] He could find in his brain texts that corresponded, more-or-less well, to the words and ideas that he needed when he needed them. This comes, of course, from repeated reading. Whether he could have begun with the first book of Moses and recited the entire text through is another issue. All we know about his memory is that he could do what his quotations reveal that he could do: quote texts containing certain words when he needed them.

Secondly, for all we know, Paul knew the Bible equally well in Hebrew. We can prove only that he usually quoted it in a form very close to the Septuagint as it has come down to us. But this does not disprove the theory that he studied in Jerusalem and knew the Bible in Hebrew. I once knew a young rabbinic student from North Africa who said that if he preached in Hebrew he quoted the

---

[15] For the usual curriculum, see Marrou, *History of Education*, 162–164.

[16] For evidence of such schools beginning early in the second century and continuing into the fourth, see Saul Lieberman's *Greek in Jewish Palestine* (New York: Philipp Feldheim, 1965). Lieberman does not deal with the first century, but his general statements seem to exclude the possibility of Greek-language schools that early (see 1, 16).

[17] Albert I. Baumgarten, "Metaphors of Memory," in Ronen Reichman (ed.), *Der Odem des Menschen ist eine Leuchte des Herrn. Aharon Agus zum Gedenken* (Heidelberg: Universitätsverlag, 2006), 77–90, here 78.

Hebrew Bible, whereas if he preached in English he quoted the English translation—both from memory. I do not favor the view of Acts that Paul was educated in Jerusalem, but it does not appear to me to be impossible that part of his education was there and that he knew Hebrew.

2. Four Topics in Summary

I wish now to describe a few of the larger aspects of Paul's thought very briefly. I believe that none of these requires much elaboration or much proof of quintessential Jewishness, but I wish to put on the record the fact that the major categories of Paul's thought are Jewish.

1. Paul's theology in the strict sense of the word was a Jewish form of modified monotheism. "Modified" means that besides the true or high God room was found for other gods, lords, and spiritual powers (as in 1 Cor 8:5 and 2 Cor 4:4). As Paula Fredriksen has recently emphasized, lots of people, not only Jews, shared this sort of monotheism.[18] What was Jewish about Paul's version was the fact that the true God was the God of Israel. Within Jewish sources, Paul's views of other spiritual beings are closest to the Dead Sea Scrolls and some of the Apocalypses. He also joined his Jewish contemporaries in denouncing the worship of idols.

2. Paul's view of time and history was Jewish. The most common Greek view was that history is cyclical.[19] In Judaism, history begins with creation and moves towards a conclusion that is determined by God. That was Paul's view precisely, as we shall see more

---

[18] Paula Fredriksen, *Augustine and the Jews: A Christian Defense of Jews and Judaism* (New York: Doubleday: 2008), 42–43 and elsewhere.

[19] See e.g. J. M. Rist, *Stoic Philosophy* (Cambridge: Cambridge University Press, 1969), 93. Note also that, according to Diogenes Laertius, God (=the world) "at stated periods of time absorbs into himself the whole reality and again creates it from himself" [in J. von Arnim, *Stoicorum veterum fragmenta* (Leipzig, 1905–24, 4 vols.), vol. 2, p. 526], quoted in Jason L. Saunders, *Greek and Roman Philosophy after Aristotle* (London: Collier-Macmillan, 1966), 90.

fully in the next section of this paper. To give a little more definition here: Paul's view of history was highly eschatological, focused on the imminent arrival of the climax of ordinary history. Lots of cultures had views of individual eschatology: rewards and punishments after death. Many forms of Judaism, however, following portions of the Bible, tended towards the view of a grand climax of this age, after which the elect would enjoy peace, prosperity, and security. Paul's expectations are, again, closest to what one finds in some of the Apocalypses. I wish to emphasize that basic to this worldview was that God determined the entire process from creation to ultimate redemption.

3. Paul's view of his own career—he was apostle to the Gentiles in the last days—was part and parcel of his eschatology. Though apostles to Gentiles do not figure in the predictions of Hebrew prophets, who seem to have expected Gentiles spontaneously to turn to the God of Israel, Paul's mission was in the service of a Jewish vision of the world.

4. Paul's ethics were Jewish. Everyone opposed murder, adultery, theft, robbery, and so on. The largest distinction between Judaism and the rest of the world was the attitude towards homosexual activity. Paul joined other Jews in being entirely against it (1 Cor 6:9; Rom 1:26–27). He discusses a few ethical topics in some detail, but a majority of his ethical opinions, including denunciation of homosexual activity, appears in *lists* of vices. The home of Paul's vice lists seems to be the Diaspora synagogue: idolatry and sexual immorality always head the series. Paul's catena of Gentile vices in Rom 1 is especially close to the list in Wisdom of Solomon 14.[20]

Thus Paul's education, youth, theology, worldview, career, and opinions about correct behavior were all distinctively and deeply Jewish.

---

[20] It is conceivable that Paul had read (without memorizing) the Wisdom of Solomon, but I think it more likely that the connection between idolatry and sexual immorality and the elaboration of resulting sins were common in Diaspora Judaism.

3. THE DISTINCTION BETWEEN JUDAISM AND CHURCH

Despite the origin of the Christian movement as a Jewish sect, and Paul's thorough Jewishness, we should not overlook the indications in his letters that he distinguished his own group from what he called "Judaism" (*Ioudaïsmos*).

First we note the passage where the word "Judaism" appears: Paul uses the noun twice, in Gal 1:13–14, and the verb "to Judaize" once, in Gal 2:14. This is not a lot of evidence, but in Galatians "Judaism" appears to be an entity from his past, not the same as his own present in-group: in Gal 1:13–14 he speaks of "his earlier life in Judaism." In the next verse, 1:15, the revelation of Christ to him interrupts this life in Judaism and leads to the result, a chapter later, that he no longer lives, but rather Christ lives in him (Gal 2:20). In this section of Galatians he also represents himself as accusing Peter of wanting the Gentile Christians in Antioch to "Judaize" (*Ioudaïzein*), which Paul regards as the wrong thing for Gentiles who believed in Christ to do.

Secondly, I note that Paul had terms for his own group—not the word "Christian" or "Christianity," but nevertheless a distinct terminology. Scholars frequently ignore or undervalue this evidence. In Gal 6:6, he uses the phrase "the Israel of God," possibly meaning his own group. Even if the ambiguous wording of that passage does apply the word "Israel" to Paul's group, the notion of a "true Israel" is otherwise not explicit.[21] Paul calls his group, rather, "the

[21] After the full emergence of the idea that "those in Christ" constitute the "true Israel" and that Jews were falsely so called and were in fact "a synagogue of Satan" (Rev. 2:9; 3:9), it became possible to find in Paul's letters support for the church as "true Israel." Apart from one of the possible interpretations of Gal 6:16, the strongest case is Gal 3:16-29: the promises were made to Abraham, but (only?) those who belong to Christ are descendants of Abraham. One might also construct the following argument: just as Paul's converts are "Christ's," Christ is "God's" (1 Cor 3:23). Paul's converts are "sons of God" through their faith in Christ (Gal 3:26). "God" in both cases is the God of the whole world, who is the God of Israel. So Paul's converts are the people of God, who were classically called "Israel." Despite the logic of these connections between Paul's group and

church" or, better, "the congregation" (*ekklêsia*), a word that occurs alone and in a variety of phrases, such as "the congregation[s] of God" in 1 Thess 2:14 and elsewhere (1 Cor 10:32; 11:16). A second term that appears in 1 Thessalonians, which is Paul's earliest surviving letter, is "those who believe," *hoi pisteuontes* (1 Thess 1:7; 2:10, 13; also Rom 1:16.)

He often designates his group by a phrase that includes the word "Christ," such as those who are "called of Jesus Christ" (Rom 1:6); those who are "baptized in Christ Jesus" (Rom 6:3); those in whom Christ is (Rom 8:10); "joint heirs with Christ" (Rom 8:17); "one body in Christ" (Rom 12:5); "the body of Christ" (1 Cor 12:27); those who are "sanctified in Christ" (1 Cor 1:2); "members of Christ" (1 Cor 6:15); those who are "Christ's" (2 Cor 10:7; Gal 3:29); those who are "in Christ" (Gal 3:27, 28); and "the saints in Christ Jesus" (Phil 1:1). The "dead in Christ" have a special status when the Lord returns (1 Thess 4:16). It is easy to call these people "Christians," and I see no reason to avoid the use of the term when discussing Paul's converts: they are "Christians," people "in Christ," not "Jews" or "Israelites."

Thirdly, in the surviving letters Paul occasionally uses tri-partite terminology: "Give no offense to Jews, or to Greeks, or to the church of God" (1 Cor 10:32). In Rom 9:32 he distinguishes "us"—his group—from the Jews and the Gentiles, who are the groups from which "we" were called. "Jews" and "the congregation of God" are distinct entities. Terminologically, then, Paul distinguished his in-group from both Jews and Gentiles, from both Judaism and paganism.

---

the title "Israel," I still would not say that we have evidence that Paul viewed his churches as the "true Israel." The idea is only incipient and is not explicitly stated. The inferences that may be derived from such passages as Gal 3 cannot overwhelm the numerous cases in which Paul distinguishes his group from Jews and Judaism. We should note Paul's direct statements that his own people are "Israelites" and that they still have the "adoption" and the promises (Rom 9:2–5). An alternative later definition of the Christians was that they constituted a "third race." The Pauline background of this conception is much clearer—though his goal was a unified new humanity.

The terminology reflects the *social fact* that Paul inhabited a tri-partite world: there were Jews, pagans and those who belonged to Christ, some of whom had belonged to Judaism, and some to paganism.

Paul's converts, as far as we know, were the latter: they were Gentiles, former pagans or idolaters. He states this explicitly in the case of the Thessalonian and Galatian Christians (1Thess 1:9; Gal 4:8), and the desire of his Corinthian converts to attend idolatrous festivals points towards a background of paganism (1 Cor 8, 10). In autobiographical statements he depicts himself as apostle to Gentiles (*ta ethnê*) (Rom 11:13; 15:16, 18), and there is no indication of Jewish converts within his own churches. Acts depicts Paul as originally an apostle to Diaspora Jews, who turned to Gentiles only out of disappointment with his Jewish mission (e.g. Acts 13:46; 18:6). Paul's own view, however, was quite different: Christ sent him to Gentiles.[22]

We find the same point when we consider his political settlement with the Jerusalem apostles. He and Peter divided up the world—Peter would go to the Jews, Paul to the Gentiles (Gal 2:7–10). Some scholars have construed this as a geographical division, but the most natural interpretation of the language, which refers to the "circumcised" and the "uncircumcised," is an ethnic division. According to this agreement, as well as his description of himself, Paul was not apostle to everyone from the Levant to Europe, but rather apostle to pagans. I do not mean that he would have refused opportunities to propose the gospel to Jews, but that was not his mission.[23]

There is no hint that Paul's converts attended synagogues.[24]

---

[22] This view appears once even in Acts (see 22:21).

[23] Ronald Hock, *The Social Context of Paul's Ministry: Tentmaking and Apostleship* (Philadelphia: Fortress, 1980), gives a convincing discussion of how Paul approached pagans, which provides a useful alternative to the view of Acts, that he found God-fearers in Jewish synagogues.

[24] This is the one point in Fredriksen's depiction of early Christianity with which I disagree. She insists that early Christian groups formed in Synagogues and constituted Hellenistic Jewish communities that, like synagogues, welcomed Gentiles. See *Augustine and the Jews*, pp. xiii, 28; cf. 50. Curiously, she distinguishes the church in Rome as a Gentile Christian community (8).

They had their own meetings, aspects of which Paul describes in chapters 11 and 14 of 1 Corinthians. Had they also attended synagogue, issues would have arisen that required discussion in Paul's letters. The church in Rome—which Paul did not found—helps make the point. Paul's letter to Rome implies that the congregation included both Jews and Gentiles, or at least his letter allows for that possibility: in 11:13 he writes, "Now I am speaking to you Gentiles." In writing to a mixed or possibly mixed congregation, he found it useful or necessary to discuss observance of "the day," presumably the Sabbath (14:5–6), and food laws (14:13–23). These issues of Jewish law and practice do not arise as problems in the letters addressed to the churches that he himself founded, except for Galatians.[25] In Galatia, however, outsiders, other apostles of Christ, apparently neither members of his congregation nor local Jews, introduced the topic of circumcision and the rest of the law. It seems very likely that such topics would have arisen in (for example) Corinth, had the Corinthians been attending synagogues. They asked about pagan sacrifices, not about observance of the Sabbath.

The social distinctiveness of his converts was obvious to Paul, sometimes painfully obvious. Since they were neither Jew nor pagan, they were isolated, without a recognizable social identity.[26] This lack of identity could lead to harassment and persecution for

---

[25] There is an attack on circumcisers in Phil 3:2, but no hint that this is a problem in Philippi. The likeliest explanation is that this is an echo of his dispute with the Galatians. See Gregory Tatum, *New Chapters in the Life of Paul: The Relative Chronology of His Career* (CBQMS 41; Washington, D.C.: Catholic Biblical Association, 2006), 73–83.

[26] E. P. Sanders, "Paul," *Enyclopedia Brittanica* (Ultimate CD ROM, 2007): "Moreover, since Paul's converts did not become Jewish, they were, in general opinion, *nothing*: neither Jew nor pagan. Religiously, they could identify only with one another, and frequently they must have wavered because of their isolation from the well-established and popular activities of both Jew and pagan. It was especially difficult for them to refrain from public festivities, since parades, feasts, theatrical performances, and athletic competitions were all connected to idolatry. This social isolation intensified their need to have rewarding spiritual experiences within the Christian communities." See also Fredriksen, *Augustine and the Jews*, 36–38.

not supporting the local cults. Even in the absence of persecution, his followers had to do without many of the pleasures of civic life that were afforded by the public religious celebrations, such as feasting on red meat.

Thus we see that Paul's vocabulary for his group accurately reflects the *new social reality* that resulted from his preaching the gospel of Christ—congregations of Gentiles who renounced idolatry, who worshipped the God of Israel outside of the synagogue, who counted as neither Jew nor pagan, and who accepted Jesus as their savior and Lord.

I suppose that someone will think that this social and terminological distinction between Paul's group and Judaism means that I have just claimed that Paul stopped being Jewish. His self-identity is another issue entirely. He was Jewish and regarded himself as the Jewish apostle to Gentiles in the last days. He states his own identity explicitly in Rom 9:2–5. His "own people" are "Israelites," to whom belong "the adoption… the covenants… and the promises."

On the other hand, we must note his strong conviction that he and other members of the body of Christ acquired a new identity. Paul was a Jew who had become one person with Christ. And, as he wrote, if anyone is in Christ, he is a "new creation" (2 Cor 5:17). Nevertheless, being one person with Christ, part of a new creation, did not make Paul himself a non-Jew. Jesus was a Jew (Rom 9:5), and we cannot think that at any point Paul would have rejected his ethnic identity. He was a Jew who was in Christ, and his converts were Gentiles who were in Christ.[27]

The present point, however, is not to define Paul's own identity, but rather to point out the fact that he did not think of his in-group as "Judaism." The only way he could have claimed or thought that his churches constituted part of "Judaism" would

---

[27] I leave aside here the question of whether or not there is any contradiction between Paul's speaking of his "former life in Judaism" and being part of a "new creation," on the one hand, and still belonging to the people of Israel, on the other. He states both, which I take at least to prove that in his own mind he did not stop being Jewish. Many Jews may have regarded him as a lapsed or renegade Jew.

have been to make a clear distinction between false Israel and true Israel. He could have written that the new creation was the true Judaism, but as far as we know he did not do so. Unfortunately, we cannot consider "true Israel" here, beyond the brief discussion in note 21, where I proposed that the future notion of the church as "true Israel" was no more than incipient in Paul's terminology. I doubt that such a definition of the churches ever rose to the level of consciousness. Thus *he* was Jewish as well as a new person in Christ, but his congregations did not constitute "Judaism," which was a separate entity.

While Paul recognized the social distinction that he and others were creating on the ground—a new spiritual identity, neither Jewish nor pagan—this division was neither what he wanted nor what he expected as the final outcome. His *theology* and his *intention* had quite a different focus. There should be one universal group, including Jew, Greek and Barbarian, all of whom were in Christ. It was not acceptable to him for the Gentile members of his movement to Judaize, thus reducing the number of groups by one. His opposition to Judaizing led to the strongest invective in his letters (Galatians and Philippians). His group should not Judaize; rather, everyone else should join his group.

With regard to the *designation* of this future totally inclusive group, the most obvious choice is "new creation," because of Gal 6:15, "neither circumcision nor uncircumcision is anything, but a new creation." We earlier saw that those who are "in Christ" are a "new creation" (2 Cor 5:17). In more traditional terms, 1 Cor 15:25 suggests the phrase "the kingdom of God."

Paul knew theologically what the outcome should be, but he also saw that the present plan for getting there was not working perfectly. The present plan, we recall, was that he (and apparently others) would convert Gentiles to faith in Christ. Peter and presumably the other Jerusalem apostles would persuade Jews to put their faith in Jesus as well. Then everyone would be part of the people of God in the last days, united by faith in Christ.

By his own estimation, Paul was nearing the end of his labors. Churches in Syria had preceded his call to be an apostle. Someone else had reached Rome before him. He himself had covered the territory from Syria to Macedonia and Greece, bumping up against Illyricum when he was in Macedonia. He did not want to preach where anyone had preceded him: building on someone else's foundation was not his style (Rom 15:20; cf. 1 Cor 3:5–15). Since he had no further room in "these regions," he wrote from Corinth, he planned to deliver a collection of money to Jerusalem, visit the church at Rome briefly, and then go on to Spain (15:25–29). The collection, conceived as the prophetically predicted tribute of the Gentiles to the Israelites, clearly marked a time near the end. He seems not to have thought of North Africa; thus several months or a few years in Spain, and his own work would be done.

Following a triumph in a debate with the Corinthians, Paul expressed an overly optimistic view of his own apostolic success: "Thanks be to God, who in Christ always leads us in triumphal procession, and through us spreads in every place the fragrance that comes from knowing him" (2 Cor 2:14). He was almost equally optimistic in Rom 15: "In Christ Jesus, then, I have reason to boast of my work for God" (15:17). His success was that he had "completed" the gospel from Jerusalem to Illyricum (15:19).

In Paul's estimation, Peter had done much less well. Paul does not say this explicitly, but it is evident from the innovation of Rom 11. The common expectation of the end-time re-gathering of the people of Israel and the turn of Gentiles towards God had followed the obvious sequence: first Israel, then the Gentiles. This is in fact a theme of the first two chapters of Romans: "the Jew first and also the Greek" (1:16; 2:9, 10).[28] So Peter should have prepared the Jews while Paul was carrying out his successful mission to the Gentiles.

But the Jews were not ready. This led Paul to develop an ingenious plan: his Gentiles would enter the new creation first. This would make the Jews jealous, and they would rush in, which would mean that Paul could indirectly save "some" Jews as well as

---

[28] This theme is balanced by repeated assertions of the equality of Jew and Gentile: Rom 2:9–11; 3:9, 22; 10:12.

Gentiles (Rom 11:13–14). He repeats the scheme in verses 25–26: the "full number of Gentiles" will come in and *thus*, in that manner, "all Israel will be saved." To make sure that the reader grasps his brilliant discovery, he repeats it a third time. The Jews have been disobedient, "*in order that*, by the mercy shown to you [Gentiles], they too [Jews] may now receive mercy" (11:30–31).

The term "in order that"—*hina* in Greek—points towards the divine intention: God made the Jews disobedient for a time, in order to allow the Gentiles to have access first, which would then bring the Jews in. Paul has recently discovered God's own true plan for saving everyone, which is a revision of what he and others had previously thought. Now he sees that his own Gentile mission will cause the Jews to come in, *so that* all will receive mercy. But Paul did not leave the implication that this is the divine plan hanging on a single *hina*. He wrote one more verse with a *hina*: "For *God* has imprisoned *all* in disobedience *in order that* he may be merciful to all" (Rom 11:32).

Well, we may think, Paul's success as an apostle and his theory of Jewish jealousy is rather a thin thread from which to hang the hope of eternal salvation for all. I am very pleased that Paul seems to have realized this. He immediately offers a brief panegyric on the wisdom of God: "O the depth of the riches and wisdom and knowledge of God! How unsearchable are his judgments and how inscrutable his ways!" Then he quotes, "Who has known the mind of the Lord?" (11:33–34).

From Rom 11:13 through 11:32, Paul three times offers a rational way in which God can save the world—a sequence in which his own mission plays the crucial role. But in the end, he has to trust that God himself will in any case figure out a way. God's mind can do it, even if Paul's fertile and inventive brain cannot figure it all out. Finally, he leaves universal salvation to God.

This section of the lecture started with the social distinctions between Jew, pagan, and Christian as seen in Paul's letters and has ended up with Paul's theological/eschatological solution to the social partition of humans, namely, all will be one people. The apostles should do their best to bring everyone into the body of

Christ while normal history runs on, though the time is very short. But at the end of time, when the redeemer comes from Mt Zion, God will accomplish the goal—the salvation of the world—in a way that we cannot comprehend.

Since this discussion of universal salvation will have raised questions, I should here add a further comment: yes, I have read all of the exclusivist passages in Paul's letters about the destruction of the unbelievers. I have written about universalism and exclusivism in Paul more than once. Here, unfortunately, I cannot give Paul's exclusivist side. In any case, Paul's last recorded hope and vision were universal.[29]

We return to the end of Rom 11 and the salvation of humanity: I cannot imagine a plan that is more entirely Jewish. In the background is the Jewish doctrine that God created the world and declared it good; that is the principle that is obvious in Paul's first burst of universalism, 1 Cor 15:22: "for as all die in Adam, so all will be made alive in Christ." That passage immediately moves on to the subjection to God of "all things," *ta panta*, at the end (1 Cor 15:27–28). Just as, according to Rom 11:32, God locked up all people in disobedience *in order* to save them all, so in Rom 8 God subjected the entire creation to futility *in order* to set it "free from its bondage to decay" when he brings ordinary history to its end (Rom 8:20–21).

That God has a beneficent long-term plan for a happy end to normal history is a deeply Jewish thought, though the beneficiaries varied in different bodies of literature—from all Israel to a select group of sectarians.[30] That the plan includes sin and suffering along

[29] In *Paul, the Law, and the Jewish People* (index *s.v.* "universalism"), I favored the exclusivist side as Paul's dominant view. In *Paul* (Oxford: OUP, 1991, 2001, 2009), chapter 11, I swung towards emphasizing the universalist side. Most recently, see my emphasis on universalism in "Paul Between Judaism and Hellenism," *St. Paul Among the Philosophers* (ed. Linda Martin Alcoff and John D. Caputo Bloomington: Indiana University Press, 2009), 84–88.

[30] The issue is often complicated. See e.g. E. P. Sanders, *Paul and Palestinian Judaism* (London: SCM, 1977), 257–270; 360–362; 369–71; 378; 408–409. For criticisms that do not take adequate account of these discussions, see Mark Adam Elliott, *The Survivors of Israel: A Reconsideration of the Theology of pre-*

the way is equally Jewish. Similarly, according to Josephus, God planned the transfer of power to Rome, and he planned the destruction of the temple, which had to be purged because of bloodshed and sin. But, Josephus suggested, if you read the passage in Daniel about the Stone, you will know that the redemption of Israel is God's ultimate goal: Josephus, at least, hints at this outcome in *Antiquities* 10.210.[31] Divine control of the ultimate outcome, an outcome that includes redemption, life and freedom on the other side of punishment, suffering and death, is part and parcel of the Jewish idea of divine providence, *pronoia*.

To summarize: Paul lived and worked in the Greek-speaking world. Whatever his knowledge of that environment, his education and upbringing were Jewish; the main categories of his thought were Jewish; his mission was set in the framework of Jewish eschatology; the final outcome for which he longed was a universal form of Jewish hope. Temporarily, he thought, he was creating a third group, distinguishable from both Judaism and paganism, as part of the new creation that would fully arrive when the God of Israel, who was the only true God, brought ordinary history to its conclusion.

Christian Judaism (Grand Rapids: Eerdmans, 2000); Daniel Falk, "Prayers and Psalms," *Justification and Variegated Nomism*, vol. 1, *The Complexities of Second Temple Judaism* (ed. D. A. Carson, Peter T. O'Brien, and Mark A. Seifrid; WUNT, 2 Reihe 140; Tübingen: Mohr Siebeck 2001), 7–57. Most recently, see E. P. Sanders, "Covenantal Nomism Revisited," *JSQ* 16 (2009) 23–55; here 36–38.

[31]See E. P. Sanders, "God Gave the Law to Condemn: Providence in Paul and Josephus," in *The Impartial God: Essays in Biblical Studies in Honor of Jouette M. Bassler* (ed. Calvin J. Roetzel and Robert L. Foster; Sheffield: Phoenix Press, 2007), 78–97; on Josephus, see 82–87.

CHAPTER 2
PAUL'S STANCE ON THE TORAH REVISITED: GENTILE ADDRESSEES AND THE JEWISH SETTING

Serge Ruzer

1. INTRODUCTION

According to Acts, there seems to be no contradiction in the time of messianic redemption between the exemption from the Torah's ritual precepts of those Gentiles who have become part of the Jesus movement and the continuing faithfulness of Jewish believers in Jesus to these precepts (Acts 15:1–29; 21:18–25).[1] Moreover, the tragic Stephen episode in Acts 7 notwithstanding, the author's balancing act aims to establish that not only the first Jerusalem-based apostles but also Paul – even after his impressive missionary successes among the non-Jews in the Diaspora – remained faithful to the Temple, undoubtedly the core element of Jewish ritual observance of the day (Acts 2:46; 21:26).[2]

Paul's Epistles, however, appear to present a different picture, and it is on them that the traditional interpretation of Paul's

---

[1] The English quotations from the Old and New Testaments throughout this paper are from the RSV.

[2] See Hanz Conzelman, *Acts of the Apostles: A Commentary on the Acts of the Apostles* (Hermeneia; Philadelphia: Fortress, 1987), 24. For discussion of the strategies employed here and throughout Acts, see, for example, Steven G. Wilson, *The Gentiles and the Gentile Mission in Luke-Acts* (Cambridge: Cambridge University Press, 1973); Robert L. Brawley, *Luke-Acts and the Jews: Conflict, Apology, and Conciliation* (Atlanta, Ga: Scholars Press, 1987); Serge Ruzer, "Crucifixion: The Search for a Meaning vis-à-vis Biblical Prophecy. From Luke to Acts," in idem, *Mapping the New Testament: Early Christian Writings as a Witness for Jewish Biblical Exegesis* (Leiden: Brill, 2007), 187–99. See also Justin Taylor's study in this volume.

stance on the Torah, to be outlined further on, is mainly based. The apostle's emphasis seems to have been on denying the capacity of Judaism's ritual precepts to contribute to the cleansing of hearts. These precepts might have had such a capacity in the past; but in the messianic era, it is exclusively identification with and "sharing" in the Messiah's expiating death, and belief in his resurrection, that constitute the path leading to salvation – by grace and not by acquired merit. Moreover, those who still put their hope in the "works of the Torah" are thereby bringing upon themselves "the Torah's curse" (Gal 3:10–11, 6:15). Even if Torah still has a very important function to fulfill—namely, to highlight and strengthen the awareness of one's sins (Rom 3:20)—it may also expose one to the cunning of the evil impulse and, most important, it does not provide the means to overcome humanity's built-in sinful inclinations and follow God's commandments (Rom 9:31). As a result, those of Israel who cling to the pre-messianic understanding of the Torah, find themselves entrapped by "the god of this world" (2 Cor 3:14–4:4).

It should be noted that there are also statements emphasizing the holiness of the Torah and placing the blame not on it but rather on humanity's own weak nature (Rom 7). Moreover, when Paul has to address the moral lapses and unruly behavior in the communities he is communicating with, he evokes certain Torah precepts and warns that they are fully obligatory, and without following them one has no chance to be a part of the kingdom (1 Cor 6:9–10; Gal 5:19–21). These fluctuations in Paul's attitude to the Torah, which sometimes seem to amount to outright contradictions, have repeatedly drawn the attention of recent research. In what follows, I shall first briefly discuss the various solutions to this conundrum and then suggest a tentative synthesis. My focus will be on the problematic aspects of the Torah's status in the intra-Jewish discourse itself and thus on the possible intra-Jewish setting of what is perceived as Paul's anti-Torah statements.

2. THE TRADITIONAL VIEW OF PAUL

For the sake of our discussion, what—following John Gager—will be called here the traditional view of Paul[3] may be summarized as ascribing to the apostle the conviction that the dawn of the messianic era in its very essence heralded a divorce from the Jewish religious outlook centered on the Torah and its commandments. Statements on the Torah's (partial) validity and absolute holiness are correspondingly explained away as secondary and/or dictated by the needs of the mission. This appraisal had a long history in theological thought—both among Christians, who embraced this position as their own and among Jews (those who paid attention), who disapproved of it, including Judeo-Christians of the early centuries. Its various modifications have also been adopted, *mutatis mutandis*, by many influential scholars.[4]

To give just one instructive example, Martin Hengel has argued that the underlying insight of Paul's thinking is that nowadays the fulfillment of Torah ritual demands in general and, more specifically, those rituals connected to Temple worship have lost their ability (even if they had such in the past) to effect one's redemption—e.g., forgiveness of sins, a place in the world-to-come. From now on this is the exclusive prerogative of Jesus' salvific death. Moreover, according to Hengel, this basic understanding not only characterized Paul but, in fact, almost from the very beginning, constituted a salient faith marker of the early Jesus movement and thus what distinguished it from broader Judaism.[5]

---

[3] John J. Gager, *Reinventing Paul* (Oxford: Oxford University Press, 2000), 21ff.

[4] For a review, see Gager, *Reinventing Paul*, 3–42. Characteristically, even Alan F. Segal ("Torah and *Nomos* in Recent Scholarly Discussion," *SR* 13:1 (1984): 19–27) subscribed to this view at an earlier stage, claiming that "Paul deliberately revalued Torah" following "his radical conversion experience" (ibid., 27). The scholar seems to have later modified this assessment; see Alan F. Segal, *Paul the Convert: The Apostolate and Apostasy of Saul the Pharisee* (New Haven, Conn.: Yale University Press, 1990).

[5] See Martin Hengel, "The Beginnings of Christianity as a Jewish-Messianic and Universalistic Movement," in *The Beginnings of Christianity: A Collection of Articles*

It is noteworthy, however, that according to Hengel's general perception, even when Christianity subscribed to certain belief patterns having their source in the Greco-Roman world of ideas and practices, this was conditioned by the fact that they had already been internalized by the Jewish tradition and were thus perceived as belonging to it. One may therefore surmise that the controversial "anti-Torah" messianic inclination of Paul (and others) might have relied—while developing them—on certain tendencies present in pre-Christian Judaism. In this context, a study by Shlomo Pines should be mentioned: Pines discussed Paul's call to freedom from the yoke of Torah's ritual laws as taking one step further the liberation impulse present already in proto-rabbinic tradition and attested in early rabbinic sources where it was applied to other yokes of human existence.[6] I find intriguing the potential openness of the "traditional appraisal" of the apostle's message to the possibility that the "Pauline revolution" was linked to a broader contemporaneous Jewish setting.

3. MITIGATED TRADITIONAL VIEW

There have been a number of inroads in recent research that somehow alleviate the above picture of a substantial reversal of the attitude to the Torah supposedly propagated by Paul. Thus E. P. Sanders has forcefully argued that, in fact, the issue of Torah observance or deeds-grace controversy was not a part of the true core of Paul's teaching of messianic salvation, constituting rather one of those secondary themes evoked by the apostle—according to varying circumstances, rhetorical needs and an occasional change of message—in the service of his main insight.[7]

(ed., J. Pastor and M. Mor; Jerusalem: Yad Ben-Zvi, 2005), 85–100; idem, *The Atonement: The Origins of the Doctrine in the New Testament* (Philadelphia: Fortress, 1981).

[6] See Shlomo Pines, "Metamorphoses of the Notion of Freedom," *Iyyun* 33 (1984): 247–65 (in Hebrew).

[7] E. P. Sanders, *Paul and Palestinian Judaism* (Philadelphia: Fortress, 1977).

It has also been suggested that the "works of the law, ἔργα νόμου," about whose effectiveness Paul expresses doubts[8] should be understood in the context of Pauline epistles in a limited sense—e.g. as "ritual precepts" or, more specifically, those practices prescribed by the Torah that serve as "identity badges" distinguishing between Jews and their gentile neighbors and thus as differing from the core commandments defining God's covenant with Israel or the Torah (νόμος) proper: the Decalogue, Lev 19:18, passages that according to the apostle's interpretation speak of messianic salvation in Jesus, etc.[9] Such an understanding of the "works of the law" finds corroboration in the מעשי התורה usage attested in 4QMMT from Qumran, where the expression "to be reckoned as righteousness" is likewise used in this connection.[10] This would mean that in Paul's writings the word "Torah" (νόμος) when coupled with "works" and/or "doing" may have a distinctive and limited meaning—a fact that may explain what are perceived as contradictions in the apostle's stance on the Torah.[11]

---

[8] See, for example, Gal 2:15–21.

[9] See James D. G. Dunn, "Works of the Law and the Curse of the Law (Galatians 3:10–4)," *NTS* 31:4 (1985): 523–42. For a criticism of Dunn's thesis, see Charles E. B. Cranfield, "The Works of the Law in the Epistle to the Romans," *JSNT* 43 (1991): 89–101; Dunn's response is found in his "Yet Once More 'The Works of the Law': A Response," *JSNT* 46 (1992): 99–117.

[10] 4Q398 (4QMMT e), Frags. 14–17, 2:2–8; 4Q399 (4QMMT f), 1:11. See Dunn, "Works of the Law"; Joseph A. Fitzmyer, "Paul's Jewish Background and the Deeds of the Law," in idem, *According to Paul: Studies in the Theology of the Apostle* (Mahwah, NJ: Paulist Press, 1993), 18–35, esp. 21–23. For a variety of appraisals – mostly differing from Dunn's—of the nature of the link observed here between Paul and 4QMMT, see Martin G. Abegg, Jr., "Paul, 'Works of the Law' and MMT," *BAR* 20:6 (1994): 52–61, 82; "4QMMT, Paul, and 'Works of the Law'," in *The Bible at Qumran: Text, Shape, and Interpretation* (Studies in the Dead Sea Scrolls and Related Literature, ed. Peter W. Flint; Grand Rapids: Eerdmans, 2001), 203–16, esp. 205–6; Tom N. Wright, "Paul and Qumran," *BR* 14:5 (1998): 18–54, esp. 54; Jacqueline C. R. de Roo, "The Concept of 'Works of the Law' in Jewish and Christian Literature," in *Christian-Jewish Relationships through the Centuries* (ed. Stanley E. Porter and Brook W. R. Pearson; Sheffield: Sheffield Academic Press, 2000), 116–47.

[11] See, for example, Frederick Avemarie, "Paul and the Claim of the Law according to the Scripture: Leviticus 18:5 in Galatians 3:12 and Romans 10:5," in Pastor and Mor, *The Beginnings of Christianity*, 125–148, esp. 146–48.

One should note one more idea featuring prominently in Qumran—namely, that the true fulfillment of the Torah is possible only when based on its distinctive, and novel, exegesis (1QS 1, *Damascus Document* 6).[12] So the interpretations suggested within the mitigated traditional approach enable us to reconstruct a possible underlying intra-Jewish context of Paul's reasoning. Indeed, without the core conviction/ true interpretation of the Torah (in Paul's case, in light of the messianic Jesus-centered belief), the ritual gestures themselves are of no value; but it is not unthinkable that with that conviction even the "works of the law" may acquire renewed meaningfulness.[13] It has also been demonstrated that the

---

[12] Both these foundational texts present the sectarian idea of separation from the "sons of darkness" as the true interpretation of the Torah's core precept valid for the pre-eschatological "times of trial." 1QS 1:1-13: "1 For [the Instructor] [book of the Rul]e of the Community: in order to 2 seek God [with all (one's) heart and with all (one's) soul; in order] to do what is good and just in his presence, as 3 commanded by means of the hand of Moses and his servants the Prophets; in order to love everything 4 which he selects and to hate everything that he rejects....8 so as to be united in the counsel of God and walk in perfection in his sight, complying with all 9 revealed things concerning the regulated times of their stipulations; in order to love all the sons of light, each one 10 according to his lot in God's plan, and to detest all the sons of darkness, each one in accordance with his blame 11 in God's vindication. All those who submit freely to his truth will convey all their knowledge, their energies, 12 and their riches to the Community of God in order to refine their knowledge in the truth of God's decrees and marshal their energies 13 in accordance with his perfect paths and all their riches in accordance with his just counsel." CD-A 6: "And the staff is the interpreter of the Torah, of whom 8 Isaiah said (*Isa 54:16*): «He produces a tool for his labor». *Blank* And the nobles of the people are 9 those who have arrived to dig the well with the staves that the sceptre decreed, 10 to walk in them throughout the whole age of wickedness, and without which they will not obtain it, until there arises 11 he who teaches justice at the end of days. *Blank* But all those who have been brought into the covenant 12 shall not enter the temple to kindle his altar in vain. They will be the ones who close 13 the door, as God said (*Mal 1:10*): «Whoever amongst you will close its door so that you do not kindle my altar 14 in vain!». Unless they are careful to act in accordance with the exact interpretation of the Torah for the age of wickedness: to separate themselves 15 from the sons of the pit; to abstain from wicked wealth which defiles, either by promise or by vow, 16 and from the wealth of the temple..."

Deuteronomy 27:26-related notion of the "curse of the Torah" (Gal 3:10)—expressed in what is perceived as Israel's continuing exile—also finds its proper contextualization within broader trends of Second Temple Jewish thought.[14] Thus among the advantages of this approach is the fact that it allows addressing more seriously the evidence of Acts on the basic compatibility of the Jesus' followers' messianic belief with loyalty to the ritual gestures of Jewish tradition. Its salient disadvantage, however, shared with the traditional interpretation of Paul, is that it does not sufficiently take into account the particularities of Paul's (Gentile) audience.

4. THE NEW APPROACH

Another influential line of revision has been propagated in the course of the last few decades by a number of scholars, among them Krister Stendahl, John Gager, and Paula Fredriksen, who have emphasized the specific context in which Paul's harsh statements concerning the Torah were meant to resonate—namely, the non-Jewish addressees of the apostle's writings.[15] Within this approach, inter alia, a number of basic theses have been formulated. (1) The contradictions between the high evaluation of the Torah and the denial of the salvific effectiveness of its commandments can be explained if the sayings of the former kind are seen as addressed to the Jews and the latter as addressed to the Gentiles, who from the beginning had not been destined to follow the ritual instructions of

---

[13] See Avemarie, "Paul and the Claim of the Law," 145–46; John O'Neill, "'Did You Receive the Spirit by the Works of the Law?' (Gal 3:2): The Works of the Law in Judaism and the Pauline corpus," *ABR* 46 (1998): 70–84, esp. 74–76.

[14] See James M. Scott, "For as Many as Are of Works of the Law Are under a Curse (Galatians 3:10)," in *Paul and the Scriptures of Israel* (JSNT Suppl. 83; ed. Craig A. Evans and James A. Sanders; Sheffield: Sheffield Academic Press, 1993), 187–221.

[15] See, for example, Krister Stendahl, *Final Account: Paul's Letter to the Romans* (Minneapolis, MN: Augsburg Fortress, 1995); Gager, *Reinventing Paul*, 43–75; Paula Fredriksen, "Judaism, the Circumcision of Gentiles, and Apocalyptic Hope: Another Look at Galatians 1 and 2," *JTS* 42 (1991): 532–64.

Judaism. This suggestion has sometimes been taken even further, to the effect that, in Paul's view, what Torah is for the Jews—namely, the means of salvation—Jesus is for the Gentiles who join the messianic movement. (2) Arguing that pious Gentiles do not have to observe the ritual precepts of the Torah—e.g., perform circumcision—Paul in fact followed an accepted, particularly in the Hellenistic Diaspora, Jewish perception—namely, that even at the end of days, the Gentiles will join the redemption in accordance with the pattern found in the biblical prophecy, that is, as Gentiles, without blurring the borderline between Israel and the nations. In other words, the nations come to the mountain of the Lord to serve him together with the Jews and become privy to the core messages of God's Torah while remaining ethnically and culturally distinct from the people of Israel.[16] Correspondingly those are, in fact, Paul's opponents within the Jesus movement, those insisting on "Judaizing" Gentiles who have embraced Jesus as the Messiah of Israel, who act as innovators here. Their stance may be seen as a reaction to the perceived delay in the arrival of the end and the corresponding changes in the projected redemption scenario—a longer historical perspective or, alternatively, the upcoming catastrophic phase of wars and disasters—with both perspectives engendering a need for socially consolidating the Jesus movement.[17] In any case, Paul did not introduce any drastic reevaluation of the Torah vis-à-vis Jews.

According to this new approach, the age-long erroneous perception of Paul as a rebel against the Torah is a result of an anachronistic reading of his epistles in light of a later Christian outlook that emerged in different socio-historical circumstances of a clear-cut division and border marking. For example, Fredriksen has highlighted that some later notions emerging in the wake of and as a reaction to the destruction of the Temple, with Jewish followers of Jesus being gradually marginalized, were completely foreign to Paul's thinking.[18]

---

[16] See Isa 2:1–4; Frederiksen, "Judaism, The Circumcision of Gentiles."

[17] Fredriksen, "Judaism, the Circumcision of Gentiles," 558–61.

[18] See Paula Fredriksen, "Paul, Purity, and the 'Ekklesia' of the Gentiles," in Pastor and Mor, *The Beginnings of Christianity*, 205–17, esp. 215–16.

One may also classify under the rubric of the new approach some other attempts at a pointed contextualization and, correspondingly, at reducing the scope and the volume of the apostle's "anti-Torah" sayings. One such tendency presents the discussion of "the works of the law" issue as a whole as an *ad hoc* elaboration subjugated to and derived from the needs of Paul's urgent practical task—namely, the creation of a new religious community comprising Jews and Gentiles.[19] There has even been a readiness to claim that within this task also, Paul managed to remain a Jew faithful to the Torah-related rulings of his time and milieu.[20]

The emphasis of the new approach on the specific context of Paul's reasoning—a Pharisaic Jew bringing the messianic message/the good news of the God of Israel to the Gentiles—has proved most challenging and productive, opening a new and promising line of investigation. At the same time, the perception of Paul's intended audience as exclusively non-Jewish is not devoid of problematic elements. It is here, with the issue of Paul's audience, that the remarks that follow start—the remarks that are to lead to suggesting a tentative synthesis of the above approaches.

5. HIDDEN JEWISH AUDIENCE

In my opinion, it is not always justified to see the "anti-Torah" statements as directed exclusively to Paul's Gentile addressees, since the epistles clearly presuppose the presence of a third party to the discussion—namely, Jewish agitators from within the Jesus movement, whose arguments exercised an influence on the apostle's non-Jewish listeners/readers and thus had to be repelled by

---

[19] See Segal, *Paul the Convert*; Mark D. Nanos, "What Was at Stake in Peter's 'Eating with Gentiles' at Antioch"; "The Inter- and Intra-Jewish Political Context of Paul's Letter to the Galatians," in *The Galatians Debate: Contemporary Issues in Rhetorical and Historical Interpretation* (ed. Mark D. Nanos; Peabody, Mass.: Hendrickson, 2002), 282–318, 396–407.

[20] See Mark Nanos's recent publications on his website: http://www.marknanos.com.

him.[21] The "conversation" with that third party seems to have found its expression, inter alia, in the adoption — and adaptation — of patterns of contemporaneous Jewish exegetical discourse, which were part of Paul's own Jewish education.[22] In light of this, Paul's famous first-person sayings—such as "We ourselves, who are Jews by birth and not gentile sinners, yet who know that a man is not justified by works of the Torah but through faith in Jesus Christ, even we have believed in Christ Jesus, in order to be justified by faith in Christ, and not by works of the Torah, because by works of the Torah shall no one be justified" (Gal 2:15–16)—can hardly be dismissed as mere rhetoric.[23]

Therefore, an undoubtedly most productive attempt to clarify the exact, and by necessity limited, meaning of Paul's arguments may at times lead to a tendency to disregard the implicit Jewish component of the apostle's intended audience and thus to automatically "cleanse" him from any doubt whatsoever about the validity of the Torah with regard to the Jews. Such a tendency has the potential pitfall of ignoring the fact that, as will be argued below, awareness of the problematic efficacy of the Torah commandments as a means of attaining redemption was not foreign to the intra-Jewish religious discourse of Paul's days, both in the Hellenistic Diaspora and in the Land of Israel.

---

[21] See, for example, Paul's extensive treatment of the challenge coming from this group in Galatians 1–2.

[22] See, for example, Berndt Schaller, "1 Kor 10,1-10(13) und die jüdischen Voraussetzungen der Schriftauslegung des Paulus," in idem, *Fundamenta Judaica: Studien zum antiken Judentum und zum Neuen Testament* (Göttingen: Vanderhoeck & Ruprecht, 2001), 167-189; Serge Ruzer, "Negotiating the Proper Attitude to Marriage and Divorce," in *Mapping the New Testament*, 142-145; Menahem Kister, "Romans 5:12-21 against the Background of Torah-Theology and Hebrew Usage," *HTR* 100.4 (2007): 391-424.

[23] The same seems to apply to the famous exclamation in Rom 7:21: "Wretched man that I am!"

6. Torah Precepts as a Path for Redemption

If the above observation concerning an additional (Jewish) intended audience of Paul's reasoning is accepted, one may further ask what patterns of intra-Jewish discourse on the feasibility or usefulness of the "way of the commandments" Paul might possibly have adapted to the needs of his polemic. In this regard, it should first be remarked that Paul's rhetoric presupposes a distinction between the hard-core demands of God's covenant (or the true meaning of those demands) and, as it were, peripheral or secondary commandments—"works of the law." It appears that fateful divisions of this kind featured also in broader Judaism, whereas the distinguishing criteria and the corresponding Torah observance strategies might have varied from one tradition to another. Thus Philo bears witness to a variety of Jewish attitudes toward the "external" precepts of the Torah—from neglecting to upholding them—all of which share the conviction that the true meaning of the commandments is the "internal" one. Philo himself surely subscribes to this consensual appraisal; unlike some of his Jewish contemporaries, however, as a responsible member of the community who recognizes the constraints of our physical and social existence, he upholds the validity of the ritual side of Jewish tradition as befitting external means for "gradually educating one's soul." People whom Philo criticizes in this context seem inclined to drop ritual observance altogether and deal directly with the mending of their "inner man."[24]

There is much to be said about general Hellenistic ideas that provided the setting for such a tendency, but dichotomic perceptions of the kind did not characterize only the Greco-Roman Diaspora. Admittedly, evidence about the early proto-rabbinic tradition is scarce and attested relatively late, but it indicates that the idea of a two-fold division of the bulk of religious precepts was known in the Land of Israel also and duly discussed. It will suffice to quote one tradition attested in the Mishnah, where it is ascribed to none other

---

[24] See Philo, *Migr.* 89–93.

than the second-century codifier of the Mishnaic law himself (*m.Abot* 2:1):[25]

> R. Judah the Prince said: Which is the proper course that a man should choose for himself? That which is an honor to him and elicits honor from his fellow men. Be as scrupulous about a light precept (מצוה קלה) as of a weighty one (בחמורה), for you do not know the reward allotted for each precept. Balance the loss incurred by the fulfillment of a precept against the gain and the accruing from a transgression against the loss it involves. Reflect on three things and you will never come to sin: Know what is above you – a seeing eye, a hearing ear, and all your deeds recorded in a book.[26]

One may first note a partial overlap of terminology between our early third-century Mishnah and Matt 5:19 (τῶν ἐντολῶν τούτων τῶν ἐλαχίστων, "the least of these/ the light commandments") – an overlap that points to the terminology's early provenance. Second, not unlike Philo (and Jesus in Matthew 5 and 23!),[27] the Mishnah votes for the importance of the efforts to fulfill precepts ostensibly not belonging to the core of the Torah. Though the reasons may be different, the "peripheral" commandments are seen here too as being in the final account expedient for a person's "balance of merits." Third, again like Philo, the Mishnah seems to bear witness to—polemically rejected—alternative perceptions. Fourth, while the dichotomy itself emerges as a shared feature of a whole spectrum of traditions, its character—namely, what commandments are seen as belonging to either category—may vary considerably. Thus as distinct from Philo with his dichotomy between internal/spiritual

---

[25] Cf. Matt 23:23 "Woe to you, scribes and Pharisees, hypocrites! For you tithe mint and dill and cummin, and have neglected the weightier matters of the law, justice and mercy and faith; these you ought to have done, without neglecting the others."

[26] The English translation of Mishnaic material in this paper follows Herbert Danby, *The Mishnah* (Oxford: Oxford University Press, 1950).

[27] See Matt 5:21–37 and above note 25.

and external meaning of the commandment, the Mishnah seems to understand both categories as pertaining to the realm of deeds.[28]

If in the tractate *Abot* the "light" commandments are presented as **potentially** expedient for God's approval, another telling Mishnaic tradition speaks of the fateful eschatological transformation of the individual—i.e., the gift of the Holy Spirit and the resurrection—as **conditioned** by the sequence of efforts at fulfilling, inter alia, ritual (external, secondary) observances (*m. Sotah* 9:15):

> R. Pinhas son of Yair says: "Expediency brings to cleanness, cleanness brings to purity, purity brings to chastity, chastity brings to holiness, holiness brings to meekness, meekness brings to the fear of sin, fear of sin brings to righteousness, righteousness brings to the spirit of holiness (holy spirit), and the holy spirit brings to the resurrection of the dead, and the resurrection of the dead comes through Elijah of blessed memory. Amen."

The historical context here is that of the destruction of the Temple and anticipation of redemption. Yet it stands to reason that both the singling out of certain ritual observances and a claim for their crucial importance for obtaining righteousness and eventually salvation are linked and point to an older topic—as does the previously discussed Mishnaic passage.

7. The Voice of a Seasoned Pessimism

However, by the time Paul was addressing the topic, a substantially different idea had also been probed in Jewish tradition. One may see it as derived from an essentially pessimistic appraisal of a person's ability to gradually build the edifice of righteousness by

---

[28] Cf. *Abot* 1:1, 3:13 ("the fence around the Torah"). The nature of the dichotomy—or hierarchy—indicated in Matthew 5 warrants further discussion. See Serge Ruzer, "Antitheses in Matthew 5: Midrashic Aspects of Exegetical Techniques," in *Mapping the New Testament*, 11–34.

his/her own efforts.[29] Later rabbinic sources also bear witness to such a tendency, with the sometimes inevitable conclusion that nothing short of death can cure one's sinful inclination. I have dealt at length elsewhere with such patterns of thought; here it will suffice to say that in such a context great emphasis is put on last-minute repentance, an instantaneous change of heart that has not necessarily been preceded by a long history of pious effort.[30]

This basically pessimistic assessment is, in fact, rather ancient and goes back to classical biblical prophecy. A famous example is provided by Jeremiah 31:31–34, where a "change of heart" imposed by God from outside—and not the steadfast effort invested in pious ritual actions, temple sacrifices included—is presented as the only way to righteousness, remission of sins and redemption:

> 31 "Behold, the days are coming," says the LORD, "when I will make a new covenant with the house of Israel and the house of Judah, 32 not like the covenant which I made with their fathers when I took them by the hand to bring them out of the land of Egypt, my covenant which they broke, though I was their husband, says the LORD. 33 But this is the covenant which I will make with the house of Israel after those days," says the LORD: "I will put my law within them, and I will write it upon their hearts; and I will be their God, and they shall be my people. 34 And no longer shall each man teach his neighbor and each his brother, saying, – 'Know the LORD,' for they shall all know me, from the least of them to the greatest, says the LORD; for I will forgive their iniquity, and I will remember their sin no more."

---

[29] Ellis Rivkin ("Pharisaic Revolution," in idem, *The Shaping of Jewish History: A Radical New Interpretation* [New York: Scribner, 1971]) presented this pessimistic appraisal as derived from the Pharisaic religious outlook.

[30] See Serge Ruzer, "The Death Motif in Late Antique Jewish Teshuva Narrative Patterns and in Paul's Thought"; "The Seat of Sin in Early Jewish and Christian Sources," in *Transforming the Inner Self in Ancient Religions* (ed. J. Assman and G. G. Stroumsa; Leiden: Brill, 1999), 151–65, 367–91.

It is only this God-imposed inner transformation that makes the observance of the core stipulations of God's covenant possible.[31] In another famous oracle (Ez 36:24–29), this eschatological transformation is further described in terms of receiving the gift of Spirit:

> 24 For I will take you from the nations, and gather you from all the countries, and bring you into your own land. 25 I will sprinkle clean water upon you, and you shall be clean from all your uncleannesses, and from all your idols I will cleanse you. 26 A new heart I will give you, and a new spirit I will put within you; and I will take out of your flesh the heart of stone and give you a heart of flesh. 27 And I will put my spirit within you, and cause you to walk in my statutes and be careful to observe my ordinances. 28 You shall dwell in the land which I gave to your fathers; and you shall be my people, and I will be your God. 29 And I will deliver you from all your uncleannesses; and I will summon the grain and make it abundant and lay no famine upon you.

Compared to *m. Sotah* 9:15, the passage from Ezekiel appears to outline an inverted sequence—not righteousness, forgiveness of sins, gift of Spirit and redemption as the crowning result of earnest efforts to fulfill God's precepts, including the ritual ones focused on the cleanness-uncleanness dichotomy, but the very ability to act righteously is presented here as derived from the preceding redemptive intervention by God that changes one essentially with the "stroke of spirit." This perception was later picked up at Qumran, where it was drastically modified in accordance with the belief in double predestination. One of the classical expressions of

---

[31] It has been suggested that, in fact, Jeremiah already did not perceive certain elements of the ritual—namely, those pertaining to Temple sacrifices—as part of the obligatory core stipulations. See Moshe Weinfeld, "Jeremiah and the Spiritual Metamorphosis of Israel," *ZAW* 80 (1976): 17–56, esp. 32, who suggests that the prophet might have perceived the new covenant as associated not with formal statutes but exclusively with the "circumcision of the heart." Of course, Jeremiah belongs here to a broader prophetic tendency to harbor reservations toward the priestly aspect of the Jewish religion.

that pattern of religious thinking is found in the closing section of the *Rule of the Community* (1QS 11:7–19):[32]

> To those whom God has selected he has given them as everlasting possession; until they inherit them in the lot of the holy ones. 8 He unites their assembly to the sons of the heavens. . . to be an everlasting plantation throughout all future ages. 9 However, I belong to evil humankind to the assembly of wicked flesh;. . . the assembly of worms…of those who walk in darkness. . . 10 For to man (does not belong) his path, nor to a human being the steadying of his step; since judgment belongs to God, 11 and from his hand is the perfection of the path. By his knowledge everything shall come into being, and all that does exist he establishes with his calculations and nothing is done outside of him. . . . 13 he will free my soul from the pit and make my steps steady on the path; 14. . . in his justice he will cleanse me from the uncleanness of the human being and from the sin of the sons of man, . . . so that I can extol God for his justice. . . Blessed be you, my God, who opens the heart of your servant to knowledge! 16 Establish all his deeds in justice,. . . to be everlastingly in your presence, as you have cared for the selected ones of humankind. 17 For beyond you there is no perfect path and without your will, nothing comes to be. You have taught all knowledge. . . 19 to gaze into the abyss of your mysteries . . .

In Qumran, the God-imposed transformation (a) is the only possible avenue to achieving righteousness; (b) is conditioned on predestined election; and (c) reveals God's mysteries. The flesh-spirit dualism characteristic of the Dead Sea Scrolls is only hinted at here (the "flesh" being incapable of following God's will, line 9, cf. Matt 26:41 and par.); but the Spirit is clearly perceived as both cleansing the person's "inner man" and revealing God's ultimate mysteries elsewhere in the same *Rule* (1QS 4:20):

[32] The English translation of Qumranic material in this paper follows Wilfred G. E. Watson in *The Dead Sea Scrolls Translated* (ed. F. García Martínez; Leiden: Brill, 1994) (electronic version).

> Meanwhile, God will refine, with his truth, all man's deeds, and will purify for himself the configuration of man, ripping out all spirit of deceit from the innermost part 21 of his flesh, and cleansing him with the spirit of holiness from every irreverent deed. He will sprinkle over him the spirit of truth like lustral water (in order to cleanse him) from all the abhorrences of deceit and from the defilement 22 of the unclean spirit. In this way the upright will understand knowledge of the Most High, and the wisdom of the sons of heaven will teach those of perfect behaviour. For these are those selected by God for an everlasting covenant 23 and to them shall belong all the glory of Adam.

The heavenly mysteries revealed to those "refined by God" are identified as a new interpretation of the Torah pertaining to the pre-eschatological "age of wickedness" in the *Damascus Document* 6, whereas both the necessity of the initially imposed action of the Holy Spirit for obtaining righteousness and its cardinal effect as preventing one from sinning against God in the future are again highlighted in the Qumranic *Thanksgiving Hymns* (1QH 4:17–26):

> **[I give you thanks, Lord,] for the spirits you have placed in me….to confess my former sins, to bow low and beg favour** 19 **for [. . .] of my deeds and the depravity of my heart. Because I wallowed in impurity, [I separated myself] from the foundation [of truth] and I was not allied with** [. . .] 20 To you does justice belong, blessing belongs to your Name for ever! [Act according to] your justice, 21 free [the soul of your servant,] the wicked should die! However, **I have understood that [you establish] the path of the one whom you choose** 22 **and in the insight [of your wisdom] you prevent him from sinning against you**, you restore his humility through your punishments, and by your ord[eals streng]then his heart. 23 [You, Lord, prevent] your servant from sinning against you…. 25 [. . .] **for your servant is a spirit of flesh**. *Blank* 26 [I give you thanks, Lord, because] **you have spread your holy spirit upon your servant** [. . .] his heart…

Moreover, the gift of the Spirit features in some Qumranic texts as a self-definition of the covenanters. Thus, for example, in fragments of the *Damascus Document* found at Qumran, "the anointed/messiahs by his/the Holy Spirit" or "the messiahs of (his) Holy Spirit" (משיחי רוח הקודש/משיחי רוח קודשו) serve as the community's collective self-definition.[33] In other passages, a shorter title, "the anointed of the holiness" (משיחי הקודש), denotes the whole community of the covenanters—as distinguished from the Qumranic priestly elite, those belonging to the "Aaronic anointing."[34]

The emphasis on election/gift of the Spirit as the precondition for fulfilling the Torah precepts is expressed with particular force and clarity in Qumranic texts—not least thanks to its being linked there to the double predestination concept. There is no particular reason, however, to believe that it was restricted in the Second Temple period to a sectarian eschatologically oriented milieu; but the issue warrants further investigation.[35]

The Gift of the Spirit and Jesus' Salvific Death in Paul's Writings

Belief in the gift of the Holy Spirit was at the heart of the nascent Jesus movement outlook. Its equation with the promised eschatological restoration of prophecy and the accompanying

---

[33] See 4Q266 ii, 2:12 (= CD-A 6) and 4Q 270 ii, 2:14.

[34] See, e.g., 4Q266 iii, 2:9; 4Q267 2, 6; 4Q269 iv, 1:2; Serge Ruzer, "The New Covenant, the Reinterpretation of Scripture and Collective Messiahship," in *Mapping the New Testament*, 215–39.

[35] The following passage by Philo seems to indicate that a similar emphasis, albeit without a characteristic link to the Spirit, was probed also in a non-eschatological Hellenistic Jewish context: "God has . . . promoted goodly natures apart from any manifest reason, pronouncing no action of theirs acceptable before bestowing his praises upon them. . . . the prophet says that Noah found grace in the sight of the Lord God (Gen 6:8) when as yet he had . . . done no fair deed, etc." (Philo, *Leg.* 3.77–79).

ecstatic elements are greatly emphasized in Acts.[36] Paul, however, as witnessed, inter alia, in 1 Corinthians 12–13,[37] seems to have certain qualms about this emphasis, highlighting instead the reforming power of the Spirit (Gal 5:5–26):

> 15 **For through the Spirit, by faith, we wait for the hope of righteousness. . . .** 16 **But I say, walk by the Spirit, and do not gratify the desires of the flesh.** 17 For the desires of the flesh are against the Spirit, and the desires of the Spirit are against the flesh; for these are opposed to each other, to prevent you from doing what you would. 18 But if you are led by the Spirit you are not under the law. . . . 22 But the fruit of the Spirit is love, joy, peace, patience, kindness, goodness, faithfulness, 23 gentleness, self-control; against such there is no law. **24 And those who belong to Christ Jesus have crucified the flesh with its passions and desires.** 25 **If we live by the Spirit, let us also walk by the Spirit.** 26 Let us have no self-conceit, no provoking of one another, no envy of one another.

It is this "cleansing by the Spirit" imposed from outside that is propagated by Paul—resembling the patterns of belief discerned in both biblical and Qumranic sources—as the only true remedy against the sinfulness of the flesh. As such, it is counterposed in the epistle to the "works of the law" as incapable of bringing about the desired transformation. The quoted passage is most telling in one more important respect: it demonstrates how this motif of the "cleansing by the Spirit," an inherited motif of a broader Jewish circulation, is collated by Paul with another belief, this time a "sectarian" one—namely, characteristic of Jesus' followers only—the belief in the salvific, and cleansing, function of Jesus' death (Gal 5:24).

---

[36] For example, in the foundational episode reported in the Pentecost (Shavuot) setting of Acts 2.

[37] See, for example, 1 Cor 13:1–2: "If I speak in the tongues of men and of angels, but have not love, I am a noisy gong or a clanging cymbal. 2 And if I have prophetic powers, and understand all mysteries and all knowledge, and if I have all faith, so as to remove mountains, but have not love, I am nothing."

A similar collation, or doubling, reappears in the Epistle to the Romans, where we read (Rom 7:14–8:11):

> [*before*] 14 We know that the law is spiritual; but I am carnal, sold under sin. 15 I do not understand my own actions. For I do not what I want, but I do the very thing I hate....[*and now*] 8:1 There is therefore no condemnation for those who are in Christ Jesus. 2 For the law of the Spirit of life in Christ Jesus has set me free from the law of sin and death. 3 For God has done what the law, weakened by the flesh, could not do: **sending his own Son** in the likeness of sinful flesh and for sin, he condemned sin in the flesh, 4 in order that the **just requirement of the law** might be fulfilled in us, who walk not according to the flesh but **according to the Spirit**....9 But you are not in the flesh, you are in the Spirit, if in fact **the Spirit of God dwells in you**. Any one who does not have the Spirit of Christ does not belong to him. 10 But if **Christ is in you**...11 If the Spirit of him who raised Jesus from the dead dwells in you, he who raised Christ Jesus from the dead will give life to your mortal bodies also through his Spirit which dwells in you.

A strong flesh-spirit dichotomy is deserving of notice here, with the statement in Romans 8:9 echoing the Qumran-like saying in an earlier Pauline epistle (1 Thess 5:4–5: "But you are not in darkness, brethren, for that day to surprise you like a thief. For you are all sons of light and sons of the day; we are not of the night or of darkness").[38] Even more telling, however, are the "stitches" in Romans 8:3–4, 9–11, indicating the characteristic doubling of the Spirit- and Jesus' death-related avenues of achieving righteousness—in other words, justification. It may be suggested that here, as in Galatians, these stitches mark a collation of inherited Jewish motifs of a broader circulation with a particular outlook focusing on the salvific meaning

[38] For an exhaustive discussion of Qumran-like patterns of thought in earliest Christianity, see David Flusser, "The Dead Sea Sect and pre-Pauline Christianity," in *Judaism and the Origins of Christianity* (Jerusalem: Magnes, 1988), 23–74.

of the crucifixion. It is also noteworthy that another Qumran-like function of the Spirit mentioned above—namely, disclosing the ultimate eschatological, previously hidden, meaning of the Torah—is evoked by Paul in 2 Corinthians 3–4, where the doubling discussed above is also attested: the veil that has previously hidden the true, Christ-centered, meaning of the Torah is removed by the Spirit, who is identified with Christ.[39]

8. SUGGESTION FOR A SYNTHESIS

As a starting point, one may accept the suggestion that Paul distinguishes between the core Torah commandments, intrinsically linked to justification, and the auxiliary ones belonging to the ritual, or external, sphere of identity badges ("the works of the law"), and argues against the efficacy of the latter in "educating a person's soul"—because of one's being hopelessly "flesh." In this he differs, for example, from Philo in *De migratione Abrahami* (but not from Philo in *Legum allegoriae*),[40] who, in his former treatise, for that very reason recommends that the precepts of ritual continue to be followed.[41]

The issue does not seem to have been of central importance in Paul's earliest surviving communications with the community at Thessaloniki,[42] where the closely approaching glorious return of the

---

[39] 2 Cor 3:14–3:18: "But their minds were hardened; for to this day, when they read the old covenant, that same veil remains unlifted, because only through Christ is it taken away. 15 Yes, to this day whenever Moses is read a veil lies over their minds; 16 but when a man turns to the Lord the veil is removed. 17 Now the Lord is the Spirit, and where the Spirit of the Lord is, there is freedom. 18 And we all, with unveiled face, beholding the glory of the Lord, are being changed into his likeness from one degree of glory to another; for this comes from the Lord who is the Spirit."

[40] See above note 35.

[41] See above note 24.

[42] See Werner G. Kümmel, *Introduction to the New Testament* (tr. H. C. Kee; Heidelberg: Quelle & Meyer, 1973), 257–60. See also Karl P. Donfried, "1 Thessalonians, Acts and the Early Paul," in *The Thessalonian Correspondence* (ed.

Messiah and the necessity to turn to God, to achieve the remission of sins and be prepared for the upcoming day of judgment and resurrection of the dead, were still the themes of utmost urgency.[43]

The issue, however, did become acute—possibly imposed on Paul—in the context of the mission to the gentiles, in view of the delay in the *parousia*. Thus Paul's response—namely, that there is no need to uphold the ritual obligations—is, strictly speaking, addressed to the gentiles, not to the Jews, and as such it corresponds to the attitude prevalent in the Hellenistic Jewish circles of the time (along the lines of the New Approach). It is in the heat of the argument that Paul formulates his famous rhetorical opposition in Galatians 2:21: "For if justification [δικαιοσύνη] were through law, then Christ died to no purpose."

Yet, thanks to the important insight of the New Approach, which has sharpened our awareness of the issue of the intended audience, one is encouraged to further develop the above insight, discerning additional (hidden) addressees of Paul's—those Jewish agitators or "false brethren" who are with James (Gal 1:19, 2:6–11, 12–14), who exercise an influence on the gentile segments of the Jesus movement and whose claims the apostle has to repel. Paul's arguments then should be viewed as somehow addressing the intra-Jewish concerns also (back to the Traditional Approach). It means, inter alia, that one cannot (against the New Approach) automatically dismiss as mere rhetoric the apostle's "we" language—e.g., in Gal 2:15–16: "We ourselves, who are Jews

R. F. Collins; Leuven: Leuven University Press, 1990), 3–26; Delbert Burkett, *An Introduction to the New Testament and the Origins of Christianity* (Cambridge: Cambridge University Press, 2002), 345.

[43] See 1 and 2 Thess; cf. Acts 11–14. For a discussion of the apocalyptically flavored eschatological focus of the Thessalonians correspondence, see, for example, Karl P. Donfried, "Paul and Judaism: 1 Thessalonians 2:13–16 as a Test Case," *Int* (July 1984): 242–53; John C. Hurd, "Paul Ahead of His Time: 1 Thess. 2:13–16," in *Anti-Judaism in Early Christianity* (ed. P. Richardson; Montreal: Wilfrid Laurier University Press, 1986), 21–35, esp. 33–35. See also the discussion in G. E. Okeke, "1 Thessalonians 2:13–16: The Fate of the Unbelieving Jews," *NTS* 27 (1981), 127–36, esp. 130–31.

by birth and not Gentile sinners, yet who know that a man is not justified by works of the law but through faith in Jesus Christ, even we have believed in Christ Jesus, in order to be justified by faith in Christ, and not by works of the law, because by works of the law shall no one be justified."

In other words, while one has reason to believe that it is the concrete polemical situation vis-à-vis his gentile addressees that first triggered Paul's elaboration on the issue of the (ritual) commandments, the issue eventually acquired a broader importance—thanks both to the rhetorical strength of the apostle's formulations and to the existence of the additional intended audience, the intra-Jewish concerns of which with regard to the efficacy of the commandments Paul had to engage with. I have tried to show that in the context of those intra-Jewish concerns, the ability of ritual and/or external commandments to bring about true righteousness and justification was likewise **a matter of contention**, and Paul might have related to various aspects of this contention. The above discussion highlighted one such intra-Jewish motif—namely, the function of the Spirit (imposed from outside) providing for righteousness, as distinct from the way to righteousness via the efforts of the individual. Of course, these two avenues were not necessarily always perceived and/or presented as explicitly contradicting one another, but the tension between them is undeniable. I suggest that Paul engaged with this inherited tension of broader circulation in his polemic, coupling it with the specific/sectarian argument from Jesus' salvific death.

Paradoxically, one may say that the "Pauline threat" to contemporaneous formative Judaism was not in the extremely revolutionary character of his claims but in the fact that they were highlighting insights concerning the problematic aspects of Torah observance, inherent in the Torah-centered world itself.

Chapter 3
Paul, the Pharisee, and the Law

Antonio Pitta

1. Introduction

Even if the Pharisees are often mentioned in the Gospels, Paul is the only Pharisee that, boasting of his past, declares himself "... Pharisee, according to the Law" (Phil 3:5).[1] And in Acts he defines himself as a Pharisee not only referring to his past, before the encounter with Christ on the Damascus Road, but also in the last part of his life: "I am a Pharisee, a son of Pharisees" (Acts 23:6),[2] he says during the dispute on the resurrection between the Sadducees and the Pharisees.

Also Flavius Josephus remembers the frequency of the Pharisees in his *Autobiography*: "So when I had accomplished my desires, I returned back to the city, being now nineteen years old, and began the political life according to the rules of the sect of the Pharisees,

---

[1] On the pharisaic matrix of Paul cf. K. Berger, "Jesus als Pharisäer und frühe Christen als Pharisäer," *NT* 30 (1988): 231–262; L. J. Lietaert Peerbolte, *Paul the Missionary* (Leuven: Peeters, 2003); J. A. Overman, "κατὰ νόμον Φαρισαῖος: A Short History of Paul's Pharisaism," in *Pauline Conversations in Context: Essays in Honor of Calvin J. Roetzel*, (ed. J. C. Anderson, P. Sellew, and C. Setzer; London and New York: Sheffield Academic Press, 2002), 180–193; R. Penna, "Un fariseo del secolo I: Paolo di Tarso," in *Vangelo e inculturazione: Studi sul rapporto tra rivelazione e cultura nel Nuovo Testamento* (Cinisello Balsamo: San Paolo, 2001), 297–322; A. Pitta, "Paolo e il giudaismo farisaico," *RSB* 11 (1999): 89–106; C. Tassin, "Paul dans le monde Juif du Ier siècle," in *Paul de Tarse: Congrès de l'ACFEB (Strasbourg 1995)* (ed. J. Schlosser; LD 165; Paris: Cerf, 1996), 176–181; M. Tiwald, *Hebräer von Hebräer: Paulus auf dem Hintergrund frühjüdischer Argumentation und biblischer Interpretation* (HBS 52; Freiburg im Breisgau: Herder, 2008).

[2] J.C. Lentz Jr., *Luke's Portrait of Paul* (SNTS MS 77; Cambridge: Cambridge University Press, 1993), 51–56.

which is of kin to the sect of the Stoics, as the Greeks call them."[3]

We will take up Flavius Josephus's testimony which offers precious information on the Pharisees.[4] For now it is important to say that, unfortunately, Paul does not explain his belonging to the school of the Pharisees, a movement which was widespread until the destruction of the second temple (70 C.E.). Were the Pharisees a sect or a movement? Were they a party prevalently religious or political? And what were the dominating features which distinguished them from the Sadducees, the Zealots and the Essenes? From a historiographical perspective, a recent minimalist orientation opposes the tendency that shows a diffused relationship between Paul and Phariseeism, identifying the latter, without many specifications, with Rabbinism.[5] The minimalist tendency prefers to add only a few elements to Phil 3:5–6, excluding from analysis the rabbinic literature.[6] This is because the rabbinic literature is posterior to the

[3] *Life* 1.12: Καὶ διατρίψας παρ' αὐτῷ ἐνιαυτοὺς τρεῖς καὶ τὴν ἐπιθυμίαν τελειώσας εἰς τὴν πόλιν ὑπέστρεφον ἐννεακαιδέκατον δ' ἔτος ἔχων ἠρξάμην τε πολιτεύεσθαι τῇ Φαρισαίων αἱρέσει κατακολουθῶν ἣ παραπλήσιός ἐστι τῇ παρ' Ἕλλησιν Στωϊκῇ λεγομένη. Because of the verb πολιτεύεσθαι and the context of the paragraph, this would be better translated "began the politic/public" life than "to govern my life" (vs. H. S. J. Tackeray, *Josephus: The Life*, in LCL 186, 7. Cf. S. Mason, "Pharisees in the Narrative of Josephus," in *Josephus, Judea, and Christian Origins: Methods and Categories* (ed. Steve Mason; Peabody, Mass.: Hendrickson, 2009), 209.

[4] About the relationship between Paul, Josephus and Pharisees cf. G. P. Carras, *Paul, Josephus and Judaism: The Shared Judaism of Paul and Josephus* (Oxford: Oxford University Press, 1989).

[5] Cf. the classical studies of J. Bonsirven, *Exégèse rabbinique et exégèse paulinienne* (Paris: Gabalda, 1939); W.D. Davies, *Paul and Rabbinic Judaism: Some Rabbinic Elements in Pauline Theology*, (4th ed.; Philadelphia: Fortress Press, 1980). Cf. also P. T. Tomson, *Paul and the Jewish Law: Halakha in the Letters of the Apostle to the Gentiles* (CRINT III/1; Minneapolis: Fortress Press, 1990); P. T. Tomson, "Paul's Jewish Background in View of his Law: Teaching in 1 Cor 7," in *Paul and the Mosaic Law* (ed. J. D. G. Dunn; WUNT 89; Tübingen: Mohr, 1996), 251–270. On the Rabbinic sources about the Pharisees cf. J. Neusner, *The Rabbinic Traditions About the Pharisees Before 70* (3 vols.; Leiden: Brill, 1971).

[6] Cf. J. Sievers, 'Who Were the Pharisees?' in *Hillel and Jesus: Comparative Studies of Two Major Religious Leaders* (ed. J.H. Charlseworth and L.L. Johns; Minneapolis: Fortress Press, 1997), 137–155; G. Stemberger, *Pharisäer, Sadduzäer, Essener* (Stuttgart: Katholisches Bibelwerk, 1993); G. Stemberger, "I farisei: quadro storico e ideale," *RSB* 11/2 (1999): 22.

first century C.E., having been produced after the destruction of the second temple and in a period in which Essenism, Sadduceism and even Phariseeism did not survive. A less clear-cut position is held by those who, although recognizing radical changes after the destruction of the second temple, claim to identify in Phariseeism the tendency that imposes itself on later Judaism.[7]

Because of revisionism in progress, it is best to avoid what K. Berger calls "Pan-Pharisäismus":[8] a generalization of Phariseeism where, in reality, we have little information on the main characteristics of this movement, which begins to grow during the Hasmonean reign of John Hyrcanus I (134–104 B.C.E.). An example of *Pan-Pharisäismus* is to hold that only Pharisees believed in the resurrection, when such a belief was shared by a good part of Judaism of the second temple period, particularly by those with apocalyptic tendencies.[9] If we can assert that faith in the resurrection of the body is typical of Phariseeism, because of the debate between the Pharisees and the Sadducees described in the Acts of the Apostles (Acts 23:7), it would be misleading to attribute belief in the resurrection exclusively to it.

Before entering into the debate, it is important to specify that Paul does not deal with Phariseeism *qua talis*, presenting its features and internal variations. In Gal 1:13–15 and Phil 3:5–6 he does not remember his past in a detailed way or simply for historical memory, but rather from the perspective of his believing in Christ, resulting therefore in generic and fragmentary sentences on Judaism. For this reason the term φαρισαῖος is used only once in the Pauline Letters (Phil 3:5), whereas it compares 98 times in the rest of the NT where the term usually testifies to the conflicts

[7] F. Manns, *Il Giudaismo: Ambiente e memoria del Nuovo Testamento* (Bologna: EDB, 1993), 149; R. Perrotta, *Hairésis: gruppi, movimenti e fazioni del giudaismo antico e del cristianesimo (da Filone Alessandrino a Egesippo)* (Bologna: EDB, 2008), 320; P. Schäfer, "Der vorrabinische Pharisäismus", in *Paulus und das antike Judentum* (ed. M. Hengel and U. Heckel; WUNT 58; Tübingen: Mohr, 1991), 125–172.

[8] Berger, 'Jesus als Pharisäer', 231–262.

[9] Stemberger, 'I Farisei', 20.

between Jesus and the Pharisees, being used with a negative connotation, and within the plural rather than singular form.[10]

From the etymological side, the noun φαρισαῖος is connected with the verb ἀφορίζειν (to separate, to put aside), it is used in the participial forms in Gal 1:15 (ὁ ἀφορίσας, part. aorist) and in Rom 1:1 (ἀφωρισμένος, perfect part.), and recalls the Hebrew participle פָּרוּשׁ or the Aramaic פְּרִישׁ, פְּרִישָׁה, meaning separation from the others. There are therefore two contrasting connotations of the word: one slanderous that defines the Phariseess as sectarians and hypocrites, and the other eulogistic because of the search for sanctification, reached through the separation from impurity. It is not accidental that, using the language of "separation" (ἀφορίζειν and φαρισαῖος),[11] Paul always intends it in a positive meaning (cf. also ἀφορίσθητε technique quotation of Is 52:11 in 2 Cor 6:17),[12] in contrast with the larger part of the synoptic tradition (cf. Mk 2:16,18; Matt 9:11; 23:2–29; Lk 5:20; 11:42; 12:1).

The vagueness with which Paul represents his past in Judaism should protect us from the tendency that wants us to see his discourses, or part of them, as given in synagogues and then shifted into his letters. We believe that it is illusory to consider the section of Rom 2:1–29 or the macro-sections of Rom 1:18–4:25 and Rom 9:1–11:36 as homilies relocated from the synagogue into the Letter to the Romans.[13]

---

[10] R. Meyer and H. F. Weiss, Φαρισαῖος, GLNT IX, 857–956; Overman, 'κατὰ νόμον Φαρισαῖος', 180–193.

[11] A. Pitta, *Lettera ai Romani: Nuova versione, introduzione e commento*, 3rd ed. (LB NT 6; Milano: Paoline, 2009), 46.

[12] C. D. Stanley, *Paul and the Language of Scripture. Citations Technique in the Pauline Epistles and Contemporary Literature* (SNTS MS 69; Cambridge: Cambridge University Press, 1992), 221–222.

[13] *Pace* E.P. Sanders, *Paul, the Law and the Jewish People* (Philadelphia: Fortress Press, 1983), 204 on Rom 2; and R. Scroggs, "Paul as Rhetorician: Two Homilies in Romans 1–11," in *Jews, Greeks and Christians: Religious Cultures in Late Antiquity* (ed. R. Hamerton Kelly and R. Scroggs; Festschrift W.D. Davies; Leiden: Brill, 1976), 271–298.

2. PHARISEEISM IN GAL 1:13–17 AND PHIL 3:2–6

The two autobiographical sections of Gal 1:13–17 and Phil 3:2–6 represent the principal sources on Paul's "pre-Christian" life.[14] We can add the brief mention in 1 Cor 15:9 where Paul remembers having persecuted τὴν ἐκκλησίαν τοῦ θεοῦ, and 2 Cor 11:22 where, debating with his opponents, Paul clarifies that he too is a Hebrew, an Israelite and a descendant of Abraham, and lastly Rom 11:1 which confirms his provenance from the tribe of Benjamin.

The first common trait between the two sections of Galatians and Philippians is Paul's past in Judaism (cf. Gal 1:13a; Phil 3:5). While in Gal 1:13 he recalls, in generic terms, his conduct in Judaism, in Phil 3:5 he specifies his belonging to Phariseeism. Such a connection induces us to recognize that with the generic noun Ἰουδαϊσμός Paul refers not to Sadduceeism or other political-religious movements, but instead to Phariseeism, the school of thought to which he belonged before the "Revelation of the Son of God" (Gal 1:15–16). The overlap between Ἰουδαϊσμός in Gal 1:12–14 and φαρισαῖος in Phil 3:5 should however avoid a simple merger of the two terms according to which every one of Paul's statements on the Jews should be directed to the Pharisees. In fact, the clash in 1 Thess 2:14–15 and 2 Cor 3:13 is with the Jews and the "children of Israel," not with the Pharisees.

We should make a few clarifications about the term Ἰουδαϊσμός. Because of one of the New Perspectives, some scholars of early Christianity prefer to speak of "Judaisms" and of "Christianisms."[15] As a result Sadduceeism, Essenism, apocalyptic, and Jewish wisdom tendencies should also be considered alongside Phariseeism. And that the "Christianisms" of Peter, Matthew, James, and other vari-

---

[14] M. Hengel, *The Pre-Christian Paul* (London: Trinity Press, 1991); M. Hengel, *Paulus zwischen Damaskus und Antiochien: die Unbekannten Jahre* (WUNT 108; Tübingen: Mohr, 1998).

[15] G. Boccaccini, *Middle Judaism: Jewish Thought, 300 B.C.E. to 200 C.E.* (Minneapolis: Fortress Press, 1991); and A. Destro and M. Pesce, 'Come è nato il cristianesimo', in *ASE* 21 (2004): 533–543.

ous "Christianisms" of first- and second-century sources should be regarded alongside the Christianity of Paul. Except the use of Ἰουδαϊσμός in Gal 1:13–14 (and only in these verses in the whole NT),[16] it is not by chance that in all of the Septuagint the noun is always used in the singular, but never in the plural. It is used only five times and only in the Maccabean literature,[17] namely in a *corpus* that tends to safeguard the political-religious identity of Judaism during the expansion of Hellenism. For that reason it is valuable to distinguish the noun "Judaism," which refers to the religious sphere, from "Hebraism," which refers to the ethnic origin of a people.[18] With the use of "Judaisms" and "Christianisms" – the latter noun is not testified until Ignatius of Antioch (at the beginning of the second century C.E.) and only in the singular,[19] never plural – there is the risk of creating a misunderstanding of Judaism of the Second Temple period and of the early Christian movement which were not as fragmented as the plural terms imply.[20] It is one thing not to find

---

[16] Cf. also the use of ἰουδαΐζειν in Gal 2:14, NT *hapax legomenon.*

[17] 2 Mac 2:21 (καὶ τὰς ἐξ οὐρανοῦ γενομένας ἐπιφανείας τοῖς ὑπὲρ τοῦ Ιουδαϊσμοῦ φιλοτίμως ἀνδραγαθήσασιν ὥστε τὴν ὅλην χώραν ὀλίγους ὄντας λεηλατεῖν καὶ τὰ βάρβαρα πλήθη διώκειν); 8:1; 14:38; 4 Mac 4:26. Cf. Ignatius of Antioch, *To the Philadelphians* 6.1: "But if any one preach the Jewish law unto you, listen not to him. For it is better to hearken to Christian doctrine from a man who has been circumcised, than to Judaism from one uncircumcised"; *To the Magnesians* 10.3: "It is absurd to speak of Jesus Christ with the tongue, and to cherish in the mind a Judaism which has now come to an end. For where there is Christianity there cannot be Judaism."

[18] R. Penna, 'Che cosa significava essere giudeo al tempo e nella terra di Gesù: Problemi e proposte', *Vangelo e inculturazione*, 65; *pace* S.C. Mimouni, 'Les «origines» du mouvement chrétien entre 30 et 135: Des réflexions et des remarques', *ASE* 21/2 (2004): 463.

[19] Ignatius, *To the Romans* 3.3: οὐδὲν φαινόμενον καλόν ὁ γὰρ θεὸς ἡμῶν Ἰησοῦς Χριστὸς ἐν πατρὶ ὢν μᾶλλον φαίνεται οὐ πεισμονῆς τὸ ἔργον ἀλλὰ μεγέθους ἐστὶν ὁ Χριστιανισμός, ὅταν μισῆται ὑπὸ κόσμου; *To the Philadelphians* 6.1: Ἐὰν δέ τις Ἰουδαϊσμὸν ἑρμηνεύῃ ὑμῖν μὴ ἀκούετε αὐτοῦ ἄμεινον γάρ ἐστιν παρὰ ἀνδρὸς περιτομὴν ἔχοντος Χριστιανισμὸν ἀκούειν ἢ παρὰ ἀκροβύστου Ἰουδαϊσμόν ἐὰν δὲ ἀμφότεροι περὶ Ἰησοῦ Χριστοῦ μὴ λαλῶσιν οὗτοι ἐμοὶ στῆλαί εἰσιν καὶ τάφοι νεκρῶν ἐφ' οἷς γέγραπται μόνον ὀνόματα ἀνθρώπων.

[20] On Judaism vs. Judaisms cf. T. Laato, *Paul and Judaism: An Anthropological Approach* (Atlanta: Scholars Press, 1995); A.F. Segal, *Rebecca's Children: Judaism and Christianity in the Roman World* (Cambridge, Mass.: Harvard University Press, 1986).

a normative Judaism or a unified Christianity, but it is quite another to consider every christological and ethical pattern as an autonomous form of Judaism or Christianity.[21]

On the other side there is the pattern of "Common Judaism" chosen by E. P. Sanders, who uses the category of "Common Judaism."[22] It must be pointed out however that it is difficult to identify common features among the various Jewish tendencies of the first century.[23] This raises the question with regard to the main elements of Judaism and the Christian movement with respect to other religions.[24] Limiting ourselves to some contributions that attempt to define the identity of second temple Judaism, from the historic-religionist perspective E. P. Sanders coined the "covenantal nomism" formula. As unifying factors, Sanders sees monotheism, the theology of creation, the system of sacrifices, the love for God and for neighbor as the synthesis of the entire Law, and prayer.[25] J. D. G. Dunn concludes with four basic grid references: monotheism (God is one), the election, the covenant founded on the Torah, and the land in relationship to the temple.[26] From the religious view, F. Manns considers the temple, the law and the gift of the land to be the "soul" of Judaism.[27] From a sociological prospective, E.W. Stegemann and W. Stegemann list monotheism, election, Law, temple, synagogue, and family.[28] Finally, M. Casey includes eight iden-

---

[21] P. Sacchi, *Storia del Secondo Tempio: Israele tra VI secolo a.C. e I secolo d.C.* (Turin: SEI, 1994), 282.

[22] E. P. Sanders, *Judaism: Practice and Belief 63 BCE–66 CE* (London: SCM Press, 1992).

[23] M. Hengel and R. Deines, "E.P. Sander's 'Common Judaism', Jews, and the Pharisees," *JTS* 46 (1995), 39–40.

[24] G. Theissen, "Judentum und Christentum bei Paulus: Sozialgeschichtliche Überlegungen zu einem Beginnenden Schisma," in *Paulus und das Judentum* (ed. Hengel and Heckel), 331–356.

[25] Sanders, *Judaism*, 64–104.

[26] J.D.G. Dunn, *The Partings of the Ways Between Christianity and Judaism and their Significance for the Character of Christianity* (London and Philadelphia: SCM Press, 1991), 18–36.

[27] Manns, *Giudaismo*, 28.

[28] E. W. Stegemann and W. Stegemann, *Urchristliche Sozialgeschichte: Die Anfänge im Judentum und die Christusgemeinden in der mediterranen Welt* (Stuttgart, Berlin, Köln: Kohlhammer, 1995) .

tifying characteristics of second temple Judaism: ethnicity, Scripture, monotheism, circumcision, observance of the Sabbath, dietary law, purity laws, and the major feasts.[29] While I do not want to add a new hypothesis, I think that the multiple uses of the Scripture, the Law and several systems of worship should be added to the centrality of monotheism.

As for the tendencies of Christianity, one should at least recognize that with Jesus of Nazareth begins the process that will bring about the parting of the ways after 70 CE.[30] Among the principal factors should be mentioned his messianic "pretension"—otherwise it becomes impossible to identify the main reason that led to his death on the cross.[31] The fact that the "worship of Christ" developed in a fairly rapid way at the dawn of the Christian movement can only be explained by the relation with this stage of Jesus' life.[32]

In its own turn, the decisive and original contribution of Paul hangs on the development of justification without the Law and its works,[33] but only by faith in Christ, with the consequential involvement of the Gentiles without passing through the "works of the Law."[34] These are the two extremes or the two "craters" upon which

---

[29] P. M. Casey, *From Jewish Prophet to Gentile God: The Origins and Development of New Testament Christology*, (Louisville: Westminster-John Knox, 1991), 12.

[30] S. Guijarro Oporto and E. Miquel Pericás, "Il cristianesimo nascente: delimitazione cronologica, fonti e metodologia," in *ASE* 21/2 (2004): 478; Penna, "Essere giudeo," 87.

[31] G. Jossa, *Giudei o cristiani? I seguaci di Gesù in cerca di una propria identità* (SB 142; Bresceia: Paideia, 2004).

[32] L.W. Hurtado, *Lord Jesus Christ: Devotion to Jesus in Earliest Christianity* (Grand Rapids, Mich.: Eerdmans, 2003); C. Perrot, *Gesù Cristo e Signore dei primi cristiani: Una cristologia esegetica* (Rome: Borla, 2000).

[33] S. Westerholm, *Israel's Law and the Church's Faith: Paul and His Recent Interpreters* (Grand Rapids, Mich.: Eerdmans, 1988); M. A. Seifrid, *Justification by Faith: The Origin and Development of a Central Pauline Theme* (NT Sup. 68; Leiden: Brill, 1992).

[34] A. Schweitzer, *Die Mystik des Apostels Paulus* (Tübingen: Mohr, 1930); K. Stendhal, *Paul Among Jews and Gentiles and Other Essays* (Philadelphia: Fortress Press, 1976); E. P. Sanders, *Paul and Palestinian Judaism: A Comparison of Pattern of Religion*, (2nd ed.; London: Fortress Press, 1984); J. D. G. Dunn, "The New

the greater part of contemporary exegesis is debated and that, if one looks close enough, are more related than one may think.

Also outstanding is Paul's contribution to the centrality of the cross in his gospel, mentioned implicitly in the pre-Pauline fragments of 1 Cor 11:23–25; 15:3–5; Gal 1:4; Rom 1:3–4; 3:25 and in the so-called "hymn" or better *elogium* of Phil 2:6–11, from which the bracket θανάτου δὲ σταυροῦ (v. 8b), which is of Pauline origin, should be excluded. Perhaps, without the Jewish matrix, the first Christian movement would have professed the uselessness of the Scriptures of Israel and faith in a threefold divinity of a religionist pattern; a profession which is critical for the following history of Christianity! The rooted monotheism is owed to the fact that in his main letters Paul attributes only to God the noun θεός (including the doxological sentence of Rom 9:5) and not to Jesus Christ, nor to the Spirit, without denying the "Lordship" of either one. Only when the parting of ways between Judaism and Christianity will become deeper will the Pauline tradition begin to label, *expressis verbis*, Jesus Christ as "our great God and savior" (1 Tim 2:13–14).

From the literary sources, the presence of different currents within the Judaism of the Second Temple period hinders the defining of the writings which belonged to Phariseeism: the Psalms of Solomon seem close to both Phariseeism and the apocalyptic current; and the same goes for 4 Esdras and for 4 Maccabees. Such complexity shows the need to drop the attempts to find some writings properly belonging to the Pharisees: unfortunately the only Pharisee whose writings we still have, even until today, remains Paul of Tarsus! At the most one may assume the presence of Pharisaic influences on 2 Maccabees, the Psalms of Solomon, the pseudo-phylonian *Liber Antiquitatum Biblicarum*, 2 Baruch, *Targum Neophiti*, and even the treatise *Aboth* of the Mishna.[35]

Perspective on Paul," *BJRL* 65/2 (1982): 95–122; F. Watson, *Paul, Judaism and Gentiles: A Sociological Approach* (SNTS MS 56; Cambridge: Cambridge University Press, 1986).

[35] G. Boccaccini, "Esiste una letteratura farisaica?," *RSB* 11/2 (1999): 23–41.

On the side of the polemics with the Pharisees, perhaps *4QPesherNahum*, which in different propositions alludes to their movement, has not been given enough attention: "Its interpretation refers to Demetrius, king of Yavan, who wanted to enter Jerusalem on the advice of those looking for smooth interpretations" (4QpNah fr. 3–4 col. I). The allusion proceeds with the paragraph dedicated to Alexander Hyanneus who crucified 800 Pharisees that had plotted against him:

> Its interpretation concerns the Angry Lion 7 [who filled his cave with a mass of corpses, carrying out revenge] against those looking for smooth interpretations, who hanged living men 8[from a tree, committing an atrocity which had not been committed] in Israel since ancient times, for it is [hor]rible for the one hanged alive from a tree (4QpNah fr. 7–8 Col I).[36]

With all of the complexities and the diversifications pointed out, the correspondence between Gal 1:13 and Phil 3:5 permits one to think of Phariseeism as one of the most representative currents of Judaism in the first century CE,[37] while the skepticism of those who, because of the difficulties pointed out, do not take into consideration the Pharisees' consistency in the Herodian period, should be corrected.[38] On this point the declaration of Josephus is indicative: "Of the other two (schools), before noted, one is that of the Pharisees; they enjoy a fame for interpreting exactly the laws, they make up the most important school" (*Jewish War* 2.162).[39]

---

[36] Cf. D. Flusser, "Pharisees, Sadducees, and Essenes in Pesher Nahum," in *Judaism of the Second Temple*, 214–257.

[37] L.H. Feldman, *Jew and Gentile in the Ancient World: Attitudes and Interaction from Alexander to Justinian* (Princeton: Princeton University Press, 1993), 39.

[38] D. Goodblatt, "The Place of Pharisees in First Century Judaism: The State of the Debate," *JSJ* 20 (1989): 29.

[39] S. Mason, *Flavius Josephus on the Pharisees: A Composition-Critical Study* (Leiden: Brill, 1991), 372; Schäfer, "Der vorrabbinische Pharisäismus," 132–171.

According to the same historian, "so great is their influence with the masses that even when they speak against a king or high priest, they immediately gain credence" (*Jewish Antiquities* 13.288).[40]

With regard to the expression κατὰ νόμον Φαρισαῖος (Phil 3:5), we must observe that Paul's belonging to Phariseeism is more consistent than that of Josephus as reported in his *Autobiography* (1.12), as we pointed out in the introduction. In fact Josephus does not claim, contrary to Paul, to have been a "Pharisee"; rather, he asserts that he was educated at the school of the Pharisees in a period of his childhood training. In the same context of the *Autobiography*, he also remembers having frequented the other more notable schools of his time, recognizing however that he did not identify with any of them:

> And when I was about sixteen years old, I had a mind to make trim of the several sects that were among us. These sects are three – The first is that of the Pharisees, the second that of the Sadducees, and the third that of the Essenes, as we have frequently told you; for I thought that by this means I might choose the best, if I were once acquainted with them all; so I contented myself with hard fare, and underwent great difficulties and went through them all. Nor did I content myself with these trials only; but when I was informed that one, whose name was Banus… I imitated him in those things, and continued with him three years.
>
> (*Life* 1.10–12)

This memory shows us that, unlike Paul, Josephus considers his "experience unsatisfactory" in the three principal Jewish schools of thought, and for this reason some scholars rightly tend to downplay Josephus' belonging to Phariseeism.[41] In reality some scholars esteem groundless the sentence of Phil 3:5, considering Paul not as a

---

[40] Cf. also Flavius Josephus, *Jewish Antiquities* 18.15: "Because of these views they are, as matter of fact, extremely influential among the townsfolk; and all prayers and sacred rites of divine worship are performed according to their expositions."

[41] Mason, *Flavius Josephus*, 374.

Pharisee but as emissary of the Sadducees.[42] However they do so with scarce historical proof since the hypothesis rests only on the quotation of Acts 9:1 – 2:21, where Luke remembers that Paul "asked the high priest … for letters for the synagogues of Damascus." Instead it is better to give credit to Luke himself who mentions the Pharisaic origin of Paul: "They (the Jews), if they want to give testimony, have known for some time that I lived in the most demanding school of our religion" (Acts 26:5).

In the attempt to further specify the features of the Pharisaic identity of Paul, it has been supposed that he had a familiarity with the school of Hillel or that of Shammai. Accepting information given by the Acts of the Apostles (cf. Acts 22:3), some scholars retain the idea that Paul was a Hillelite,[43] namely that he followed the progressive wing of Phariseeism. Still others, basing themselves on the rigor with which Paul treats ethical issues, presume that he belonged to the conservative wing of Shammai.[44] Besides Paul's presumed strictness on ethical questions,[45] on the one hand the distinction is purely theoretical or "goat's wool," as M. Hengel put it,[46] while on the other it takes on the connotations of an incorrect projection into the past and a lack of assim-

---

[42] H. Maccoby, *The Mythmaker: Paul and the Invention of Christianity* (London: Weidenfeld & Nicolson, 1986), 59.

[43] J. Jeremias, "Paulus als Hillelit," in *Neotestamentica et Semitica* (ed. E.E. Ellis and E. Wilcox; Edinburgh: T&T Clark, 1969), 88–94. About the relationships between Gamaliel, Paul and the rabbinic sources cf. B.D. Chilton and J. Neusner, "Paul and Gamaliel," in *In Quest of the Historical Pharisees* (ed. J. Neusner and B.D. Chilton; Waco: Baylor University Press: 2007), 175–223.

[44] H. Hübner, *Das Gesetz bei Paulus: Ein Beitrag zum Werden der paulinischen Theologie* (Göttingen: Vandenhoeck & Ruprecht, 1982), 40–41; N. T. Wright, *The New Testament and the People of God* (vol. 1; London and Minneapolis: SPCK, 1992), 201–202.

[45] Against the strictness in ethical questions see the Pauline solution for the strong and weak in 1 Cor 8:1–10:33 and Rom 14:1–15:13. A. Pitta, "The Strong, the Weak and the Mosaic Law in the Christian Communities of Rome (Rom 14:1–15:13," in *Christians as a Religious Minority in a Multicultural City* (ed. J. Zangenberg and M. Labahn; JSNT SS 243; London and New York: T&T Clark: 2004), 90–102.

ilation regarding the historical development of Phariseeism before 70 C.E. and Rabbinism afterwards.[47] Indeed the breakaway between the Hillel and Shammai schools marks a polarization of rabbinism in the second century; not of the previous Phariseeism which does not present itself so ideologically.[48] For this reason, there are those, like J. Sievers, who prefer not to enumerate Hillel and Shammai among the 12 Pharisees listed according to the NT and the corpus of Flavius Josephus, because in the rabbinic literature itself they are never defined as "Pharisees" much less "rabbis."[49] Thus we think it makes sense not to go beyond Paul's Pharisaic identity, without proceeding towards further specifications about his belonging to one or the other school.

Regarding the spread of Phariseeism in the Jewish Diaspora, Acts 23:6 seems to claim its presence in Tarsus of Cilicia: "Brothers, I am a Pharisee and son of Pharisees." However, the proposition is evaluated with scepticism by historiography.[50] It is known that Phariseeism grew up in Palestine with a concentration in Jerusalem, while there are no outside witnesses about its extension beyond the boundaries of Israel. If the Lucan sentence is explained by the rhetorical point of view, in as much as he intends to simply assert that Paul belongs in every respect to the Pharisaic movement, it is not necessary to assume the presence of the Pharisaic movement in Tarsus, unless we accept the information from Jerome who considers Giscala Paul's birthplace.[51] But leaving behind the incongruencies that jump out from the comparison of Jerome's two statements, it makes no sense of why Luke would have placed Paul's birth in Tarsus, if he had really been born in Palestine. In reality we have no knowledge about Paul's relatives except that they come from the

---

[46] Hengel, *The Pre-Christian Paul*, 85.

[47] Rightly Penna, *Vangelo e inculturazione*, 313–314.

[48] D.F. Craffert, "The Pauline Movement and the First-Century Judaism: A Framework for Transforming the Issue," *Neot* 27 (1993): 247.

[49] Sievers, "Who were the Pharisees," 137–155.

[50] Lentz Jr., *Luke's Portrait of Paul*, 54–56.

[51] Jerome, *In Epistolam ad Philemon*, PL 26.617; *De viris illustribus* 5.1.

Tribe of Benjamin (Phil. 3.5): we don't know when or why he was in Tarsus, how he gained the privilege of Roman citizenship or his economic status in the diaspora. For this reason, it is impossible to ascertain how Paul's family could have continued in the Pharisaic movement while in the Diaspora. At least for Paul, it seems that from his youth he was in Jerusalem and joined the Pharisaic movement at the school of Gamaliel I.[52]

3. PERSECUTOR OF THE CHURCH

The second point common to the autobiographical passages in Galatians and Philippians regards Paul's past persecution of the Church: "You have surely heard how I lived in the past, within Judaism, and how there was simply no limit to the way I persecuted the Church of God in my attempts to destroy it; and how, in Judaism, I outstripped most of my Jewish contemporaries in my zeal for the traditions of my fathers" (Gal 1:13–14);[53] "... As for zeal, I was a persecutor of the Church" (Phil 3:6). Already in 1 Cor 15:9 Paul had remembered his persecution against the first Christian movement.[54] From the comparison between Gal 1:14 and Phil 3:6 a different orientation in Paul's zeal is revealed. But the two statements are related when one recognizes "the Church of God" not so much as an autonomous religious identity but as a movement within Judaism, and for this very reason Paul persecuted it for its faith in the crucified Messiah.

In this way Paul's insistence on his zeal for the traditions of his fathers seems to recall the model of Phinehas who had killed a Jew

---

[52] A.J. Saldarini, *Pharisees, Scribes and Sadducees in Palestinian Society: A Sociological Approach* (Edinburgh: T&T Clark, 1989), 137–138.

[53] The imperfect ἐπόρθουν should be intended like "de conatu" corresponding to "I did try to destroy." A. Pitta, *Lettera ai Galati: Introduzione, versione e commento* (3rd ed.; SOC 9; Bologna: EDB, 2009), 93.

[54] On the formula "church of God" cf. 1 Cor 1:2; 10:32; 2 Cor 1:1; 1 Tim 3:15; Acts 20:28. The expression does not refer to a building but to an assembly of people.

and his wife of pagan origins (cf. Num 25:7–15). In different sources of the Judaism of the Second Temple Phinehas will be chosen as the model of adhering to the Law precisely because of his zeal.[55] Thus is Mattathias' zeal described at the beginning of the Macabbean revolt: "In his zeal for the Law he acted as Phinehas had against Zimri son of Salu. Then Mattathias went through the town, shouting at the top of his voice: Let everyone who has any zeal for the Law and takes his stand on the covenant come out and follow me" (1 Mac 2:26–27). Also Ps 106:30–31 exalts the merits of Phinehas in view of his final salvation actualizing the important accrediting of divine justice towards Abraham (cf. Gen. 15:6).

As far as Paul's persecution of the first Christian movement or what he calls "the church of God" (1 Cor 15:9; Gal 1:13),[56] specifying later that he is alluding to the "churches of Judea who are in Christ" (Gal 1:23; cf. also the use of the plural "churches of God that are in Judea" in 1 Thess 2:14), some scholars tend to minimize the value, claiming that on the one hand Paul's opposition excluded violence and on the other that "the picture of Paul as persecutor of the Church as it appears in Acts 7– 9 seems... false."[57] In reality even if the verbs διώκειν (persecute) and πορθείν (destroy) used in the cited passages do not necessarily allude to violence, they at least denote attempts at open opposition towards the "Church of God." But what leads towards an interpretation of a persecution which is anything but peaceful or simply ideological against the believers in Christ, are the references to the adversities faced later by Paul himself for Christ: beatings suffered for the Gospel and the reference to the five times in which he received thirty-nine lashes from the Jews (2 Cor 11:23–24) do not refer to a purely ideological persecution against the Christian movement, but a politico-religious one understood

[55] G. Barbaglio, *Gesù di Nazaret e Paolo: Confronto storico* (Bologna: EDB, 2006), 89; Penna, *Vangelo e inculturazione*, 309.

[56] In Phil 3:6 the witnesses F, G, 0282 e 629 add θεοῦ in order to specify the relationship with the Church of God and so to simplify the text.

[57] Lietaert Peerbolte, *Paul the Missionary*, 176–178.

as within Judaism itself. Therefore even if the Lucan report of Acts 7–9 reflects the contrasts between Judaism and the Christian movement, exacerbated after 70 C.E., it should not be eliminated too quickly in historiographic analysis, nor out of a prejudiced mistrust with respect to Pauline autobiography.

4. THE TRADITIONS OF THE FATHERS AND THE LAW

With the third point connecting Gal 1:14 and Phil 3:6 we come to the second reason for our analysis: the relationship between Paul, pharisaic Judaism, and the Mosaic Law. Paul remembers his observance of the traditions of the fathers and the Law. The two sentences are linked by Paul's "zealous" (ζηλωτής, ζῆλος) and "irreprehensible" (ἄμεμπτος) behaviour regarding the traditions and the mosaic Law. What does he mean by the "traditions of the fathers" (τῶν πατρικῶν μου παραδόσεων)?

In the NT the term παράδοσις refers in general to the pharisaic tradition (Mk 7:3–13)[58] or to the first Pauline communities (1 Cor 11:2).[59] The first case finds a typical synoptic expression τὴν παράδοσιν τῶν πρεσβυτέρων (Mk. 7,3; Matt. 15.2) while the syntagma τῶν πατρικῶν μου παραδόσεων is used only in Gal 1:14 in the NT. The connection between the tradition of the fathers and pharisaic Judaism is revealed again by Flavius Josephus, who considers it as one of the main reasons of contrast between Pharisees and Sadducees.[60] He writes in his *Jewish Antiquities* (13.297): "For the present I wish merely to explain that the Pharisees had passed on to the people certain regulations handed down by former generations and not recorded in the Law of Moses, for which reason they are rejected by the Sadducean group, who hold that only those regulations should be considered valid which were written down (in Scripture), and that those

---

[58] Cf. also Mk 7:3, 5, 8; Mk 9:13; Matt 15:2.

[59] Cf. also 2 Thess 2:15; 3:6.

[60] Cf. A.I. Baumgarten, "The Pharisaic Paradosis," in *HTR* 80 (1987): 63–77.

which had been handed down by former generations need not be observed."[61] The historian will again underline this feature of the Pharisees in *Antiquities* (17.41): "For there was a certain sect of men that were Jews, who valued themselves highly upon the exact skill they had in the law of their fathers, and made men believe they were highly favored by God… These are those who are called the sect of the Pharisees, who were in a capacity of greatly opposing kings."[62]

According to the same Josephus, the Pharisaic traditions were refused by John Hyrcanus, when he forsook the movement to ally himself with the Sadducees,[63] but they returned in vogue under the reign of Salome Alexandra who governed thanks to the unwavering support of the Pharisees.[64] Regarding the truthfulness of Josephus' witness perhaps it is important to mention that his description of the Pharisees, Sadducees, and Essenes is often schematic and biased because he is trying to present to Gentile readers the various branches of Judaism as the best philosophical schools of the time, among

---

[61] Flavius Josephus, *Antiquities* 13.297: περὶ μέντοι τούτων αὖθις ἐροῦμεν νῦν δὲ δηλῶσαι βούλομαι ὅτι νόμιμά τινα παρέδοσαν τῷ δήμῳ οἱ Φαρισαῖοι ἐκ πατέρων διαδοχῆς ἅπερ οὐκ ἀναγέγραπται ἐν τοῖς Μωυσέως νόμοις καὶ διὰ τοῦτο ταῦτα τὸ Σαδδουκαίων γένος ἐκβάλλει λέγον ἐκεῖνα δεῖν ἡγεῖσθαι νόμιμα τὰ γεγραμμένα τὰ δ' ἐκ παραδόσεως τῶν πατέρων μὴ τηρεῖν.

[62] Flavius Josephus, *Antiquities*17.41: καὶ ἦν γὰρ μόριόν τι Ἰουδαϊκὸν ἀνθρώπων ἐπ' ἐξακριβώσει μέγα φρονοῦν τοῦ πατρίου καὶ νόμων οἷς χαίρει τὸ θεῖον προσποιουμένων οἷς ὑπῆκτο ἡ γυναικωνῖτις Φαρισαῖοι καλοῦνται βασιλεῖ δυναμένῳ μάλιστα πράσσειν προμηθεῖς κἀκ τοῦ προὔπτου εἰς τὸ πολεμεῖν τε καὶ βλάπτειν ἐπηρμένοι.

[63] Flavius Josephus, *Antiquities* 13.296: "That he made him leave the party of the Pharisees, and abolish the decrees they had imposed on the people, and to punish those who observed them. From this source arose that hatred which he and his sons met with from the multitude."

[64] Flavius Josephus, *Antiquities* 13.408: "So she made Hyrcanus high priest, because he was the older, but much more because he cared not to meddle with politics, and permitted the Pharisees to do everything; to whom also she ordered the multitude to be obedient. She also restored again those practices which the Pharisees had introduced, according to the traditions of their forefathers, and which her father-in-law, Hyrcanus, had abrogated."

which Phariseeism excels on the same level as the Stoics; and this is particularly true in his *Jewish Antiquities*.[65] In reality even the Essenes and the Sadducees could not appeal to the Mosaic Law without reference to their own traditions.[66] However this does not deny that the reference to oral tradition characterizes the Pharisaic movement so that expressions like "the traditions of the fathers" or "the traditions of the elders" acquire the power of technical formulas for oral tradition to set beside the written Torah. To avoid further confusion about sources, I think that it is worthwhile to use the category of "oral tradition" rather than "oral Torah"[67] because only later rabbinic literature speaks of an oral Torah.[68]

Because of the importance of tradition in the pharisaic school, the verbs παραλαμβάνειν and παραδίδωμι (which correspond to the Semitic מסר and קבל) refer to the transmission of the oral tradition that developed from what is contained in the Torah. The famous treatise Aboth 1.1 of the Mishnah begins: "Moses received the Law from Sinai and handed it on to Joshua; and Joshua to the elders; and the elders to the prophets; and the Prophets handed it to the men of great congregation."[69] In this context we can understand Paul's use of the same verbs both for describing the first preaching of his communities and for evoking Jesus' words at the Last Supper (1 Cor 11:23–25: Ἐγὼ γὰρ παρέλαβον ἀπὸ τοῦ κυρίου, ὃ καὶ παρέδωκα ὑμῖν, v. 23) and the first kerygma on Christ's death and resurrection (1 Cor. 15:3-5: παρέδωκα γὰρ ὑμῖν ἐν πρώτοις, ὃ καὶ παρέλαβον,

---

[65] Mason, *Flavius Josephus*, 374–375.

[66] Baumgarten, "Paradosis," 66; J. Neusner, "The Rabbinic Tradition About the Pharisees Before 70: The Problem of Oral Transmission," in *JJS* 22 (1971): 11.

[67] *Pace* P. Lenhardt , "À l'origine du mouvement Pharisien, la tradition orale et la résurrection, " *Le judaïsme à l'aube de l'ère chrétienne, XVIIIe congrès de l'ACFEB (Lyon, septembre 1999)* (ed. P. Abadie and J.-P. Lémenon ; Paris: Cerf, 2001), 136.

[68] Rightly Hengel and Deines, "Common Judaism," 29–35; K. Müller, "Beobachtungen zum verhältnis von Torah und Halaka in frühjudischen Quellen," *Jesus und das jüdische Gesetz* (ed. I. Broer; Stuttgart 1992), 105–155; E. Rivkin, "Defining the Pharisees: the Tannaitic Sources, " in *HUCA* 40–41 (1969–1970): 248.

[69] Baumgarten, "Paradosis," 67–71.

v. 3). Therefore the expression ἀπὸ τοῦ κυρίου does not allude to what Paul received directly from the Risen Lord during a post-Easter vision, of which we have no trace of the words of the Last Supper,[70] but to the παράδοσις of the first Christian communities which goes back to the historical Jesus and was very probably transmitted in the community of Antioch in Syria.[71] In practice it is as if from (ἀπό and not the usual παρά) Jesus himself Paul had received the living tradition of the words that he passed on to the Corinthians during his first preaching in that city (51–52 C.E.) and that he later repeated in 1 Cor (54–55 C.E.). Thus the expression "tradition of the fathers" (Gal 1:14) and the process of the transmission of the Christian faith give witness to the presence and permanence of the Pharisaic model in the Pauline letters.

The Pharisaic assimilation between the written Torah and oral tradition will become fundamental for the Pauline vision of the Law.[72] Against the distinctions between the "Torah as revelation" that remains and the "Torah as legislation" that passes away for believers in Christ,[73] it is important to recover the holistic or global vision of the Torah in Pauline thought.[74] The distinction is not found in Paul's

---

[70] *Pace* H. Maccoby, "Paul and the Eucharist," in *NTS* 37 (1991): 262–265 and F. Watson, "I Received from the Lord… Paul, Jesus and the Last Supper," in *Jesus and Paul Reconnected: Fresh Pathways into an Old Debate* (ed. T.D. Still; Grand Rapids and Cambridge: Eerdmans, 2007), 103–124.

[71] G. Barbaglio, *La prima lettera ai Corinzi: Introduzione, versione e commento* (SOC 16; Bologna : EDB 1995), 486–487; J.M. van Cangh, "L'évolution de la tradition de la cène (Mc 12,22-26 et par.), " in *Lectures et relectures*, Festschrift P.-M. Bogaert (ed. J.-M. Auwers and A. Wénin; BETL 144; Leuven : Leuven University Press, 1999), 257–285; X. Léon-Dufour, *Condividere il pane secondo il Nuovo Testamento* (2nd ed.; Leumann : LDC, 2005), 97–116.

[72] Cf. J. Massonnet, "Les pharisiens et le sens communautaire," in *Judaïsme* (ed. Abadie and Lémenon), 177–204.

[73] *Pace* B.L. Martin, *Christ and the Law in Paul* (NT Sup. 62 ; Leiden: Brill, 1989), 32–34; S. Romanello, "Paolo e la Legge : Prolegomeni a una riflessione organica," in *RivB* 54 (2006): 352–353.

[74] R. Penna, *I ritratti originali di Gesù Cristo: Inizi e sviluppi della cristologia neotestamentaria. Gli sviluppi* (vol 2; San Paolo: Cinisello Balsamo, 1999), 179; L.T. Thurén, *Derhetorizing Paul: A Dynamic Perspective on Pauline Theology and the Law* (WUNT 124; Tübingen: Mohr, 2000), 109–110.

language and risks causing a sort of "canon within the canon" that the Christian tradition rejected in the first two centuries of its formation. In fact the noun νόμος (with or without the article, cf. in particular Gal 2:19; 4:21; Rom 3:21), generally refers to the Judaic law. The holistic concept of the Law is especially valuable for complex sections of the Pauline letters like Gal 2:14–21; 4:21–5:1 and Rom 1:18–3:20 and calls into question a separation between the Law as revelation and the Law as legislation, the former abrogating the latter. In its turn the importance of oral tradition together with the written Law comes out in Paul's exegesis and his free method of citing the OT according to a few specific argumentative goals that start from the event of the death and resurrection of Christ in order to reinterpret any passage of Israel's Scriptures.[75] So it seems to me that the formulas "traditions of the fathers" in Gal 1:14 and "traditions of the elders" in Matt 15:2 are different expressions for referring to the oral traditions of the Law, typical of, if not exclusive to, pharisaic Judaism. And perhaps it is significant to note the connection between these traditions and the fathers or the elders refers not only to the ancient prophets but also the current leaders of the pharisaic movement whose authority is recognized in the transmission of the oral tradition of the Law.[76]

Before these traditions Paul boasts of his own "zeal" and of his "irreproachability" in the justice of the Law (Phil 3:6): the two terms are linked and related to the noun ἀκρίβεια that Luke and Flavius Josephus use to describe the devotion of the Pharisees for the Law and the oral traditions. The Lucan Paul remembers his own pharisaic training in Acts 22:3: "I am a Jew… and was born at Tarsus in Cilicia. I was brought up here in this city. It was under Gamaliel that I studied and was taught the exact observance of the Law of our ancestors (κατὰ ἀκρίβειαν τοῦ πατρῴου νόμου)". Unfortunately a distorted vision of the pharisaic movement has often been produced, because it was considered uncompromising

[75] A. Pitta, *Paolo: La Scrittura e la Legge* (SB 57; Bologna: EDB, 2009).
[76] Baumgarten, "Paradosis," 75–77.

in the observance of the Law. On the contrary, the term ἀκρίβεια and derivatives indicate the exact opposite, namely the acute ability and flexibility in adapting the Law and oral traditions to the various situations of social and religious life.

Speaking of Flavius Josephus, it is necessary to clarify that he uses the semantic field of ἀκρίβεια in different contexts.[77] Nevertheless, in his texts the language of ἀκρίβεια characterizes the Pharisees' dedication in interpreting the Law: "And now the Pharisees joined themselves to her (the queen Alexandra), to assist her in the government. These are a certain sect of the Jews that appear more religious than others, and seem to interpret the laws more accurately".[78] About the ἀκρίβεια or the constant commitment of the Pharisees for the Law and the oral traditions Flavius Josephus writes in his *Jewish War*: "But then as to the two other orders at first mentioned, the Pharisees are those who are esteemed most skilful in the exact explanation of the laws ...".[79] And in the *Antiquities* 17.41 he adds: "There was also a group of Jews priding itself on its adherence to ancestral custom and claiming to observe the laws of which the Deity approves, and by these men, called Pharisees, the women (of the court) were ruled."[80] Finally in his *Autobiography* he will remember: "This Simon was of the city of Jerusalem, and of a very noble family, of the movement of

---

[77] Flavius Josephus, *Jewish War* 1,17.22.26; 2,162; 3,138; 6,268; 6,410; *Antiquities* 1,214.325; 9:208; *Life* 1,191.358.360; *Against Apion* 1,218; 2,149.

[78] Flavius Josephus, *Jewish War* 1.110: Παραφύονται δὲ αὐτῆς εἰς τὴν ἐξουσίαν Φαρισαῖοι σύνταγμά τι Ἰουδαίων δοκοῦν εὐσεβέστερον εἶναι τῶν ἄλλων καὶ τοὺς νόμους ἀκριβέστερον ἀφηγεῖσθαι. On the political influence of the Pharisees during the government of the queen Alexandra cf. Mason, *Josephus*, 100–101.

[79] *Jewish War* 2.162: Δύο δὲ τῶν προτέρων Φαρισαῖοι μὲν οἱ μετὰ ἀκριβείας δοκοῦντες ἐξηγεῖσθαι τὰ νόμιμα καὶ τὴν πρώτην ἀπάγοντες αἵρεσιν εἱμαρμένῃ τε καὶ θεῷ προσάπτουσι πάντα.

[80] *Antiquities* 17.41: καὶ ἦν γὰρ μόριόν τι Ἰουδαϊκὸν ἀνθρώπων ἐπ' ἐξακριβώσει μέγα φρονοῦν τοῦ πατρίου καὶ νόμων οἷς χαίρει τὸ θεῖον προσποιουμένων οἷς ὑπῆκτο ἡ γυναικωνῖτις Φαρισαῖοι καλοῦνται βασιλεῖ δυναμένῳ μάλιστα πράσσειν προμηθεῖς κἀκ τοῦ προὔπτου εἰς τὸ πολεμεῖν τε καὶ βλάπτειν ἐπηρμένοι.

the Pharisees, which are supposed to excel others in the accurate knowledge of the laws of their country."[81]

This last positive description of the Pharisees is very similar to that of Gal 1:14, in which Paul compares his zeal to the traditions of the fathers, those traditions which we have identified with the oral tradition of the Law. The common element with regard to the Pharisees' accuracy, found in the Acts of the Apostles and in Flavius Josephus, induces one to consider it as a characteristic of Phariseeism,[82] so that even when the Pharisees are not explicitly mentioned, like in *Jewish Antiquities* 20.201, we can think of their school of thought: "Those of the inhabitants of the city who were considered the most fair-minded and who were exact in observance of the law were offended at this."[83] Therefore both the terms "zealous" in Gal 1:14 and "irreproachable" in Phil 3:6 express the accuracy of Paul and the Pharisees with respect to the law and the relative oral tradition: it is not a question of the moral rigidity, but rather the ethical commitment of Paul and of the Pharisees towards the Law and their oral traditions.

5. CONCLUSION

The relationship between Paul and Pharisaic Judaism is well articulated, especially for the generalization present in the Pauline letters. Paul never treats the Pharisees and their school of thought, nor the other Judaic movements of his time. On the other hand, the rereading of his past starts from his encounter with and his being in Christ and then goes back in time. For this reason it is difficult, if not impossible, to establish the trademark of Phariseeism from the Pauline corpus. Together with fundamental reasons concerning the Mosaic Law and the oral tradition of the fathers, we could have spent time on: the typology of Israel's election, the relationship

---

[81] *Life* 1.191: ὁ δὲ Σίμων οὗτος ἦν πόλεως μὲν Ἱεροσολύμων γένους δὲ σφόδρα λαμπροῦ τῆς δὲ Φαρισαίων αἱρέσεως οἳ περὶ τὰ πάτρια νόμιμα δοκοῦσιν τῶν ἄλλων ἀκριβείᾳ διαφέρειν.

[82] Berger, "Jesus," 235.

[83] A. I. Baumgarten, "The Name of the Pharisees," *JBL* 103 (1983): 411–428.

between destiny and individual responsibility for final salvation, the resurrection of the body, and the dietary laws, since various scholars have considered these aspects typical of Phariseeism and of the Pauline letters. In this field there are valuable contacts between Paul, Flavius Josephus and the author of the *LAB*, in addition to the author of the Psalms of Solomon. In reality the Pharisaic influence on the Psalms of Solomon, the typologies on the universality of guilt and the divine impartiality, is debatable as it seems that this influence can be attributed just as much to the Jewish apocalyptic movements as to Phariseeism.

For this reason we have preferred to begin with what emerges from the comparison between Gal 1:13–14 and Phil 3:5–6, i.e. with what Paul underlines of his past in Phariseeism in order to reveal the meaningful facts. Perhaps with respect to other contributions on Paul and Phariseeism our conclusions will seem little more than minimal; in reality they are those that result from the comparison of the principal sources, without falling into either the assumption that the Jews of whom Paul speaks were Pharisees or that which is even more misleading, which considers that Phariseeism before 70 C.E. corresponds to later Rabbinism. Only from the overlap of Gal 1:13–14 and Phil 3:5–6 can we deduce that the Judaism cited in Gal 1:13–14 is pharisaic Judaism and not that of apocalyptic, Essene or Sadducean matrix. The deduction seems to be confirmed by the mention of zeal and irreproachability towards the Mosaic Law and the traditions of the fathers: common elements between Paul and the descriptions that Flavius Josephus adds to the history of the Pharisaic movement.

For this, even if from the historical point of view various scholars prefer to speak of "Judaisms" because of the lack of unifying criteria among the multiple tendencies of the first century, we think it is better to recover the category of "Judaism" that in Phariseeism previous to 70 C.E. found one of its principal tendencies. In the NT context, the Pauline declaration on periautology (i.e. self-boasting)[84] for his

[84] For periautology in the classical environment and in the Pauline letters cf. A. Pitta, "Il "discorso del pazzo" o periautologia immoderata? Analisi retorico-letteraria di 2 Cor 11,1–12,18," *Bib* 87 (2006): 493–510.

past spent in Phariseeism persuades us to reconsider the negative connotation that with time has assimilated the terms "Pharisee" and "Phariseeism" as hypocrisy, formalism, and legalistic rigidity. On the contrary, we were able to see that the Pharisees at Qumran were considered as those who search for "the smooth interpretations."

The positive perspective from which Paul remembers his past renders even more unexpected and gratuitous his adherence to Christ: he did not have anything to reproach or blame himself about with regards to his past in Judaism, nor concerning what led him to choose Jesus Christ and consider all the rest as refuse (Phil 3:8). For this we cannot apply to Paul a religious experience of conversion like that of Augustine of Hippo or of Martin Luther:[85] Paul was not Augustine before Augustine—and much less Luther before Luther—but rather one who had gained various credentials before meeting Christ!

---

[85] *Pace* S. Westerholm, *Perspectives Old and New on Paul.* The "Lutheran" Paul and His Critics (Grand Rapids, Mich.-Cambridge, U.K. 2004: Eerdmans).

CHAPTER 4

PAUL AND THE *GEZERAH SHAWAH*: A JUDAIC METHOD IN THE SERVICE OF JUSTIFICATION BY FAITH

Pasquale Basta

In the last five years I have devoted most of my studies to a single question: Why, from time to time, in the New Testament and especially in the *corpus paulinum*, do we find two consecutive quotations from the Old Testament? Isn't a single quotation sufficient to support an argument or thesis? Why two? What does the second quotation add to the first? Let us take as an example Romans 4, the famous example of Abraham. The text says:

> Romans 4:1 What then shall we say that Abraham, our forefather
> according to the flesh, discovered? 2 If, in fact, Abraham was justified
> by works, he had something to boast about—but not before God. 3
> What does the Scripture say? "*Abraham believed God, and it was cred-*
> *ited to him as righteousness.*" 4 Now when a man works, his wages are
> not credited to him as a gift, but as an obligation. 5 However, to the
> man who does not work but trusts God who justifies the wicked, his
> faith is credited as righteousness. 6 David says the same thing when
> he speaks of the blessedness of the man to whom God credits right-
> eousness apart from works:
> 7 "*Blessed are they whose transgressions are forgiven, whose sins are covered.*
> *8 Blessed is the man whose sin the Lord will never count against him.*"
> 9 Is this blessedness only for the circumcised, or also for the uncir-
> cumcised? We have been saying that Abraham's faith was credited to
> him as righteousness. 10 Under what circumstances was it credited?
> Was it after he was circumcised, or before? It was not after, but before!
> 11 And he received the sign of circumcision, a seal of the righteous-
> ness that he had by faith while he was still uncircumcised. So then, he
> is the father of all who believe but have not been circumcised, in order
> that righteousness might be credited to them. 12 And he is also the

father of the circumcised who not only are circumcised but who also walk in the footsteps of the faith that our father Abraham had before he was circumcised.

In order to show that his argument about justification by faith is already contained in the Old Testament, why does Paul mention not only Genesis 15:6, but also the proclamation in Psalm 32:2? In the latter, David asserts his state of blessedness after God has forgiven him for the adultery with Bathsheba and the killing of Uriah the Hittite. How is this second passage connected to justification by faith?

The results of my research have merged in two works[1], about which I am going to give a brief account here. This will also be a way of introducing the vast world of intrabiblical exegetics, the movement internal to the Bible, which assumes that a biblical text is born out of the interpretation of a text that precedes it.

What I want to say can be divided into three major parts:

- in the first, I will briefly analyse the method of interpreting the Bible used by the rabbis of Israel, starting from an exemplary case: the use of Hillel's second rule, the so-called *gezerah shawah*;
- in the second, I will concentrate on how Paul uses the same method in at least one page of his epistolary;
- in the third, I will offer some brief and pertinent conclusions.

The aim is to understand *how the apostle situated himself in relation to the Old Testament when he reinterpreted it in the light of what had happened in the end times with the coming of Christ, which forced a re-reading of several passages of the ancient Scriptures.*

---

[1] Pasquale Basta, *Gezerah Shawah: storia, forme e metodi dell'analogia biblica* (*SubBi* 26; Roma: Editrice Pontificio Istituto Biblico, 2006); Pasquale Basta, *Abramo in Rm 4: l'analogia dell'agire divino nella ricerca esegetica di Paolo* (AnBib 168; Roma: Editrice Pontificio Istituto Biblico, 2007).

1. Rabbinical hermeneutics in the light of *gezerah shawah*

We can start from two texts by the Pontifical Biblical Commission:

> "All this serves to show that within the one Christian Bible the relationships that exist between the New and the Old Testament are quite complex. When it is a question of the use of particular texts, the authors of the New Testament naturally have recourse to the ideas and procedures for interpretation current in their time. To require them to conform to modern scientific methods would be anachronistic. Rather, it is for the exegete to acquire a knowledge of ancient techniques of exegesis so as to be able to interpret correctly the way in which a Scriptural author has used them."[2]

> "Traditional Jewish methods of scriptural argumentation for the purpose of establishing rules of conduct — methods later codified by the rabbis — are frequently used in the words of Jesus transmitted in the Gospels and in the Epistles. Those occurring most often are the first two *middoth* ("rules") of Hillel, *qal wa-homer* and *gezerah shawah*. These correspond *more or less* to arguments *a fortiori* and by *analogy* respectively."[3]

Here in brief outline, on the other hand, are the seven hermeneutic rules used by Hillel to interpret Scripture:

1. *Qal wa-ḥomer* (from the lightest to the heaviest) – if something is true in a minor case, then it is true in the major one and vice versa.
2. *Gezerah shawah* (same order) – argument based on an analogy between two similar passages.
3. *Binyan ab mi-katub ehad* (establishment of a family) – a specific aspect found only in one text from a series of correlated biblical passages is applied to all of them; this way the basic text gives all the others a common character setting them up as a family.

---

[2] J. A Fitzmyer, *The Biblical Commission's Document "The Interpretation of the Bible in the Church"*. Text and Commentary (Subsidia Biblica 18; Editrice Pontificio Istituto Biblico, Roma 1995) 138-139.

[3] Pontifical Biblical Commission, *The Jewish People and their Sacred Scriptures in the Christian Bible* (Libreria Editrice Vaticana, Roma 2002) 37.

4. *Binyan ab mi-shene ketubim* (establishment of a family from two passages) – it is like the third middah, with the difference that the general rule is grounded in two passages and not in just one.
5. *Kelal u-perat u-perat u-kelal* (general and particular, particular and general) – the general can be defined through the particular and vice versa.
6. *Ke-yoze bo be-maqom aher* (something similar in another passage) – it is like the GS, but with much less restrictive use.
7. *Dabar ha-lamed me-inyano* (argument from the context) – the passages are explained also on the basis of passages nearby.

1.1 Hillel's example

In a significant and defining passage, Hillel set a new milestone for rabbinical hermeneutics (*yPes* 33a; *bPes* 66a):

> "These are the things concerning Passover, etc."[4] This *halakah* had been forgotten by the elders of Beteira.[5] It happened once that the 14th (Nisan) fell on a Saturday, and they did not know if the Paschal sacrifice could override the Sabbath or not. They said: "Here is a Babylonian called Hillel, who assisted Shemajah and Avtalion. He maybe knows if the Passover overrides the Sabbath or not. It is possible that some hope might come from him."
> They sent for him and asked him: "Have you ever heard in your life if, when the 14th (Nisan) falls on a Sabbath, it overrides the Sabbath or not?" He replied: "Do we have a Passover occurring only once a year that overrides the Sabbath? Are there not many *pesaḥim* overriding the Sabbath during the year?" (Someone says they are one hundred, someone says they are two hundred, others they are three hundred, etc.). Then they said: "We were right in saying that from you comes hope." He then started to explain (*darash*) the question by means of the "similarity among concrete things" (*heqqesh*), the "deduction from the

[4] The text of *mPes* 6,1 is here implied, about the prescription that the Passover prevails against the Sabbath restrictive rules.
[5] This expression was used to indicate the leaders of the Pharisees within the Sanhedrin.

lightest to the heaviest" (*qal wa-ḥomer*) and the "textual correspondence" (*gezerah shawah*).

By "similarity among concrete things": since the perpetual offering (*tamid*) is a communal sacrifice, it overrides the Sabbath, and also the *pesaḥ*, which is a communal sacrifice, overrides the Sabbath.

By "deduction from the lightest to the heaviest": if perpetual offering, whose omission does not bring excommunication (from community= *karet*), overrides the Sabbath, then, shall not the Passover offering, whose omission entails excommunication, logically (*eino din*) override the Sabbath?

By "textual correspondence": about the perpetual offering it is said "at its appointed time" (Num 28:2), so about the Passover "at its appointed time" (Num 9:2). Therefore, if the *tamid*, about which it is said "at its appointed time", overrides the Sabbath, also the *pesaḥ*, about which it is said "at its appointed time", must override the Sabbath.

Then, they said: "We were right in saying that hope might come from a Babylonian! However, an objection can be raised to the similarity you explained. It is not possible for you to refer to the *tamid*, whose quantity is limited, to draw conclusions about the *pesaḥ*, whose quantity is not. There is an objection as well to the deduction from the lightest to the heaviest you claimed. It is not possible for you to refer to the *tamid*, which is something extremely holy, in order to draw conclusions about the *pesaḥ*, whose holiness is lighter. Finally, regarding your textual correspondence, nobody can use a textual correspondence on his own account (*me'azmo*[6]) ..."

Rabbi Jose, Rabbi Bun's son, says in the name of Rabbi Abba bar Mamal: "A man can use a textual correspondence to 'carry out' the lesson he has been taught (*leqajjem talmudo*), not to 'repeal' the lesson he has been taught (*levattel talmudo*)..."

And even though (Hillel) would sit explaining all day long (*darash*), they did not accept (*leqabbel*) his (lesson) until he said to them: "May it come upon me (the curse) if this is not what I heard from Shemajah

---

[6] The rest of this tale shows how the elders of the Sanhedrin mean, through this expression, that the *gezerah shawah* (GS, hereafter), can be used only to confirm a traditional verity, and not to innovate or to confute.

and Avtalion!" Having heard this, they got up and appointed him as their head (*nassi*). As they had elected him as their head, he started to scold them by saying: "Why did you need this Babylonian? Is it not because you did not attend to the two greats of this generation, Shemajah and Avtalion, who were still "sitting" (= teaching) next to you?" But since he was angry, he forgot a *halakah*. They asked him: "What shall people do if they have not brought knives? "[7] He said to them: "I heard this *halakah*, but I forgot it! Anyway, let Israel do that: when they are not prophets, they are prophets' sons!" And indeed, those who had a lamb as their Passover sacrifice, had stuck their knife in its wool, and those who had a kid had stuck it between its horns, they were thus the Passover victims who brought the knives with themselves! When he saw this, he remembered the *halakah* and said: "This is what I learned from Shemajah and Avtalion!"

By means of a *gezerah shawah*, Hillel provided here the answer to the initial question related to the Paschal offering, starting from two different biblical passages. It thus becomes clearly evident how a new precept can be attained, a precept which goes beyond the limited statements of a single passage, a precept which is based on two identical terms occurring in different parts of Scripture:

- Num 9:2: "Let the Israelites keep the Passover sacrifice at its appointed time"

  וְיַעֲשׂוּ בְנֵי־יִשְׂרָאֵל אֶת־הַפָּסַח **בְּמוֹעֲדוֹ**
- Num 28:2: "Command the Israelites, and say to them: My offering, the food for my offerings by fire, my pleasing odor, you shall take care to offer to me at their appointed time"

  אֶת־קָרְבָּנִי לַחְמִי לְאִשַּׁי רֵיחַ נִיחֹחִי תִּשְׁמְרוּ לְהַקְרִיב לִי **בְּמוֹעֲדוֹ**

The expression at its appointed time (בְּמוֹעֲדוֹ), related to both forms of sacrifice, is the key to this demonstration. Since the same temporal specification appears in two different passages of

---

[7] They are the knives for the Passover sacrifice, which could not be carried on the Sabbath.

Scripture (Num 9:2 and Num 28:2), an analogy can be drawn: just as the daily sacrifice overrides the Sabbath rules, being offered twice every day including the Sabbath, so also the Passover sacrifice is allowed on the Sabbath. Consequently, the Paschal sacrifice possesses the same kind of obligation as the daily one regardless of whether it occurs on the Sabbath or not. The fact that in both texts there is an insistence on the temporal deadline makes them in some way equal.

The logical scheme underlying this complex hermeneutical operation is more or less the following one:

- if a + b occur in a text
- and in another text we find c + b
- a and c can then be related to one another so that a new assertion can be made, which is not directly expressed in either passage.

1.2 Analogical logic

An interesting example to explain the logic underlying a GS can be found in *bShab* 96b. In this haggadic *midrash*, Aquiba connects by textual correspondence:

- Num 15:32: "When the Israelites were in the wilderness, they found a man gathering sticks on the Sabbath day";
  וַיִּהְיוּ בְנֵי־יִשְׂרָאֵל **בַּמִּדְבָּר** וַיִּמְצְאוּ אִישׁ מְקֹשֵׁשׁ עֵצִים בְּיוֹם הַשַּׁבָּת
- Num 27:3: "Our father died in the wilderness. He did not belong to the people of Korah, who banded together against the Lord, but he died because of his own sin, and left no sons";
  אָבִינוּ מֵת **בַּמִּדְבָּר** וְהוּא לֹא־הָיָה בְּתוֹךְ הָעֵדָה הַנּוֹעָדִים
  עַל־יְהוָה בַּעֲדַת־קֹרַח כִּי־בְחֶטְאוֹ מֵת וּבָנִים לֹא־הָיוּ לוֹ

Num 15:32 tells of a man who was executed, on God's explicit order, because he was gathering wood in the wilderness (**בַּמִּדְבָּר**) on the Sabbath day. In Num 27:3 Zelophehad's daughters claim an inheritance, even though they have no brothers and their father is now dead in the wilderness (**בַּמִּדְבָּר**).

In the first text we do not know who is the man who gathers wood on the Sabbath day, while the Israelite community is in the desert (wilderness), and who dies as a result, because the text does not tell us. But in Num 27:3 we find the same indication about a man who had died some time before and had left inheritance problems. Now, the mention of the desert (wilderness), common to both the texts, suggests to Aquiba the analogical conclusion: it must have been the same person in both cases.

But another Rabbi does not agree with the identification of Zelophehad as the desecrator of the Sabbath and uses hard words in case *gezerah shawah* should prove to be forcing things. Here is the *haggadah*:

> The Rabbanans taught: Zelophehad was the wood gatherer. And so [Scripture] says: "While the Israelites were in the wilderness, they found a man who was gathering wood on the Sabbath day" (Num 15:32). Then it says: "Our father died in the wilderness" (Num 27:3). Since it was Zelophehad there, here is Zelophehad as well. The words of Rabbi Aquiba. Rabbi Jehudah ben Batyra said [to Rabbi Aquiba]: "Aquiba, true or not, you will have to account for it. If it is as you say – the *Torah* hid it and you found out about it. If not, then you slandered this just person."

But did the great Aquiba really run into this danger and so expose himself to a legitimate protest? The truth is that from a logical point of view, his proposal is in fact open to simple objections: the deduction is only probable and, in addition, not verifiable. Besides, the expression "in the wilderness" recurs 141 times in the whole Hebrew Bible and as many as 60 times just within the *Torah*, with the consequence that the interchanges can be multiplied according to the whims of every single interpreter and to follow his desire to make the biblical text say whatever he wants it to say. The *rabbanans* would then be right to warn against the dangers of such an approach.

However, if we go into this question in greater depth, we see that the way Aquiba reasons and compares texts is not superficial at all. In fact, this great Rabbi did not confine himself just to finding a banal terminological connection, which he later expanded unduly and whose value he overestimated, even though it might appear that he did this at first glance. Instead, he proceeded with great intelligence and skill, even though he did not manifest this skill in an obvious or explicit way. Not only do the two passages at issue have the mention of the wilderness in common, but they also have in common at least two other analogous elements.

- In *both cases* people report to Moses, Aaron (who, in the second episode that follows his death, is replaced by his son Eleazar), and the community to ask for a decision: Num 15:22 and Num 27: 1–2.
- In *both cases* Moses brings the case to the Lord, who resolves it: Num 15: 35 and Num 27: 5–7.

As can clearly be seen, beyond a simply terminological connection, Aquiba considered above all the circumstantial analogy: the two verses can be compared because the textual correspondence is located within a series of similar circumstances, such that the interpretation can be situated within a relatively specific domain. This is an important detail, since it proves decisive in developing a good *gezerah shawah.*

1.3 Fields of application of analogical logic

The preferred area for questions concerning the GS are discussions related to these problems, even though the solution to these problems presents considerable difficulties. These difficulties are due to the lack of deployment of important terms. In this respect, textual correspondence has the great merit of introducing known elements into partially unknown topics, thanks to its intrinsic capacity to discover requisites present in what is already known and transfer them to future and different hermeneutical possibilities. At this level, the analogy presents itself as a connecting bridge between passages that are far from each other, between distinct concepts, between episodes which apparently have nothing in common. To put it succinctly, it is a link between the old and the new, to the extent that what is being investigated now has already been answered in the past. It is only necessary to know how to look for it in the correct way—and through the labour of a long and strenuous investigation, which can yield surprising results. Talmudic literature, then, with its vast spaces, is the place where most of the research carried out by means of the GS has converged. Here the analogical conclusion plays a vital and leading role, both in the **haggadic** parts and in the **halakhic** ones.

In fact its field of action extends from simple biblical reflection, typical of the school-synagogue circles, to the creation of new *halakot*, a work of the Sanhedrin alone. The only difference between these two approaches seems to be connected to the fact that the criteria for creating a GS appear more rigorous in the legal sections and less so in the narrative ones.

1.3.1 *GS and haggadah*

The haggadic deductions, typical of the homiletic explanations of historical and moral passages of Scripture, are usually less attentive to the need for formal analogical accuracy. In fact, they mostly tend to highlight connections within biblical stories that are not directly explicit and they make use of GS because of its unique capacity to establish connections between biblical figures and events that cannot otherwise be related. Moreover, this phenomenon recurs in all the homiletic genres, where an even marginal contact between two distant elements allows the preacher to perform a series of variations on a theme, which would otherwise be unthinkable. At this level, the listener does not care very much about the legitimacy of the combinations, because the intention of the homily is not to demonstrate a logical truth, but elicit interest in order to encourage agreement with the content of the text. Consequently, the analogy is here submitted to the requirements of preaching, to the extent that it demands imitation, a change in moral behaviour, personal reflection or even the simple contemplation of beauty, factors which have always characterized hagiography.

A good example of haggadic approach is the *midrash* about Joshua, as in *bTaan* 20a. The *darshan* outlines his GS by making the most of the small connection between:

- Deut 2:25: "**This day I will begin** to put the dread and fear of you upon the peoples everywhere under heaven; when they hear reports of you, they will tremble and be in anguish because of you";

הַיּוֹם הַזֶּה אָחֵל תֵּת פַּחְדְּךָ וְיִרְאָתְךָ עַל־פְּנֵי הָעַמִּים תַּחַת
כָּל־הַשָּׁמָיִם אֲשֶׁר יִשְׁמְעוּן שִׁמְעֲךָ וְרָגְזוּ וְחָלוּ מִפָּנֶיךָ

- Josh 3:7: "The Lord said to Joshua: '**This day I will begin** to exalt you in the sight of all Israel, so that they may know that I will be with you as I was with Moses'";

וַיֹּאמֶר יְהוָה אֶל־יְהוֹשֻׁעַ **הַיּוֹם הַזֶּה אָחֵל** גַּדֶּלְךָ בְּעֵינֵי כָּל־
יִשְׂרָאֵל אֲשֶׁר יֵדְעוּן כִּי כַּאֲשֶׁר הָיִיתִי עִם־מֹשֶׁה אֶהְיֶה עִמָּךְ

It can easily be seen that both passages have the *incipit* of the phrase (הַיּוֹם הַזֶּה אָחֵל) in common. On the basis of this simple similarity, the homilist infers a complete analogy between the two figures, with the consequence that he can then compare almost all the characteristics between them as well as the events regarding Moses and Joshua. Again we should not laugh at the apparently illogical nature of this measure. In fact, when we look carefully at the GS of *bTaan* 20a, it is at least excellent, since the verb "begin" occurs only three times in the Hebrew Bible: apart from Deut 2:25 and Josh 3:7 it also appears in Ezek 39:7. But in the latter instance the connection is fleeting:

- Ezek 39:7: "My holy name I will make known among my people Israel; and I will not let my holy name be profaned any more; and the nations shall know that I am the LORD, the Holy One in Israel";

וְאֶת־שֵׁם קָדְשִׁי אוֹדִיעַ בְּתוֹךְ עַמִּי יִשְׂרָאֵל **וְלֹא־אַחֵל** אֶת־שֵׁם־
קָדְשִׁי עוֹד וְיָדְעוּ הַגּוֹיִם כִּי־אֲנִי יְהוָה קָדוֹשׁ בְּיִשְׂרָאֵל

It is clear that in Ezek 39:7 the meaning of the verb is already different. Though, more interesting still, the semantic series where חלל occurs does not correspond at all to the two previous cases. There is no mention of הַיּוֹם הַזֶּה and the verb is formulated in a negative manner (וְלֹא־אַחֵל). Consequently, the only two passages where the term really occurs (for the sake of creating a GS), are Deut 2:25 and Josh 3:7, which offer also the best chance of analogical inference: what is said twice (δὶς λεγόμενα). Furthermore, another detail of no little importance is that the comparison between Moses and Joshua is also suggested by the same word of God in Josh 3:7: "so that they may know that I will be with you as I was with Moses." Obviously, the midrashic extension of the comparison between the two figures to the span of their whole lifetimes, of their affairs and their own personalities goes beyond the realm of inference. The procedure, though, once started, falls into the homilist's hands, who draws out of it a beautiful *haggadah*, in which Joshua truly appears as Moses restored once again to life, who continues his presence in the midst of the people of Israel through the works and person of his successor.

1.3.2 *Gezerah shawah and halakah*

In the legal realm, however, the analogy serves most of all with reference to the law of Sinai, for the purpose of establishing new *halakot*. In the service of this purpose it appears as a precious instrument of reflection with regard to legal questions that are difficult to solve; it appears as a forum whose quality is even comparable to the Law itself. For this same reason what is found through an analogical conclusion is *halakah* and by this very fact a binding norm. Besides, when new jurisprudence is created, the analogy helps to determine the meaning of ambiguous expressions, compensating for the defective elements of a law by referring to other places capable of offering more precise indications, in order to decide upon cases not directly considered in the *Torah*. However, unlike the Greek-Hellenistic legal culture, the Judaic one maintains a unique curiosity. It does not in fact contemplate the deduction of new laws solely from real analogies, but it also acknowledges the possibility of inferring juridical frameworks from exclusively formal analogies, as happens in the case of the *gezerah shawah*. Besides, the textual correspondence does not require that the laws to be compared are of the same nature, or with strong similarities in concrete aspects and fundamental relationships. It is usually sufficient for the connection to amount to minimal and formal elements, like common words or similar expressions. It is even not always necessary for the same terms that form the basis of a GS to be perfectly identical. This was particularly true in the haggadic *midrash*, where the formal validity of an inference did not exact full rigour. But the same thing happens in the halakhic context, where, in order to establish new norms, one uses passages which have different words in common, even if they are at least similar in meaning.

But this should not lead to the supposition that Judaic jurisprudence is a purely illogical realm of empty fantasy. On the contrary, it is necessary to keep in mind that the source of the halakhic law is not a code of juridical procedures, from which administrative and penal articles reverberate in a cold way with their burden of sanctions, but is in fact the Bible itself, with its life and its history, its faith and its memory. Consequently, even if the way of proceeding of rabbinic-talmudic logic in haggadic and halakhic territory seems strange to us, the theological-rational principle to which it is subject is beyond reproach: *all of Scripture is traversed in every part by the same Spirit, even in the smallest and most insignificant part.* In this sense, the Bible asserts its unity, the fact that it is a unique book, as unique as the One who guided it through its varied history. It is up to the human interpreter, who lives within a limited portion of time, to find the harmony linking apparently distant pages. This research will sometimes be characterized by polemics, controversy and hard dialectical confrontations. But in the search for a global meaning, many texts can dialogue with one another, with the aim of obtaining and transferring information about aspects that are common, but not at all obvious at first sight. In so doing, every linguistic sign within Scripture is not simply treated as the outcome of chance, but as the result of a clear intentionality that simply calls for analysis.

We can obviously raise many questions and objections with regard to this conceptual horizon. What weight can we give to such an elaborate procedure? Was it really God's Spirit who foresaw all the possible GSs, in order to help the haggadic and halakhic exegesis of posterity? Isn't there a danger of manipulating Scripture, by submitting it too often to the necessities and demands of the Rabbis?

At this point an important observation is in order. The hermeneutical rules deployed in Judaic hermeneutics were approved by prestigious exegetical authorities of the highest order, and given the prestige and standing of these authorities, all objections lack force and credibility. In this sense, the very names of Hillel, Ishmael, and Eliezer were the best guarantees of all, since it was in fact these fathers of Hebrew hermeneutics who shaped and ordered the numerous *middoth* then in circulation, by fixing once and for all the limits within which a sound and valid biblical exegesis was to be performed. The extent to which their works received unanimous acknowledgement and praise is also evident in the introduction to Ishmael's list inside the prayer book used by the Jewish people. Together with hymns and blessings, the pious Israelite habitually repeated, regularly and in a context of prayer, the 13 fundamental rules of scriptural interpretation. Beyond its logical worth, then, GS was regarded as an exegetical operation that was not only licit, but also endowed with an intrinsic sacredness.

1.4 Working levels for *gezerah shawah*

The final part of the journey in this first section involves the examination of the foundational hermeneutical principles upon which *gezerah shawah* usually works.

1. **First level: same statute, same prescription (the analogy allows us to point out how two texts which have in common the same internal regulations are also characterized by the presence of the same final rule).**

An excellent example of this working method is the postponement of Passover decided by king Hezekiah, in 2 Chr 30: 1–3. Here, Hezekiah and his court's decision to defer the Passover date, by moving it to the second month, is taken on the basis of Num 9: 6–14.

From a first rough comparison between the two texts, the common features easily emerge. Num 9 allows (1) anyone who touched a corpse, or (2) is away on a journey at the appointed time of the Passover, to postpone its celebration to one month later. In 2 Chr 30 Hezekiah and his court extend this possibility of postponing the feast until the 14th of the second month also, to (1) priests who have been made unclean by objects coming from pagan worship; and (2) those who are far from Jerusalem's central sanctuary.

It is obvious that here everything moves at the level of concrete situations. In both cases, there are people who cannot keep the Passover at its appointed time, either because of *impurity* or a *long journey*. It follows that the same statute produces the same prescription: in both cases the date can be postponed to one month later.

2. Second level: *support for the defective elements (the analogical inference allows us to attach to a single term in a passage the whole sequence of ideas, concepts or words occurring in the other one, in order to compensate for any defective elements in the first one, the second one or both).*

Within the sacrificial ritual two rules are provided regarding the sacrificing of birds:

Lev 1:15: "The priest shall bring it to the altar and wring off its head, and turn it into smoke on the altar; and its blood shall be drained out against the side of the altar";

וְהִקְרִיבוֹ הַכֹּהֵן אֶל־הַמִּזְבֵּחַ **וּמָלַק אֶת־רֹאשׁוֹ** וְהִקְטִיר הַמִּזְבֵּחָה
וְנִמְצָה דָמוֹ עַל קִיר הַמִּזְבֵּחַ

Lev 5:8: "You shall bring them to the priest, who shall offer first the one for the sin offering, wringing its head at the nape without severing it";

וְהֵבִיא אֹתָם אֶל־הַכֹּהֵן וְהִקְרִיב אֶת־אֲשֶׁר לַחַטָּאת רִאשׁוֹנָה
וּמָלַק אֶת־רֹאשׁוֹ מִמּוּל עָרְפּוֹ וְלֹא יַבְדִּיל

The expression **מָלַק אֶת־רֹאשׁוֹ** (= wringing its head) occurs only twice in the Pentateuch, thus guaranteeing an optimal degree of inference. In Lev 5:8, though, the expression מָלַק אֶת־רֹאשׁוֹ is accompanied by a further specification (מִמּוּל עָרְפּוֹ= at the nape). It follows that the specification "at the nape" can be connected to the "wringing its head" of Lev 1:15, thus compensating for the defective element, in such a way that also in the case of the simple sacrifice the procedure of expiatory sacrifice applies.

3. Third level: the analysis of contexts and its application (the analogy, when it connects two equal expressions in a biblical text, does not limit itself to a terminological connection, but often fully involves also the two overarching legal or narrative frameworks, in such a way that by means of one of the two sequences, the context and the application of the other can also be explained).

In order to confirm this last aspect—which, it must be noted, always intersects with the previous two—a helpful illustration is found in the synoptic story of the ears of wheat plucked on the Sabbath:

Mt 12:1–8: At that time Jesus went through the grainfields on the Sabbath (τοῖς σάββασιν); his disciples were hungry (ἐπείνασαν), and they began to pluck heads of grain and to eat (ἐσθίειν). When the Pharisees saw it, they said to him, "Look, your disciples are doing what is not lawful to do (ὃ οὐκ ἔξεστιν ποιεῖν) on the Sabbath (ἐν σαββάτῳ)". He said to them, "Have you not read what

> David did when he and his companions were hungry (ἐπείνασεν)? He entered the house of God and ate (ἔφαγον) the bread of the Presence, which it was not lawful for him or his companions to eat (ἔφαγον), but only for the priests. Or have you not read in the law that on the sabbath (τοῖς σάββασιν) the priests in the temple break the sabbath and yet are guiltless? I tell you, something greater than the temple is here. But if you had known what this means, 'I desire mercy and not sacrifice,' you would not have condemned the guiltless. For the Son of Man is lord of the Sabbath."

Without entering into a specific exegesis of Matthew's pericope, let us simply observe the criteria underlying the analogy created by Jesus. First of all, it must be said that, because of a peculiarity of great importance, only Mt 12:1–8 can be used for the purposes of our discussion. In fact, differently from

Mk 2:23: "One Sabbath he was going through the grainfields; and as they made their way his disciples began to pluck heads of grain";

Καὶ ἐγένετο αὐτὸν ἐν τοῖς σάββασιν παραπορεύεσθαι διὰ τῶν σπορίμων,
καὶ οἱ μαθηταὶ αὐτοῦ ἤρξαντο ὁδὸν ποιεῖν τίλλοντες τοὺς στάχυας.

and Lk 6:1: "One Sabbath while Jesus was going through the grainfields, his disciples plucked some heads of grain, rubbed them in their hands, and ate them";

Ἐγένετο δὲ ἐν σαββάτῳ διαπορεύεσθαι αὐτὸν διὰ σπορίμων,
καὶ ἔτιλλον οἱ μαθηταὶ αὐτοῦ καὶ ἤσθιον τοὺς στάχυας ψώχοντες ταῖς χερσίν,

only Mt 12:1 specifies that the disciples were plucking grain because they "were hungry" (ἐπείνασαν). The other two synoptics, instead, confine themselves, while describing the background, to the indication that it was on the Sabbath, adding nothing more. However, the Pharisees remember only this contextual aspect, from which they deduce the illicit nature of the disciples' action. In itself, the action of plucking ears of corn was not legally inappropriate, as proved by:

Deut 23:26: "If you go into your neighbour's standing grain, you may pluck the ears with your hand, but you shall not put a sickle to your neighbour's standing grain."

The problem is that this happens on the Sabbath, as the Pharisees correctly underline. Usually, ignoring the GS, it is thought that Matthew added the verb ἐπείνασαν in order to clear the disciples from the accusation of carelessly performing a forbidden action.[8] But this is not the case. Actually, Matthew, who is the most careful synoptic when it is a question of the confrontation with the synagogue, wants to precisely define the context: it was not only on the Sabbath, but there was also the necessity of hunger. The Pharisees, on the contrary, totally ignore the situation within which the action is performed. They stop at the Sabbath infringement, not taking into account the wider overall view. The hermeneutical debate between the two opposing parties is then about contexts. What is more important? Sabbath or hunger? Faced with the accusation addressed against him, Jesus posits an analogy that retrieves and explains the context of hunger within which the legally forbidden behaviour has taken place, retrieving for this purpose the following episode:

1Sam 21:1–7: David came to Nob to the priest Ahimelech. Ahimelech came trembling to meet David, and said to him, "Why are you alone, and no one with you?" David said to the priest Ahimelech,

[8] So, for instance, Joachim Gnilka, *Il vangelo di Matteo: testo greco e traduzione* (trans. S. Cavallini and V. Gatti; CTNT I/I; Brescia: Paideia, 1990), 645.

> "The king has charged me with a matter, and said to me, 'No one must know anything of the matter about which I send you, and with which I have charged you.' I have made an appointment with the young men for such and such a place. Now then, what have you at hand? Give me five loaves of bread, or whatever is here." The priest answered David, "I have no ordinary bread at hand, only holy bread—provided that the young men have kept themselves from women." David answered the priest, "Indeed women have been kept from us as always when I go on an expedition; the vessels of the young men are holy even when it is a common journey; how much more today will their vessels be holy?" So the priest gave him the holy bread; for there was no bread there except the bread of the Presence, which is removed from before the Lord, to be replaced by hot bread on the day it is taken away. Now a certain man of the servants of Saul was there that day, detained before the Lord; his name was Doeg the Edomite, the chief of Saul's shepherds.

It is clear that the GS with 1Sam 21:1–7 does not draw attention to the holy day, but to the material need. What links the situation of Jesus and his disciples to that of David and his men is that, in both cases, only the need to fulfil a physiological need like hunger can justify the clear legal infringement. David and Jesus, with their respective companions, act within a similar context: For both of them an objective necessity is resolved by eating forbidden food. Once the context has been analogized, the application acquires a different ratification as well. What was forbidden by the Pharisees is authorized by Jesus: the illicit eating, allowed to David and his men, is in a similar way allowed to the disciples. Matthew has thus made a great GS between two episodes: 1 Sam 21 makes clear the context of hunger clear within which the ears were plucked, and sanctions the consequent relativization of the Sabbath. The presence of a similar scene thus generates a common application.

Also in the case of the third working approach, the differences do not militate against the course of the *gezerah shawah*. In the case of David, in fact, it was the food itself that was not permitted, since the loaves from the offering are reserved to Aaron and his children alone, according to the rule of:

> Lev 24:9: "They shall be for Aaron and his descendants, who shall eat them in a holy place, for they are most holy portions for him from the offerings by fire to the LORD, a perpetual due."

In the case of Jesus, on the other hand, the problem is not the food, which is licit, but the fact that it has been taken by breaking the law about the Sabbath rest, as stated in Ex 20:10: "But the seventh day is a Sabbath to the Lord your God; you shall not do any work—you, your son or your daughter, your male or female slave, your livestock, or the alien resident in your towns."

Strictly speaking, it is not Jesus who breaks the Sabbath, but only his disciples, which is different from the case of David, who is united with his soldiers in their transgression (but this is a subtlety of the evangelists that has nothing to do with *gezerah shawah*). Now, the fact that the nature of the violation is not exactly the same does not affect its essence; what was allowed to David—a breach of the *halakah*—is equally allowed to the Son of Man. The identification of Jesus as the figure of Dan 7:13—"As I watched in the night visions, I saw one like a human being coming with the clouds of heaven. And he came to the Ancient One and was presented before him"—is then aimed again at the clarification of context and practice. At a contextual level, in fact, both David in

> 1Sam 15,28: "And Samuel said to him, "The LORD has torn the kingdom of Israel from you this very day, and has given it to a neighbour of yours, who is better than you""

and the Son of Man in

> Dan 7,14: "To him was given dominion and glory and kingship, that all peoples, nations, and languages should serve him. His dominion is an everlasting dominion that shall not pass away, and his kingship is one that shall never be destroyed"

received a kingdom from God. Consequently, at the practical level, neither can be considered guilty when together with his men he breaks the law together in analogous circumstances.

But the game of context and application does not stop at this point; it progresses continually. In fact, from the point of view of strict rabbinical logic, the arguments Jesus produces look weak from the beginning, for at least two reasons: (1) David's episode does not appear in the *Torah* and so has not normative force in terms of establishing a law; and (2) the episode of 1 Sam 21 is not very relevant to the extent that the problem there is whether they can eat the bread of the Presence, which is intended for liturgical use, and not the fact that it occurs on the Sabbath.

These two possible objections probably touched on the GS of Jesus. As in the addition of ἐπείνασαν, Matthew distinguishes himself once again from Mark and Luke by introducing an important detail. In Mt 12:5–6, in fact, a reference is made to a *halakah* taken from Num 28:9–10:

> On the sabbath day: two male lambs a year old without blemish, and two-tenths of an ephah of choice flour for a grain offering, mixed with oil, and its drink offering—this is the burnt offering for every sabbath, in addition to the regular burnt offering and its drink offering.

In this passage of the *Torah* the priests are required to offer a double offering on the Sabbath, the daily one and the perpetual, without thereby breaking the rules of the Sabbath rest (and for that reason they are ἀναίτιοι. This second reference definitively explains both the Sabbath context and how it may be superseded, a question that is not at all resolved by David's example. Also here, some elements are dissimilar: in the priests' episode the matter is the offering on the Sabbath, while for the disciples the difficulty concerns the way the food is prepared on the Sabbath. But the two situations can be incorporated under a single perspective: the rejection of the Sabbath law. The new GS, established in this way, becomes the basis for the following *qal wa-ḥomer*.

It is interesting to note the mastery of Matthew's rereading of the episode of the ears of wheat plucked on the Sabbath: Matthew searches for overlapping contextual and practical links, in order to best guarantee the lawfulness of the behaviour of Jesus's disciples. Following exegetical procedures, it is possible to show a pattern that has three phases:

I. Basic comparison in Mt 12:1–4:

Jesus + his disciples	**Hunger, followed by eating in an unlawful context (Sabbath)**
David + his companions	**Hunger, followed by eating in an unlawful context (Lev 24:9)**

II. The reference to the priests in 12:4 brings up a new comparison:

David + his companions	**in the house of God**	**break a law (Lev 24:9**
Priests	**in the temple**	**break the Sabbath but remain guiltless (Num 28:9–10)**

III. Finally, the context and the application can be definitively clarified:

Priests	**break the Sabbath**	**but remain guiltless (ἀναίτιοι)**
Jesus + his disciples	**break the Sabbath**	**but remain guiltless (ἀναίτιοι)**

Ultimately, Matthew's GS is very complex, but exemplary in terms of our theme: David's episode explains the context of hunger; the priests' situation explains the infringement of the Sabbath. At the same time, both references to the Old Testament broaden the horizons of the debate, giving credence to Jesus' practice and not to that of the Pharisees. Many passages and scenes have thus been brought together thanks to a transposition that has operated in a contextual way more than in terms of individual phrases. The final inference is that David and his companions, the priests and the disciples prove to be indisputably ἀναίτιοι in all three cases.

With this last reference we have entered the New Testament and it is time to look at the horizon and context of Paul. First, though, it should be noted how at least three fundamental hermeneutical presuppositions are concealed behind this technical rule:

- the first, of a theological character, is born from faith in Scripture's literal inspiration, to whose truth the analogical paths pay homage: it was God's Spirit himself who foresaw the future GSs, by prearranging perfect terminological connections for this purpose; the interpreter's only task is to find and analyse them; consequently to the Rabbi is left the dignity of research;

- the second, of a juridical kind, comes from the awareness that the legislator, that is God, cannot contradict himself, which is why Scripture can interpret itself (*Scriptura sui ipsius interpres*), on account of the very unity of Scripture; this is the principle, accepted by the Romans as well, of the *intentio Legislatoris*;

- the third, purely methodological, leads to the hypothesis that there exists a work which is lateral to the *gezerah shawah*, as Stemberger affirms:

The procedure assumes that the Torah, or the Bible, is an organic whole complete in itself, where everything is mutually related and the linguistic expression not only follows stylistic criteria, but also builds a network of relations and is formalized for research purposes. The choice of terms is not casual, it is not subject to one's free judgment. From a technical point of view, the rule requires that lists of expressions and rare formulas are prepared, procedures that are assigned to the soferims, whose name not only means "scriveners, scribes", but also "counters". If we have not a text that is fixed in every single detail (also in its handwriting), the rule cannot be applied.[9]

2. PAULINE USE OF *GEZERAH SHAWAH*

The first Christian authors also reinterpreted the Scriptures of Israel, but in the light of the long awaited definitive event of the Messiah's appearance. Within this context, the *midrash* became a particularly fertile ground for a Christological re-reading of the whole Bible. Consequently, the rabbinical hermeneutical rules found in the New Testament a new and fruitful field of application, to the extent that they facilitated a connection between the old and the new. Because the *gezerah shawah* was a widely known and practised Jewish exegetical method, it was also used with a certain frequency in primitive Christian hermeneutics. Besides, the already mentioned episode of the ears of wheat plucked on the Sabbath, as reported by Matthew, in some sense foretold such a development. Furthermore, dating problems apart, until today and until proved otherwise, we can say that Paul is the first author in whom is found the formal use of *gezerah shawah*, an exegetical method which will also appear regularly in Qumran and in rabbinical sources.[10] It is now time to look at some Pauline examples of the use of this rule.

---

[9] Günter Stemberger, *Ermeneutica ebraica della Bibbia* (trans. V. Gatti; StBi 127; Brescia: Paideia Editrice, 2000), 124.

[10] For a first good introduction, cf. Solomon Zeitlin, "Hillel and the Hermeneutic Rules," *JQR* 54 (1963/1964): 161–173; Waine S. Towner, "Hermeneutical Systems of Hillel and the Tannaim: A Fresh Look," *HUCA* 53 (1982): 101–135; Rimon Kasher, "The Interpretation of Scripture in Rabbinic Literature," in *Mikra: text, translation, reading and interpretation of the Hebrew Bible in ancient judaism and early Christianity* (ed. M. J. Mulder; CRINT 2;. Assen: Van Gorcum; Philadelphia: Fortress Press, 1988), 547–594; Michael L. Chernick, "Internal Restraints on *Gezerah Shawah*'s Application," *JQR* 80

2.1 1 Cor 3:18–20: The GS about the wise

In 1 Cor 1–4 the apostle to the Gentiles develops in a paradoxical manner the subject of wisdom and foolishness regarding the preaching of the Cross: "For the message about the cross is foolishness to those who are perishing, but to us who are being saved it is the power of God" (1:18).

Starting from 3:5 Paul then shows how in the Church the same foolishness of the Cross is reproduced. Among the many proofs that support his thesis, one proof is constructed by means of a GS. In fact, it can be read in 3:18–20:

> Do not deceive yourselves. If you think that you are wise in this age, you should become fools so that you may become wise. For the wisdom of this world is foolishness with God. For it is written,
> "*He catches the wise in their craftiness,*"
> and again,
> "*The Lord knows the thoughts of the wise, that they are futile.*"

The apostle here quoted

> Job 5:13a: "He takes the wise in their own craftiness";
>
> לֹכֵד חֲכָמִים בְּעָרְמָם
> ὁ καταλαμβάνων σοφοὺς ἐν τῇ φρονήσει
>
> Ps 93:11: "The Lord knows our thoughts (but in Paul: τῶν σοφῶν = the wise), that they are but an empty breath";
>
> יְהוָה יֹדֵעַ מַחְשְׁבוֹת אָדָם כִּי־הֵמָּה הָבֶל
> κύριος γινώσκει τοὺς διαλογισμοὺς τῶν ἀνθρώπων ὅτι εἰσὶν μάταιοι.

(1990): 253–282; Arne J. Hobbel, "Hermeneutics in Talmud, Midrash and the New Testament," *Imm* 24/25 (1990): 132–146. For the GS in Qumran cf. Elieser Slomovic, "Toward an Understanding of the Exegesis of the Dead Sea Scrolls," *RevQ* 7 (1969–1971): 3–15.

Now, Paul wants to show how Scripture already manifests his paradox, a paradox which sets the wisdom of the world against the foolishness of the Cross. However, looking back through the pages of the Bible, it turns out that the two terms σοφία and μωρία never occur in a semantic series that could help Paul in any way. In fact, the only passage where this happens is a single *mashal* repeated, though twice, and in a perfectly identical way, in Sir 20:31 and 41:15:

"Better are those who hide their folly
than those who hide their wisdom";

κρείσσων ἄνθρωπος ἀποκρύπτων τὴν **μωρίαν** αὐτοῦ
ἢ ἄνθρωπος ἀποκρύπτων τὴν **σοφίαν** αὐτοῦ.

As one can easily deduce, the apostle cannot find help in this passage, since it does not fit in with his objective. And no other passage from the OT works better, at least when it comes to the term σοφία. This term never occurs together with the idea of "foolishness" in the whole Hebrew Bible, in the way that Paul intends it. Consequently, the paradoxical combination of wisdom and foolishness must be deduced in another way, for instance by taking the path of an inference like *gezerah shawah*. In this regard, Job 5:13 and Ps 93:11 are quite helpful, since they can be combined for different reasons. In fact, in the case of both of these passages we are facing a sapiential proclamation of God's justice against the challenge issued by the fools. Furthermore, Paul is able to obtain also a terminological connection which enables the two texts to work in combination, following a very simple norm, which shows that if

- in Job 5:13a **a + b**: the wise / craftiness
- in Ps 93:11 **a + c**: the wise / vain
- consequently **b + c**: craftiness (of the wise) is vain.[11]

[11] Cf. Christoph Plag, "Paulus und die *Gezera schawa*: Zur Übernahme rabbinischer Auslegungskunst," *Jud* 50 (1994): 138–139.

But this new statement, not directly present in any of the two quoted texts, is nothing but the paradox of 1 Cor 3:19—"For the wisdom of this world is foolishness with God"—with the difference, though, that now it has received adequate scriptural support.

2.2 1 Cor 9:9—10: GS and right of the ministers of the Gospel

Still in 1 Cor, but this time in the context of things offered to idols, Paul deals with the legal criteria concerning the right to use or renounce freedom in view of the greater good of not creating an obstacle to the Gospel, especially because of the difficulties of conscience that might occur in the other person (1 Cor 8–10). In this connection, the apostle refers to his right to be supported because of his ministry, already from the starting point of questions such as 9:7:

> "Who at any time pays the expenses for doing military service? Who plants a vineyard and does not eat any of its fruit? Or who tends a flock and does not get any of its milk?"

Thus, even though those who preach the Gospel live on the Gospel itself, the apostle renounces his right to a reward because, paradoxically, he already recognizes a reward in the chance to preach the Gospel for free, without exploiting that very right given him by the Gospel. However, before explaining his renunciation to any support whatever for reasons founded on his own life experience, Paul states that income of this kind is fully authorized on the basis of Scripture:

> Do I say this on human authority? Does not the law also say the same? For it is written in the law of Moses, "*You shall not muzzle an ox while it is treading out the grain.*" Is it for oxen that God is concerned? Or does he not speak entirely for our sake? It was indeed written for our sake, for "*whoever plows should plow in hope and whoever threshes should thresh in hope of a share in the crop*" (1 Cor 9: 8–10).

What is interesting here is the double appearance of the verb ἀλοάω in Deut 25:4, "*You shall not muzzle an ox while it is **treading*** *out the grain*" (Οὐ φιμώσεις βοῦν **ἀλοῶντα**.), versus the unknown text's "*whoever plows should plow in hope and* ***whoever threshes*** *should thresh in hope of a share in the crop*" (ὀφείλει ἐπ' ἐλπίδι ὁ ἀροτριῶν ἀροτριᾶν καὶ ὁ **ἀλοῶν** ἐπ' ἐλπίδι τοῦ μετέχειν). The analogical reasoning is at this point easy to follow:

- in Deut 25:4 **a + b**: if while threshing / no muzzle;
- in unknown text **a + c**: if while threshing / a right to get a share of it;
- consequently **b + c**: no muzzle is a right to get a share of it.[12]

But Paul's exegetical progression goes further if we consider that 1 Cor 9:13—"Do you not know that those who are employed in the temple service get their food from the temple, and those who serve at the altar share in what is sacrificed on the altar?"—recalls the rule of Deut 18: 1–8:

> The levitical priests, the whole tribe of Levi, shall have no allotment or inheritance within Israel. They may eat the sacrifices that are the Lord's portion but they shall have no inheritance among the other members of the community; the Lord is their inheritance, as he promised them. This shall be the priests' due from the people, from those offering a sacrifice, whether an ox or a sheep: they shall give to the priest the shoulder, the two jowls, and the stomach. The first fruits of your grain, your wine, and your oil, as well as the first of the fleece of your sheep, you shall give him. For the Lord your God has chosen Levi out of all your tribes, to stand and minister in the name of the Lord, him and his sons for all time. If a Levite leaves any of your towns, from wherever he has been residing in Israel, and comes to the place that the Lord will choose (and he may come whenever he wishes), then he may minister in the name of the Lord his God, like all his fellow-Levites who stand to minister there before the Lord. They shall have equal portions to eat, even though they have income from the sale of family possessions.

---

[12] Cf. Plag, "Paulus, " 139.

It is clear that the Pauline exegetical method proceeds by inferences. Through a *gezerah shawah* he could demonstrate that the command not to muzzle the threshing ox (Deut 25:4) is analogous to getting a share of the crop by the thresher (in the unknown text). But having a share also characterizes the command of giving a quota of the sacrifices to the priests of the temple (Deut 18:1–8). The final result is that Gospel ministers have a right to receive support.

2.3 Rom 4:3–8: GS and justification

An excellent GS can be found within the famous example concerning Abraham. The analysis of this example is among the most instructive for determining the forms and methods with which the apostle used the rabbinical rule.[13] The two texts to be compared are:

Gen 15:6: "And Abraham believed the Lord; and the Lord reckoned it to him as righteousness";

ἐπίστευσεν δὲ Ἀβραὰμ τῷ θεῷ καὶ **ἐλογίσθη** αὐτῷ εἰς δικαιοσύνην

Ps 32:1–2"Happy are those whose transgression is forgiven, whose sin is covered.

Happy are those to whom the LORD imputes no iniquity";

μακάριοι ὧν ἀφέθησαν αἱ ἀνομίαι
καὶ ὧν ἐπεκαλύφθησαν αἱ ἁμαρτίαι·
μακάριος ἀνὴρ οὗ οὐ μὴ **λογίσηται** κύριος ἁμαρτίαν.

[13] On the matter cf. Joachim Jeremias, "Zur Gedankenführung in den paulinischen Briefen," in *Abba: Studien zur neutestamentlichen Theologie und Zeitgeschichte* (Göttingen: Vandenhoeck & Ruprecht, 1966), 269–276; Plag, "Paulus," 135–140; Marie-Jo Porcher, "Quelques considérations sur l'usage du Psaume 32 dans l'Épître aux Romains (Rm 4:1–12)," *RevScRel* 77 (2003): 552–564; Jean-Noël Aletti, "Romains 4 et Genèse 17: Quelle énigme et quelle solution?," *Bib* 84 (2003): 305–325.

The apostle needs to explain that justification is provided by faith, not by works. But the mere quotation of Gen 15:6 is not sufficient to achieve this aim, since in two passages, which moreover sound like a reinterpretation of Gen 15:6, Judaism interpreted Abraham's faith in the same way as any kind of work:

1 Macc 2:52: "Was not Abraham found faithful when tested, and **it was reckoned to him as righteousness**?";

Αβρααμ οὐχὶ ἐν πειρασμῷ εὑρέθη πιστός καὶ **ἐλογίσθη αὐτῷ εἰς δικαιοσύνην**;[14]

Ps 105:30–31: "Then Phinehas stood up and interceded, and the plague was stopped. And **that has been reckoned to him as righteousness** from generation to generation forever";

καὶ ἔστη Φινεες καὶ ἐξιλάσατο, καὶ ἐκόπασεν ἡ θραῦσις· καὶ **ἐλογίσθη αὐτῷ εἰς δικαιοσύνη** εἰς γενεὰν καὶ γενεὰν ἕως τοῦ αἰῶνος.[15]

Now, according to Paul Gen 15:6 has not been correctly interpreted by Judaic tradition. But how can he advance his thesis of justification by faith alone when in the OT it is never said that someone has been justified without the actions of Law? In order to demolish this well-established school of interpretation, Paul needs to demonstrate that works have no importance at all for

[14] Here to the question "why God justified Abraham?" the text answers: "because he was πιστός (=faithful)!"; being πιστός is therefore what determines the ἐλογίσθη according to a thought pattern: Abraham = πιστός = ἐλογίσθη αὐτῷ εἰς δικαιοσύνην.

[15] Here, to the question "why God justified Phinehas?" the text answers: "because he had zeal for God"; being zealous is therefore what determines the ἐλογίσθη according to an identical thought pattern: Phinehas = he takes actions which are full of zeal = ἐλογίσθη αὐτῷ εἰς δικαιοσύνην.

the interpretation of Gen 15:6. In fact, the only way is to prove that believing can be counted as justice, without the act of faith being considered a good deed, for which God is forced to bestow a reward, like the wage paid to a worker. But how will he go about proving this? Paul needs another text, which allows him to separate the πιστεύειν from the ἔργα νόμου and the μισθός and so to move in an opposite direction to the Judaic interpretation of his time.

Therefore, in order to achieve his exegetical and theological aim, Paul reads Gen 15:6 starting from Ps 32:1–2, through a GS outlined on the basis of λογίζομαι, the term common to both passages. But why did the apostle consider necessary the comparison between precisely these two passages? By reviewing the LXX, it is evident that the verb λογίζομαι occurs more than 100 times. It often means, however, "think, consider", which is why the number of comparable passages already decreases drastically. And the reduction continues even further if instead of stopping at only terminological proximity we instead examine only those passages that display the same semantic sequence, a fact which is of decisive importance for the GS. Now the sequence:

God → counts (= λογίζομαι)

→ to the man

→ what he did/believed → in positive/negative

can be found only in nine passages: Gen 15:6; Lev 7:18; 17:4; Num 18:26, 30; Job 31:27–28; Ps 31:1–2; Ps 105:30–31; 1 Macc 2:52.

So the number of occurrences drops from more than one hundred down to nine:

Text	Area of the λογίζομαι
1. Gen 15:6: "And Abraham believed the Lord; and the Lord reckoned it to him as righteousness (ἐλογίσθη αὐτῷ εἰς δικαιοσύνην / ויחשבה לו צדקה)."	Faith was counted for Abraham as justice.
2. Lev 7:18: "If any of the flesh of your sacrifice of well-being is eaten on the third day, it shall not be acceptable, nor shall it be credited to the one who offers it (οὐ λογισθήσεται αὐτῷ / לא יחשב לו); it shall be an abomination, and the one who eats of it shall incur guilt (ἁμαρτίαν)."	Who disobeys the cultural prescription requiring to consume within the first two days the meat coming from the communion sacrifice and to burn the remains in the fire by eating it on the third day, instead, will be negatively counted by God.
3. Lev 17:3–4: "If anyone of the house of Israel slaughters an ox or a lamb or a goat in the camp, or slaughters it outside the camp, and does not bring it to the entrance of the tent of meeting, to present it as an offering to the Lord before the tabernacle of the Lord, he shall be held guilty of bloodshed (λογισθήσεται τῷ ἀνθρώπῳ ἐκείνῳ αἷμα / דָּם יֵחָשֵׁב לָאִישׁ) he has shed blood, and he shall be cut off from the people."	Who disobeys the law requiring to butcher an animal only at the meeting tent, in order to let the blood pour from it only according to the religious law, will be negatively counted by God.
4. Num 18:25–27: "Then the Lord spoke to Moses, saying: You shall speak to the Levites, saying: When you receive from the Israelites the tithe that I have given you from them for your portion, you shall set apart an offering from it to the Lord, a tithe of the tithe. It shall be reckoned to you as your gift (καὶ λογισθήσεται ὑμῖν / וְנֶחְשַׁב לָכֶם) the same as the grain of the threshing floor and the fullness of the wine press."	The Levite who offers a tenth of a tenth will be positively counted by God.
5. Num 18:30: "Say also to them: When you have set apart the best of it, then the rest shall be reckoned to the Levites (καὶ λογισθήσεται τοῖς Λευίταις / וְנֶחְשַׁב לַלְוִיִּם) as produce of the threshing floor, and as produce of the wine press."	The Levite who offers a tenth of a tenth will be positively counted by God.
6. Job 31:27–28: "…and my heart has been secretly enticed, and my mouth has kissed my hand; this also would be an iniquity to be punished by the judges (καὶ τοῦτό μοι… λογισθείη) (ἀνομία ἡ μεγίστη), for I should have been false to God above."	Job, talking in his own defence, says that if he had committed sin, God would have negatively counted his sin.
7. Ps 32:1–2: "Happy are those whose transgression is forgiven,(ἀφέθησαν αἱ ἀνομίαι), whose sin is covered (ἐπεκαλύφθησαν αἱ ἁμαρτίαι). Happy are those to whom the LORD imputes no iniquity (οὗ οὐ μὴ λογίσηται κύριος ἁμαρτίαν / לֹא יַחְשֹׁב יְהוָה לוֹ עָוֹן)."	God does not count sin.
8. Ps 105:30–31: "Then Phinehas stood up and interceded, and the plague was stopped. And that has been reckoned to him as righteousness (καὶ ἐλογίσθη αὐτῷ εἰς δικαιοσύνην / וַתֵּחָשֶׁב לוֹ לִצְדָקָה) from generation to generation forever."	Phinehas's zealous acting is positively counted by God.
9. 1 Macc 2:52: "Was not Abraham found faithful (εὑρέθη πιστός) when tested (ἐν πειρασμῷ), and it was reckoned to him as righteousness (καὶ ἐλογίσθη αὐτῷ εἰς δικαιοσύνην)?" ἐλογίσθη αὐτῷ εἰς δικαιοσύνην)?"	Abraham's faithful acting is positively counted by God.

Analyzing the semantic series, we notice that among those nine passages the ones that best match on the basis of the LXX are Gen 15:6 and Ps 32:2. In fact, they are the only two texts where the verb λογίζομαι is closely and clearly combined with the explicit mention of God, while in the other seven cases this mention is to be presumed rather as the subject of the theological passive:

text	*semantic series*
Gen 15:6	καὶ ἐπίστευσεν Αβραμ **τῷ θεῷ** καὶ **ἐλογίσθη** αὐτῷ εἰς δικαιοσύνην.
Ps 32:2	μακάριος ἀνήρ οὗ οὐ μὴ **λογίσηται κύριος** ἁμαρτίαν.
Lev 7:18	ἐὰν δὲ φαγὼν φάγῃ ἀπὸ τῶν κρεῶν τῇ ἡμέρᾳ τῇ τρίτῃ οὐ δεχθήσεται αὐτῷ τῷ προσφέροντι αὐτό, οὐ **λογισθήσεται** αὐτῷ...
Lev 17:4	καὶ **λογισθήσεται** τῷ ἀνθρώπῳ ἐκείνῳ αἷμα·
Num 18:27	καὶ **λογισθήσεται** ὑμῖν τὰ ἀφαιρέματα ὑμῶν ὡς σῖτος ἀπὸ ἅλω καὶ ἀφαίρεμα ἀπὸ ληνοῦ.
Nm 18:30	καὶ **λογισθήσεται** τοῖς Λευίταις ὡς γένημα ἀπὸ ἅλω καὶ ὡς γένημα ἀπὸ ληνοῦ.
Job 31:28	καὶ τοῦτό μοι ἄρα ἀνομία ἡ μεγίστη **λογισθείη**...
Ps 105:31	καὶ **ἐλογίσθη** αὐτῷ εἰς δικαιοσύνην εἰς γενεὰν καὶ γενεὰν ἕως τοῦ αἰῶνος.
1Macc 2:52	Αβρααμ οὐχὶ ἐν πειρασμῷ εὑρέθη πιστός, καὶ **ἐλογίσθη** αὐτῷ εἰς δικαιοσύνην;

In Hebrew, then, the perfect identity of the syntactic-semantic construction is seen more clearly.

Text	*semantic series*
Gen 15:6	יַחְשְׁבֶהָ לוֹ צְדָקָה
Ps 32:2	לֹא יַחְשֹׁב יְהוָה לוֹ עָוֹן
Lev 7:18	לֹא יֵחָשֵׁב לוֹ
Lev 17:4	דָּם יֵחָשֵׁב לָאִישׁ
Num 18:27	וְנֶחְשַׁב לָכֶם תְּרוּמַתְכֶם כַּ
Num 18:30	וְנֶחְשַׁב לַלְוִיִּם כִּ
Job 31:28	חשב it does not appear
Ps 106:,31	וַתֵּחָשֶׁב לוֹ לִצְדָקָה
1Macc 2:52	only in Greek

As we can see, only in Gen 15:6 and Ps 32:2 is the series perfectly identical (חשב + לו + direct complement with no preposition), while in the other five cases, the identity stops at חשב + ל.

We are then in the presence of a GS, which has drawn the texts together in an excellent way: any Jewish expert in exegetical methods would have appreciated the apostle's ability to narrow down in a plausible way the nine passages to just two in which the following sequence appears

God → counts (=λογίζομαι)

→ to the man

→ what he did/believed → positively/negatively.

But what is behind this series of texts centered on the verb λογίζομαι? Obviously, it is the classic vision of retribution, since as many as seven of them are born of the Judaic idea according to which God counts human deeds by giving them positive or negative value, depending on whether one acts for good or evil. In the face of such a well-established theological construct, how can Paul declare the truth of justification by faith alone, and at the same time reject passages that seem to go in the opposite direction? What can be said about the fact that Gen 15:6 has been reinterpreted in Ps 105:31 and 1 Macc 2:52 as an indication of justification by works? In the midst of these difficulties Ps 32:2 appears as a witness to something other than traditional retribution, since it is the only text where it is said that God does not count sin. Furthermore, even more interesting is the fact that *David's declaration has the same semantic series as Gen 15:6.* That is why, for Paul, *the psalm can explain Gen 15:6 as a justification χωρὶς ἔργων, being supported by an excellent GS, which is also the only possible one.*

3. CONCLUSIONS

3.1 An overall observation

The analysis of *gezerot shawot* in the New Testament could be carried further by considering at least twenty other cases. However, here I confine myself to some concluding remarks.

By comparing 2 Sam 24:1 and 1 Chr 21:1 we notice how one of the most important goals of intrabiblical exegesis is the attempt to decontaminate as much as possible the image of God in certain texts. The same concern to highlight what is more opportune for the most purified possible idea of God emerges from many of the reinterpretations of the OT on the basis of the NT. It could not be otherwise, if we consider the degree of development that the Christ event imparts to the debate about God. In this context, the hermeneutical rules play an enormous role to the extent that they contribute to outlining a renewed understanding of a great part of the ancient Scriptures. It is not surprising, then, that some *gezerot shawot* of the NT are broken up by invitations, even ironical sometimes, to modify already established interpretative schemes. But this does not mean that the authors of the NT want to manipulate Scripture by means of the *gezerah shawah*, but instead shows that they want to use the GS as a place to investigate its meaning, in order to connect new and old, Scripture and life, written *Torah* and its present developments. With regard to Paul, his biblical argumentations focus on Scripture, starting from the present time when a lot of new questions are arising. After the Christ event and the faith response to it on the part of the pagans, what can we say about the promises made to the fathers, about Law, circumcision and covenants, about ethical questions and many other issues, and ultimately about God himself and his way of acting? G*ezerah shawah* offers an excellent instrument to answer these questions, to the extent that it favours the reinterpretation and possibly the resulting reconciliation between new and old, Scripture and present.[16]

[16] Concerning the peculiar characteristics of Pauline exegesis, with specific reference to its midrashic quality, cf. Joseph Bonsirven, *Exégèse rabbinique et exégèse*

But even if Paul and the New Testament in general only turned to the rabbinical rules because these rules offered encouragement

---

paulinienne (Paris: Beauchesne et ses fils,1939); Hans-Joachim Schoeps, *Paulus: die Theologie des Apostels im Lichte der jüdischen Religionsgeschichte* (Tübingen: Mohr, 1959); William D. Davies, *Paul and Rabbinic Judaism: some Rabbinic Elements in Pauline Theology* (3d ed.; London: SPCK, 1970); David Daube, *The New Testament and Rabbinic Judaism* (Salem: Ayer Company, 1984); Augustín Del Agua Pérez, *El método midrásico y la exégesis del Nuevo Testamento* (BibMid 4; Valencia: Soler, 1985); Peter J. Tomson, *Paul and the Jewish Law: Halakha in the Letters of the Apostle to the Gentiles* (CRINT 3.1; Assen/Maastricht: Van Gorcum, 1990); Jean-Noël Aletti, "Saint Paul, exégète de l'Écriture," in *L'Écriture âme de la théologie: actes du Colloque tenu à Bruxelles du 17 au 19 septembre 1989* (ed. R. Lafontaine et al.; IET 9; Bruxelles: Institut d'Études Théologiques, 1990), 37–59; Edward E. Ellis, *Paul's Use of the Old Testament* (TwBS; Grand Rapids, Mich.: Baker Book House, 1991); Romano Penna, "Atteggiamenti di Paolo verso l'Antico Testamento," in *L'Apostolo Paolo: studi di esegesi e teologia* (Parola di Dio. Seconda Serie 12; Cinisello Balsamo: Edizioni Paoline, 1991), 436–469; Christopher D. Stanley, *Paul and the Language of Scripture: citation technique in the Pauline Epistles and contemporary literature* (SNTSMS 74; Cambridge: Cambridge University Press, 1992); Craig A. Evans and James A. Sanders, eds., *Paul and the Scripture of Israel* (JSNTSup 83; Sheffield: Academic Press, 1993); James W. Aageson, *Written Also for Our Sake: Paul and the Art of Biblical Interpretation* (Louisville, KY: Westminster John Knox, 1993); Rinaldo Fabris, "La Scrittura in Paolo e nelle comunità paoline," in *La Bibbia nell'antichità cristiana* (ed. E. Norelli; La Bibbia nella storia 15/I; Bologna: Edizione Dehoniane Bologna, 1993), 87–103; Brian S. Rosner, "'Written for Us': Paul's view of Scripture," in *A Pathway into the Holy Scripture* (ed. P. E. Satterthwaite and D. F. Wright; Grand Rapids, Mich.: Eerdmans, 1994), 81–105; Thomas Söding, "Heilige Schriften für Israel und die Kirche: Die Sicht des Alten Testaments bei Paulus," in *Das Wort vom Kreuz: Studien zur paulinischen Theologie* (WUNT 93; Tübingen: Mohr, 1997), 222–247; Kenneth D. Litwak, "Echoes of Scripture? A critical survey of recent works on Paul's use of the Old Testament," *CurBS* 6 (1998): 260–288; Frédéric Manns, "Paul e la lecture juive des Écritures, " in *Atti del V Simposio di Tarso su S. Paolo Apostolo* (ed. L. Padovese; TurCs 12; Roma: Pontificio Ateneo Antoniano. Istituto Francescano di Spiritualità, 1998), 29–39; Gerbern S. Oegema, *Für Israel und die Völker: Studien zum alttestamentlich-jüdischen Hintergrund der paulinischen Theologie* (NovTSup 95; Leiden: Brill, 1998); Marco Nobile, "Le citazioni veterotestamentarie di Paolo," in *Atti del VII Simposio di Tarso su S. Paolo Apostolo* (ed. L. Padovese; TurCs 16; Roma: Pontificio Ateneo Antoniano, Istituto Francescano di Spiritualità, 2002), 21–27.

and scriptural support for their new and innovative views, we still would not be close to exhausting the full import of their use by Paul and the early Christians. Certainly the first Christian writers were intent on appealing to the authority and example of the Jewish Bible in order to legitimate and confirm the value of their theological vision. It is also true that behind this need was concealed the desire to keep open the dialogue with Israel, as well as with its history, its traditions and its Scriptures. In this sense, the adoption and employment by Paul and the New Testament of rabbinical exegetical methods, and particularly of *gezerah shawah*, demonstrates how extensive, and sometimes also how polemical and angry, was the attempt to keep together old and new believers, synagogue and church, Israel and the Gentiles. Consequently, the first decades of the Christian era, characterized by a strong sharing of the rules of Judaic hermeneutics, still encourage us not only with their content but also with the way they present the Christian event. They invite us to re-appropriate cultural contexts and Judaic themes in order to wholly retrieve the horizon within which the original Church preached the Gospel, *first of all* to the children of Israel and only afterwards to all the other people of the world.

3.2. Gezerah shawah and the Pauline method of reading the OT

Turning in conclusion to Paul, what can we say at the end of this journey, after having analysed at such length some of his *gezerot shawot*? Until some years ago the study of the methods and forms of the apostle's biblical exegesis used to generate clear and unambiguous opinions. Dietzfelbinger, for instance, thought that Paul's uniqueness was not to be found in the application of rabbinical methods, or in the desire to update the Scripture. In his view, the Judaic methodologies would at most characterize the formal levels of the apostle, but without touching his ideas. These ideas were to be found rather in the Damascus experience, where Paul understands, based on his own experience, that God justifies the human being in Jesus Christ, apart from the works of the Law. But is it really like that? Or are there other keys with which to enter the vast world of Pauline exegesis of the OT, keys such as Christocentrism,[17] ecclesiocentrism,[18] theocentrism,[19] or the evidence given to the εὐαγγέλιον.[20]

What can we say? Pauline *gezerot shawot* and particularly the one of Rom 4 can help in this debate. In fact in this regard, a typical expression of rabbinical exegetic discussion was: *how can I fulfil (mà ani meqajjem) what is written?* Behind this question was concealed a constant desire for study and self-actualization. In a certain sense, the Scripture was thought of as lacking a foundation until a practical way of realizing it in the now was discovered. The *midrash* with its *middoth*, was the favourite instrument of this investigation, which the NT authors, even Paul, used as well. In this sense, by recovering Rom 4 the apostle does not deny Gen 15:6; instead he clarifies it, remembers it and reaffirms it, starting from the search for a more complete meaning than that offered by tradition, a meaning at the same time more open and accessible to the Gentiles. Paul has, then, a relationship with the νόμος characterized by true completion, and not arbitrary diminishment. He wants to fulfil the Scripture, confirm it in the light of what has emerged in the end times, to the extent that the new illuminates the old and vice versa. Consequently, every accusation levelled against the apostle of distancing himself from the νόμος proves to be a mistaken understanding of his biblical hermeneutics. Paul repeals nothing that God's will has already manifested in the Law and the Prophets regarding justice, Law, faith and works.

Yet given all this, the most burning issue still remains. How did Paul proceed from a methodological point of view? Confronted with the theological approach of justification by works adopted by

---

[17] Cf. Anthony T. Hanson, "Paul as Exegete and Theologian," in *Studies in Paul's Technique and Theology* (London: SPCK, 1974), 201–224.

[18] As in Richard B. Hays, *Echoes of Scripture in the Letters of Paul* (New Haven, Conn.: Yale University Press, 1989), 84–87.

[19] Cf. James A. Sanders, "Paul and Theological History", in Evans and Sanders, *Paul and the Scripture of Israel*, 53–54.

[20] As in Dietrich-Alex Koch, *Die Schrift als Zeuge des Evangeliums: Untersuchungen zur Verwendung und zum Verständnis der Schrift bei Paulus* (BHT 69; Tübingen: Mohr, 1986), 341–353.

Judaism toward Abraham, the apostle went back directly to the biblical text, almost *ex abrupto*. In fact, Paul did not look for a direct comparison with those interpretations he regarded as wrong, but he looked straight at God's intention and meaning in the OT. The *gezerah shawah* method he used can be seen as questionable, but this is the method he had at his disposal. *Paul reasoned and wrote according to the directions his time provided.* He "cryptogrammed" the OT by comparing text portions related to Abraham and David that were united by means of a verb. Therefore, we can understand that the apostle meant to ground his thesis on justification by faith in the OT through using the analogical inference.

Concerning his attempt to methodologically legitimate his arguments, Paul cannot be accused of distorting and manipulating the OT, since his way of reading it is perfectly in line with biblical dictates. By linking Gen 15:6 and Ps 32:1–2, the apostle did not connect two disparate texts, but he remained perfectly within the methodological limits respected by those who do not annul the Law, but search for a more reliable foundation for it, from an exegetical point of view as well. Besides, the hermeneutical debate opposing Paul to the pious Judean does not focus on Gen 15:6, but on the way tradition has received it. Paul warns against a wrong interpretation of the Genesis text, as happened within Judaism: justification by works is nothing but a reduced and weakened understanding of the importance of Gen 15:6. *Everything depends on something written that could be explained differently even from the exegetical point of view. In this sense, Gen 15:6 becomes new in the light of Pauline interpretation, but its thesis of justification by faith alone would not be acceptable if it were not a new formulation of what is already written.* It is his very fidelity to the OT that drives Paul to reread it in the light of the most recent circumstances. *The result is that his arguments do not abolish the νόμος, they do not replace it, but they provide it with a foundation which confirms it again on the basis of new elements that have emerged.*

Reading the OT in this way, then, Paul retrieves all its power and in this way his message acquires the flavour of the fullness of revelation. What was already attested in the Law and Prophets starts to be completely revealed through the Gospel. *The apostle is thus able to connect Rom 4 with much of the content of the OT, in a dialectic of witness and manifestation which finds its full illumination only in the current situation. But at the same time his hermeneutical approach does not close off questions, does not limit areas of investigation, and does not pigeonhole situations. On the contrary it opens up new paths, it provokes thought, instils hope and trust in some, while it leaves others in doubt and uncertainty. The Paul of Romans 4 is truly a messenger of the Spirit for the Roman community to which he offers his authoritative contribution. But he also allows space so that each one can look at the paths that God is indicating, paths that lead forward from the departure point of the Christ event.* Such a hermeneutical exercise, then, helps both the Judeans and the Gentiles to understand their own history, to the extent that it reveals certain hidden dimensions of this history. So Abraham, the father of believers, he who was the first in this world to base his relationship with God on faith, becomes the father of a huge family. Everything started when he believed in the promise of a son. But the process inaugurated by Abraham continued throughout the whole OT, passing through David and the circumcised believers, until the present time. The acceptance of the uncircumcised Gentiles into the heart of Abraham's family testifies to the power and loyalty of the God of Israel.

3.3 Pauline hermeneutics as compared with the Jewish heritage

In conclusion, what are the final words we can pronounce at the end of this encounter with Paul the interpreter of the Scriptures? Metaphorically speaking, we can certainly affirm that Paul appears to us like a bridge. In fact, through the whole course of his elaborate debate in Rom 4, the apostle was constantly setting himself against historical rigidity and looking for instances of unity, without thereby resorting to complacent or facile mediations with his Jewish brothers and sisters. In this work of his, GS was the powerful hermeneutical instrument used by Paul in his attempt to forcibly break with everything that contaminated God's distinctive will, as witnessed to in the pages of the OT and reaffirmed in the last times. In this sense, then, Paul is a man helping other human beings, Jewish like him, to walk a specific way, which he has already walked and which is called the God of Israel. It is the reader who crosses the bridge, and after the bridge there is God: Paul, by himself, has built that bridge. In this work the apostle also shows himself to be an extraordinary architect. His construction is of the finest material, yet simultaneously of the strongest: it is a bridge that everybody can cross, both the circumcised and the uncircumcised. However, one concern reigns supreme: that on this path everyone may feel at ease, without being distracted by the difficulties of a theology which could paradoxically hinder the ways of grace. This is the ultimate reason why the semantic bridge that Paul built should not be filled too much with words and concepts. The apostle's main task, in fact, was to remove obstacles which blocked the path toward God, in order to favour as much as possible human acceptance of divine grace.

So, Paul appears as a *complex whole* whose words and reasoning urge us to question ourselves in a deep and profound way. But why does the Judean find it difficult to perceive the fact that God, also with regard to the Gentiles, is absolute grace, a grace free from any human activity that is deprived of faith? Compared with his blood relations and the Greeks, Paul *is a dove, a messenger of the Spirit, a builder of possibilities*. Furthermore, in this proclamation he does not align himself with either of the two parties that are in disagreement because of historical events involving Gentile and Jew. On the contrary, Paul analyses the historical situations of the circumcised and uncircumcised solely because behind them lies hidden the anguish of every human being who is distant, yet nevertheless reached by God. In this sense, the apostle is also a true connoisseur of the Jewish soul, since he understands all the possibilities exercised by the latter just in order not to surrender to the proclamation of the supremacy of grace over all human beings irrespective of ethnic identity (for example Law, circumcision, privileged positions, ancestors' merits, etc.). The logical demonstration of the untenability of any boast, though, does not bring

Paul to take his stand on one side or the other; instead it is exclusively aimed at removing obstacles so that the Jew may also see the bridge and walk across it. This means that the apostle does not construct just causes for opposing parties. The Jew does not have a just cause, but neither does the ethno-Christian have one. The only just cause both of them have is the God of Israel. Paul, though, does not place himself in non-historical or disincarnate places, but he tries, starting from these kinds of places, to minimize any contamination of salvific truth. Precisely because the theological, ethnic and religious debates that oppose the Judeans to the Gentiles is significantly affected by historical and juridical criteria, the apostle enters into these debates. But his goal is the proclamation of absolute grace for every human being. And this is the main purpose of GS in Rom 4. Within this context, Paul pays attention in a matchless way to the communicative tension engendered by this debate. Yet Paul never backs away in any passage from being always highly evangelical and magnanimous towards his blood relations. In the order of mercy and grace, he never speaks menacingly to the Judean. First, because he would contradict himself. Second, because this is the only true Law of the One who has given his life for all human beings. This, though, does not mean that the apostle indulges in a facile conciliatory rhetoric. On the contrary, his words sting Israel according to the flesh.

In fact, the Jew with whom Paul reasoned in Rom 4 still remains attached to his convictions; even though the apostle showed himself capable of harmonizing his argument with the most rabbinical of exegetical sensibilities. Indeed, we could say regarding this matter that the Pauline way of argumentation did not give rise to the desired effects. The Jew did not agree with the apostle's statements, as indeed the whole of subsequent history has shown. But why? Maybe we are going beyond Rom 4, but it is necessary to draw attention to one final factor. The Judean preferred to remain within a context of permanence, constancy and stability, by virtue of the logic of conservation that characterized that tradition: the GS on Gen 15:6 and Ps 32:2 did not convince him. Paul, instead, adopted a criterion of change and evolution, showing how this is actually more faithful to biblical dictates, which form the real tradition. Probably the Jew reading Rom 4 accused, and still today accuses the apostle of the Gentiles of having changed the very meaning of Scriptures.[21] The debate has never shown great development forward from this point of fundamental disagreement, and it does not seem to me that Jews share the Pauline reading and application of Gen 15:6. Perhaps this is a goal that will be attained in future centuries, in the knowledge that God's times and grace differ radically from the *chronos* to which we are accustomed.

[21] A good sample of the accusations of heresy made against the Pauline argumentations about Rom 4 is in Lillian C. Freudmann, *Antisemitism in the New Testament* (Lanham: University Press of America, 1994), 132–133, 166–169; Bruce S. Feiler, *Abraham: A Journey to the Heart of Three Faiths* (New York: William Morrow and Company, 2002), 139–148.

CHAPTER 5

THE HEAVENLY JOURNEY IN PAUL: TRADITION OF A JEWISH APOCALYPTIC LITERARY GENRE OR CULTURAL PRACTICE IN A HELLENISTIC-ROMAN CONTEXT?

Adriana Destro and Mauro Pesce

1. INTRODUCTION

1. In Second Corinthians Paul speaks of a journey to the third heaven that he himself experienced:

> I will go on to visions (*optasiai*) and revelations (*apokalypseis*) of the Lord.[1] I know (*oida*) a man in Christ who fourteen years[2] ago — whether in (*en*) the body or out of (*ektos*) the body I do not know; God knows—was caught (*arpagenta*) up to the third heaven. And I know that such a man—whether in (*en*) the body or without (*chôris*) the body I do not know; God knows—was caught (*êrpagê*) up into Paradise and heard inexpressible words[3] (*arrêta rêmata*), that no man is permitted to pronounce (12:1–4).[4]

---

[1] On the relevance of revelations in Paul see 1 Cor 1:7; 14:6–26; 2 Cor 12:1–7; Gal 1:12–16; 2:2; Phil 3:15 and also Eph 1:17.

[2] The motif of fourteen years in relation to a revelation is also present in Gal 2:1–2: "after fourteen years I went up again to Jerusalem with Barnabas [...] I went up in response to a revelation."

[3] See Pap.Graec.Mag. XIII, 763 (Preseindanz). *Papyri graecae magicae. Die griechischen Zauberpapyri* (Herausgegeben und übersetzt von Karl Preisendanz unter Mitarbeit von Erich Diehl, Sam Eitrem, Aldolf Jacobi. Leipzig und Berlin, 1931), 122; H.-D. Betz, ed. *The Greek Magical Papyri in Translation, Including the Demotic Spells* (2d ed. Chicago: University of Chicago Press, 1992).

[4] The subject of our analysis is the heavenly journey of Paul as a religious phenomenon and is primarily concerned neither with the reasons why Paul speaks of his experience, nor its Pauline specificity. On 2 Cor 12:1–4 and the heavenly journey in Paul, see: M. D. Goulder, "Visions and Revelations of the Lord (2 Corinthians 12:1–10)," in *Corinthians: Studies on a Community in Conflict;*

The so-called "heavenly journey" is a religious phenomenon present in a large number of cultural areas, and is also encountered in texts that are not specifically religious (such as the *Poem of Parmenides* or Lucian's *Dialogues*). Alan F. Segal could write that "it is possible to see the heavenly journey of the soul, its consequent promise of immortality and the corollary necessity of peri-

---

Essays in Honour of Margaret Thrall (ed. T. J. Burke and J. K. Elliott; Leiden: Brill, 2003), 303–312; P. H. Menoud, "L'écharde et l'ange satanique (2 Cor 12:7)," in idem, *Jésus-Christ et la foi: recherches néotestamentaires* (Neuchâtel: Éditions Delachaux & Niestlé, 1975), 23–29; C. R. A. Morray-Jones, "Paradise Revisited (2 Cor 12:1–12): The Jewish Mystical Background of Paul's Apostolate, Part 1: The Jewish Sources; Part 2: Paul's Heavenly Ascent and its Significance", *HTR* 86 (1993): 177–217, 265–292; B. Heininger, *Paulus als Visionär: Eine religionsgeschichtliche Studie* (HBS 9; Herder: Freiburg u.a., 1996); V. Jegher-Bucher, "'The Thorn in the Flesh'/'Der Pfhal im Fleisch': Considerations About 2 Corinthians 12:7–10 in Connection with 12:1–3," in *The Rhetorical Analysis of Scripture: Essays from the 1995 London Conference* (ed. S. E. Porter and T. H. Olbricht; JSNT SS 146; Sheffield: Sheffield Academic Press, 1996), 388–397; G. Quispel, "L'extase de Saint Paul", in *Ascension et Hypostases initiatiques de l'âme: Mystique et eschatologie à travers les traditions religieuses, Vol. I. Acts du Colloque internationale d'histoire des religions "Psychanodia"* (ed. A.A. Shismanian and D.Shismanian; Paris: Les Amis de I. P. Couliano, 2006), 381–392; V. K. Robbins, "The Legacy of 2 Corinthians 12:2–4 in the Apocalypse of Paul", in *Corinthians: Studies on a Community in Conflict; Essays in Honour of Margaret Thrall* (ed. T. J. Burke and J. K. Elliott; Leiden: Brill, 2003), 327–339 ; J. D. Tabor, *Things Unutterable: Paul's Ascent to Paradise in its Greco-Roman, Judaic, and Early Christian Contexts* (Lanham, MD: University Press of America, 1986); O. Wischmeyer, "2 Korinther 12:1–10: Ein autobiographisch-theologischer Text des Paulus," in *Von Ben Sira zu Paulus: Gesammelte Aufsätze* (ed. E.-M. Becker; Tübungen: Mohr Siebeck, 2004), 277–288; J-P. Ruiz, "Hearing and Seeing but not Saying: A Look at Revelation 10:4 and 2 Corinthians 12:4," in *SBLSP, 1994* (Atlanta, GA: Scholars Press, 1994), 182–202; J. M. Scott, "The Triumph of God in 2 Cor 2:14: Additional Evidence of Merkabah Mysticism in Paul," *NTS* 42 (1996): 260–281; A. F. Segal, "Paul and Ecstasy," in *SBLSP, 1996* (Atlanta, GA: Scholars Press, 1996), 555–580; M. Smith, "Ascent to the Heavens and the Beginning of Christianity," in Idem., *Studies in the Cult of Yahweh, Volume Two: New Testament, Early Christianity, and Magic* (ed. S. J. D. Cohen; Leiden: Brill, 1996), 47–67; M. Smith, "Two Ascended to Heaven: Jesus and the Author of 4Q491," in Idem., *Studies in the Cult of Yahweh, Volume Two: New Testament, Early Christianity, and Magic* (ed. S. J. D. Cohen; Leiden: Brill, 1996), 68–78.

odic ecstatic journeys to heaven as the dominant mythical constellation of late antiquity."[5] This type of experience "had been further popularized and is found everywhere in the literature of the late republic and early empire."[6]

Some scholars tend to interpret the presence in Paul of the pattern of the heavenly journey as an influence of a previous, especially 'apocalyptic', Jewish tradition. The wide diffusion of this kind of experience, however, obliges us to look for a different interpretation. The questions we pose are the following. To what extent was Paul's model of the heavenly journey drawn from a Greco-Roman environment or on the contrary from a Jewish one? And, did he draw upon one religious milieu alone or upon many interrelating environments?

In a celebrated issue of *Semeia,* edited in 1979 and entitled *Apocalypse: The Morphology of a Genre,*[7] John Joseph Collins drew up an inventory of Persian, Jewish, Christian, Gnostic and Greco-Roman texts of revelation for a period of time of about ten centuries. Collins considered the heavenly journey as just one among the various ways of obtaining supernatural knowledge: he made a distinction between revelation *with* or *without* a heavenly journey. His system of classification tended to identify a literary genre, rather than a religious practice or ritual. We will instead examine the heavenly ascent in terms of a religious *form* and *practice* in all its experiential and social aspects.

2. The fact that the heavenly journey was a universally recognised mythological concept in the early centuries of the Common

---

[5] A. Segal, "Heavenly Ascent in Hellenistic Judaism, Early Christianity and their Environment," (ANRW II.23.2: Berlin, de Gruyter, 1980), 1388.

[6] Smith, "Ascent to the Heavens," 51; see also Idem., "Observations on Hekhalot Rabbati," in *Biblical and Other Studies* (ed. A. Altmann; Cambridge, MA: Cambridge University Press, 1963), 142–60; Idem., "Prolegomena to a Discussion of Aretologies, Divine Men, the Gospels and Jesus," *JBL* 90 (1971): 174–99.

[7] J. J. Collins (ed.), *Apocalypse: The Morphology of A Genre* (*Semeia* 14, Atlanta, Ga.: Society of Biblical Literature, 1979).

Era is confirmed by the dialogue *Icarus-Menippus or Above the Clouds*,[8] written around 160–165 by Lucian of Samosata.[9] The heavenly journey was so widely known that Lucian could use it to channel his criticisms of the philosophy of the time. His irony focuses first of all on the absurdity of a man ascending to the home of Zeus (above all heavenly bodies):

> First stage, Earth to Moon three thousand stades [560 kilometers]; Second stage, up to the Sun five hundred parasangs circa [2775 kilometers], Then the third, to the actual Heaven and Zeus's citadel, might be put at a day's journey for an eagle in light marching order.
>
> (*Icaro-Menippus*, 1)[10]

Lucian makes fun of this statement, precisely because it is a *topos* of ascension texts. In fact, Lucian reveals a knowledge of several aspects of ascension texts: for example, that access to the upper heavens is overseen by guardians and that there is an entrance door:

> Three days' flight through the stars, with the Sun on my right hand, brought me close to Heaven; and my first idea was to go straight in as I was; I should easily pass unobserved in virtue of my half-eagle-ship; for of course the eagle was Zeus's familiar; on second thoughts, though, my vulture wing would very soon betray me. So, thinking it better not to run any risks, I went up to the door and knocked. Hermes opened, took my name, and hurried off to inform Zeus.

---

[8] "Icaromenippo o l'uomo sopra le nubi," in *Dialoghi di Luciano a cura di Vincenzo Longo* (vol. 2; Torino: UTET, 1986), 847–885. E. Talbot, *Oeuvres complètes de Lucien de Samosate: Traduction nouvelle avec une introduction et des notes* (Paris: Hachette, 1912).

[9] J. Schwartz, *Biographie de Lucien de Samosate* (Collection Latomus, Vol. 83; Bruxelles: Latomus, 1965).

[10] See Aristarchus of Samos (310–230 B.C.E.), *On the Sizes and Distances of the Sun and Moon.* Aristarchus of Samos, *A History of Greek Astronomy to Aristarchus, Together with Aristarchus's Treatise on the Sizes and Distances of the Sun and Moon, a new Greek text with translation and notes* (ed. Sir Thomas Heath; Oxford: Clarendon Press, 1913).

> After a brief wait I was asked to step in; I was now trembling with apprehension, and I found that the Gods, who were all seated together, were not quite easy themselves. The unexpected nature of the visit was slightly disturbing to them, and they had visions of all mankind arriving at my heels by the same conveyance.
>
> (*Icarus-Menippus*, 20)

Lucian then moves on to a whole series of themes, normally found in religious texts dealing with the heavenly journey. How can the Earth and life thereon be seen from on high? How is it possible to know from on high what happens below? How can the Gods hear the prayers of men? What is man's ultimate destiny and what is the structure of the universe?

Overall, Lucian presents a radical criticism of the heavenly journey. Instead of constituting a founding and legitimizing element of philosophical and religious truth, it becomes the clear demonstration of the crisis of philosophy and religion.

Recounting Menippus' ascension to the heavens, Lucian speaks only of the Moon, the Sun and the higher heavens. He therefore refers, like Paul in Second Corinthians, only to three heavens, and not the nine of Cicero's *Dream of Scipio* (the seven planets, the Earth and the heaven where the divinity resides). Neither is he implying the astronomical vision of Ptolemy, also writing around that time.[11] If Lucian had known the Ptolemaic astronomy, he would not have

[11] M.-P. Lerner, *Le monde des sphères. I. Genèse et triomphe d'une représentation cosmique* (Paris : Les Belles Lettres, 2008), 70 : "Abordant [...] le problème de la position de Mercure et de Vénus dans la série des planètes, Ptolémée avait estimé plus probable l'opinion des astronomes anciens qui les plaçaient entre la lune et le soleil. " On ancient astronomy see A. Jeremias, *Babylonisches im Neuen Testament* (Leipzig : Hinrichs'sche Buchhandlung, 1905); G. Luck, *Arcana Mundi : Magic and the Occult in the Greek and Roman Worlds: A Collection of Ancient Texts* (Baltimore: John Hopkins University Press, 1985); O. Neugebauer, "The 'Astronomical' Chapters of the Ethiopic Book of Henoch (72 to 82): Translation and Commentary", in *The Book of Enoch or I Enoch* (ed. M. Black; Leiden: Brill, 1985), 386–415; J.-P. Verdet, *Histoire de l'astronomie ancienne et classique* (Paris: PUF, 1998).

placed the Sun so close to the Moon without any planets (Mercury and Venus) in between. The dialogue of Lucian shows in any case that the motif of the three heavens could be associated with the heavenly journey in a Greek context, exactly as it was associated with the heavenly journey in a Jewish context as we shall see below.

2. The heavenly journey in some Christian and Gnostic texts: A Jewish "tradition"?

1. The issue of the heavenly journey in Paul cannot be isolated from its widespread presence in early Christian and Gnostic texts. We find it for example in Revelation (4:1), in the *Ascension of Isaiah* (6–11), in the *Gospel of Thomas*,[12] in the *Gospel of the Savior*, or in Gnostic texts like *The Paraphrase of Sem* (NHC VII,1); the *"Zostrian" tractate* (NHC VIII,1); the *Coptic Apocalypse of Paul* (NHC V,2). How is this evidence situated in relation to the Greek, Hellenistic, and Roman texts dealing with the heavenly journey, on the one hand, and with antecedent, contemporary, and later Jewish texts, on the other?[13]

---

[12] Following A. De Conick, *Seek to See Him. Ascent and Vision Mysticism in the Gospel of Thomas* (Supplements to Vigiliae Christianae, 33; Leiden: Brill, 1996) in the *Gospel of Thomas* the heavenly journey is presupposed in vv. 50, 15, 83,59, 27, 37, 84.

[13] On the heavenly journey in ancient Jewish literature see L. Arcari, "Sui rapporti tra Apocalissi 'con viaggio ultraterreno' e 'senza viaggio ultraterreno'. Indagine per una 'storia' del 'genere apocalittico'," *Hen* 26 (2004): 64–84; C. A. Evans and Peter W. Flint, eds. *Eschatology, Messianism, and the Dead Sea Scrolls* (Grand Rapids, Mich.: Eerdmans, 1997); I. Gruenwald, *Apocalyptic and Merkavah Mysticism* (AGSU 14; Leiden: Brill, 1980); D. J. Halperin, *The Merkabah in Rabbinic Literature* (*AOS* 62; New Haven: American Oriental Society, 1980); M. Himmelfarb, *Ascent to Heaven in Jewish and Christian Apocalypses* (New York and Oxford: Oxford University Press, 1993); I. Knohl, "'By Three Days, Live': Messiahs, Resurrection, and Ascent to Heaven in *Hazon Gabriel*," *The Journal of Religion* 88 (2008): 147–158; N. Janowitz, *The Poetics of Ascent, Theories of Language in a Rabbinic Ascent Text* (Albany: SUNY Press, 1989); P. L. Lanfranchi, "Il sogno di Mosè nell'Exagoge di Ezechiele il tragico," Materia Giudaica 8 (2003): 103–112; R. Macy Lesses, *Ritual to Gain Power:*

In the Jewish literature of Antiquity there are several texts that speak of the heavenly journey. Some of them are antecedent to Second Corinthians, for example: Enoch 1–36; 40:52–54; 60–61 (*Book of Parables*); 72–82 (*Book of Luminaries*); *Testament of Levi* 2–5 (this latter is difficult to date, given the possibility of "Christian" insertions); the *Exagoge of Ezechiel* 68–89. On the heavenly journey at Qumran see 1QApGen II:23; 4Q534; 4Q529; see also 4Q491 fr. 11; 1Q16:4–26; 4Q286; 4Q405. Some are more or less contemporary, such as the texts of Philo. Others come immediately after Paul, and more or less contemporary to the *Ascension of Isaiah*, such as, the *Apocalypse of Abraham* 15–32; *2 Baruch*; *2 Enoch* 8:1; *Testament of Abraham* 10–15 (8–12 in version B); *Apocalypse of Zephaniah*. Others, again, are clearly later, such as *3 Enoch*, the hekhalotic texts, and Rabbinic passages recounting the journey to *pardes* (*tHag.* 2:2–5; *yHag.* 77b; *bHag.* 14b–15b; Cant.R. 1:28).

2. Are Second Corinthians and the early Christian and Gnostic texts part of an intra-Judaic linear *transmission* of the religious practice (or the literary *topos*) of the heavenly journey, as maintained by many specialists in Jewish and Christian literature? Or, conversely, do we need to make recourse to another model of

---

Angels, Incantations, and Revelation in Early Jewish Mysticism (Harvard Theological Studies; Harrisburg, Pennsylvania: Trinity Press International, 1998); G. W. E. Nickelsburg, *Resurrection, Immortality and Eternal Life in Intertestamental Judaism* (HTS 26; Cambridge, MA: Harvard University Press, 2006); A. J. Saldarini, "Apocalypses and 'Apocalyptic' in Rabbinic Literature and Mysticism," in Collins, *Apocalypse: The Morphology of A Genre*, 187– 205; G. Scholem, *Jewish Gnosticism, Merkabah Mysticism and the Talmudic Tradition* (2nd edn; New York: Jewish Theological Seminary of America, 1965); J. D. Tabor, "Returning to the Divinity: Josephus's Portrayal of the Disappearance of Enoch, Elijah, and Moses," *JBL* 108 (1989): 225–38; J. E. Wright, *The Early History of Heaven*, (New York: Oxford University Press, 2000); J. E. Wright, "Bibical Versus Israelite Images of the Heavenly Realm," *JSOT* 93 (2001): 55–71; Idem., "Whither Elijah? The Ascension of Elijah in Biblical and Extrabiblical Traditions," in *Things Revealed: Studies in Early Jewish and Christian Literature in Honor of Michael E. Stone* (ed. E. G. Chazon, D. Satran and R. A. Clemente; Leiden: Brill, 2004), 123–147; A. J. Saldarini, "Apocalypse and 'Apocalyptic' in Rabbinic Literature and Mysticism", in *Semeia* 14 (1979): 187–205.

interpretation, different from that of linear diachronic *tradition*? Can Paul's heavenly journey be understood within his Greco-Hellenistic, and Roman environment, of which Jewish groups and texts are also part?

Tradition is normally understood in terms of a linear diachronic transmission of particular concepts and practices within a given group. Through the idea of tradition, a community, people, or group of people, affirms its identity in time, and supports its claim to be the legitimate continuity with a community, people, of group of persons in the past. It presupposes that, in spite of modifications and variations, a given group maintains, through a traditional transmission, its identifying characteristics. Loyalty to and continuity with tradition therefore guarantee the maintenance of identity. However, the concept of tradition necessarily implies something more: that conceptions and practices transmitted within a given group are different from those of other groups that are characterized by other traditions. Thus, each group has a tradition of its own. This assumption has a number of important repercussions. Scholars who uphold the validity of the concept of tradition maintain, for example, that a particular text belongs to a particular group each time they encounter in it an element thought to belong to its particular tradition. Our aim is to examine critically the concept of linear diachronic tradition within the same group, at least in one particular regard.

Religious groups interact with each other in places where they live together, especially cities. In such contexts of religious and cultural plurality, the groups intercommunicate and the diverse religious conceptions and practices are mutually influential. In many cases, the effects resulting from contact with other contemporary groups are more important than traditions inherited from previous generations of the same community.

3. The heavenly journey in Greek and Latin texts

Within Greco-Roman culture the "heavenly journey" is attested in numerous texts.[14]

1. Poem of Parmenides[15]

The poem narrates a journey undertaken by Parmenides on a horse-drawn chariot, guided by young women. The chariot leaves the regions of the night and proceeds towards that of light. A bolted door is opened and Parmenides is received by a Goddess, who makes a fundamental philosophical revelation:

> you must be instructed on everything: on the heart without variation of the persuasive truth and on the opinions of mortal men in which there is no true certitude (vv. 28–30).[16]

It does not describe a crossing of the heavens, but rather an ascension and a passage from night to day, a transition from dark to glory. There is the description of the bolted door and of the heaven, seat of the divinity and place of revelation. Extraordinarily revealing in terms of relationships among different cultures, is the description of the chariot on which Parmenides travels: its wheels are of fire. It will not

---

[14] See H.W. Attridge, "Greek and Latin Apocalypses," in *Apocalypse: The Morphology of A Genre, Semeia* 14 (1979): 159–186. On the *Corpus Hermeticum*, see A. D. Nock and A. J. Festugière, *Corpus Hermeticum* (I–XIII, 1945. III–IV, 1954; Milano: Bompiani, 2005).

[15] M. Conche, *Parménide: Le poème: Fragments, Texte grec, traduction, présentation et commentaire* (Paris: PUF, 2004), 41–64; See also H. Diels and W. Kranz, *I presocratici: Testimonianze e frammenti*, (vol 1.; Ottava ed.; Bari-Roma: Laterza, 2004), 268–271.

[16] See the translation of L. Couloubaritis, *La pensée de Parménide: Troisième édition modifiée et augmentée de Mythe et Philosophie chez Parmenide* (Bruxelles: Ousia, 2008), 540: "tu dois t'enquérir de toutes choses, d'une part, du coeur inflexible d'Alètheia bien-arrondie, d'autre part, des considerations des mortels, en lesquelles il n'y a pas de créance vraie."

escape us that the chariot on which Elijah travels to heaven has wheels of fire (2 Kgs 2:11), and that the four wheels of the cherubim in Ezekiel (10:1–18) are also of fire. It cannot be merely coincidence that the heavenly journey in these two such different cultures is undertaken on chariots characterized by fire. A contact or an indirect relation must be hypothesized.

2. *Plato,* Republic *614b–621d*[17]

This is a fundamental text on which, however, we cannot dwell at length. The heavenly journey of Er, son of Armenius, is undertaken by him in the ten days between his being killed in battle and coming back to life, seemingly suggesting that only the dead can make such a journey or that only physical conditions can permit it. It is the soul of Er that makes the journey after its detachment from him (614b). The heavens are described, and mention is made of the harmonious music they emit (617b). The revelation concerns the destiny of man: the punishments and rewards awaiting him, and the reincarnation undergone by souls.

3. *Cicero,* Somnium Scipionis[18]

In this text, written almost a century before Second Corinthians, we find ourselves in a Roman setting. In heaven, Scipio has the vision of his ancestor and his father; he sees the heavens and listens to the music of the heavenly spheres. It is interesting that Macrobius, who transmits Cicero's *De Republica,* sets the *Somnium Scipionis* in relation to Plato's story of Er (Cicero, *Republic* VI, 8). It is hardly by chance that both heavenly journeys are situated at the end of two works that deal with political life (Plato's, with the story of Er, and Cicero's, with Scipio's dream). The description of the beginning of

---

[17] Plato, *La repubblica* (ed. Giuseppe Lozza; Milano: Mondadori, 1990), 822–845.

[18] Cicero, *La république* (Tome II, Livres II-VI ; tr. Esther Bréguet, (Paris: Les Belles Lettres, 2002), 103–118.

the heavenly journey shows a certain interest on the part of Cicero in the physical condition that can induce a revelatory dream.[19] In his journey Scipio obtains the revelation of the meaning of life: the body is a prison from which man must be freed, after death, in order to return to the place where souls originate, the highest heaven. It is therefore necessary to know "the way that leads to heaven." This way consists of the exercise of justice and piety, especially towards the fatherland (*patria*):

> But, Scipio, like this your grandfather, like me, your father, cherish justice and that sacred observance of duty to your kind, which, while of great worth toward parents and family, is of supreme value toward your fatherland (*patria*). Such a life is the way to heaven (*ea vita via est in caelum*), and to this assembly of those who have already lived, and, released from the body, inhabit the place which you now see,—it was that circle that shines forth among the stars in the most dazzling white,—which you have learned from the Greeks to call the Milky Way (*Somnium Scipionis*, 16).

There is no description of any journey through the heavens. In his dream he finds himself already in heaven. The heavens are however described in sections 17–19. They are formed of seven spheres or circles, above which is the highest heaven—the Milky Way—which is God himself (*summus ipse deus*). The seven spheres "have a retrograde movement, opposite to that of the heavens" (*Somnium Scipionis*, 17). As they move, the spheres emit a cosmic music (as is the case in many texts, from Plato to the hermetic writings).

> tantus est totius mundi incitatissima conversione sonitus, ut eum aures hominum capere non possint
>
> (*Somnium Scipionis*, 19)

---

[19] On the dream as a means of revelation see *De Divinatione*, XX, 39 ff.

We cannot avoid underlining the similarity between the sentence *ut eum aures hominum capere non possint* and Paul's words in 2 Cor 12:4: "(he) heard inexpressible words, that no man is permitted to pronounce." In these chapters of the *Dream* we encounter also the description of a range of psychosomatic experiences undergone by Scipio in the heavens.[20]

4. *Plutarch's* The Demon of Socrates[21]

Written around 90 C. E., this work is roughly coeval with the Gospel of Luke, and the *Vision of Isaiah* (in chapters 6–11 of the *Ascension of Isaiah*, discussed below), and was probably written a little before the Gospel of John. It tells of Timarchus descending into the crypt of Trophonius.[22]

> Timarchus… in his desire to learn the nature of Socrates' demon, … descended into the crypt of Trophonius, first performing the rites that are customary at the oracle. He remained underground two nights and a day… He said that on descending into the oracular crypt his first experience was a profound darkness; next, after a prayer, he lay a long time not clearly aware whether he was awake or dreaming. It did seem to him, however, that at the same moment he heard a crash and was

---

[20] On the ascent of the soul of the just man to the heaven where the just men of the past live, see also Seneca, *Consolatio ad Marciam* 25.1–2. Lucio Anneo Seneca, *I Dialoghi* (vol. 2; ed. Giovanni Viansino; Milano: Mondadori, 1993), 89. See Seneca, *Dialogues: Consolations* (tr. René Waltz; Paris : Les Belles Lettres, 2003), 50–51.

[21] Plutarch, *On the Sign of Socrates* (*De genio Socratis*) in *Moralia* (vol. 7 ; tr. P. H. De Lacy and B. Einarson (Loeb Classical Library; Cambridge, MA: Harvard University Press, 1968), 361–598; Plutarch, *Oeuvres Morales* (vol. 8 ; tr. Jean Hani (Paris : Les Belles Lettres, 2003); Plutarch, *Il Demone di Socrate : I ritardi della punizione divina, con un saggio di Dario del Corno* (Milano: Adelphi, 2005).

[22] Plutarch, *Il Demone di Socrate*, 102; see J. Hani, *Plutarque: Le Démon de Socrate* (*Moralia* vol. 8 ; Paris : Les Belles Lettres, 2003), 108. Plutarch reports another description of a heavenly journey in *The Delays in Divine Vengeance* 22–33; Plutarch, *Il Demone di Socrate*, 164–175. See also Segal, "Heavenly Ascent," 1346.

> struck on the head, and that the sutures parted and released his soul (*psychê*). As it withdrew and mingled joyfully with air that was translucent and pure, it felt in the first place that now, after long being cramped, it had again found relief, and was growing larger than before, spreading out like a sail.
>
> (*The Demon of Socrates*, 590B)

He then lies down and, half-awake, for two nights and a day, experiences a journey through the heavens. During the journey, he learns the structure of the cosmos (Hades, the Earth, and the heavens above), how the heavenly bodies were generated, and the identities of their guardians and protectors. Above all, he learns of the nature of man (soul, intellect, and the demon), the destinies of souls, how they are united with and freed from the body, and the cognitive capacities of man.

At the end of the journey, Plutarch once again describes Timarchus' psychosomatic experience:

> When the voice ceased Timarchus desired to turn (he said) and see who the speaker was. But once more he felt a sharp pain in his head, as though it had been violently compressed, and he lost all recognition and awareness of what was going on about him; but he presently recovered and saw that he was lying in the crypt of Trophonius near the entrance, at the very spot where he had first laid himself down.
>
> (*On the Demon of Socrates*, 592 E)

Throughout this array of texts, there are important references to the actual psychosomatic experience that take place during the initial moment or preparation, the "journey" itself, and the final moment of reawakening.

Not surprisingly, the journey always leads to the knowledge of an esoteric doctrine concerning the cosmic structure, man's nature and ultimate destiny. We shall return to this and see that the doctrine may end up counterbalancing popular representations or traditional visions of the world, conferring authority on specific persons (who become specialists) and legitimizing their doctrine and functions.

5. *The Liturgy of Mithras*

We also wish to mention the so-called Liturgy of Mithras. The text explains to the initiates who are to ascend to the heavens how the journey unfolds. It has often been challenged that this text concerns Mithraic ritual. The soul's ascent to the heavens was in any case envisaged by Mithraic ritual, as was also suggested by Celsus and Porphyry (Origen, *Contra Celsum* 6.21–22; Porphyry, *De antro nympharum*, 5–6). According to Celsus, in the initiation of Mithras

> here is a symbolic representation of the two movements in the heavens, that of the stars and that of the planets, and also of the passage of the *psychê* through them. The figuration is that of a ladder with seven doors. Above them there is an eighth door (*Contra Celsum* 6.22).[23]

The Mithraic theory of the initiate's ascension through the seven heavens[24] had certainly been well known from the first century B. C. E., as proven by its depiction in the mosaic of Mithras at Ostia Antica.[25]

What is important is that according to many studies[26] the heavenly journey in Jewish hekhalotic texts seems to depend on Greek texts that have clear connections with the *Mithras Liturgy*. This is another demonstration of the fact that the Judaic experience of

---

[23] See Origen, *Contro Celso* (ed. Pietro Ressa; Brescia: Morcelliana, 2000), 446–449 and 447 note 125; see also E.V. Gallagher, *Divine Man or Magician?: Celsus and Origen on Jesus* (SBLDS 64; Missoula, MT: Society of Biblical Literature, 1982); Porfirio, *L'antro delle ninfe* (ed. Laura Simonini; Milano: Adelphi, 1986).

[24] See G. Sfameni Gasparro, "I misteri di Mitra," in *Il Rito segreto: Misteri in Grecia e a Roma* (ed. A. Bottini; Milano: Electa, 2005), 99–101. See also D. M. Ulansey, *Mithras and Perseus: Mithraic Astronomy and the Anatolian Perseus Cult* (Ph.D. Diss, Princeton University, 1984).

[25] *Papyri Graecae Magicae: Die griechischen Zauberpapyri* (ed. Karl Preisendanz, 2nd edn., ed. Albert Henrichs; vol. 1; Stuttgart: Teubner, 1973), 88–101; H. D. Betz, *The "Mithras Liturgy": Text, Translation, and Commentary* (Studien und Texte zu Antike und Christentum,18; Tübingen: Mohr Siebeck, 2003); A. Dieterich, *Eine Mithrasliturgie* (3rd edn., ed. O. Weinreich; Leipzig: Teubner, 1923).

[26] See Macy Lesses, *Ritual Practices to Gain Power*, 336–344.

the heavenly journey is not independent from Greek and Roman religious practices.

6. *Philo of Alexandria*

The experience of the heavenly journey is encountered in another first-century Jew, perhaps a generation older than Paul, Philo of Alexandria, a figure steeped in Hellenic culture.[27]

In *De opificio mundi*, commenting the passage in Genesis according to which God made man in his own "image and likeness," Philo states that the intellect (*nous*) of man

> is invisible (*aoratos*), though it sees everything itself; and it has an essence which is indiscernible (*adêlon*), though it can discern the essences of all other things, and making for itself by art (*technais*) and science (*epistêmais*) all sorts of roads leading in divers directions, and all plain; it traverses land and sea, investigating everything which is contained in either element.
>
> (*Opif.* 69)

In fact,

> *being raised* up on wings, and so surveying and contemplating the air, and all the commotions to which it is subject, *it is borne upwards* to the higher firmament, and to the revolutions of the heavenly bodies. And also being itself involved in the revolutions of the planets and fixed stars according to the perfect laws of music, and being led on by love, which is the guide of wisdom, it proceeds onwards till, having surmounted all essence intelligible by the external senses, it comes to aspire to such as is perceptible only by the intellect.
>
> (*Opif.* 70)

---

[27] Cf. P. Borgen, "Heavenly Ascent in Philo: An Examination of Selected Passages," in *The Pseudepigrapha and Early Biblical Interpretation* (ed. J. H. Charlesworth and C. A. Evans; Sheffield: Sheffield Academic Press, 1993), 246–268; M. Dean-Otting, *Heavenly Journeys: A Study of the Motif in Hellenistic Jewish Literature* (Frankfurt: Peter Lang, 1984).

On contemplating tangible things in all their reality and beauty, the soul, says Philo, is invaded by a state of enthusiasm:

> it becomes *seized* with a sort of sober intoxication like the zealots engaged in the Corybantian festivals, and *yields to enthusiasm, becoming filled with another desire*, and a more excellent longing, by which *it is conducted* onwards to the very summit of such things as are perceptible only to the intellect, till it appears to be reaching the great King himself.
>
> (*Opif.* 71)

Finally, the intellect is filled with divine splendour:

> And while it is eagerly longing to behold him pure and unmingled, rays of divine light *are poured forth upon it* like a torrent, so as to bewilder the eyes of its intelligence by their splendour
>
> (*Opif.* 71)

The verbs in the passive—uplifted, carried, grasped, filled, driven (*artheis*, *pheretai*, *kataschetheis*, *gemistheis*, *parapemphtheis*)—denote the actions through which the intellect is forced upwards, even if what moves it is its own internal divine desire. The ascent is not only produced by the intellect, but is induced by the divine power that resides within it, a power set free by philosophical contemplation and by the heavenly journey itself, which brings the intellect within a profoundly different environment from that of the earth.[28]

It is also crucial to note that the description of the soul's psychosomatic state is understood in the light of the religious practice of corybants. It is this current religious practice (and not only middle-Platonic philosophy) that allows the interpretation of the intellect's experience. It is therefore clear that Philo moved outside of any presumed Jewish "tradition" of the heavenly journey.

Philo also speaks of the heavenly journey in *De Specialibus Legibus* 3.1–2, where he reports a personal experience. His jour-

---

[28] See also *Det.* 89 and M. Dean-Otting, *Heavenly Journeys*, 32–33.

ney consists of his soul being carried to "the sun the moon, and to the whole heaven, and the whole world":

> I appeared to be raised on high and borne aloft by a certain inspiration (*epitheiasmos*) of the soul (*psychê*), and to dwell in the regions of the sun and moon, and to associate with the whole heaven, and the whole universal world.
>
> (*Spec. Leg.* 3.1)

From on high, Philo looks down upon earthly things:

> looking down from above, from the air, and straining the eye of my mind as from a watchtower, I surveyed the unspeakable contemplations (*tas amythêtous theôrias*) of all the things on the earth, and looked upon myself as happy as having forcibly escaped from all the evil fates
>
> (*Spec. Leg.* 3.2)

Certainly the "unspeakable" contemplations, or ones that "cannot be told in a story," show a similarity with the "unutterable words" of Paul. However, we must guard against any ingenuous direct comparison between the two texts.

Philo's heavenly journey is no sudden occurrence, but one that is prepared for and induced by a philosophical meditation focusing only on divine objects (*theiois logois kai dogmasin*). It is an experience that arises at a certain point within this philosophical quest. It is aroused by the soul's urge towards the divine: "I appeared to be raised on high and borne aloft by a certain inspiration (*epitheiasmos*) of the soul (*psychê*)" (*Spec.* 3,1). The journey permits a vision of all the world's affairs, contemplated from the highest heavens. The soul perceives that it is in the heavens, within a co-natural state, and understands that it has escaped the mortal dimension of the world. We are not far from the spiritual and religious atmosphere of Cicero's *Dream of Scipio*. The heavenly journey appears in Philo at the center of a religious experience profoundly rooted in a widely diffused religious atmosphere. It is not an eccentric or marginal practice.

Cities are the place *par excellence* in which different groups could participate in this common religious atmosphere. In the cities different communities coexisted and interacted, reinterpreting in their own ways sensibilities and issues, behavioural models and common religious practices. The plurality and religious coexistence of different groups in the same city (with all the inevitable issues of comparison, identity change, transformations and conflicts) constitute the context that justifies the use of widespread cultural schemes.

In our argumentation the case of Philo also has the function of demonstrating that a first-century Judean could speak of the heavenly journey as the centre of his own religious experience without referring to the apocalyptic "tradition" of the heavenly journey, but simply because he was in deep relation with Hellenistic religious practices and philosophy.

4. Paul's heavenly journey

1. Only three heavens?

A long-standing question is whether Paul speaks of one heavenly journey to the third heaven, and of a second journey to paradise, or whether he is referring to a single experience.[29] In favor of a single journey is the fact that some Jewish texts locate paradise in the third heaven.[30] Now, according to the Gospel of Luke

---

[29] Also in support of the hypothesis of two journeys could be the explicit mention of a journey to the third heaven and another to paradise, and the fact that Paul speaks twice of a plurality of visions and revelations (12:1–7). However, the plural could mean that Paul wants to speak here of only one journey, even though he had the experience of many other heavenly ascents. See M. E. Thrall, *The Second Epistle to the Corinthians* (vol. 2; Edinburgh: T&T Clark, 2000), 783; P. Barnett, *The Second Epistle to the Corinthians* (Grand Rapids Michigan: Eerdmans, 1984); Ph.E. Hughes, *Paul's Second Epistle to the Corinthians* (London and Edinburgh: Marshall, Morgan & Scott, 1962).

[30] See J. D. Tabor, "Heaven, Ascent to," in *ABD*, vol. 3: 91–94; See also I. De Vuippens, *Le Paradis Terrestre au troisième ciel: Exposé historique d'une conception chrétienne des premiers siècles* (Paris: Librairie Saint-François d'Assise – Freiburg Suisse, Librairie de l'Oeuvre de S.-Paul, 1925).

paradise is the place where Christ and the just men reside ("today you will be with me in Paradise," Luke 23:43). In Rev 2:7, it is the place where the just believers, the "victors," will eat the fruit of the tree of life. According to Luke 16:22, it is probably the home of the Patriarchs: the poor man of the parable is carried by angels on his death to eat at the place of honor, near Abraham. The numerous Jewish texts that speak of paradise are far from agreeing on its location and on the people who reside there. It is therefore difficult to establish to what extent Paul shares the opinions expressed in the various texts.[31] If during his heavenly journey Paul sees the Lord Jesus and receives his revelations, must we suppose that the location of the Lord, for him, is paradise? In this case, paradise could be for Paul the highest heaven, and this means that he shares an astronomy of the three heavens. Or, is the Lord's location in the third heaven provisional, with him remaining in that heaven while struggling for the final victory? No element allows us to resolve this hypothesis.

A cosmology of only three heavens (as also found in Lucian, with the Moon, Sun and the supreme heaven where God abides), is more probable in Paul than the idea that other heavens exist above the third heaven. The *Coptic Apocalypse of Paul* (NHC V, 19. 20–25) seems to attribute the latter meaning to the passage, but that depends on the fact that its author has a different cosmology from that of Paul. The later *Ascension of Isaiah*, deeply rooted in Judaic cosmological conceptions, speaks of seven (or better nine heavens). In the *Testament of Levi* 2–3 (version a), the third heaven is the highest.[32] The *Second Book of Enoch* (version a, 3–22) has seven

---

[31] See J.H. Charlesworth, "Paradise," in *ABD*, vol. 5: 154–155.

[32] See 2: 9–10; 3,4. See P. Sacchi, *Apocrifi dell'Antico Testamento* (vol. 1 ; Torino : UTET), 790–793. In 3:5–8 the text speaks of three heavens under God's heaven. The holy astronomy of the *Testament of Levi* is therefore unclear. It seems that the saints live in the third heaven, which could mean that paradise is located in the third heaven. "Le texte primitif du Testament de Lévi ne comportait, en effet, que trois cieux, puisque, selon I,8, le troisième ciel, dont la hauteur est infinie, ne peut, de toute évidence, être que le dernier" (M.Philonenko, *Testament des douze patriarches*, in *La Bible: Écrits Intertestamentaires I* (ed. A.Dupont-Sommer and M.Philonenko; Paris: Gallimard, 1987), 836.

heavens, but paradise is located in the third heaven (8.1), while the moon and sun are situated in the fourth (11.1). In the *Third Book of Baruch* (7:2), which visualizes seven heavens, the third is that of the Sun.[33] In the Apocalypse of Moses (*Life of Adam and Eve*) 37.40, paradise is also in the third heaven. All this confirms that different cosmologies could coexist within Jewish culture.

According to A. Panaino the division into three heavens is Mesopotamian in origin and influenced Iran, India, and also Greece, starting with Anaximander and Parmenides.[34] Basically, many observations converge towards the affirmation that the three-heaven astronomy supposed by Paul is Mesopotamian in origin, and influenced various cultural areas, including the Greek one, as seen in Lucian. At the very least, as a minimum conclusion, it can be asserted that the presence of a three-heaven cosmology does not confine Paul's statements in 2 Cor 12:2 exclusively within a Jewish environment.

2. Paul's journey as an experience

The description of the heavenly journey of Paul in Second Corinthians is the narration of a real experience[35] and not a purely

---

[33] See the translation of J. Riaud, *Apocalypse grècque de Baruch*, in *La Bible: Écrits Intertestamentaires I* (A. Dupont-Sommer and Marc Philonenko, eds.; Paris: Gallimard, 1987), 1157.

[34] A. Panaino, "Uranographica Uranica 1: The Three Heavens in the Zoroastrian Tradition and the Mesopotamian Background," in *Au carrefour des religions: Mélanges offerts à Philippe Gignoux, Res Orientales* (vol. 7; 1995), 215–219. See also W. Boussett, "Die Himmelsreise der Seele," *ARW* 4 (1901): 136–69 [228–273 (repr. Darmstadt. 1960)]; L. Bieler, *THEIOS ANER: Das Bild des "Göttlichen Menschen" in Spätantike und Frühchristentum* (2 vols.; Vienna, 1935–36); C. Colpe, "Die 'Himmelreise der Seele' als philosophisches und religionsgeschichtliches Problem," in *Festschrift für Joseph Klein zum 70. Geburtstag* (ed. E. Fries; Göttingen: Vandenhoeek Vandenhoeck und Ruprecht, 1967), 85–104; R. Reitzenstein, *Hellenistic Mystery-Religions: Their Basic Ideas and Significance* (tr. J. E. Steely; PTMS 15; Pittsburgh: Pickwick, 1978); E. Rohde, *Psyche: The Cult of Souls and Belief in Immortality Among the Greeks* (New York: Harper and Row, 1966).

[35] M. E. Thrall, *The Second Epistle to the Corinthians*, vol. 2, 775–776 ("actual personal experience"); A. Pitta, *La seconda lettera ai Corinzi* (Roma: Borla, 2006), 483.

literary representation or a story about the heavenly journey of some person from the past. It is one of the few direct testimonies reporting what a person has really undergone, also providing far from secondary details of how it came to pass. "Since he is reckoning his own experience, he can date the event: '14 years ago.'"[36] The experience reported by Paul must have taken place around the beginning of the forties, if this part of Second Corinthians was written in August or September of 56, as dated by Margaret Thrall.[37]

It is likely, although not certain, that the object of the visions and revelations obtained through the heavenly journey is Jesus himself. In 12:1 Paul speaks of "*visions* and [...] *revelations* of the Lord." Is the genitive subjective or objective?[38] Is it Jesus who permits the visions and revelations, or do they have the Lord himself as their object? We lean towards the latter hypothesis, but without certainty.

Paul's claim that he does not know whether the heavenly journey took place with his body or not may mean either that his bodily perception was suspended, or that a loss of memory was subsequently undergone. We are very close to Plutarch's description of Timarchus' experience. Paul does remember, nonetheless, that he heard "unutterable words, *arrêta rhêmata*."[39]

---

[36] Thrall, *The Second Epistle to the Corinthians*, vol. 2, 782.

[37] M.E. Thrall, *The Second Epistle to the Corinthians* (vol. 1; Edinburgh: T&T Clark, 1994), 3–77; see also B. Heininger, "Paulus und Philo als Mystiker? Himmelreisen in Vergleich (2 Kor 12,2–4; SpecLeg III 1-6)," in *Philo und das Neue Testament: Wechselseitige Wahrnehmungen* (ed. R. Deines and K.-W. Niebuhr; Tübingen: Mohr Siebeck, 2004), 191. We do not agree with the opinion that the intention of Paul is to reduce the importance of the experience of the heavenly ascent or of the revelation of "unspeakable" words (against, e.g., Heininger, "Paulus und Philo," 192). The opinion of Smith in "Ascent to the Heavens" (63–67) that Paul speaks here not of his heavenly journey, but of Jesus's seems to us unsustainable.

[38] We disagree with the suggestion of a "general" genitive in which Jesus would be in the same time subject and object (Pitta, *La seconda lettera ai Corinzi*, 487).

[39] On *arrêta rhêmata* see Thrall, *The Second Epistle to the Corinthians*, vol. 2, 795–796 and G. Lo Russo, *La Seconda Lettera ai Corinzi: Introduzione, versione e commento* (Bologna: EDB, 2007), 292.

Paul's description of his experience is of extreme importance. First and foremost, he is aware of the existence of different ways of experiencing and speaking of the fact of being displaced to the heavens. As A. A. Orlov rightly notes, Paul shows a "knowledge of the two types of ascent, inside the body and also outside it."[40] Paul does not avoid representing his experience to the Corinthians, as if the soul alone could have made the journey, while his body stayed on earth, exactly as imagined by Philo. If Philo imagined that the eyes of the soul could contemplate supernatural phenomena, why can we not think that Paul also imagined the ears of the soul hearing those unspeakable words? It is possible that Paul makes reference to a distinction that was known and discussed in Corinth. Resorting to the affirmation that only God knows, he seems to show the intention to avoid a confrontation on this subject. The body is, however, involved in both cases. In the first case, when the journey takes place "outside" or "without" the body, the body remains on earth, and undergoes particular modifications. In the second, it is the whole body that journeys through the heavens, and its functions are necessarily altered in the otherworldly situation.[41] The deep division of cases is intended to avoid the necessity for any further clarification but it also allows for a wide range of variations. Every other experience may be included within the two extremes.

In 2 Cor 12:1–4 the double confession of an imperfect knowledge of how the journey came about ("in the body (*en sômati*) I do not know; or out of (12:2) (or without, 12:3) the body I do not know") reveals a complex state of mind that arises during the

---

[40] A. A. Orlov, *The Enoch-Metatron Tradition* (Tübingen: Mohr, 2005), 183. P. Schäfer (in "New Testament and Hekhalot Literature: The Journey into Heaven in Paul and in Merkavah Mysticism," in Idem., *Hekhalot Studies* (Tübingen: Mohr, 1988), 237) thinks that for Paul both solutions are possible. See also Pitta, *La seconda lettera ai Corinzi*, 489. In *2 Enoch*, following Orlov (*The Enoch-Metatron Tradition*, 182–184) the ascent to the heavens takes place with the body, but this fact represents an evolution in the so-called Enochic tradition.

[41] The use of the third person derives from the nature of the experience itself, that is from the ecstatic phenomenon of dislocation of the ego (Thrall, *The Second Epistle to the Corinthians*, vol. 2, 782).

heavenly journey, in which pure intellectual knowledge is challenged. Paul experiences knowledge in a specific form. He knows that he cannot understand. The affirmation is of key significance, precisely because it is repeated twice.

The fact that Paul speaks of his own experience as if it were that of another person is intended to underscore the idea that the subject is governed by a supernatural power. An experience that takes place during a lack of consciousness of the subject may easily be attributed to the intervention of supernatural forces. Thrall suggests that the use of the third person "originally derives from the nature of the experience itself, that is, from the ecstatic phenomenon of self-dislocation."[42]

All these remarks about body and bodily experience lead us to exclude those interpretations that see this passage purely as a literary motif.

3. The centrality of the heavenly journey in Paul's experience

Pauline communities discussed at length about prophetic collective liturgies (1 Cor 12–14), and in First Corinthians 2:6-16 Paul explicitly speaks of revelations experienced together with a close group of "perfect ones." The fact that the heavenly journey of 2 Cor 12:1–4 seems to take place as an individual experience, without a community participation, does not mean that we have to distinguish it too sharply from the collective supernatural manifestations of the Pauline churches. *Glossolalia* also can arise without any community function (in this case, the speaker does not even have to convey the received revelation to the assembly, 1 Cor 14:27–28). The polemical and apologetic context of 2 Cor 12:1–4 shows that Paul is playing on his experience of the heavenly journey in a relational community context. The passage is *polemical* insofar as Paul is arguing against his opponent preachers who have arrived in Corinth, boasting to be "*Ebraioi, israêlitai,* [...] *minis-*

---

[42] Thrall, *The Second Epistle to the Corinthians,* vol. 2, 782.

ters of Christ" (2 Cor 11:22–23). But the passage is also *apologetic*, since Paul defends himself by highlighting his extraordinary career as a preacher devoted to his mission until death, and by claiming to have had extraordinary revelations and visions "of the Lord" as well as a personal revelation of Jesus.

In any case the heavenly journey of 2 Cor 12:1–4 cannot be considered as an exceptional event in Paul's life. Supernatural revelations are at the center of his experience as Jesus' follower. His decision to adhere to Jesus Christ depends on a supernatural revelation (Gal 1:16). The content of his "gospel" is given to him by a special revelation (Gal 1:12). When Paul must decide something relevant to his apostolic activity he makes appeal to a revelation (Gal 2:2). He receives personal direct revelations from the Kyrios Jesus (2 Cor 12:7), he declares that he has received many visions and revelations from the Lord Jesus (2 Cor 12:1), he wants the members of his churches to receive supernatural knowledge through the gift of the Spirit (1 Cor 1:4–7), he encourages them to seek the gift of prophecy (1 Cor 14:1–5); he recognizes that the prophets of his churches can have revelations from Christ (1 Cor 14:37; Phil 3:15). The passage of 1 Cor 2:6–16 shows that particular members of the Pauline churches ("the perfect ones") could have access, under the guidance of Paul, to a collective supernatural knowledge of the mind of Christ, through which they received a special "God's wisdom, secret and hidden, which God decreed before the ages for our glory… And we speak of these things in words not taught by human wisdom but taught by the Spirit, interpreting spiritual things to those who are spiritual" (1 Cor 2:7). The knowledge received by Paul in his heavenly journey seems not so different from this kind of wisdom, since what it is possible to learn in the third heaven or in Paradise is not so different from "God's wisdom, secret and hidden, which God decreed before the ages."

2 Cor 12:1–4 shows the presence of a profound combination of Greco-Roman and Judaic elements. The pattern of the heavenly journey, the motif of the third heaven, the presence of just men of the past in heaven, the bodily and mental modifications at the beginning, during and after the experience, the fact of hearing

unutterable words and knowledge during the journey, the relevance of this kind of experience are all widespread elements in Greco-Roman culture. The mention of paradise is the only element that we cannot find in Greco-Roman texts. This shows how a common religious pattern could be adapted in a particular religious context like Corinth, where Judeans, Romans, and Greeks coexisted, also in the Pauline house-churches.

It is therefore probable that the recourse of 2 Cor 12:1–4 to the "heavenly journey"—with an apologetic and legitimating function—sprang from the fact that members of the Corinth *ekklêsia* practiced this type of religious experience, on account of their connection with a Greco-Roman form of religiosity, or from the likelihood that the Jewish adversaries themselves had boasted of such experiences. Whatever the case, the scenario is one of a religious form that was quite widespread among the various religious groups present in Corinth.[43]

The twentieth-century debate on Paul's mysticism is indeed quite impressive. In our opinion in 2 Cor 12:1–12 there emerges a religiosity whose fundamental objective is to attain a direct contact with the supernatural that takes place in the interiority of the human being. The formula "I know in Christ, *en christô*" may justify a mystic interpretation of Paul's religiosity. The fact of being incorporated "in Christ" places the individual under the action of a supernatural power. In 2 Cor 12: 1–4 the effect of this incorporation is that the power of Christ transports Paul to the third heaven. Of extreme significance is the religious theory according to which "'My grace [it is Christ that speaks] is sufficient for you, for power is made perfect in weakness.' I [it is Paul that speaks] will therefore boast all the more gladly of my weaknesses, so that the power of Christ may dwell in me" (2 Cor 12:9).

[43] We can also add that in later time Apuleius locates precisely in Corinth his initiation in Isis' mysteries (in which he seems to have made the experience of the heavenly journey). On the religious relation between Jews, early Jesus followers and the so-called "Pagans" see also G. Sfameni-Gasparro, *Oracoli. Profeti. Sibille. Rivelazione e salvezza nel mondo antico*, (Roma: Libreria Ateneo Salesiano, 2002), 61–112.

The weakness/power opposition is formulated in theological terms. But, through it, Paul refers to the concrete facts of his experience. The weakness of the flesh, of the body and bodily functions, is exemplified by his autobiographical experiences. The experiential basis of such theological formulations lies in the fact of setting oneself in a condition of weakness in order to be possessed by the supernatural power (through revelations, thaumaturgical and prophetic capacities). The heavenly ascension is a manifestation, among others, of the supernatural *dynamis* which overwhelms the individual in his weakness.[44]

It would be ingenuous to object that Paul's heavenly journey is not prepared or induced as in Philo, because it occurs suddenly and by God's work. In 1 Cor 12:1–4 Paul does not set out to reveal how the experience can be obtained, nor to describe its content. The formula "in Christ" is a condensation of all kinds of religious attitudes, rituals and practices that allow the individual to be incorporated in Christ, to remain within him, and to be open to his power. The heavenly journey could be prepared or permitted by one of these practices.

---

[44] According to Heininger ("Paulus und Philo," 203) some elements are typical of Jewish apocalyptic literature: that the aim of the journey is to reach paradise, that Paul does not know whether the journey took place with or without the body, and the interest in the multiplicity of heavens (ibid., 192), but these elements are also found in Greco-Roman literature. Neither do we agree with the outlook of P. R. Gooder (*Only the Third Heaven? 2 Corinthians 12:1–10 and Heavenly Ascent* (London and New York: T&T Clark, 2006), 31), who limits himself to comparing Paul's heavenly ascent with Jewish apocalyptic texts alone, or with texts of the "Judeo-Christian tradition." His comparison excludes the *Testament of Abraham* and *Apocalypse of Abraham* on the grounds that they do not contain a proper description of the ascent through the heavens. But in reality, neither does 2 Cor 12:1–3.

5. THE ASCENSION OF ISAIAH AND THE GOSPEL OF THE SAVIOR

The profound interrelation between different cultural environments in the conception and practice of the heavenly journey is confirmed in early Christianity after Paul.

1. In this regard, the *Ascension of Isaiah* is of extreme relevance. The text is datable between the end of the first century and the beginning of the second, perhaps originating from Antioch in Syria.[45] Its historical importance lies in its detailed description of the way in which the seer experiences the heavenly journey. The phenomenon is presented as an ecstatic experience: the journey takes place during a collective prophetic liturgy in which a prophet is prophesying; he suddenly ceases to speak, his eyes open, and his breath is suspended; the journey takes place outside of the body, which remains on earth while the spirit is carried to the heavens. All this suggests the hypothesis that the text is the product of prophetic environments that are referring to their own practices, and not merely citing literary or abstract theological motifs. The fact that in the *Ascension of Isaiah* the heavenly journey takes place outside of the body allows a better understanding of Paul's assertion.

The description of the ascent through the heavens, with their physical and religious features (the guardians of each heaven, the doors, the angels living there, and so on), presents literary motifs already found in Jewish and Greco-Roman texts. Literary relationships with Jewish ascension texts are undeniable, but there is also close relationship with the Greco-Roman environment. The *Ascension of Isaiah* has a cosmology of seven heavens, which become nine if we include the "air" and the heaven where God lives, exactly as in Cicero's *Dream of Scipio*. However, the seven heavens are not conceived of as divinities: in each of them reside hosts of angels, situated to the right and left of an angelic throne

[45] P. Bettiolo, A. Kossova, C. Leonardi, E. Norelli, L. Perrone (eds.), *Ascensio Isaiae* (2 vols.; CCSA, 7–8; Turnhout: Brepols, 1995).

presiding over each heaven. The difference in relation to the cosmology of Paul demonstrates that we cannot speak of an early Christian "tradition" of the heavenly journey. Each text reacts to the influence of its cultural and historical context.

Recourse to the cultural motif of the heavenly journey arises, in the *Ascension of Isaiah*, in connection with a rather localised debate, involving discussions between early Christian groups and their Jewish milieu, or even among the different strands of early Christianity. Such debates were perhaps characteristic of the Johannine prophetic environments of Antioch in Syria.[46] One reason why recourse to the heavenly journey becomes necessary is the need to show that the highest heaven is not only the abode of God and the Holy Spirit, but also (and always) of the Beloved, who will descend to earth transforming himself into various angelic figures, until eventually assuming the human form of Jesus. The fact that the biblical prophet Isaiah, on arriving in heaven, finds the Beloved next to God, aims to demonstrate the pre-existence of Jesus Christ, consequently legitimating faith in him, and the christological interpretation of the biblical prophecy. However, Isaiah's encounter with the Beloved above the heavens, many centuries before his incarnation, also served to settle debates concerning Jesus' identity: Messiah, man, son of Man, *logos*, pre-existing son, are some of the options available.

The medium chosen for the task—the heavenly journey and prophetic ecstasy—shows how widely accepted a practice it was among certain Jewish and early Christian groupings, and even among some Hellenistic circles in Syria around the end of the first

---

[46] The second part of the *Ascension* (chapters 6–11: the so-called *Vision*) was known by the Gospel of John 12:41; see M. Pesce, "Isaia disse queste cose perché vide la sua gloria e parlò di lui (Gv 12,41): Il *Vangelo di Giovanni* e *l'Ascensione di Isaia*", *Studia Patavina* 50 (2003): 649–666. On the constellation of Johannine writings (to which the *Ascension of Isaiah* belongs), see A. Destro and M. Pesce, "Constellations of Texts in Early Christianity: The Gospel of the Savior and Johannist Writings," *Annali di storia dell'Esegesi* 22 /2 (2005): 337–353; A. Destro and M. Pesce, "Continuity or Discontinuity Between Jesus and Groups of his Followers? Practices of Contact with the Supernatural", *Annali di Storia dell'Esegesi* 24 (2007): 37–58.

century. This cultural schema seems functional and flexible enough to assume specific roles in different specific contexts.

2. In the *Gospel of the Savior*, published for the first time in 1999 by Charles W. Hedrick and Paul A. Mirecki,[47] the heavenly journey plays a particularly important role: it is mentioned no less than three times (100. 33–35; 113.1–59; 122.61–64). The most important passage is the first (following the translation and new numeration of S. Emmel):

> *26:28–36* 28 [. . . *12± lines untranslatable* . . .] *(B 100:ii)* on the mountain. 29 We became as spiritual bodies. Our eyes opened wide in every direction. The whole place was revealed before us. 30 We [saw] the heavens, and they [opened] up one after another. 31 The guardians

---

[47] See W. Hedrick and P. Mirecki, *The Gospel of the Savior: A New Ancient Gospel* (California Classical Library; Sonora: Polebridge Press, 1999). See also S. Emmel, "The 'Gospel of the Savior': A New Witness to the Strasbourg Coptic Gospel," *Bulletin de l'AELAC* 12 (2000): 10–19; Idem., "Unbekanntes Berliner Evangelium – The Strasbourg Coptic Gospel: Prolegomena to a New Edition of the Strasbourg Fragments," in *For the Children, Perfect Instruction: Studies in Honor of Hans-Martin Schenke on the Occasion of the Berliner Arbeitskreis für koptisch-gnostiche Schriften's Thirtieth Year* (ed. H.-G. Bethge et al.; Leiden-Boston: Brill, 2000), 353–374; Idem., "The Recently Published Gospel of the Savior ("Unbekanntes Berliner Evangelium"): Righting the Order of Pages and Events," *HTR* 95 (2000): 45–72; Idem., "Preliminary Reedition and Translation of the Gospel of the Savior: New Light on the Strasbourg Coptic Gospel and the Stauros-Text from Nubia", *Apocrypha* 14 (2003): 9–53; Idem., "Ein altes Evangelium der Apostel taucht in Fragmenten aus Ägypten und Nubien auf," *ZAC* 9 (2005); 85–99. J. Frey, "Leidenskampf und Himmelresise: Das Berliner Evangelienfragment (Papyrus Berolensis 22220) und die Gethsemane-Tradition", *BZ* 46 (2002): 71–96; Ch. W. Hedrick, "Caveat to a 'Righted Order' of the Gospel of the Savior," *HThR* 96 (2003): 229–238; P. Nagel, "Gespräche Jesu mit seinen Jüngern vor der Auferstehung – Zur Herkunft und Datierung des 'Unbekannten Berliner Evangelium'," *ZNW* 94 (2003): 215–257; U.-K. Plisch, *Verborgene Worte Jesu – verworfene Evangelien: Apokryphe Schriften des frühen Christentums* (2nd edn; Die Bibel 5; Berlin: Brennpunkt, 2002), 27–34; Idem., "Zu einigen Einleitungsfragen Berliner Evangeliums (UBE)," *ZAC* 9 (2005): 64–84; H.-M. Schenke, "Das sogenannte 'Unbekannte Berliner Evangelium' (UBE)," *ZAC* 2 (1998): 27–34.

> of the gates were alarmed. 32 The angels were afraid and [fled] this [way] and that, thinking [that] they would all be destroyed. 33 We saw our Savior having penetrated all the heavens, [his] feet [placed firmly on] the [mountain with us, his head penetrating the seventh] heaven. 34 [. . . *8 lines untranslatable* . . .] *(B 101)* . . . all the heavens. 35 Then before us, the apostles, this world became as darkness. 36 We became as [those] among the [immortal] aeons, with our [eyes penetrating all] the heavens, clothed with the [power of] our apostleship, and we saw our Savior when he had reached the [seventh] heaven.[48]

The passage narrates an experience that passes through various phases: a) the apostles' transformation into spiritual bodies; b) a vision; c) an ascent through the heavens passing through doors guarded by angels; d) the apostles see the Savior who has journeyed through the heavens.

The heavenly journey returns in 113.1–59 and also in 122.61–64. In the latter passage it probably offers an explanation of the systemic function of the heavenly journey in the *Gospel of the Savior*. Through a journey undertaken by the *Soter* accompanied by his apostles, the apostles obtain religious knowledge. It seems that we are dealing with a group that develops its religious conceptions not only through an inspired exegesis of the words of the Savior and the Hebrew Sacred Scripture, as in *John*,[49] but also through the search for and experience of ecstasy.

6. Some final considerations

The examples reported seem to constitute single instances of a widespread phenomenon, each with its own distinctive and specific characteristics. This leads us to distance ourselves from the concept or scheme of a *tradition* that envisaged within Jewish cul-

---

[48] S. Emmel, "The Gospel of the Savior", 12.

[49] See the analysis of John 2:22 in A. Destro and M. Pesce, "Il profetismo e la nascita di una religione: il caso del Giovannismo", in *Carisma profetico, fattore di innovazione religiosa* (ed. G. Filoramo; Brescia: Morcelliana, 2003), 87–106.

ture the transmission of the conception, practice or literary model of the "heavenly journey" (this is valid from the *Book of Kings* to the *Book of Enoch*, to Paul, to the *Ascension of Isaiah*, the *Gospel of the Savior*, down to the Christian gnostic texts).

We propose as an hypothesis that the explicative schema should be what we might call *cultural traffic or (crossing) exchanges*, over an extended time span involving different cultural areas (Rome, Greece, Asia Minor, Syria, and elsewhere). Our hypothesis is that the "heavenly journey" corresponds to a religious practice. For this reason our approach stresses the primacy of the experience and of the ritual practice. In our perspective, the heavenly journey must be analyzed as a performance[50] that cannot take place without formally predetermined expressions of the body, defined within a particular cultural environment. This performance was widespread in different cultures and groups. The different groups interpreted the same religious-cultural pattern *in their own way*, while "preserving" some of its characteristic and recognizable traits (in spite of the changes brought by mutating situations and times).[51]

What all the forms of "heavenly journey" (considered as a practice) have in common, is that:

a) The "journey" involves a *detachment*, one that is often interpreted as a separation of a part of the person (the spirit, intellect, mind, for example) from the rest of the body. Such detachment, as we have seen, is associated with a strong physical effect: a state between sleep and waking, an inability to understand how the event actually takes place (see Plutarch, *The Demon of Socrates*, 590C) or a loss of consciousness. The *Dream of Scipio* speaks of a heavy sleep after a banquet. A situation of presumed death during

---

[50] See V. Turner, *Anthropology of Performance* (New York: PAJ Publications, 1986).

[51] A. F. Segal speaks of "a mythical structure of *katabasis* and *anabasis*, which was shared by most cultures of their time. However, the mythical structure was developed in specific ways according to individual cultural traditions" (Segal, "Heavenly Ascent," 1387).

the heavenly journey of Er is in Plato's *Republic*. The Ascension of Isaiah refers to a sudden "interruption of speaking": the body breathes but remains inert, the open eyes cannot see. This is what we call detachment of a part of the body. Only some texts state that the intellect leaves the body. Plutarch says that the soul departs from the body of Timarchus, although he also asserts that Timarchus sees and hears during the heavenly journey. Seeing, hearing, feeling pain are bodily experiences or modifications that are part of the practice, like the state between waking and sleeping. Periodic repetition of such detachment is induced by techniques and personal temperaments. Such separation leads the individual to overcome what is commonly known as the threshold of consciousness.

One essential point: personal inability. The individual loses his normal life functions during the time in which the journey experience takes place. If the journey phenomenon is intended as a *performance*, one may suppose that the "traveller" is subject to states of marginality and powerlessness, either due to his own inactivity or because of external forces (the so-called *other-than-human persons*).[52]

b) Since the performance is strategic and directed to obtaining particular goals, the detachment is not definitive, but envisages a *return* and a *re-composition* of the person's parts. The weakening and marginality are followed by reintegration—that is, restoration of the individual to full functionality. The return is characterized again by a specific physical state, marking the return to normal life. In the *Ascension of Isaiah* the angel says to Isaiah: "you will come back in your garment," that is, in your body. In Plutarch, at the end of the journey, Timarchus sees himself lying at the entrance of Trophonius' crypt, where he was at the beginning.

---

[52] See A. I. Hallowell, "Ojibwa Ontology, Behavior, and World View," in *Teachings from the American Earth* (ed. Dennis and Barbara Tedlock; New York: Liveright, 1975), 141–179; G. Harvey, *Shamanism: A Reader* (London and New York: Routledge, 2003), 9–11.

In some cases the presence of witnesses is necessary to demonstrate that a return to normal life has taken place. Sometimes, a witness to the traveller's lack of consciousness is necessary in order to demonstrate that the journey is taking place (see, for example, *Ascension of Isaiah*). The return must also be followed by a *report or a kind of explanation* by the traveller himself of what he has experienced during the journey.

c) The object of the displacement is to attain *knowledge* of hidden fundamental truths, a kind of knowledge that cannot be understood or expressed in any other way. It can only be obtained by reaching inaccessible places in the cosmos. The journey's rationale is therefore based on a dislocation that is rarely spontaneous or self-induced (the references are to abductions, to being transported). In all cases, the journey is less ambiguous that we might imagine: it leads toward a destination, which has topographical features.

d) A further aspect concerns initiation. In a number of cases the journey has the function of introducing the person into a group that posseses distinctive characteristics. This is the case of Timarchus in *Socrates' Demon* of Plutarch, where he who makes the journey becomes *theios anêr*, a divine man. In *Scipio's Dream*, Scipio goes through a ritual of passage in which he attains the knowledge that the persons who devote their lives to the good of the republic could (after death) have a place in heaven with the good politicians of the past.

In other texts, the journey has also a function of legitimitation. For instance, in Paul, it constitutes a basis of "pride." This may mean that for the group to which he belongs, authority depends on heavenly revelations. The organization of their human world is based on supernatural knowledge attained through the journey.

e) The theme of the traveller's bodily transformation *during the journey* is also present. It is found, for example, in the *Ascension of Isaiah* (transformation of the Beloved) and in the *Gospel of the Savior* (transformation of the Savior who reveals and of the apostles who make with him the experience of the heavenly journey).

Ultimately, all these elements converge towards confirming a fundamental hypothesis: in the ancient world the heavenly journey was a religious experience thought *possible* by a large number of people, who received through it initiation and legitimation, necessary for both social life and producing social meaning.

In conclusion, we believe the heavenly journey to be a religious form rich in meanings and effects. It has been continuously reshaped throughout the antique world (Middle Eastern, Greek, and Roman). It is no surprise, therefore, that we encounter it also among various Jewish groups and, subsequently, among the different early Christian communities, including that of Paul. This religious practice should be viewed together or on the same level as other very widespread practices (like prayer, or sacrifice), none of which is exclusive to a single religion or religious group. It is one of the complex range of means available to the men and women of antiquity to achieve their religious goals. In each culture, each religion and each group (along with prayer and sacrifice), it was a practice that assumed different contents, forms, functions, and purposes. What we are trying to say is that men and women of the ancient world tried constantly to place themselves in a particular bodily and psychic disposition. They tried to be open to a kind of bodily-mental scission that could produce and lead to the "heavenly journey." All this may be considered as an ordinary and widespread religious experience.

Chapter 6

Paul, Moses, and the Veil: Paul's Perspective on Judaism in Light of 2 Corinthians 3[1]

Part 1: On Paul's use of καταργέω *and* τέλος *in 2 Cor 3:7, 11, 13 and 14*

Emmanuel Nathan

To speak of Paul, Moses, and the Veil in the Second Letter to the Corinthians is to focus our attention on 12 problematic verses in the third chapter of this epistle, viz. 2 Cor 3:7-18, in which Paul seems to offer his own interpretation of the Exodus narrative recounting Moses' shining face after his descent from Mount Sinai with the second set of tablets (Exod 34:29-35). The subtitle of this paper, "Paul's Perspective on Judaism in Light of 2 Corinthians 3", fits well with a sentiment once uttered by E.P. Sanders that Paul offers something of an evaluation of Judaism in 2 Corinthians 3 (another passage being Philippians 3:3-11).[2]

In order to examine this claim further, we take as our starting point the position of Hans Windisch. In his influential 1924 commentary on 2 Corinthians, Windisch characterized the section of 2 Cor 3:7-18 as a 'Christlicher midrash' where "Christentum und Judentum, nicht Paulinismus und Judaismus, sind die größten Gegensätze" and whose "Stoff ist unabhängig von der brieflichen

---

[1] The research for this study was conducted in the context of the research project "New Perspectives on Paul and the Jews" which was made possible by a grant from the Research Foundation Flanders - FWO. Both Emmanuel Nathan and Reimund Bieringer express their gratitude for the support they received from the Research Foundation Flanders for this work.

[2] E.P. Sanders, *Paul, the Law, and the Jewish People* (Philadelphia: Fortress, 1983), 137.

Situation konzipiert".[3] There are three important aspects to this position.[4] First, Windisch maintained that Paul radically reinterpreted the Exodus narrative of Moses' glory. In this Paul's καταργέω sayings in vv. 7, 11, 13 and 14 were central to the thesis that Paul adapted the Exodus account. For Windisch these were 'targum-like entries' which ran counter to the biblical narrative. Related to this, Paul's use of τέλος in v. 13 refers to the glory on Moses' face that was coming to an end, such that the veil serves the purpose of Moses willfully hiding this fact from the Israelites. Second, this meant that Paul's reinterpretation was a *Christian* midrash. The fact that it is Christian is because Paul's experience of Christ allows him to, as it were, read Scripture against the grain. Lastly, and what has made the most impact on studies of this passage, Windisch's insight that 3:7-18 was only loosely connected to its immediate epistolary context, has led scholars to search for a pre-Pauline tradition and *Vorlage*. We can mention in this context the essay by Siegfried Schulz on Moses' veil,[5] and in more recent times the monograph by Linda Belleville on a possible Moses-Δόξα tradition.[6]

So influential has been the legacy of Windisch that all future studies of 2 Cor 3:7-18 have in some way acted as *responsa* to his position. This will become evident when we examine more closely the various exegetical options that exist when considering Paul's use of καταργέω and τέλος in this passage. Following this, we shall then briefly comment on Paul's use of κάλυμμα, the veil. Reimund Bieringer will address the more weighty issue of δόξα in Part 2 of this contribution.

---

[3] Hans Windisch, *Der Zweite Korintherbrief* (Göttingen: Vandenhoeck & Ruprecht, 1924), 112.

[4] Scott J. Hafemann, *Paul, Moses, and the History of Israel: The Letter/Spirit Contrast and the Argument from Scripture in 2 Corinthians 3* (WUNT 81; Tübingen: Mohr [Siebeck], 1995), 257.

[5] Siegfried Schulz, "Die Decke des Moses. Untersuchungen zu einer vorpaulinischen Überlieferung in II Cor 3.7-18," *ZNW* 49 (1958): 1-30.

[6] Linda Belleville, *Reflections of Glory: Paul's Polemical Use of the Moses-Doxa Tradition in 2 Corinthians 3.1-18* (JSNT SS 52; Sheffield: JSOT Press, 1991).

Examining the exegetical options of καταργέω *and* τέλος *2 Cor 3:7, 11, 13 and 14*

We need to bear in mind a tension that confronts us when reading 2 Cor 3:7-18 which increases the difficulty of its interpretation: Paul seems to be making contradictory statements. For instance, the ministry of 'death' (θανάτου) and 'condemnation' (κατακρίσεως) is also at the same time 'glorious'.[7] Second, Paul presents Moses both as representing the old covenant (3:13, 15) and as the example for unhindered access to divine glory (3:16, 18).[8] Third, Paul compares his sufficiency (ἱκανός cf. 2:16, 3:5, 6) to that of Moses but then also contrasts his ministry with Moses' (3:13).[9] These tensions are reflected when examining the exegetical options with regard to Paul's use of καταργέω and τέλος in 3:7-18. The four verses in question are:

> 7 Εἰ δὲ ἡ διακονία τοῦ θανάτου ἐν γράμμασιν ἐντετυπ-
> ωμένη λίθοις ἐγενήθη ἐν δόξῃ, ὥστε μὴ δύνασθαι ἀτενί-
> σαι τοὺς υἱους Ἰσραὴλ εἰς τὸ πρόσωπον Μωϋσέως διὰ τὴν
> δόξαν τοῦ προσώπου αὐτοῦ **τὴν καταργουμένην**,
> 11 εἰ γὰρ **τὸ καταργούμενον** διὰ δόξης, πολλῷ μᾶλλον τὸ
> μένον ἐν δόξῃ.
> 13 καὶ οὐ καθάπερ Μωϋσῆς ἐτίθει κάλυμμα ἐπὶ τὸ πρόσωπον
> αὐτοῦ πρὸς τὸ μὴ ἀτενίσαι τοὺς υἱοὺς Ἰσραὴλ εἰς τὸ
> **τέλος τοῦ καταργουμένου**.

---

[7] Sanders, *Paul, the Law, and the Jewish People*, 138: "Paul does not explain how it is that something which condemns and kills can be glorious. He is caught here as elsewhere between two convictions, but here there is no struggle to resolve them; he states them both as facts."

[8] Richard B. Hays, *Echoes of Scripture in the Letters of Paul* (New Haven, CT: Yale University Press, 1989), 144: "Moses prefigures Christian experience, but he is not a Christian. He is both the paradigm for Christians' direct experience of the Spirit and the symbol for the old covenant to which that experience is set in antithesis."

[9] Hafemann, *Paul, Moses and the History of Israel*, 34: "If Paul's authority as an apostle is based in some sense on the *parallel* between his sufficiency and the sufficiency of Moses, it is also equally supported by the *contrast* between his διακονία and the διακονία of Moses".

14 ἀλλὰ ἐπωρώθη τὰ νοήματα αὐτῶν. ἄχρι γὰρ τῆς σήμερον ἡμέρας τὸ αὐτὸ κάλυμμα ἐπὶ τῇ ἀναγνώσει τῆς παλαιᾶς διαθήκης μένει, μὴ ἀνακαλυπτόμενον ὅτι ἐν Χριστῷ **καταργεῖται**·

Καταργέω is rare in both extra-biblical Greek and the LXX. In the NT it is used almost exclusively by Paul. His usage (in the undisputed letters) accounts for 22 of the 27 occurrences in the NT, with its highest concentration (4x) in 2 Cor 3:7-18, prompting its consideration as a *terminus technicus.*[10] Determining its meaning, then, will be crucial for the interpretation of the passage. The simplex ἀργέω translates "be out of action," while the compound καταργέω in the active voice renders "cause to be out of action," In the passive it means "cease," "pass away".[11]

3:7

In 2 Cor 3:7, τὴν καταργουμένην is a feminine attributive present participle expressing repeated action in the past.[12] It modifies τὴν δόξαν, which in its immediate sense can be understood as referring to the glory on Moses' face, but some will choose to understand this as referring to the entire Mosaic dispensation, in light of the later change to a neuter substantival participle τὸ καταργούμενον in vv. 11 and 13.[13]

---

[10] *Ibid.*, 309: "Indeed, Paul's frequent and consistent use of καταργέω sayings warrants its consideration as a Pauline *terminus technicus* to express the meaning of the coming and return of Christ in relationship to the structures of this world on the one hand, and its significance for the effects of those structures on the other. Καταργέω becomes for Paul a *theological* designation in which the turn of the ages is expressed in terms of what the gospel does and does not abolish and what does and does not continue to be effective or operate as a result. Paul's characteristic use of the term therefore poses in itself the question of the continuity and discontinuity between this age and the age to come.

[11] Murray J. Harris, *The Second Epistle to the Corinthians: A Commentary on the Greek Text* (NIGTC; Grand Rapids MI and Milton Keynes: Eerdmans and Paternoster, 2005), 284.

[12] *Ibid.*, 285.

[13] *Ibid.* "It might also be noted at this point that since the verb καταργέομαι

Grammatically, the form of a present participle is identical in the middle and the passive voice.[14] Thus, one can translate it either as 'coming to an end' or 'being abolished' (the NRSV opts for "set aside"). Yet, it is more likely to be passive since in v. 14 καταργέω is certainly passive and this is also assumed to be the case in vv. 11 and 13.[15] While many English versions translate the verb with "fading" (e.g. RSV, NIV, NEB, NASB, JB, NAB, REB), it should be noted that there is no lexical evidence for καταργέω to be translated this way.[16] Rather, to translate καταργέω as "render ineffective" fits all Pauline and NT contexts. Paul is consistent in using it to refer to something invalidated or replaced.[17] Furthermore, other than in 2 Cor 3:7-18, the notion of a gradual diminishing of some former reality is never suggested,[18] since the semantic field of καταργέω appears to be the realm of legal process rather than visual imagery.[19]

It is owing to Hans Windisch and Siegfried Schulz that καταργέω has been translated in this context to mean "fading".[20] The participle is seen to convey Moses' negative critique of the Law because it is taken as synonymous with the neuter substantival participle τὸ καταργούμενον. One speaks then of "the derogatory

---

appears as a neuter substantival participle in vv. 11 and 13 in reference to the era and order of the old covenant, it is relatively insignificant that Paul attaches the participle καταργουμένη to δόξα, not διακονία. The glory on Moses' face symbolizes the whole Mosaic dispensation, including its διαθήκη and its διακονία." But, Friedrich Avemarie, "The Notion of a 'New Covenant' in 2 Corinthians 3: its function in Paul's argument and its Jewish background" (paper presented at the colloquium "Jewish Perspectives on Paul: 2 Corinthians and Late Second Temple Judaism," Leuven, Belgium, 30 March 2009), 11, disagrees: "Paul clearly does not refer to any covenant, but to the vanishing radiance of the face of Moses."

[14] Margaret E.Thrall, *A Critical and Exegetical Commentary on the Second Epistle to the Corinthians*, vol. I (ICC; Edinburgh: T.&T. Clark, 1994), 243, n. 362.

[15] Thrall (*ibid.*) points out that in Rom 6:6, 7:6 and Gal 5:4 it is also passive.

[16] See Hafemann, *Paul, Moses and the History of Israel*, 286-309 and William R. Baker, "Did the Glory of Moses' Face Fade? A Reexamination of καταργέω in 2 Corinthians 3:7-18." *BBR* 10.1 (2000), 3-5.

[17] Victor Paul Furnish, *II Corinthians* (AB 32A; Garden City: Doubleday, 1984), 203.

[18] Baker, "Did the Glory of Moses' Face Fade?", 5.

[19] Hays, *Echoes*, 134.

[20] Hafemann, *Paul, Moses and the History of Israel*, 286.

addition of τὴν καταργουμένην ...".[21] Since Exod. 34:29-35 does not refer to Moses' glory fading, Paul not only goes beyond the biblical text, but seems to intentionally misread it in light of his apologetic concerns (the defence of his ministry) and supposed Christian presuppositions (e.g. a divide between 'Law' and 'Gospel').

Yet a problem arises: if Paul is engaged in a debate with rivals at Corinth who are accusing him of preaching a 'veiled gospel' (2 Cor 4:3), would it not weaken Paul's position if he was basing his argument on his own fanciful reading of the Exodus narrative? In order to avoid this conclusion, two options are available. One either posits that there existed such a tradition of a fading glory and then seeks to recover this[22] or one suggests that καταργουμένην in v. 7, because of its present tense, should not be read as referring to the time of Moses, but to Paul's day. In this reading, Paul is asserting that it is *now* the case that the glory of the Law or ministry of Moses is "passing away".[23] (This seems to be the reading offered by the NRSV translation: "a glory now set aside".)

We reserve comment with respect to the first option of an existing tradition, but with respect to the second, it is argued that the time reference of the ὥστε-clause is determined by the main verb of the previous εἰ δέ–clause. This verb, the aorist ἐγενήθη "took place", signifies that the entire protasis is referring to the time of Moses. Hence, τὴν καταργουμένην, is most easily read as referring to the glory in Moses' day, thus "was being annulled". Besides, Paul indicates explicitly in 2 Cor 3:14b, 15 (τῆς σήμερον ἡμέρας; ἕως σήμερον) when he changes from Moses' time to his own.[24]

To resolve the issue of translating τὴν καταργουμένην in 3:7, one can begin by arguing that the emphasis here is not its time ref-

---

[21] Hafemann, *ibid.*, quoting Ralph P. Martin, *2 Corinthians* (WBC 40; Waco: Word, 1986), 62.

[22] Most recently done by Belleville in *Reflections of Glory*. Needless to say, she is a proponent of the reading of καταργέω as "fading".

[23] See Carol K. Stockhausen, *Moses' Veil and the Glory of the New Covenant: The Exegetical Substructure of II Cor. 3,1-4,6* (Analecta Biblica 116; Roma: Pontificio Istituto Biblico and Biblical Institute Press, 1989) 87, n.3.

[24] Hafemann, *Paul, Moses and the History of Israel,* 300 and Furnish, *II Corinthians*, 203.

erence but that it is passive.[25] On asking who or what is causing the action, if one claims that it is the veil of Moses, it explains in a natural way why the glory of Moses' face was "being rendered inoperative" (Hafemann) or "hindered" (Baker). One would not need to leave the time frame of the Exodus narrative which Paul is using, nor would one here in v. 7 need to posit that Paul has read against the Exodus text and introduced a notion of Moses' glory "fading".

So, to summarise, already in v. 7, several exegetical decisions need to be taken that influence the interpretation of καταργέω. One must:

1) decide whether it is synonymous with its neuter form (in later verses) with regard to its referent;
2) decide whether to interpret it as passive or middle;
3) choose between emphasizing its voice or its tense; and
4) opt for either its usual meaning of "'rendering ineffective" or an exceptional meaning of "fading".

3:11

In v. 11, the participle has become neuter and a substantive (as opposed to it being feminine and attributive in v. 7). Thus, whereas τὴν καταργουμένην referred specifically to the glory on Moses' face in v. 7, here τὸ καταργούμενον could be understood in more general terms.[26] This is bolstered by another neuter substantive participle in v.10 τὸ δεδοξασμένον).[27]

As can be expected, the referent of τὸ καταργούμενον is a matter of debate. It could refer to the Law, the ministry of Moses, or the old covenant. Minimalists would prefer to still see it as

---

[25] Hafemann, *Paul, Moses and the History of Israel,* 311.

[26] Harris, *The Second Epistle to the Corinthians*, 291 sees an allusion to Moses' face in the accompanying prepositional phrase: "Whereas in 3:7 the allusion to the Mosaic order is secondary, here in 3:11 the Mosaic economy is the focus, with Moses' face alluded to by the phrase διὰ δόξης."

[27] Furnish, *II Corinthians*, 205.

referring to the glory on Moses' face.[28] Maximalists, on the other hand, would go so far as to argue that because the participle is an abstract substantive, "it could refer to the old economy in general or the whole religious system based on the law."[29] Yet the maximalist view seems a little extreme in this case.

For those arguing that in v. 11 we see a reference to the Law, it must be pointed out that Law is here viewed as synonymous with the Mosaic ministry, or dispensation, being treated by Paul.[30] A close link is then drawn to τὸ δεδοξασμένον in v. 10, understood as "[the Law] which was [given] in glory". The discussion will then turn on what aspect of the Law in v. 11 is τὸ καταργούμενον ("being nullified") and τὸ μένον ("remaining"). It has been argued that what is abolished is obedience to the law's precepts and what remains is the Law's witness to Christ, since Paul evidently still uses scripture.[31] Alternatively, one can decide to let the ambiguity in Paul's argumentation stand: the Law remains because it can be read correctly in Christ, but it also passes away because it cannot save and only brings death and condemnation.[32] However, while the Law may be in view through the metonymic use of "Moses" in v. 15 (ἡνίκα ἂν ἀναγινώσκηται Μωϋσῆς), the lack of any explicit mention of νόμος in this passage makes a reference to the Law unlikely.

What is more likely, though, is that Paul has in view the ministry of Moses, on the basis that Paul moves to a neuter gender so

---

[28] Avemarie, "The Notion," 11: "This is now indeed a formulation which seems to lend strong support to the assumption that Paul is thinking of a cessation of the Sinai covenant. ... Quite a different interpretation results if we take καταργου'μενον to refer here to what it refers also in vv. 7 and 13, namely to the radiance of the face of Moses."

[29] Harris, *The Second Epistle to the Corinthians*, 290 citing Barrett.

[30] Since one would otherwise have anticipated a masculine form in order to justify a reference to ὁ νόμος.

[31] See Sanders' discussion of Hooker's position in Sanders, *Paul, the Law, and the Jewish People*, 139.

[32] *Ibid.*: "Hooker's explanation highlights, rather, a true ambiguity in Paul's position. ... We see, rather, the two sides of a dilemma".

as to encompass what is said in v. 7a (ἡ διακονία τοῦ θανάτου ἐν γράμμασιν ἐντετυπωμένη λίθοις ἐγενήθη ἐν δόξῃ "the ministry of death, chiseled in letters on stones took place in glory"). Thus "Paul is thinking of the Mosaic ministry with its attendant glory as being in the process of diminishment or decay rather than either Moses' facial splendor or the old covenant alone."[33] Paul's use of the neuter participle instead of the feminine encourages one to suppose that Paul is thinking now in general theological terms of what is being nullified, and thus leads others to include in this the old covenant and its ministry.[34] Interestingly, it is the broadening scope of the neuter participle that encourages them to then read the more specific feminine participle in v. 7 τὴν καταργουμένην as "Paul's retrospective judgment on that which the radiance on Moses' face symbolized. It is a theological afterthought, just as is his description – in the same sentence – of the old covenant as offering a 'ministry of death.'"[35]

2 Cor 3:11 can also lend itself to the impression that Paul is referring to the abolition of the old covenant. In this reading τὸ καταργούμενον is understood as referring to the Mosaic covenant, with its antithesis, τὸ μένον, referring in a general way to the new covenant.[36] There is discussion as to whether the difference in prepositional phrases (διὰ δόξης-ἐν δόξῃ) points to what distinguishes the two covenants.[37] In general, though, the neuter participle is understood more broadly than just encompassing the ministry of Moses, but becomes a metonymy for the entire old covenant, including its glory, results and theological

---

33 Belleville, *Reflections of Glory*, 203.

34 For instance, Hays, *Echoes*, 135.

35 *Ibid.*

36 Thrall, *A Critical and Exegetical Commentary on the Second Epistle to the Corinthians*, 1: 252-253.

37 *Ibid.* Thrall lists Allo, Klöpper, Bachmann, Plummer, Hughes, Prümm and Collange as seeing some kind of distinction. She thinks not. Neither does Harris, *The Second Epistle to the Corinthians*, 291.

purpose.[38] The Sinai covenant "was continually being hindered" (τὸ καταργούμενον, 3:11) from establishing God's presence among his people.

To summarise, the options for τὸ καταργούμενον in v. 11 differ with regard to their referent. It could refer to the glory on Moses' face, or to the Law, the ministry of Moses, or the entire Mosaic covenant. What is clear, though, is that here there is no discussion on rendering καταργέω with "fading".

3:13

The issue of translating "fading" returns, however, in 3:13. Here there is also a substantive participle as in v. 11, albeit in the genitive case, τοῦ καταργουμένου. As a genitive singular this form can be masculine or neuter, but owing to the context in which it is used it is most likely to be neuter. The arguments about its referent are thus familiar. It can refer to the glory on Moses' face,[39] the ministry of Moses,[40] or the entire Mosaic covenant.[41] An argument in favour of the radiance of Moses' face is the terminological parallelism noted between 3:7 and 3:13, since one can then suppose that Paul still has in mind the splendour of Moses' face:

---

[38] Hafemann, *Paul, Moses, and the History of Israel*, 329-330.

[39] Avemarie, "The Notion," 11: "If we want to take this as an allegory, that which was 'vanishing' might refer to the covenant at Sinai. However, nothing in the text seems to require such an allegorical reading, and taken at face value, that which was vanishing is, of course, again the radiance of Moses' face."

[40] Furnish, *II Corinthians*, 207: "Not just the radiant splendor of Moses' face was being annulled, which would require a feminine participle as in v. 7, nor the law specifically, which would require a masculine form; rather, and comprehensively, the entire ministry of the old covenant."

[41] Hafemann, *Paul, Moses and the History of Israel*, 355: "The repetition of the neuter form of the participle in 3:13 recalls its earlier inclusive referent to the old covenant *as a whole*, with its results and underlying theological purpose (3:9-10), rather than referring solely to the glory of God on Moses' face as in 3:7b. In 3:13b, Paul once again intends to assert that Moses' veil kept the old covenant ministry from accomplishing what it would have had it not been stopped by this covering."

7 μὴ δύνασθαι ἀτενίσαι τους υἱοὺς 'Ισραὴλ εἰς τὸ πρόσωπον Μωϋσέως διὰ τὴν δόξαν τοῦ προσώπου αὐτοῦ τὴν καταργουμένην

13μὴ ἀτενίσαι τοὺς υἱοὺς 'Ισραὴλ εἰς τὸ τέλος τοῦ καταργουμένου

However, the shift from feminine in v. 7 to neuter, as we have seen for v. 11, is used to argue that Paul broadens his scope from the glory of Moses' face to ἡ διακονία τοῦ θανάτου in v. 7a. It is therefore the ministry of Moses and its glory that is in view through Paul's use of the neuter.[42] As mentioned, too, others choose to see the neuter even more broadly as referring to the Mosaic covenant as a whole.

More problematic than τοῦ καταργουμένου, though, is the presence of the noun τέλος in 3:13. "All interpreters recognize τέλος as the key on which all else hinges in understanding the significance of καταργέω and what Paul is trying to get at in the passage as a whole."[43] Interpreters are caught between translating τέλος here with "goal" or "cessation".

Some of the reasons for preferring τέλος in 2 Cor 3.13 to mean "goal" is that it is supposed Paul is thinking of: (1) Christ as the fulfillment of the Mosaic law, (2) the messianic glory of the preexistent Christ, (3) the surpassing of the old covenant by the new, (4) the abolition of the old covenant and the inauguration of the new, or (5) the purpose of the Law as an expression of the will of

---

[42] Belleville, *Reflections of Glory*, 203. Belleville resists seeing the neuter as too broad or too restrictive. "Some maintain that by τοῦ καταργουμένου has in view God's entire revelation in the OT, or the whole Jewish religious system. But Paul's use of παλαιᾶς διαθήκης in v. 14 suggests that he is thinking more narrowly in terms of the Mosaic covenant. Yet not the old covenant per se but the old covenant viewed specifically from the standpoint of its ministerial role, as the parallelism between ἡ διακονία and τοῦ καταργουμένου vv. 7ff implies. Others think in terms of the old covenant to condemn. But Paul's shift to the neuter points to a more comprehensive notion."

[43] Baker, "Did the Glory of Moses' Face Fade?" 12.

God in the history of the people.[44]

By contrast, the following arguments are put forward to support the rendering of τέλος with "end":

(1) One 'understands' an intention or purpose, but here one 'sees' the glory;
(2) εἰς τὸ τέλος has a counterpart in the phrase ἀπὸ δόξης εἰς δόξαν (3:18), suggesting that the contrast is between decrease and increase;
(3) the participial construction τοῦ καταργουμένου (v. 13) is parallel to τὴν καταργουμένην (v. 7), where it is argued that one witnesses a "fading" glory;
(4) τέλος in conjunction with ἀτενίσαι εἰς as 'looking down to' produces a more unified picture – one of looking down to the end of a diminishing splendor;
(5) τέλος in the temporal phrases εἰς τέλος, ἕως τέλους, μέχρι τέλους, and ἄρχι τέλους in the NT is always used in the sense of 'end' – or in the case of adverbial counterparts, 'completely', 'continually' – and not 'goal'.[45]

Yet, it has been pointed out that those who prefer the rendering of τέλος with "end" need to assume that Paul thought of the glory on Moses' face as fading.[46] They share the belief that the veil concealed from Israel the symbolic evidence of the transitory character of the old covenant. More recent arguments for choosing τέλος as "goal" are as follows:

1. The normal meaning of the Greek word τέλος is teleological.
2. Rom 10:4 (τέλος γὰρ νόμου Χριστός) must be construed to mean that Christ is the goal and culmination of the Law.
3. Patristic interpreters understood the phrase in this way.

---

[44] As enumerated by Belleville, *Reflections of Glory*, 201.

[45] For a critical assessment of Belleville's position, see Baker, "Did the Glory of Moses' Face Fade?" 12.

[46] Hays, *Echoes*, 136-140.

4. καταργούμενον in v. 13 cannot be read as a reference to fading glory. If Paul were still thinking about the visual image of the glory, he would use the feminine participle καταργουμένη. Instead, carrying the neuter participle over from verse 11, he repeats his descriptive characterization of the old covenant ministry.
5. The internal logic of 2 Cor 3 favors this reading. What is seen when the veil is removed? The glory of God. Moses' veil conceals not the absence but the presence of glory.
6. Windisch and followers assume that Moses was hiding a fading glory. It suggests for them that the real point of the figure is the obsolescence of the old covenant and the superiority of Christianity to Judaism, themes not readily pertinent to Paul's self-defence against the charges of other Christian apostles.

As one can see, the interpretation of τέλος is closely tied up with the interpretation of καταργέω and each side has its proponents. Perhaps to problematise this even further, agreement on the rendering of καταργέω does not imply agreement on the reliance of Rom 10:4 as a supporting argument for τέλος. For instance, Scott Hafemann states: "Unlike Rom. 10:4, the τέλος in 2 Cor. 3:13b takes place within the time frame of Moses' activity, rather than referring to the future time of Christ. For this reason, in the present context Paul explicitly does *not* identify the τέλος of the old covenant with Christ, as he does in Rom. 10:4, even though the two statements are related theologically."[47] We shall briefly return to this after our final consideration of 3:14.

3:14

This verse is noteworthy for the first known use of the phrase ἡ παλαιὰ διαθήκη, believed to be a Pauline innovation. In v. 15 there is a parallel reference to "Moses" being read, and the metonymic use of Moses confirms that ἡ παλαιὰ διαθήκη is the Mosaic covenant.[48]

---

[47] Hafemann, *Paul, Moses, and the History of Israel*, 358.

[48] So Furnish, *II Corinthians*, 208.

The last occurrence of καταργέω, καταργεῖται in 3:14, is ambiguous because one needs to decide what is its implied subject. There are three options:[49]

1. If the subject is taken to be the glory of the Mosaic covenant (vv. 7, 13), then the verb will mean "is in the process of fading".
2. If the subject is the old covenant, the sense will be "is abrogated", "is abolished", "is being annulled", or "is set aside".
3. If, alternatively, κάλυμμα is the subject, the verb may mean "is set aside", "is ... abolished", or "is ... removed".

The principal reason for preferring κάλυμμα as the subject is that after τὸ αὐτὸ κάλυμμα ... μένει, the neuter μὴ ἀνακαλυπτόμενον naturally refers back to κάλυμμα. Therefore, the reader would be hard pressed to envisage a change of subject with καταργεῖται.[50] Thus the veil, and not the covenant, is being abolished.

Some brief considerations on κάλυμμα

"If the key word of 3,7-11 was δόξα, the key word for 3,12-18 would be κάλυμμα (3,13.14.15.16; cf. also ἀνακαλυπτόμενον in 3,14 and ἀνακεκαλυμμένῳ in 3,18)."[51] Since Reimund Bieringer will handle the term δόξα in the second part of this contribution, perhaps it is fitting to end with some brief considerations of the term κάλυμμα.

---

[49] Harris, *The Second Epistle to the Corinthians*, 304.

[50] *Ibid.*: "If the old covenant were, in fact, the subject of καταργεῖται, we would have expected Paul to write κατήργηται ('has been annulled,' 'is void') or κατηργήθη ('was abrogated')." See also Thrall, *A Critical and Exegetical Commentary on the Second Epistle to the Corinthians*, 266: "the subject is most naturally to be supplied from that of the participle, which must be the κάλυμμα." So too Avemarie, "The Notion," 12: "Thus, it is the veil rather than the covenant which in v.14 is said to vanish in Christ." Furnish, *II Corinthians*, 210, on the other hand, is persuaded by the overall context to opt for the abrogation of the old covenant.

[51] Jan Lambrecht, "Structure and Line of Thought in 2 Cor 2,14-4,6," in Reimund Bieringer & Jan Lambrecht, *Studies in 2 Corinthians* (BETL 112; Leuven: Leuven University Press and Peeters, 1994), 270.

It is pointed out that Paul's interpretation of the veil motif is unique and his interpretation has been understood in various ways:[52]

1. Paul may have seen this act of concealment as educational and preparatory.
2. The results of Moses' actions are not all intended by him.
3. Moses' conduct is occasioned by the Israelites so that Moses is free from blame. Moses is here regarded as concealing not the glory as such but its destined abolition.
4. Paul's view of Moses is determined by what his opponents were saying. They accuse him of preaching a veiled gospel.
5. Paul sees Moses as acting out of motives of reverence.
6. Paul uses the veiled face of the lawgiver as a warning to his readers not to allow themselves to be deceived by his opponents.
7. Moses points forward to Christ.

Of these, positions (3) and (4) are worth commenting on in light of recent studies of the passage because they are diametrically opposed to one another. With respect to (3), κάλυμμα has been understood as a metonymy for "the hard heartedness that continues to characterize those outside of Christ and which, when removed by the power of the Spirit, makes a Spirit-empowered obedience to the Law of God possible."[53] This veil of hard-heartedness could only be abolished (Hafemann's reading of καταργεῖται in 3:14c) by the new covenant inaugurated by Christ. There was no power to do so under the Sinai covenant. It was Moses therefore who mercifully shielded the Israelites from being judged owing to the hardness of their hearts. From this perspective, Paul was offering a contextual reading of Exod 34:29-35 in accordance with the original intention of the biblical text. Taken this way, Hafemann's position represents the repudiation of Windisch and the rehabilitation, albeit in nuanced form, of the position put forward by Johann Goettsberger.[54]

---

[52] Thrall, *A Critical and Exegetical Commentary on the Second Epistle to the Corinthians*, 1: 258.

[53] Scott J. Hafemann, "The Glory and Veil of Moses in 2 Cor 3:7-14: An Example of Paul's Contextual Exegesis of the OT – A Proposal," *HBT* 14 (1992): 43.

[54] Johann Goettsberger, "Die Hülle des Moses nach Exod 34 und 2 Kor 3," *BZ* 16 (1924): 1-17. See Hafemann, *Paul, Moses, and the History of Israel*, 255-265.

By contrast, it has been most recently argued that the radiance on Moses' face being abolished, and the implied end of the law, are likely to have been Pauline formulations since they are consistent with Paul's view in Gal 3:23-4:11 and Rom 10:4. "According to Paul, the law remained in effect until Christ ended it."[55] In this reading, Paul's use of 2 Cor 3:13b can be read alongside Rom 10:4 (contra Hafemann). For someone like Thomas Blanton, 2 Cor 3:7-18 represents a theological narrative that speaks of a physical and ideological move out of the synagogue into the house-church. Paul's narrative is one in which Moses as representative of the law is superseded by Christ. It is Blanton's view that Paul redeploys the motif of Moses' veil' in order to delegitimize the ideology and praxis of his rivals who preached that under the new covenant the spirit enables perfect observance of the law. Rather than attack his opponents head-on he undermines their ideology of the primacy of the Mosaic law. By way of an exegetical inversion Paul constructs a discourse that transposes the charges against him of falsifying God's word and preaching a veiled gospel (cf. 2 Cor 4:2-3) onto Moses instead and, by extension, onto the opponents advocating Torah observance. Thus Blanton represents a revival, in modified form, of the position of Windisch.

Both positions, it should be noted, are firmly situated within the new trend of Pauline scholarship that no longer sees 2 Cor 3:7-18 as offering a negative assessment of Judaism. This owes itself to the legacy of E.P. Sanders and the so-called 'New Perspective on Paul' who have helped us to appreciate Paul within his Jewish matrix.[56]

---

[55] Thomas R. Blanton, *Constructing a New Covenant: Discursive Strategies in the Damascus Document and Second Corinthians* (WUNT, 2: Tübingen: Mohr [Siebeck], 2007), 220.

[56] E.P. Sanders, *Paul and Palestinian Judaism: A Comparison of Patterns of Religion* (London: SCM Press, 1977). See Hafemann, *Paul, Moses, and the History of Israel,* 261 on the issue of opponents: "Those who want to maintain that Paul's opponents were in some sense 'Judaizers' must now contend with the challenge of E.P. Sanders, *et al.* and the 'new perspective on Paul' which it has produced. Indeed, many from this perspective doubt if Paul's polemics have anything to do with the real position of his opponents at all! But if Paul's opponents were in fact Jews who were somehow connected to Jerusalem, and if Paul did in fact understand them correctly, rather than having erected a 'straw man,' then the nature of this Judaistic opposition can no longer simply be *assumed* to be legal-

For instance, Hafemann's position does away with the need to reconstruct the identity and theology of the opponents since Paul's argument follows the inner logic of the Jewish scriptures.[57] Blanton, on the other hand, *does* reconstruct the ideology of the opponents but argues to see early pre-70 CE 'Christianity' more accurately as a Jewish sect characterized by internal division on the matter of Torah observance. Paul and his rivals were struggling to promote their own often mutually exclusive ideological views. Yet both positions lead to implications that are strikingly similar. These are:

(1) Even though Hafemann points out that νόμος is never explicitly mentioned in 2 Corinthians, and argues against looking to the use of τέλος in Rom 10:4 as a parallel for 2 Cor 3:13b, nonetheless he did concede, as seen earlier, that the two statements are related *theologically*. "It is precisely because Moses had to veil the purpose (τέλος) of the glory of the old covenant from Israel due to their hard hearts (2 Cor. 13:13b) that Christ must become the τέλος of the Law (Rom. 10:4)."[58]

(2) As for Blanton, even though he maintains that Paul's proclamation of a law-free ministry was in fact a minority position, one must reckon with the fact that if Paul's view became in time the majority position, this only renders the apostle's contribution to the later 'parting of the ways' between Judaism and Christianity all the more significant.[59] Viewed from that perspective, 2 Cor 3:7-18, as

---

istic. This is especially the case in 2 Corinthians, where it has long been observed that the issue of circumcision never appears and the Law as such is never explicitly mentioned."

[57] Hafemann, *Paul, Moses and the History of Israel*, 360: " There is no reason to suppose that v.13 represents the view of Paul's *opponents* rather than that of Exod. 34:29ff. itself as read by Paul."

[58] *Ibid.*, 358.

[59] See for instance Jörg Frey's conclusion in, "Paul's Jewish Identity," *Jewish Identity in the Greco-Roman World / Jüdische Identität in der griechisch-römischen Welt*, ed. Jörg Frey, Daniel R. Schwartz and Stephanie Gripenrung, (AJEC/AGJU 71; Leiden and Boston: Brill, 2007), 285-321, 321: "Even though Paul relentlessly worked for the unity of Jewish and Gentile Christians, it may well be the case that he actually contributed more to the later split between the increasingly Gentile church and Jewish Christianity."

the theological narrative that speaks of a physical and ideological move out of the synagogue into the house-church, would seem to occupy an important place in this separation process.

Both these considerations bring us back, at least for now, to the statement by Sanders that "when Paul speaks in a direct way about the two dispensations (2 Corinthians 3)..., his thought is dominated by the surpassing value of life in Christ."[60]

Summary

To summarise the contribution thus far, Paul's use of καταργέω and τέλος continues to vex and frustrate exegetes, particularly with regard to their referents.

In v. 7, the feminine attributive present participle is understood in its immediate sense as referring to the glory on/of Moses' face.

The change to a neuter substantive participle in vv. 11 and 13 seems to broaden the scope to something more general, but here one can choose to see it more immediately as referring to the διακονία of Moses, but then what this διακονία implies is also unclear.

In v. 13 we also have the problem of τέλος, which acts as a hinge on which the understanding of καταργέω depends, but then here we are caught between the option of rendering it as "goal" or "end". The choice for end/cessation requires a reading of Moses' glory fading, something not necessarily recommended when translating καταργέω. The reading of "goal" however places a huge reliance on Paul's later use of τέλος in Rom 10:4 and here there is discussion as to whether that is a legitimate parallel to 2 Cor 3:13.

Finally, in v. 14 we are frustrated by what is the implied subject of καταργεῖται. Is it the glory of the Mosaic covenant, the old covenant, or just the veil? Here, in a limited, restricted, sense it seems to be the veil.

The sheer ambiguity of καταργέω and τέλος, together with locating their referents, contributes to the uncertainty of what exactly Paul means. Even though Paul can, and should, be appreciated within his

[60] Sanders, *Paul, the Law, and the Jewish People*, 140.

Jewish matrix,[61] we believe that this ambiguity helped to contribute to the later understanding of the old covenant that is abolished.

Part 2: The Glory and the Veil

Reimund Bieringer

The central theological concept of 2 Cor 3:7-18 is undoubtedly δόξα. In 3:7-11.18 the noun occurs eleven times (see also the two occurrences in 4:4.6). The extra-biblical Greek meaning of δόξα as "view", "opinion", "reputation" does not occur in the NT[62]. The NT meaning of the word is rather in line with its LXX usage. There it is the translation of כבוד which "is used esp. in reference to the deity as an expression of the manifestation of his sovereign rule over nature and history, on the one hand in the powerful form of divine radiance in theophanies, but even more in the majesty of his historical acts of salvation and judgment"[63].

Analysis of the Meanings of δόξα in 3:7-18 (4:4.6)

In his EDNT article on δόξα H. Hegermann distinguishes three groups of meaning[64]: First we encounter the meaning "esteem," "honor" with ἔπαινος and τιμή as synonyms and ἀτιμία as antonym (see Rom 2:7; 3:7; 4:20; 9:23b; 11:36; 15:7; 16:27; 1 Cor 2:7; 10:31; 11:15; 15:43; 2 Cor 1:20; 4:15; 6,8; 8:19.23; Gal 1:5; Phil 1,11; 2:11;

[61] See for instance the reading by Serge Ruzer, "The New Covenant, the Reinterpretation of Scripture and Collective Messiahship," *Mapping the New Testament: Early Christian Writings as a Witness for Jewish Biblical Exegesis* (Jewish and Christian Perspectives 13; Leiden: Brill, 2007), 215-241 (ch. 8). We are grateful to the author for bringing this article to our attention.

[62] H. Hegermann, art. δόξα, in *EDNT* 1 (1990), 344-348, 345.

[63] *Ibid.*

[64] *Ibid.*

3:19; 4:20; 1 Thess 2:6; 2:20). Second somewhat less frequently δόξα has the meaning "splendor," "radiance of power" (Rom 11:36; 16:27; 1 Cor 11:7; 15:40-41; Phil 3:21; 4:19; 1 Thess 2:12. Here δόξα is often used in the same context with δύναμις, ἐξουσία, κράτος; antonym: ταπείνωσις). The third meaning of δόξα is "the nature of the deity in its manifestation" (Rom 1:20.23 [cf. θειότης]; 3:23; 5:2; 6:4; 8:18.21; 9:4.23a; 1 Cor 2:8; 2 Cor 4:4.6; 4:17).

2 Corinthians 3:1-4:6 has the highest frequency of δόξα of any Pauline text. Paul uses the noun δόξα in ways which require careful analysis. There are nine absolute occurrences of δόξα (3:7.8.9 [bis].10.11 [bis].18 [bis]). The other uses are qualified by a noun in the genitive: δόξα τοῦ προσώπου αὐτοῦ [= Μωϋσέως] (3:7), δόξα κυρίου (3:18), δόξα τοῦ Χριστοῦ (4:4) and δόξα τοῦ θεοῦ ἐν προσώπῳ ['Ιησοῦ] Χριστοῦ (4:6). When he uses δόξα without a qualifier, he explicitly relates it to διακονία τοῦ θανάτου/τῆς κατακρίσεως, to διακονία τοῦ πνεύματος/τῆς δικαιοσύνης as well as to τὸ καταργούμενον and τὸ μένον. Paul uses the verbs γίνομαι, εἰμί and περισσεύω to connect δόξα with these nouns. In three cases the clauses are elliptic (3:9.11), most probably presupposing a form of εἰμί. From a semantic point of view, the meaning of δόξα in 3:1-4:6 does not occur in the meaning "honor" nor just radiance of power, but rather in the meaning of "the nature of the deity in its manifestation." It is God's δόξα and this δόξα appears on the face of Christ (4:6). Long before that it had appeared on the face of Moses (3:7). The δόξα κυρίου is also reflected[65] on the face of the Christ believers. The main interest of 3:7-11 is how this δόξα which was on the face of Moses is related to the διακονία of the Spirit and the διακονία of death respectively. Thus because of the link with the δόξα on the face of Moses in 3:7 we assume that in 3:1-4:6 δόξα does not simply mean honor or radiance of power, but is understood as a reflection or manifestation of God's divine majesty.

---

[65] So also J. Kremer, art. κατοπτρίζομαι, in *EDNT* 2 (1990), 274-275, 274.

In the first conditional period in 3:7 ἐγενήθη ἐν δόξῃ is used in the protasis and ἔσται ἐν δόξῃ in the apodosis. While Paul uses two different verbs (γίνομαι and εἰμί), many translations use the same verb to translate both, either assimilating ἔσται to ἐγενήθη (NRSV: came – will come; NJB: occurred – will occur) or vice versa (Luther: hatte – sollte haben; TOB: a été – aura; NAB: was – will be). Fewer translations render the difference of the verbs (NIV: came – will be). The aorist verb form ἐγενήθη is the predicate of the conditional clause in 3:7a. The verb of the apodosis in 3:8 is a future form (ἔσται). This conditional clause expresses a condition of fact (realis). The contrast between the forms of γίνομαι and εἰμί suggests that the first stresses the dynamic becoming and the second the more static being (cf. NIV)[66]. The use of the more dynamic verb γινόμαι in 3:7 with regard to the διακονία of death directs the focus on its coming into being and creates a contrast with διὰ τὴν δόξαν τοῦ προσώπου αὐτοῦ τὴν καραργουμένην. When Paul speaks about the διακονία of the Spirit, he does not emphasize its coming into being, but its (future) existence. Even though the prepositional phrases ἐν δόξῃ are identical in 3:7-8, there is a difference of nuance between the verbs that are used (γίνομαι vs. εἰμί). As a result of the different meanings of the verbs, a slight shift in meaning is also notable in ἐν δόξῃ. The διακονία of death is described as having come into being by means of glory. Used with ἐγενήθη the preposition ἐν has an instrumental meaning. The διακονία of the Spirit, however, is presented as having a future existence in glory. Here, with the verb form ἔσται the preposition ἐν is understood more in its locative meaning. The relationship with glory is closer when it is expressed with ἐν than with διά. This reading is confirmed by the fact that in 3:11 where Paul succinctly (and elliptically) summarizes what preceded, he uses διὰ δόξης and ἐν δόξῃ respectively: "For if what was rendered inefficient [came] through glory, much more [will] what abides [be]

---

[66] See *BDAG* s.v. γίνομαι, 196: "Its contrast to the more static term εἰμί can be seen in Kaibel 595, 5 οὐκ ἤμην καὶ ἐγενόμην = I was not and then I came to be".

in glory" (3:11). Thus Paul says that διακονία τοῦ θανάτου came into being through glory (ἐν δόξῃ), while the διακονία τοῦ πνεύματος will have its existence in glory (ἐν δόξῃ).

In the next conditional period, Paul varies the way he expresses the relationship between ministry and glory. In the protasis of the second conditional period δόξα is the subject and διακονία τῆς κατακρίσεως is in the (possessive) dative[67] expressing a belonging[68]. Glory belongs[69] to the διακονία τῆς κατακρίσεως (3:9). In the apodosis abundant possession of glory of the διακονία τῆς δικαιοσύνης is expressed with the verb περισσεύω and a dative of respect of the noun δόξα. This idea is taken up again in the expression εἵνεκεν τῆς ὑπερβαλλούσης δόξης in 3:10. In the third conditional period in 3:11 Paul reuses the grammatical construction of the first conditional period in 3:7-8 as we have already demonstrated above.

There is only one place in 3:7-11 where δόξα is qualified in any way, namely in 3:7 where it is related to Moses: διὰ τὴν δόξαν τοῦ προσώπου αὐτοῦ τὴν καταργουμένην. Paul specifies the glory with the genitive τοῦ προσώπου αὐτοῦ and the attributive participle τὴν καταργουμένην. The genitive indicates where the δόξα is found, namely on the face of Moses. Here the meaning of δόξα is focused on a light phenomenon, namely a radiance or splendor which blinds the onlooker. On the basis of the background of this text in Ex 33:18-22 and 34:29-35 it is clear that the splendor on Moses' face is not his own, but a reflection of the glory of God. It is important not to overlook that the MT does not linguistically connect the radiance on the face of Moses and the glory of God. For the reflection of God's glory on Moses' face the verb קרן (to shine) is used (Ex 34:29.30.35). For the glory of God the Hebrew word כבוד is

[67] For a discussion of the textual problem see Harris, *The Second Epistle to the Corinthians*, 281.

[68] Other datives are less likely in the context. See Harris, *The Second Epistle to the Corinthians*, 287.

[69] For a discussion of the correct tense see below.

used (Ex 33:18-22). כבוד is semantically not connected to light phenomena, but to weight[70]. Only after the LXX translated כבוד with δόξα, it became possible to associate Moses' shining skin with the glory of God. The equivalent of קרן in the corresponding LXX text is δοξάζω (δεδόξασται in 34:29.35 and ἦν δεδοξασμένη in 34.30), thus establishing a linguistic link with δόξα of 33:18.22. Paul goes one step further by using the noun δόξα to refer to both the radiance on Moses' face and the διακονία as possessing δόξα. This linguistic choice of Paul is at the origin of the suggestion that the diminishing of the radiance (δόξα) on the face of Moses (3:7) is an indication of the fading glory of the διακονία (ministry or dispensation?) associated with Moses (3:7-11). But at the same time the fact that Paul uses the same noun δόξα for all of these realities is a strong witness to the conviction that the ministry of both the old and of the new covenants are filled with the same majesty and splendor of God.

In 3:7-11 Paul also uses the verb δοξάζω, namely in 3:10. καὶ γὰρ οὐ δεδόξασται τὸ δεδοξασμένον ἐν τούτῳ τῷ μέρει is a rather cryptic statement in many regards, as it is not clear what is the referent of τὸ δεδοξασμένον. No matter what the referent is, the perfect passive forms of δοξάζω clarify that the δόξα that has so far been talked about is a received glory. Possessing glory is the result of having been glorified.

In 3:18 Paul relates δόξα to "all of us". He first speaks about reflecting (κατοπτριζόμενοι[71]) the glory of the Lord as in a mirror, and then he refers to "being transformed into the same image ἀπὸ δόξης εἰς δόξαν" (3:18). Paul is convinced that we shall be transformed into the image which we reflect as in a mirror, namely the glory of the Lord. "It would seem to us that Paul detected

---

[70] H. Hegermann, art. δόξα, in *EDNT* 1 (1990), 344-348, 345.

[71] For the discussion whether κατοπτριζόμενοι refers to the action of beholding or reflecting as in a mirror see the discussion in Jan Lambrecht, *Second Corinthians* (Sacra Pagina 8; Collegeville MN: Liturgical Press, 1999), 55-56.

the idea of 'transformation by vision' in his reading of Exodus 34. The glorious transformation that happened to Moses becomes a possibility for every Christian"[72]. Here Paul "envisages a profound idea of unity with Christ (without loss of separate identity)"[73] which implies a sharing of the δόξα.

The Tenses and the Time References in 2 Cor 3:7-18

For a correct interpretation of 2 Cor 3:7-18 a careful study of the tenses and the time references is of crucial importance. Commentators and translators often suggest interpretations which are not necessarily backed by the grammar. Here we would especially like to draw attention to the NRSV.

In the first conditional period Paul uses the aorist ἐγενήθη and the future ἔσται in a *Qal wa-ḥomer* construction. Most translations render these tenses as past and future respectively. In light of περισσεύει in 3:9 the future ἔσται in 3:8 is often read as a logical future expressing that which is to be expected under certain specified circumstances. However, 3:12 speaks about the *Qal wa-ḥomer* conclusions of 3:7-11 as a hope, and in 3:18 the transformation into the glory of the Lord seems to be dependent on our beholding it. Therefore, it might be better to accept ἔσται as a real future which would then be evidence that Paul is aware that what he is talking about is yet to be (fully) realized.

Paul and Judaism in 2 Cor 3:7-18

In 2 Cor 3:7-18 Paul does not speak about Judaism explicitly. But does some of his terminology at least refer to Judaism implicitly? When he mentions the expression παλαιὰ διαθήκη in 3:14 he is using an antithetical term to καινὴ διαθήκη which he had men-

[72] *Ibid.*, 56.
[73] *Ibid.*

tioned in 3:6. In 1 Cor 11:25 we find this expression in the Lord's Supper paradosis: τοῦτο τὸ ποτήριον ἡ καινὴ διαθήκη ἐστὶν ἐν τῷ ἐμῷ αἵματι. Since the expression παλαιὰ διαθήκη is not found anywhere else in the Bible, a number of scholars have suggested that it is a Pauline creation[74]. In that case the use of the adjective παλαιός, ά, όν instead of ἀρχαῖος, α, ον is Paul's more or less deliberate choice which may have significant implications for the understanding of its context. Harris concisely presents what we find in the lexica: "Whereas the adjective ἀρχαῖος ("old") has the predominant sense of "ancient" or "venerable," παλαιός more often means "old" in the sense of "antiquated" or "dated."[75] In 3:14 Paul speaks about the reading of the "old covenant" and in 3:15 in a parallel expression about the reading of Moses. "Moses" seems to be used here as metonymy. This means that the referent of "old covenant" is the Pentateuch, "the books of Moses". By introducing the "veil", Paul changes his metaphor significantly. In 3:7-11, the focus was on "rendering ineffective", coming to an end. By using the metaphor of the veil, Paul does not suggest the ineffectiveness or end, but rather the hiddenness of the "old covenant". As soon as the veil is taken away, it continues to be useful, it seems, since it continues to be read, albeit in a new light. By the phrase ἐν Χριστῷ καταργεῖται Paul suggests the hermeneutical key that makes it possible for him to continue reading the "old covenant" from his new perspective.

In 3:7 Paul uses the expression ἡ διακονία τοῦ θανάτου, in 3:9 ἡ διακονία τῆς κατακρίσεως. The meaning of διακονία is disputed. Since in 3:6 Paul has just referred to himself (and the

---

[74] E.g., Windisch, *Der Zweite Korintherbrief*, 121; Furnish, *II Corinthians*, 208 and Harris, *The Second Epistle to the Corinthians*, 302.

[75] *Ibid.* See also Michael J. Gorman, *Apostle of the Crucified Lord: A Theological Introduction to Paul and His Letters* (Grand Rapids MI and Cambridge: Eerdmans, 2004), 299-300 (italics in the original): "*Thus for Paul, depending especially on the prophets Jeremiah and Ezekiel, the old covenant was never intended to be permanent but to be renewed by a covenant involving God's Spirit.*"

other apostles) as διάκονοι of the new covenant, one is spontaneously inclined to understand ἡ διακονία τοῦ θανάτου as the ministry of death. But by the very fact that it is characterized as "chiseled in letters on stone", indicates that it must refer to more than the minister (cf. the translation "dispensation"). Whatever Paul says about ἡ διακονία τοῦ θανάτου/τῆς κατακρίσεως in 3:7-11, he says about what he later calls the "old covenant". By using the word διακονία he, however, creates an ambiguity suggesting that the διάκονοι of the covenant(s) are also implied[76].

The fundamental content of what Paul says in 3:6.7-18 is a comparison between two entities which he calls ἡ διακονία τοῦ θανάτου/τῆς κατακρίσεως on the one hand and ἡ διακονία τοῦ πνεύματος/τῆς δικαιοσύνης on the other hand. The bottom line of that comparison is that δόξα belongs to both of them. This is the fundamental presupposition of his use of the *Qal wa-ḥomer* (*a minore ad maius*) argument. Paul clearly acknowledges, even presupposes that ἡ διακονία τοῦ θανάτου/τῆς κατακρίσεως possessed δόξα. But he also turns the comparison into a competition, emphasizing that the glory of the διακονία τοῦ πνεύματος/τῆς δικαιοσύνης surpasses that of the διακονία τοῦ θανάτου/τῆς κατακρίσεως, and that the latter was rendered ineffective (3:11)[77].

As we have seen above, what Paul says implicitly about central aspects of Judaism is mostly indirect and implicit. At the same time it is carefully composed, complex and subtle. By using the word διακονία in 3:7,9 instead of διαθήκη the reader is left with the impression that the rendering ineffective refers to the ministry and not the covenant. Another ambiguity stems from the fact that

[76] See Thrall, *A Critical and Exegetical Commentary on the Second Epistle to the Corinthians*, 1:241.

[77] Belleville, *Reflections of Glory*, 211: "With the exception of v. 14a, Paul's contribution is in terms of subtle shading and turn of phrase: through a change of gender, the fading glory of Moses' face becomes the fading character of the covenant itself."

the word δόξα is used to speak about the reflection of God's glory on Moses' face and about the Lord's glory as such. Moreover Paul uses elliptic syntax, not expressing the verbs. The ambiguity of his statements is also increased by the fact that he uses three neuter participles (τὸ δεδοξασμένον in 3:10; τὸ καταργούμενον in 3:11,13 and τὸ μένον in 3:11) whose referents are uncertain. It is not surprising that exegetes have been divided as to the question whether the verb καταργέω in 3:11.13 refers to the glory on Moses' face or the glory of the διακονία. And even if it refers to the διακονία it remains ambiguous whether καταργέω is about the ministry or the covenant. Finally Paul switches from the metaphor of the rendering ineffective to veiling, the latter in opposition to the former leaving open the possibility of reversibility. As is obvious, Paul's text leaves many issues unresolved and many questions unanswered. We might wonder whether this ambiguity was the result of his uncertainty about the subject or whether it is part of a rhetorical strategy with which he tried to say more than he had the courage to express explicitly at that moment.

CONCLUSION

Despite, or maybe just because of our detailed analysis of key issues in 2 Cor 3:7-18 throughout this contribution both in part 1 and part 2, we became aware of the ambiguity and complexity of the meaning of this text. This ambiguity opened the doors for misunderstandings and abuses in later centuries. As we demonstrated in this study, the Pauline text itself is less explicit about the precise perspective of Paul on Judaism than some translations and specialized studies would make us believe. In the limited scope of this contribution it was not possible to offer a detailed exegesis of this pericope. We rather focused our attention on several key concepts of 2 Cor 3:1-4:6 which are important for a better understanding of Paul's post-Damascus view of Judaism, namely καταργέω, τέλος, κάλυμμα and δόξα. We pointed out the problems with understanding καταργέω as "to fade," τέλος as end and with interpreting 3:14 as stating the abolishing of the old covenant or the ministry of the old covenant rather than the veil. We also clarified that 3:7-11 is not suggesting that only the ministry of the new covenant is characterized by δόξα. There is more continuity between the old and the new covenant in this text than many other interpretations suggest. Nevertheless this cannot blind us to the clear evidence of antithetical terminology (ministry of death vs. ministry of the Spirit; ministry of condemnation vs. ministry of justification; καταργέω vs. μένω; παλαιὰ διαθήκη vs. καινὴ διαθήκη). Even if we do not take this out of context and if we do not allow this to be read onesidedly, we need to acknowledge where Paul's preference and allegiance is found. Paul's christological and pneumatological Scriptural hermeneutics (3:14-17) needs to be read in its early Christian, first century context, but it cannot be ignored or denied. If and in as much as such christological and pneumatological hermeneutics carry dangerous potential for later readers, they need to take care not to actualize this potential. Here our own Scriptural hermeneutics is challenged.[78]

[78] See Reimund Bieringer & Mary Elsbernd *Normativity of the Future: Reading Biblical and Other Authoritative Texts in an Eschatological Perspective* (Leuven - Paris and Walpole, MA, Peeters, 2010).

Chapter 7
Paul, Deicide, and the Wrath of God: Towards a Hermeneutical Reading of 1 Thess 2:14–16

Didier Pollefeyt and David J. Bolton

1. The Text NRSV/ NA27

14a For you, brothers and sisters, became imitators	ὑμεῖς γὰρ μιμηταὶ ἐγενήθητε, ἀδελφοί,
14b of the churches of God in Christ Jesus	τῶν ἐκκλησιῶν τοῦ θεοῦ τῶν οὐσῶν ἐν τῇ
14c that are in Judea,	Ἰουδαίᾳ ἐν Χριστῷ Ἰησοῦ,
14d for you suffered the same things from your own compatriots	ὅτι τὰ αὐτὰ ἐπάθετε καὶ ὑμεῖς ὑπὸ τῶν ἰδίων συμφυλετῶν
14e as they did from the Jews,	καθὼς καὶ αὐτοὶ ὑπὸ τῶν Ἰουδαίων,
15a who killed both the Lord Jesus	τῶν καὶ τὸν κύριον ἀποκτεινάντων Ἰησοῦν
15b and the prophets,	καὶ τοὺς προφήτας
15c and drove us out;	καὶ ἡμᾶς ἐκδιωξάντων
15d they displease God	καὶ θεῷ μὴ ἀρεσκόντων
15e and oppose everyone	καὶ πᾶσιν ἀνθρώποις ἐναντίων,
16a by hindering us from speaking to the Gentiles	κωλυόντων ἡμᾶς τοῖς ἔθνεσιν λαλῆσαι
16b so that they may be saved.	ἵνα σωθῶσιν,
16c Thus they have constantly been filling up the measure of their sins;	εἰς τὸ ἀναπληρῶσαι αὐτῶν τὰς ἁμαρτίας πάντοτε.
16d but God's wrath has overtaken them at last.	ἔφθασεν δὲ ἐπ' αὐτοὺς ἡ ὀργὴ εἰς τέλος.

2. INTRODUCTION: SETTING THE PROBLEM

1 Thess 2:14–16[1] is generally acknowledged to be the most vituperative and polemical statement by Paul against "the Jews" (οἱ Ἰουδαῖοι). As Leon Morris has written, it is

> a denunciation of the Jews more severe than anything else in the Pauline writings. It is not an outburst of temper but [...] the vehement condemnation, by a man in thorough sympathy with the mind and spirit of God, of the principles on which the Jews as a nation had acted at every period of their history.[2]

Five accusations are presented: (1) that they have caused suffering to the Judean churches (v.14a–e); (2) that they have killed the Lord Jesus and the prophets (v.15a–b); (3) that they have driven out the Jewish believers in Jesus (v.15c); (4) that they do not please God or humanity (v.15d–e) and (5) that they try to prevent the Gentile mission (v.16a–b).[3] In light of this behaviour, their sins are said to have reached (or be reaching) intolerable levels with the outpouring of (divine) wrath εἰς τέλος (v.16c–d) as the inevitable result.

Owing to the difficulty of the text on a variety of issues, a wide range of scholarly responses have arisen that attempt to find a suitable 'resolution' to the problem. Is Paul the actual author of the text?; does the text refer to all Jews or just some Jews?; is it a normal example of contemporary intra-Jewish polemics?; how far is

---

[1] For an introduction to the epistle and its historical background see, e.g.: Leon Morris, *The First and Second Epistles to the Thessalonians* (Grand Rapids, Mich.: Eerdmans, 1959); F.F. Bruce, *1 and 2 Thessalonians* (WBC vol. 45; Waco, Tex.: Word Books, 1982); Robert Jewett, *The Thessalonian Correspondence: Pauline Rhetoric and Millenarian Piety* (Philadelphia, Penn.: Fortress, 1986); Carol J. Schlueter, *Filling Up the Measure: Polemical Hyperbole in 1 Thessalonians 2.14–16* (JSNTSup 98; Sheffield: Sheffield Academic Press, 1994); Earl J. Richard, *First and Second Thessalonians* (Collegeville, Minn.: Liturgical Press, 1995); David Luckensmeyer, *The Eschatology of First Thessalonians* (Göttingen: Vandenhoeck & Ruprecht, 2009).

[2] Morris, *Thessalonians*, 90.

[3] Richard, *First and Second Thessalonians*, 123.

Paul responsible for the *Wirkungsgeschichte* of this passage? Our own proposal in this paper is threefold: we shall firstly place the pericope in the context of the letter as a whole; then give an overview of the various positions taken in response to it and finally present our own hermeneutical reading.

3. CONTEXTUALIZATION

Paul's purpose in writing 1 Thess appears to be based around three main concerns: to express joy at the Thessalonians' progress in the gospel; to vindicate his own mission as shown by the genuineness of their conversion; and to deal with various eschatological and practical matters.

A broad outline, giving more attention to our specific passage, may be presented as follows:[4]

I. Salutation (1:1)

II. Paul's Relation to the Thessalonians (1:2–3:13)

- A. Thanks for the Thessalonians (1:2–10
- B. Defense of Paul's Apostleship and the Thessalonians' Conversion (2:1–16)
    - 1. Positive Defense (2:1–12)
    - 2. Negative Defense (2:13–16)
        - a. The Thessalonians' Reception of the Gospel (2:13–14a)
        - b. Their Opponents' Rejection of the Gospel (2:14b–16)
- C. Paul's Desire to Visit (2:17–3:10)
- D. Transitional Benediction (3:11–13)

III. The Lord's Return as a Motive for Sanctification (4:1–5:22)

IV. Concluding Remarks (5:23–28)

---

[4] This is largely taken from Daniel B. Wallace, "1 Thessalonians: Introduction, Outline, and Argument," 9–11 [cited 25 August 2009]. Online http://bible.org/seriespage/1-thessalonians-introduction-outline-and-argument. Wallace is Professor of New Testament Studies at Dallas Theological Seminary and maintains the above website.

First Thessalonians is virtually unanimously accepted as a genuine Pauline letter.[5] It is referenced as belonging to the Marcion canon (mid-2nd century C.E.), the Muratorian canon (c.180 CE), as well as being quoted by name by Irenaeus, Clement of Alexandria, and Tertullian. It also appears in the most ancient manuscripts such as the Old Latin, Old Syriac, as well as in fragmentary form in P30, P46, and P65.[6] Despite this external attestation our passage under consideration has often been deemed non-Pauline, even anti-Pauline. The reasons for this are many, and it is to them that we now turn.

4. VARIOUS STRATEGIES TO DEAL WITH THE PASSAGE

Let us now look to the content of the passage and present a critical overview of the various scholarly responses to it. Summaries have been given among others, by Josef Coppens (1975);[7] Robert Jewett (1986);[8] John W. Simpson (1988);[9] Jon Weatherly (1991);[10] Carol J. Schlueter (1994);[11] Earl J. Richard (1995);[12] Jonas Holmstrand

---

His outline is more thorough than that given in other commentaries, such as Bruce, *1 and 2* Thessalonians, 3; or I. Howard Marshall, *1 and 2 Thessalonians* (The New Century Bible Commentary; Grand Rapids, Mich.: Eerdmans, 1983), 10–11. Bruce has given 1 Thess 2:13–16 the unfortunate title of "Further Thanksgiving."

[5] Wallace, "1 Thessalonians: Introduction," 2.

[6] Philip W. Comfort and David P. Barrett, eds., *The Complete Text of the Earliest New Testament Manuscripts* (Grand Rapids, Mich.: Baker Books, 1999), 118–119; 193–224; 345–351.

[7] Josef Coppens, "Miscellanées bibliques. LXXX : Une diatribe antijuive dans 1 Thess., II, 13–16," *ETL* 51 (1975): 90–95, here 91–93.

[8] Robert Jewett, *Thessalonian Correspondence*, 36–37.

[9] John W. Simpson, *The Future of Non-Christian Jews: 1 Thessalonians 2:15–16 and Romans 9–11* (Ann Arbor, Mich.: University Microfilms International, 1990).

[10] Jon Weatherly, "The Authenticity of 1 Thessalonians 2:13–16: Additional Evidence," *JSNT* 42 (1991): 79–98, here 79–91.

[11] Schlueter, *Filling Up the Measure.*

[12] Richard, *First and Second Thessalonians*, 17.

(1997);[13] and David Luckensmeyer (2009).[14] It is our purpose to present a critical overview of both sides of the positions taken.

4.1 Deutero-Pauline interpolation

Treating 1 Thess 2:14–16 as an interpolation is probably the most common analysis of the text. Such an approach does indeed seem "to offer the best of both worlds" for, according to John C. Hurd, "we are allowed to keep 1 Thessalonians as an authentic letter of Paul but the historical and theological difficulties posed by our passage are resolved by resigning it to a later period."[15] The arguments marshaled go back to the work of F. C. Baur (1875) who opined that the passage was a reflection of "a post-Pauline period" when both Gentile and even Jewish Christians "had begun to regard Jews as enemies of the gospel."[16] The general approach of viewing the passage as the later work of some anti-Jewish Gentile is based on various considerations such as the polemical tone of the passage, the use of un-Pauline terms, an unusual statement about imitating the Judean churches, the un-Pauline list of accusations and a definitive condemnation of the Jews that contradicts what Paul writes in Rom 11:26 that "all Israel will be saved." In short the issues deal with textual, historical, form-critical and theological issues.

---

[13] Jonas Holmstrand, *Markers and Meaning in Paul: An Analysis of 1 Thessalonians, Philippians and Galatians* (ConBNT 28; Stockholm: Almquist & Wiksell International, 1997), 42–46.

[14] David Luckensmeyer, *Eschatology*, 162–167.

[15] John C. Hurd, "Paul Ahead of his Time: 1 Thess 2:13–16," in *Anti-Judaism in Early Christianity* (ed. Peter Richardson and David Granskou; Waterloo, Ont: Wilfrid Laurier University Press, 1986), 21–36, here 25.

[16] Simpson, *Non-Christian Jews*, 66 n. 2.

4.1.1 *Textual criticism*

Textual criticism throws up something of a surprise. Despite the strong scholarly *Tendenz* to excuse the problem by appeal to interpolation (see e.g. the works by David Wenham, Norman Beck, and Birger Pearson[17]), the text critical apparatus reveals a bias in favor of inclusion. There is virtually no manuscript evidence that the passage is an interpolation.[18] From the fourth century onwards basically all manuscripts contain the passage in its entirety. Only one eleventh-century manuscript (vatic. Lat. 5729) leaves out v.16d, yet it is highly improbable that this variant goes back to a Greek manuscript.[19] The textual variants in vv.15–16 are of a very minor nature and could not be taken as supporting an interpolation, as William O. Walker confirms.[20] The difficulty comes however, with the discovery of early papyri containing fragments of 1 Thess. According to Philip W. Comfort and David P. Barrett the earliest textual fragments we have of the epistle are P46 (ca. 125–150 C. E.); P30 (ca. 225 C. E.) and P65 (ca. 250 C. E.).[21] None of these fragments contain our passage. The nearest is P65 that has 1 Thess 2:1, 6–13, but then lacks the rest of the letter.[22] P30 has nothing of chapters 1–3[23] and P46 has 1:9–2:3 but then nothing of the rest of chapter 2, nor chapters 3–4.[24]

---

[17] David Wenham, *Paul: Follower of Jesus or Founder of Christianity?* (Grand Rapids/Cambridge: Eerdmans, 1995), 319–320; Norman Beck, *Mature Christianity in the 21st Century: The Recognition and Repudiation of the Anti-Jewish Polemic of the New Testament* (New York: Crossroad, 1994), 82.

[18] Daniel B. Wallace, *Is 1 Thessalonians 2.13–16 an Interpolation?*, 2 [cited 25 August 2009]. http://bible.org/article/1-thessalonians-213-16-interpolation. He shows that manuscripts A B D F G H I P 0208 0278 33 1739 Itala, Syriac, Coptic, Origen, Athanasius, Jerome, Augustine, Chrysostom *et plures* all contain our passage.

[19] Luckensmeyer, *Eschatology*, 162.

[20] William O. Walker, *Interpolation in the Pauline letters* (JSNTSup 213; Sheffield: Sheffield Academic Press, 2001), 211–212.

[21] Philip W. Comfort and David P. Barrett, eds., *Earliest New Testament*, 118–119; 193–224; 345–351.

[22] P65 (PSI XIV 1373) contains 1 Thess 1:3–2:1, 6–13.

[23] P30 (P. Oxy. 1598) contains 1 Thess 4:12–13, 16–17; 5:3, 8–10, 12–18, 25–28.

[24] P46 (P. Chester Beatty II and P. Mich. Inv. 6238) contains 1 Thess 1:1; 1:9–2:3; 5:5–5:9, 23–28.

Now at face value, the absence of our passage from these papyri may seem to suggest the possibility of an interpolation, but an honest appraisal has to admit that it is impossible to say, owing to the piecemeal nature of the evidence. Moreover we have discovered that Origen quotes verbatim from 1 Thess 2:14–15 in his *Commentary on Matthew* (ca. 246–248 C. E.).[25] He explicitly mentions that the words are from Paul. This places his witness to the authenticity of the text around the same time as P30 and P65. When the codices are also taken into account, it is fair to argue that textual criticism rather tends to support, more than challenge, Pauline authorship.

4.1.2 *Historical criticism*

Historical criticism presents more formidable arguments. The strongest of them may be grouped as follows: that Paul would not appeal to the churches in Judea as an example for his churches to imitate (v.14a–14c); that there is no evidence of persecutions of Christians in Judea at that time (c.50 CE); that nowhere else does Paul attribute the death of Jesus to the Jews (v.15a), and that the only possible historical referent to ἡ ὀργή (v.16d) has to be the later, post-Pauline destruction of the Temple in 70 C. E.[26]

---

[25] Origen, "Commentary on Matthew," Book II, chapter 10 in *The Anti-Nicene Fathers: Translations of the Writings of the Fathers down to A.D. 325* (ed. Allan Menzies; vol. 10; Grand Rapids, Mich.: Eerdmans, 1978), 425. The dating to 246–248 CE is based on internal evidence and the witness of Eusebius (H.E. vi. 36). Origen, commenting on Matt 13:57 here writes "And by Paul in the First Epistle to the Thessalonians like things are said: 'For ye brethren became imitators of the churches of God which are in Judea in Christ Jesus, for ye also suffered the same things of your own countrymen even as they did of the Jews, who both killed the Lord Jesus and the prophets, and drave us out, and please not God, and are contrary to all men'."

[26] Birger A. Pearson, "1 Thessalonians 2:13–16: A Deutero-Pauline Interpolation," *HTR* 64 (1971): 79–94, here 82–83, 86–88; Luckensmeyer, *Eschatology*, 162–163. Beck, *Mature Christianity*, 94, 79; Pearson, "1 Thessalonians 2:13–16," 82–83; Richard, *First and Second Thessalonians*, 120.

However, counter-arguments are also well known. Since Paul only uses the imitation (μιμητής) motif four times in the proto-Paulines (1 Cor 4:16; 11:1; 1 Thess 1:6; 2:14) referring to himself and to the Lord, it is simply too categorical to argue that its use here is un-Pauline. Paul in fact does make reference to the churches of Christ in Judea in Gal 1:22. Moreover, though less plausibly, F. F. Bruce has argued that Silas, signified as a co-author of the letter, was a leading member of the church in Jerusalem (cf. Acts 15:22) and may have been responsible for this comparison.[27] In any case, as J. W. Simpson has pointed out, the imitation mentioned here is not an imperative, telling them to follow the Judean churches, but a description of an existing situation.[28] In their long-suffering steadfastness the Thessalonians are already imitating the Judean churches.

Regarding the evidence of persecution in Judea, other scholars have put forward a series of possible options. It could refer, either singularly or collectively, to the general persecution between 41–44 C. E. under the elder Herod Agrippa (cf. Acts 12:1)[29], to the revolt of Theudas in 44–46, to the Judean famine in 46–47 C. E., or to the aftermath of the expulsion of Jews from Rome in 49 C. E.[30] As concerns the attribution of the death of Jesus to the Jews, it has been pointed out that in 1 Cor 2:8 Paul blames the rulers (οἱ ἄρχοντες) as crucifying the Lord of glory in ignorance. Though it is debated who or what this phrase refers to (spiritual powers, Roman rulers, Jewish authorities?)[31] it still shows that this may not be the only place where Paul implicates Jewish responsibility for Jesus' death.[32]

---

[27] Bruce, *1 and 2 Thessalonians*, xxxii; cf. Michael Goulder, "Silas in Thesssalonica," *JSNT* 48 (1992): 94.

[28] Simpson, *Non-Christian Jews*, 115.

[29] Ibid., 89.

[30] Ibid., 90.

[31] Pearson, "1 Thessalonians 2:13–16," 85; Bruce, *1 and 2 Thessalonians*, 47; Pieter W. van der Horst, "Omgaan met anti-joodse teksten in het Nieuwe Testament," 1–13, here 8–9. [cited 25 August 2009]. http://www.appelkerkenisrael.nl/Lezingen/pvdhorst.pdf.

[32] Acts is the only other New Testament book to charge οἱ Ἰουδαῖοι with Jesus' death (Acts 2:36; 3:15; 5:30; 7:52).

Though several scholars, most notably Birger A. Pearson, point to a necessary historical setting of post 70 C. E. and thus a post-Pauline authorship, this is not demanded by the syntax. Pearson contends that ἔφθασεν has to refer to a past event ("wrath has come"), and that only the destruction of the Temple could account for such wrath. Yet according to David Luckensmeyer, the aorist tense of the verb ἔφθασεν governing ἡ ὀργή can have both modal and temporal aspects, meaning that the wrath could be in the past, coming presently or still to come in the future, undercutting the claim that it has to refer to one specific historical referent.[33] Paul could thus still have written verse 16d.

In general then, despite the seeming strength of its arguments, historical criticism remains far from decisive in evidencing an interpolation in 1 Thess 2:14–16.

4.1.3 *Form criticism*

Turning to the arguments for interpolation from form criticism, we find that they largely centre around three things: (i) the fact that 1 Thess 2:13, often taken as a unit with 2:14–16, begins with a redundant and repetitive second thanksgiving (cf. 1:2–10); (ii) that these verses seem to interrupt the natural flow connecting 2:12 to 2:17;[34] and (iii) that the passage uses apparently un-Pauline phrases.[35] However, once again scholars have not been shy in supplying counter-arguments to these authorial challenges.

For while it is true that virtually all the Pauline thanksgivings come immediately after the opening salutations (Rom 1:8–9; 1 Cor 1:4–9; Phil 1:3–11, etc.) renewals of thanksgiving are not unknown (cf. Phil 1:3–8; 4:10–20) and in any case the two thanksgivings are dealing with two different matters, one introductory and general, the other more specific and embedded in a particular context. Furthermore, as

---

[33] Luckensmeyer, *Eschatology*, 158.

[34] Simpson, *Non-Christian Jews*, 70.

[35] Daryl Schmidt, "1 Thess 2.13–16: Linguistic Evidence for an Interpolation," *JBL* 102 (1983): 269–279.

Bruce and Murphy-O'Connor note, it is extremely difficult to be able to establish a vocabulary norm for Paul's letters.[36] In contrast to those who see an abrupt transition between 2:12–2:13 and 2:16–2:17, many scholars have also argued that 2:13–16 "is an integral part of 1 Thessalonians overall."[37] Indeed Daniel Wallace has pointed out that 2:13–16 seems to form an *inclusio* with 1:2–10 regarding the parallel themes of thanksgiving (1:2/2:13), receiving the dynamic word of God (1:5/2:13), the Thessalonians' imitation (1:6/2:14), their perseverance in the midst of suffering (1:6/2:14), and the deliverance from wrath contrasted with the inescapability of wrath (1:9–10/2:16).[38] All this goes to show that while form criticism offers perhaps the strongest arguments for an interpolation, it is still far from enjoying a scholarly consensus since the counter-arguments for many are equally persuasive.

4.1.4 *Theological criticism*

As Jon Weatherly has in fact pointed out, most scholars base their interpolation theories on theological grounds rather than on textual, historical or form critical grounds.[39] One could summarize this approach as pitting 'Paul against Paul,' playing off his theology regarding the Jews in other authentic letters against the picture presented here. The main argument centers around the incompatibility of a wrath coming upon the Jews that is εἰς τέλος with what Paul writes about seven years later in Rom 9–11, especially 11:26 that

---

[36] Luckensmeyer, *Eschatology*, 164; Schmidt, "Interpolation," 269–70; Bruce, *1 and 2 Thessalonians*, xxxii; Jerome Murphy-O'Connor, *Paul the Letter-Writer: His World, His Opinions, His Skills* (GNS 41; Collegeville, Minn.: Liturgical Press, 1995), 34–35.

[37] Luckensmeyer, *Eschatology*, 164; Jewett, *The Thessalonian Correspondence*, 86; Charles A. Wanamaker, *The Epistles to the Thessalonians: A Commentary on the Greek Text* (Grand Rapids, Mich.: Eerdmans, 1990), 90; Schlueter, *Filling Up the Measure*, 25; Simpson, *Non-Christian Jews*, 76.

[38] Daniel B. Wallace, "1 Thessalonians: Introduction," 3 n. 6.

[39] Jon Weatherly, "The Authenticity of 1 Thess 2.13–16: Additional Evidence," *JSNT* 42 (1991): 79–98, here 82–83.

"all Israel will be saved." In 1 Thess 2:16 he appears to be damning the Jews while in Rom 11:26 he is heralding their redemption. Such blatant contradiction is seen to call for either an inconsistent Paul à la Heikki Räisänen[40] or a pseudo-Paul by way of interpolation. Owing to the unattractiveness of the first option, many scholars choose for the second.

However, both options have their problems. For while the former seems to overlook the contextual nature of Paul's writings and the fact that his is a theology 'on the run' and 'in the making', the latter is an argument based on the need for theological harmonization, and a tendency to take the good and dismiss (as interpolation) the ugly. A third option is put forward by Hurd, that though Paul's "diatribe against the Jews quite properly offends us" yet "we are not thereby justified in improving his letter by removing the offending passage. The passage is part of the apocalyptic logic which is woven into the fabric of the whole letter."[41] Hurd has pinpointed the heart of the problem for theologically-based interpolative readings. Dismissing a passage as an interpolation because it seems to contradict Paul's theological discourse elsewhere is tenuous at best. Each letter has to be taken in its own right and allowed to speak with its own voice.

Taking stock of all the interpolation positions presented above, we are struck by the following question: in what way do these various approaches solve the anti-Jewish problem present in our text? It seems clear that any form of the interpolation argument has the effect, either implicitly or explicitly, of saving Paul from being anti-Jewish, at least in this letter. He cannot be held responsible for what he did not write. Yet when we see that the collective evidence in favor of an interpolation is far from being clear-cut, one wonders whether such an outcome, in its potential desirability, has overly

---

[40] Heikki Räisänen, *Römer 9–11 Analyse eines geistigen Ringen* (*ANRW* II 25.4 1987), 2891–2939, esp. 2925. With regard to our passage Räisänen argues that Paul makes two inconsistencies. Firstly that in 1 Thess 2:14–16 the Jews prevent him speaking to the Gentiles whereas in Rom 11:11f. it is actually Jewish unbelief that spurs him on to speak to them. Secondly that Paul ends with wrath in 1 Thess 2:16 whereas he ends with Israel's salvation in Rom 11:26.

[41] Hurd, "Paul Ahead of his Time," 35.

influenced the call to label our text as an interpolation. Cataloging a text or passage as an interpolation should be a matter of last resort. We simply raise the question, therefore, of whether the extreme polemical nature of this passage has led to an overhasty categorization by some considering the ambiguity of the evidence.

4.2 Canon within the canon

Related to this issue is whether any or all of the above approaches may in fact lead to the practical creation of a canon within the canon. That is, overlooking or disregarding those parts of Paul's letters that one now finds distasteful and emphasizing only those passages that please. This is so whether one calls those unpleasant parts interpolations or not.

J. Louis Martyn, for example, makes a good case of showing that the influential 1980 Resolution of the *Landessynode der Evangelischen*, a document by German Protestants seeking to renovate their relationship with Jews, falls into this trap. In its confession it puts ample weight on Rom 9–11 to the utter exclusion of 1 Thess 2:14–16 and other difficult passages such as Gal 4:21–5:1 and 2 Cor 3:6, 14.[42] Martyn remarks that such exclusion by silence results in the creation of an "inner-canonical canon." He writes,

> Small wonder that a group of European Christians, living after the Holocaust, and admirably intent on rectifying some of the most grievous wrongs done to Jews by Christians, should concentrate their attention on certain parts of the Pauline corpus, to the practical exclusion of others. All exegetes work with an operative canon within the canon, their own context and thus their own history inevitably playing a significant role in their interpretive labors.[43]

---

[42] J. Louis Martyn, *Theological Issues in the Letters of Paul* (Edinburgh: T&T Clark, 1997), 192–193.

[43]Ibid.,193.

This marginalizing of difficult texts in favor of universal ones raises several issues of its own. Firstly, it is clear that selecting those texts that one thinks present Paul in the best light, offers an incomplete portraiture at the very least. Secondly, the working assumption that the message in Rom 9–11 is primarily a positive one vis-à-vis the Jews is seriously open to question.

In Rom 9:22–23 NRSV Paul appears to be equating the Jews (whom he terms his brethren and kinsmen κατὰ σάρκα Rom 9:3) with "objects of wrath that are made for destruction"; in 9:31–33 he charges them with a form of covenantal legalism (and not covenantal nomism) in that they fail to attain to a Torah-based righteousness since they pursue it through works and not faith; in 10:21 NRSV he forthrightly declares, roughly quoting Isaiah 65:2, that they are a "disobedient and contrary people"; and in 11:9–10 he cites a curse coming from David in Psalm 69:22–24 that the Jews' table may become a trap and a snare, that their eyes may be darkened and their backs bent continually; and finally in 11:19 he announces that the unbelieving Jews are broken branches out of the olive tree of Israel. This is quite a litany in itself, and actually reveals a certain amount of theological continuity with 1 Thess 2:14–16. Indeed it is only Paul's supreme conviction that God remains true to his previously elected people (Rom 11:1–2) and to his covenantal promises (11:26–27) that gives Paul the further hope in Romans that all will be well with Israel in the end (11:26–29).

It is therefore doubtful that the canon within the canon position, though well-meaning and sensitive to its times, suffices as a legitimate response to this problematic text. It is undertaken, as Walker argues, by those "who wish to use the biblical writings as a basis for Christian faith and practice" but it is not a valid "path for literary-historical scholarship."[44] It is the gap between these two worlds that our own hermeneutical approach seeks to address at the end of this paper.

Let us now consider other non-interpolation responses to the passage.

---

[44] Walker, *Interpolation*, 242.

4.3 Referent limitation

Taking Pauline authorship for granted, this position argues that Paul is referencing *some* Judean Jews, not all Jews non-restrictively. It is contended that Paul used the articular participial phrase translated in (v.15a) "who killed both the Lord Jesus and the prophets" to restrict the range of those Jews involved.[45] It is only those Jews who carried out these acts and those enumerated in the following verse that are referenced, not all Jews. In this way it is again put forward that there is no theological anomaly with what he says collectively about ethnic Israel's salvation in Rom 9–11.[46] Gilliard[47] and Koenig[48] in separate works all argue that the comma inserted in many translations between vv.14 and 15—"for you suffered the same thing from your own compatriots as they did from the Jews, who killed both the Lord Jesus and the prophets [...]"—illegitimately removes the restrictive limitation regarding the deeds of some Judean Jews to universally referring to all Jews without distinction. This move from the restrictive to the descriptive, it could be argued, raises questions of scholarly pre-understanding or prejudice.[49]

Nonetheless, despite its grammatical veracity on this point, the referent limitation model overlooks the fact that the rest of the charges in v.15b–e are unrestricted in nature and take on a supra-temporal tone.[50] For taking the one long clause that defines οἱ Ἰουδαῖοι as solely referring to a contemporary group of Paul "stretches the historical

---

[45] Frank D. Gilliard, "The Problem of the Antisemitic Comma between 1 Thessalonians 2.14 and 15," *NTS* 35 (1989): 481–502, here 491–2.

[46] Ibid., 492.

[47] Gilliard, "Antisemitic Comma," passim.

[48] John Koenig, *Jews and Christians in Dialogue: New Testament Foundations* (Philadelphia, Penn.: Westminster, 1979), 47–48.

[49] A similar thing happens in 2 Cor 11:24–26 where Paul writes that he received lashes Ὑπὸ Ἰουδαίων and that he has been in danger ἐξ ἐθνῶν. While the latter is translated in the NRSV "from Gentiles," the former is translated as "from the Jews". The insertion here of a definite article similarly universalises the designated group from some Jews, to all Jews in general. See Gilliard, "Antisemitic Comma," 493.

[50] Richard, *First and Second Thessalonians*, 18; Luckensmeyer, *Eschatology*, 141.

context of 1 Thess 2:13–16 to breaking point."[51] It is the Jewish people throughout history whom Paul is targeting as constantly resisting God's purposes to their own hurt. Paul is judging the whole historical people and not just the acts of some Jewish contemporaries. So we see that limiting the referent only addresses part of the problem, and not the whole.

4.4 Referent expansion

In the opposite direction to the above position, this approach contends that the phrase οἱ Ἰουδαῖοι should be theologized to refer abstractly to "hostility to God in general," rather than to any specific Jewish party or people. Yet this use of "the Jew within" as a trope for human evil conveys the troublesome idea that the Jew represents that part of human nature that needs to be overcome. Ernst Käsemann for example talks of "the hidden Jew in all of us," as "the man who validates rights and demands over against God on the basis of God's past dealings with him and to this extent is serving not God but an illusion."[52] The problems inherent to this model are self-evident. It is unjustifiable, even from the basis of our passage in question, to portray the Jews as the archetype for evil in humanity. For though this position may actually think it is delivering a blow to any kind of dangerous anti-Jewishness by claiming that "we are all Jews," it actually has the opposite effect of demonizing the Jew as the enemy of God.[53]

4.5 Intra-Jewish polemic

This brings us to our next model, that of intra-Jewish polemic. This position argues that it is better to understand the pericope as

---

[51] Luckensmeyer, *Eschatology*, 142,

[52] E. Käsemann, "Paul and Israel," *New Testament Questions of Today* (Philadelphia: Fortress, 1969), 186.

[53] See Daniel Boyarin, *A Radical Jew: Paul and the Politics of Identity* (Berkeley: University of California Press, 1997), 213.

an intra-Jewish literary motif rather than as anti-Jewish or anti-Semitic.[54] It puts forward the idea that "heated rhetoric in the service of religious disputes was quite the norm in ancient times." David Turner comments that "such rhetoric was used in Jewish circles since the days of the biblical prophets, and that it continued to be used in the days of the Second Temple as various Jewish groups critiqued the religious establishment in Jerusalem."[55] In fact, he goes so far as to tell us that the use of such a motif was "a valid expression of authentic Jewish spirituality."[56]

Turner gives a convenient overview of the rejection and even killing of the prophets in the Tanakh that includes "Ahab and Jezebel's rejection of Elijah and Micaiah (1 Kgs 18–19, 22), Amaziah's rejection of Amos (Amos 7:10–17), Pashhur's persecution of Jeremiah (Jer 20), Jehoiakim's murder of Uriah son of Shemaiah (Jer 26:20–23), and Zedekiah's imprisonment of Jeremiah (Jer 37–38)." He also references the Second Temple Book of Jubilees (c. 150 B. C. E.) that "predicts the judgment which will come to Israel when they refuse to listen to the prophets (here called "witnesses") but instead kill them (1:12–14)."[57]

The similarly construed "Woe oracles" announcing an impending negative divine judgement, are, according to Turner, also found in Second Temple Jewish literature, especially throughout the Apocrypha (Jdt 16:17; Sir 2:12–14; 41:8; 2 Esd 13:16,19; 1 Macc 2:7.23), in Josephus (*The Jewish War* 6.301–11) and in Qumran (1QPHqb 10:5; 11:2).[58] Others have similarly noted the striking parallel between Paul's language of wrath in v.16d–e and that contained in the Testament of Levi (6:11).[59]

---

[54] E. P. Sanders, "Reflections on Anti-Judaism in the New Testament and Christianity," in *Anti-Judaism and the Gospels* (ed. William R. Farmer; Harrisburg, Pa.: Trinity Press International, 1999), 265–286, here 268–269.

[55] David L. Turner, "Matthew 23 as a Prophetic Critique," *JBS* 4.1 (January 2004): 23–42, here 24.

[56] Ibid., 25.

[57] Ibid., 39.

[58] Ibid., 33–34.

[59] Jeffrey S. Lampe, "Is Paul Anti-Jewish? Testament of Levi 6 in the

As a result, Charles Wanamaker writes, "[f]rom [Paul] and his contemporaries' viewpoint, the persecution of the Christians in Judea represented a continuation of the phenomenon going back to the prophets of the OT period and recently manifested in the experiences of Jesus and Paul himself (cf. 2 Cor. 11:24)."[60] Consequently Linda McKinnish Bridges states that "Paul is not providing fuel for hatred – neither for the first century nor for the twenty-first." While it is admitted that "Paul is very angry" and "his language is harsh and negative, hurtful and spiteful," one must realize that "[t]his is language [...] from the inside to the inside. These words come from one faction of the Jewish-Christian debate to another in the first-century world. Language used by family members against other family members can often be more violent and harmful than language used by outsiders. These words belong to family conflict in the world of Paul."[61]

As Luke T. Johnson has pointed out, the apparent purpose of such rhetoric was primarily to define community self-identity by polarizing the other, and had much less to do with the actual facts or the supposed deeds of the other.[62] In the words of Carol Schlueter, "Paul, a skilled debater, used polemical hyperbole to polarize issues and to move his readers to his side while casting his opponents (in this case, the Jews) completely on the wrong side."[63]

Thus we may summarize this approach as arguing that Paul, in listing Jewish sins and proclaiming divine wrath, is simply continuing a Jewish tradition that is a motivated self-critique, not done out of hatred, but out of grief for his own people. It is not to be feared for it "is in keeping with both the spirit of the prophets and the rhet-

Interpretation of 1 Thess 2:13–16," *CBQ* 65.3 (2003): 408–427. Testament of Levi 6:11 reads "But the wrath of the Lord came suddenly upon them to the uttermost."

[60] Charles Wannamaker, *Epistles to the Thessalonians*, 31.

[61] Linda McKinnish Bridges, *1 & 2 Thessalonians* (SHBC; Macon: Smyth & Helwys, 2008), 56.

[62] Luke T. Johnson, "The New Testament's Anti-Jewish Slander and the Conventions of Ancient Polemic," *JBL* 108 (1989): 419–441.

[63] Schlueter, *Filling Up the Measure*, 11.

oric of the times."[64] Based on such a premise, this position also assumes that Paul remains a Jew within Judaism, even if on the margins, and that the parting of the ways has not yet occurred.[65]

However, at this point several questions need to be raised. For example, does the fact that Paul writes as a Jew deflate or defuse the polemical discourse? In light of the sheer extent of the critique and condemnation given against the Jews, is it not possible to classify Paul here as a Jew acting anti-Jewishly? That is not to say, of course, that he is a self-hating Jew,[66] but it is to say that he found little with which to identify in the mainstream or common Judaism of his day. In fact there is nothing in the passage itself that identifies Paul with οἱ Ἰουδαῖοι as his own people. He appears to speak of himself as an outsider and an accuser, rather "than as a member of penitent Israel."[67] One could easily assume that this passage actually supports an early parting of the ways rather than disproves it. Paul, it would appear, has been able to distance himself from his own kind to such an extent that he is able to condemn them without a blush.

Similarly, one can also ask if this intra-Jewish position overlooks the issue of conflictual ethics, and whether one has the right, even in an intra-familial conflict, to neglect or negate a basic ethic for enemies? Paul himself writes in 1 Thess 5:15 NRSV "See that none of you repays evil for evil, but always seek to do good to one another and to all." Further, it can also be argued that Paul ought to have been aware of the dangerous potential that he embedded in this text, especially in light of the revelatory claims that lay at the basis of his missionary activity and the integral role his letters played in that enterprise (cf. 1 Thess 2:13). Finally, the fact that

---

[64] Turner, "Prophetic Critique," 41.

[65] Schlueter, *Filling Up the Measure*, 187. On the parting of the ways between Judaism and Christianity see James D. G. Dunn, ed. *Jews and Christians: The Parting of the Ways, AD 70 to 135* (Cambridge: Eerdmans, 1992).

[66] Pamela Eisenbaum, "Is Paul the Father of Misogyny and Antisemitism?" *Cross Currents* 50.4 (Winter, 2000): 506–524.

[67] Simpson, *Non-Christian Jews*, 100.

the Thessalonian community was largely or predominantly Gentile in composition moves Paul's words away from operating on an intra-Jewish level to functioning on a Gentile versus Jewish level, with all the perilous possibilities that that transition brings. In the end, the intra-Jewish polemic position, though valuable for its insights, leaves many questions unasked and unanswered.

4.6 The mysterious plan of God

This position, largely dependent upon Johannes Munck[68] and Karl Donfried,[69] puts forward the case that εἰς τέλος, the climax of the passage, should not be understood as conveying a finality or eternal state of condemnation, but rather that it means until the end of the age, that is the παρουσία.[70] Read in this light, it actually agrees theologically with Rom 11:25f. in that the current stubbornness of Israel vis-à-vis the gospel (equated with the outpouring of God's wrath in 1 Thess 2:16d) will ultimately be removed and Israel will be redeemed. In this sense εἰς τέλος carries the idea of the wrath as having a functional goal or purpose in the greater salvific plan of God.

Yet the problem with Paul's text in 1 Thess 2:14–16 is rather that there is no hope or promise of redemption once the τέλος or goal of the wrath has been reached. It is this very lack of hope that convinces scholars to see the wrath as final and forever. J. W. Simpson, for example, has argued that Paul is foregoing any further chance of repentance as he assumes such an imminent παρουσία in his own lifetime (1 Thess 4:15; 5:23) that he simply saw no time left for such repentance.[71] Yet we need to ask, how does the Church today deal with this lack of hope now that the supposed early παρουσία has not

---

[68] Johannes Munck, *Christ and Israel: An Interpretation of Rom 9–11* (tr. I. Nixon; Philadelphia: Fortress, 1967), 64.

[69] Karl P. Donfried, "Paul and Judaism: 1 Thessalonians 2:13–16 as a Test Case," *Int* 38 (1984) 242–253, here 252.

[70] Cf. Simpson, *Non–Christian Jews*, 151.

[71] Ibid., 158.

come? Does the Church still translate the εἰς τέλος as lasting for 2,000 years and continuing with no anticipation of remittance?

Or should we agree with C. Williamson that to read Paul "in good faith" is to read him forwards from Thessalonians to Romans, in tandem with his positive evolution regarding ethnic Israel, and that "to read him backward is to read him in bad faith"?[72] This may be to pre-judge the issue, for the real question needing to be asked is whether Paul ever distanced himself from what he wrote in 1 Thess 2:14–16. As we have seen above, Rom 9–11 does not offer a profound theology of discontinuity with 1 Thess 2:14–16, but rather brings a severe critique with the hope of a final salvation based not on Israel's deeds, but actually despite them, on God's grace. So while the mysterious plan of God approach offers an alternative reading of εἰς τέλος, one that is functional and temporary rather than final and eternal, we still find that its advocates have to look outside 1 Thess 2:14–16 to Rom 11:25–36 to try to find a solution to the problem and build on the rather brittle idea of Paul's supposed u-turn vis-à-vis the Jews.[73]

4.7 Intent and effect

This brings us to another type of argument, intent and effect. This position advocates that there is a distinction to be made between the intentionality governing a text and the effect it may have on its readers.[74] Two main points need to be made here. Firstly, that the author may or may not be self-consciously aware of that intentionality when speaking or writing, and secondly, that one's discourses (whether spoken or written) may "have unintend-

---

[72] Clark Williamson, *Has God Rejected His People? Anti-Judaism in the Christian Church* (Nashville: Abingdon, 1982), 63

[73] See E.P. Sanders, "Did Paul's Theology Develop?" in *The Word Leaps the Gap: Essays on Scripture and Theology in Honor of Richard B. Hays* (ed. J. Ross Wagner, A. Katherine Grieb, C. Kavin Rowe; Grand Rapids, Mich.: Eerdmans, 2008), 325–350.

[74] Daniel Patte, "Anti-Semitism in the New Testament: Confronting the Dark Side of Paul and Matthew's Teaching," *CTSR* 78 (1988): 31–52, here, 33–44. Cited and used by Luckensmeyer, "Eschatology," 170–171.

ed effects."[75] If a person's rhetoric does in fact have an "unexpected effect" upon the reader(s), then that person tends to complain that he or she has "been misunderstood" since people are often satisfied that their "discourses express [their] good intentions."[76]

In light of this approach, Luckensmeyer argues that while the effects of 1 Thess 2:14–16 have admittedly been adverse, Paul's intentionality remains pure.[77] Indeed, because of Paul's position within Judaism, and his self-conscious awareness that he writes as a Jew, Luckensmeyer maintains that any negative effects of the text cannot be charged to his account. Being within Judaism is again an appeal to the literary motif of intra-Jewish polemic discussed above (see 4.5) and it again side-steps the question raised there of whether a Jew within Judaism can also be anti-Jewish. In any case, Luckensmeyer finishes his argument by highlighting that Paul is not only limiting the charge of persecutors to 'some Jews' instead of all but is also including the Thessalonians own compatriots (v.14d) in the claim, stressing in turn that he is actually not anti-Judaistic, nor anti-Gentile but simply "anti-anyone-against-Christ-as-Kyrios."[78] So the argument goes that Paul's intention is not against the Jews per se but against every opponent of Christ, Jewish or non-Jewish.

Evidently, this is a very interesting position in that it takes not just the world of the text, but also the world of the author and the world of the reader into account. It makes it clear that these three entities are all interdependent to a certain degree. Further, a link is made between the author and the (potentially negative) consequences of his or her writings. But, once again, does this model go far enough? If Paul is equally against all those not accepting Jesus as Kyrios, why does he not equally list the sins of the Gentile compatriots in comparable terms, including the certainty of divine doom? Additionally, the quest to keep Paul's intention sacrosanct and thus divorced from the text's negative effects raises issues.

---

[75] Patte, "Anti-Semitism," 41.

[76] Ibid.

[77] Luckensmeyer, "Eschatology," 171.

[78] Luckensmeyer, "Eschatology," 169.

Does this not separate the author too much from any dangerous potential in his text? Indeed, just how far is the author responsible for the effects of the text, whether intended or not? Was Paul fully aware of the intentionality governing his text at this point? This brings us to our next position, that of resistant reading.

4.8 Resistant readings

This model suggests that Paul's human side is clearly seen in this passage, and that he is openly writing in anger and frustration against those Jews who have personally persecuted and prevented him from evangelizing the nations. Van der Horst[79] reminds us that Paul is not immune from venting his emotions on vellum, as his caustic remark about castration in Gal 5:12 reveals. Nonetheless, Van der Horst also notes that this text is part of our New Testament and is read in our Churches. Indeed he remarks that the statement that the Jews "displease God and oppose everyone" (v.15b) is very similar to classical pagan anti-Jewish comments by Tacitus and others and gives the impression that Paul is joining in pagan condemnation of his own people. Van der Horst is direct in his judgement: "Paul, (or whoever) you ought not to have written that!"[80] He is convinced that we have the right to "rap the fingers" of the Bible writers, if only in the sense of distancing ourselves from such comments while realizing their contextual character. He argues that it is only in recognizing and responding to the *Umwelt* of these statements that one can do good theology and at the same time relativize the author's polemics. According to him, such an approach will save us from the danger of biblicism (a kind of fundamentalist reading of the text) that eternally keeps alive the anti-Jewish feelings of any given biblical writer.

This method is clearly more critical of the author per se. In the name of the reader it judges that it was unwise for Paul to write what he did and so the Church should take distance from it. This

---

[79] Van der Horst, "Omgaan met anti-joodse teksten," 8 [cited 25 August 2009]. http://www.appelkerkenisrael.nl/Lezingen/pvdhorst.

[80] Ibid., 9 "Paulus (of welk ander dan ook), dat had je niet moeten schrijven!"

position seeks to resist what it considers an oppressive use of power in the discourse. Where is the alternative Jewish voice in this passage? Why is it silenced? Once more, however, one can ask if this position really does adequate justice to Paul himself. Is Paul simply to be left with bruised fingers for writing a bad text or does the idea of him imparting revelation through his letter writing not go deeper than this? The resistant reader model seems to leave us in a kind of binary opposition to the text and its author. Is there no room for moving beyond such a reading to a fresh engagement with the text that can lead us to a type of Ricoeurian second naïveté?[81] This brings us to our third and final section: revelation in Pauline texts and how God writes straight on crooked lines.

5. REVELATION IN PAULINE TEXTS – GOD WRITES STRAIGHT ON CROOKED LINES[82]

This has been no easy journey. We have seen that various attempts have been made to deal with this passage, with the majority trying either to justify Paul or limit the damage of the text. Some have gone so far as to make a connection between negative effects and Paul's intent, but only one model (that of resistant reading) has actually said that Paul was misguided to write what he did.

---

[81] Central to Paul Ricoeur's work is a strong conviction that theological interpretation of the Bible ought to deal with the text's message, more than just its meaning. In other words, one ought to be concerned with engaging the divine reality to which the text bears witness. This is reflected in his method of observation, reflection and appropriation (coming to a second naïveté). In this desire he has similarities with Karl Barth and the post-liberal movement. See Mark I. Wallace, *Second Naïveté: Barth, Ricoeur, and the New Yale Theology* (Studies in American Biblical Hermeneutics, 6; 2nd edn; Macon, Ga.: Mercer University Press, 1995).

[82] The phrase "God writes straight on crooked lines" is taken from Reimund Bieringer, Didier Pollefeyt, and Frederique Vandecasteele-Vanneuville, "Wrestling with Johannine Anti-Judaism: A Hermeneutical Framework for the Analysis of the Current Debate," in *Anti-Judaism and the Fourth Gospel: Papers of the Leuven Colloquium, 2000* (ed., Reimund Bieringer et al.; Assen: Van Gorcum, 2001), 3–37 here 34.

An honest appraisal would take all these positions into consideration and grant that all of them have something of value to say. Yet it is our evaluation that none of them is capable of dealing with all the issues on its own. Regarding the various interpolation theories, we have seen that the balance of arguments is very tight, with, in our view, a bias in favor of inclusion. Nevertheless, no matter which side a scholar chooses in the debate, it still does not negate the fact that the text, as it now is, remains part of the Christian canon and thus scripturally authoritative.

Regarding the practical fall-back position of a canon within the canon approach, we would caution that the subjective and selective use of some Pauline texts as normative while neglecting other parts of the whole corpus is openly questionable. As regards referent limitation, it is true that while Paul should not be falsely accused, and the universalizing anti-Jewish comma ought to be removed from translations, the rest of the sweeping charges against "the Jews" still stands.

As concerns the referent expansion option, it presents a troubling caricature of the Jew as the basest part of human nature and simply needs to be rejected outright. Likewise, the literary motif of the intra-Jewish position only succeeds in displacing the problem but not removing it altogether. The author is still responsible for the passage, whatever its genre or type, and cannot, merely by being a Jew, avoid all responsibility for its history of effects.

With regard to the mysterious plan of God, it is important to note that εἰς τέλος can be interpreted in non-final ways. That it can indeed point to a goal beyond itself is significant. Unfortunately though, this further horizon is missing from the text. As for the intent and effect position, it is an important step forward. Yet its application in this case leaves other questions unanswered. It too quickly seeks to defend the author's intention and blame the interpreters for any negative effects of the text.

Finally, rapping the author's fingers for writing such polemic is a bold and controversial step yet one that is defended in the interest of good theology that disallows contextual outbursts of anger to become sacralized truths. While we would agree that divine inspiration does not do away with the humanness of the authors, such an upbraiding of Paul and subsequent distancing from the text seem to disengage too much from the text as revelation. Can we honestly say that this is in the interests of good theology?

This is the point where hermeneutical approaches may go beyond the limits of the historical-critical method. While the latter remains an indispensible tool, it stops short of asking crucial questions that do deal with the revelatory nature of the text and its dialogue with the historical Church community.

In varying degrees of contrast to all the above approaches, we believe that "[a] hermeneutical approach will allow us to accept the normativity of a seemingly oppressive text."[83] It can enable us to do this by seeking a way that both includes, but goes beyond, the historical-critical approach, with its almost exclusive focus on authorial intention, and equally includes, but goes beyond, the reader response approach, with its rather exclusive interest in the meaning given by the reader.[84] In this regard we follow the hermeneutist Paul Ricoeur who escapes the polarization between authorial intent and the reader monopoly by stressing the importance of the text as a mediating and creative factor in the relations between both author and reader.[85] All three elements (text, author, reader) need to be taken into consideration, yet a certain priority is to be given to the text as *primus inter pares.*[86]

According to Ricoeur, a text can in fact escape the finite horizon lived by its author.[87] In his joint work with A. LaCoque, *Penser La Bible,* he frames the biblical text as largely autonomous and in need

---

[83] R. Bieringer, "'Come and you will see' (John 1:39): Dialogical Authority and Normativity of the Future in the Fourth Gospel and in Religious Education," in *Hermeneutics and Religious Education* (ed. H. Lombaerts & D. Pollefeyt; Leuven: Peeters Press, 2004), 179–202, here 186–7.

[84] Gregory J. Laughery, "Reading Ricoeur: Authors, Readers, and Texts," *European Journal of Theology* 9.2 (2000): 159–170.

[85] Laughery, "Reading Ricoeur,"161.

[86] Ibid., 163.

[87] Paul Ricoeur, *Interpretation Theory: Discourse and Surplus of Meaning* (Fort Worth, Tex.: Christian University Press), 30.

of fulfilment by the reading community.[88] For whereas historical-critical methods often focus exclusively on the historical world *behind* the text or the semantic world *in* the text, Ricoeur highlights the world projected *out in front of* the text. This unfolding of the world of the text in front of itself is most important.[89] On the one hand, the text, as revelation, though dependent on its author for mediation, goes beyond its author in its unfolding of the transcendent. On the other hand, the reader is "called to dialogue with the text,"[90] especially with this world as thrown out in front of the text.

So what is the unfolding world of 1 Thess 2:14–16? Is it unending eschatological wrath for the Jewish people? Remarkably, just two verses prior to our passage Paul's kerygma actually centred on "God, who calls you into his own kingdom and glory" (1 Thess 2:12b). In a real way that divine invitation openly challenges what he most likely wrote four verses later in 2:16d. While 2:12b holds forth the universal and eschatological dimension of God's call to participate in his glorious reign, our passage of 2:14–16 leaves us with a text of dangerous potential that seems to replace that universal call with unremitting wrath for the Jews. It appears to offer a frightening apocalyptic dualism that has apriori and unconditionally condemned those who have not (yet) positively responded to that call.

It is our opinion that the author of 2:14–16 risks losing sight of the universal horizon of God's call in the heat of his immediate contextual conflict. It may be a very human and understandable response in the face of suffering, but limiting the horizon in 2:16d to one of utter condemnation is theologically hazardous to say the least. It has to be admitted that the negative use of this passage,

---

88 Paul Ricoeur and A. LaCoque, *Penser La Bible* (Paris: Seuil, 1998), 12. See also Paul Ricoeur, "Hermeneutics and the Critique of Ideology" in idem., *From Text to Action* (tr. Kathleen Blamey and John B. Thompson; Evanston, Ill.: Northwestern University Press, 1991), 270–307.

89 Ricoeur, *Temps et Récit*, I, 22. Cited in Laugherty, "Reading Ricoeur," 162.

90 Angus Paddison, *Theological Hermeneutics and 1 Thessalonians* (SNTSMS 133; Cambridge: Cambridge University Press, 2005), 48.

among others, in the formation of the 'theology of contempt' towards the Jewish people, chief among which is the charge of deicide, gives pause for thought.[91] Are the interpreters solely to blame, or does the evidence not point to the author's own humanity, in all its fragility? It is at just such a moment that the Church community may be called upon *not* to distance itself from the author and his work, but to challenge the author to see the bigger picture and the larger horizon, as revealed almost despite himself, within that same mediated text. So we need to ask, is there a further redemptive horizon in this text itself, unfolding with eschatological purpose and waiting for readers to perceive it and interact with it as providing an eschatological norm? We need to ask, theologically and pastorally, what is "the eschatological potential" of the text?[92] To which ultimate end does it point? According to us, 1 Thess 2:14–16's own widest eschatological horizon is unfolded in the word σῴζω (2:16b).

Σωτηρία is God's salvific will extending to all. Such is evidenced in Paul's own probable proclamation of the gospel in the synagogue in Thessalonica (Acts 17:1–2) and in his salvific proclamation in this letter whose audience undoubtedly contained many Gentiles.[93] And it is this divine will to save all, though somewhat hidden in this pericope, that throws up another horizon. A horizon that can be recognized by the reader and be seen to transcend the narrower usage of it here as applying only to Gentiles (2:16b) and which is in fact overtaken in importance by an apocalyptic ὀργή (2:16d). Instead, we are persuaded in dialoguing with the text that God's call, God's σωτηρία, presents itself as the further and stronger horizon, one that can certainly include what is written in 2:16b, i.e. that

[91] Blaming the destruction of Jerusalem on the Jewish crime of pressing for Jesus' death is already evidenced as early as Tertullian *Adv. Jud.* 13; Gospel of Peter 7:25, Barn. 5:12 etc. For a recent work on Paul's use of Kyrios to declare Jesus' deity, see Gordon Fee, *Pauline Christology: an Exegetical-Theological Study* (Peabody, Mass.: Hendrickson, 2007).

[92] Angus Paddison, *Theological*, 52.

[93] Wanamaker, *The Epistles to the Thessalonians*, 7. Cf. Acts 17:4.

salvation is for the Gentiles, but it cannot stop there. 1 Thess 1:10 and 5:9 highlight that within this epistle as a whole, ὀργή is not God's ultimate horizon for humanity, including the Jews, but σωτηρία is.[94] God's salvation reaches beyond God's wrath.

In our reading then, the revelatory text itself in 2:16b presents another horizon in tandem with 1:10, 5:9 and 2:12b that lies beyond what is mediated by the author in 2:16d. The inviting horizon thrown up by σῴζω ultimately transcends any myopic vision on its author's behalf. In this way, through reader recognition of the revelatory nature of the text, and the text's own ability to unfold its fullest eschatological dimension even beyond the original authorial intention, the passage, over time, can actually recontextualize itself. In this particular case, we discovered that the text does contain a universal redemptive horizon that the author either missed or deliberately ignored. As a result we find that the pericope itself ends up challenging the author's confinement of the text to an apocalyptic dualism (salvation to the Gentiles, wrath to the Jews) that neglects to offer an ongoing salvific invitation to the Jews.

Hermeneutically speaking, it is the revelatory Word in Paul's words that should be our interest and enable us to discern where the wider redemptive horizon of the text lies in its ongoing unfolding of God's revelation.[95] In our theological-hermeneutical perspective, we find that this passage's own ultimate horizon of σῴζω shoots beyond ἡ ὀργὴ εἰς τέλος, highlighting that God's covenantal faithfulness is greater than his wrath. In our view, the author should have been aware of this. As such, this position does

[94] 1 Thess 1:10 NRSV "and to wait for his Son from heaven, whom he raised from the dead — Jesus, who rescues us from the wrath that is coming"; 1 Thess 5:9 NRSV "For God has destined us not for wrath but for obtaining salvation through our Lord Jesus Christ." The 'us' here includes Jews as much as Gentiles in its scope and shows that the will of God for both is salvation, not wrath.

[95] As Paul Ricoeur, "Contribution d'une réflexion sur le langage à une théologie de la parole," in *Exégèse et herméneutique : Parole de Dieu* (ed. Xavier Léon-Dufour; Paris: Seuil, 1971), 301–320, here 303, where he writes "All theology is a theology of the Word."

not need to fall back onto ambiguous interpolation theories to justify the author, nor does it need to look further afield to another letter to redeem this pericope's contents. Instead, it maintains the author's responsibility for what is written, while looking to the text as a source of continual unveiling to see what it is ultimately telling us about the kingdom of God. It thus allows that text, in dialogue with the contemporary reader, to be read eschatologically, recognizing it as a signpost to the kingdom that we are convinced offers σωτηρία for all.

CHAPTER 8
FROM PERMISSION TO PROHIBITION: PAUL AND THE EARLY CHURCH ON MIXED MARRIAGE

Shaye J. D. Cohen

Numerous ancient Jewish texts speak out against mixed marriage, the marriage of a Jew with a non-Jew. The poet Theodotus, the Temple Scroll, the book of Jubilees, the Testaments of the Twelve Patriarchs, Philo, Josephus, and other works, written in Greek or Hebrew, in the land of Israel or the diaspora, clearly state that Jews are not to marry non-Jews. Rabbinic literature continues along the same trajectory. The reasons given for the prohibition usually reduce themselves to two: the non-Jewish spouse may turn the Jewish spouse away from the one true God and towards the worship of other, false gods; Jews constitute a "holy" people that cannot tolerate foreign admixture. Some of these texts attempt to ground the prohibition in passages from the Bible, especially the Torah, while others are content to argue without scriptural support. Jewish endogamy caught the eye of outsiders. *Alienarum concubitu abstinent* ("they abstain from sleeping with foreign women"), writes Tacitus. This material is well known and well studied.[1]

Strikingly absent from these discussions is the New Testament. It is not surprising, I suppose, that Jesus did not say anything about mixed marriage: he lived his entire life among Jews in the ethnic homeland and for most of them mixed marriage was a distant problem of little concern.[2] More surprising, however, is the

---

[1] See e.g. Menahem Stern, *Greek and Latin Authors on Jews and Judaism* (vol. 2; Jerusalem: Israel Academy of Sciences, 1980), 40 (on Tacitus Histories 5.5.2); Shaye J.D. Cohen, *The Beginnings of Jewishness* (Berkeley: University of California, 1999), esp. 241–262; Christine Hayes, *Gentile Impurities and Jewish Identities* (New York: Oxford University Press, 2002), 24–33 and 68–91.

[2] Paul says explicitly that he does not have any statement of Jesus on the subject (1 Cor 7:12)

near total silence of Paul on the subject. Here is a Diaspora Jew much concerned about Jewishness and identity, about the boundary between Jews and Greeks, about circumcision and non-circumcision, but who says almost nothing—explicitly, at least—about mixed marriage, whether between Jews and non-Jews or, what is the subject of this essay, between believers in Christ and non-believers. Paul, of course, re-defined the concept of God's people; for him the new Israel of God consists not only of Jews but of Greeks as well, all those who have come to have faith in Christ. Therefore we understand why Paul would have discarded one of the old arguments against mixed marriage. Since ethnic Israel is no longer the real Israel, the real people of God, then laws and practices intended to safeguard the purity of ethnic Israel no longer have any meaning for Paul. This seems clear enough. But the other source for the prohibition of mixed marriage, the concern that members of the people of God may be led astray by those who worship false gods—this concern should have been as relevant to Paul as it was to other Jews. Was it?

Many writers of the early church assert that Paul did, in fact, transfer the prohibition of mixed marriage from the old Israel to the new. Tertullian (ca. 160–220) is the first Christian to state that Christians may not marry non-Christians, and the first exegete to find this prohibition in the writings of Paul.[3] By the middle of the third century C.E. Christian writers had a standard collection of scriptural texts to document the prohibition of mixed marriage. So, for example, to support the proposition that "Marriage is not to be joined [by Christians] with gentiles," the author of the tract *To Quirinus,* probably Cyprian of Carthage (ca. 250 C.E. or a little later), adduces the following evidence: Tobit 4:12; Genesis 24; Ezra 9-10; 1 Cor 7:39–40; 1 Cor 6:15–17; 2 Cor 6:14; and 1

[3] There is no survey of mixed marriage in early Christianity. The fullest study remains J. Köhne, *Die Ehen zwischen Christen und Heiden in den ersten christlichen Jahrhunderten* (Paderborn: Bonifacius, 1931), which is not a history but a commentary on book 2 of Tertullian *Ad Uxorem.*

Kings 1:4.[4] The citation of the Hebrew Bible by a Christian author in order to justify the prohibition of marriage between a Christian and a "gentile"—this is fascinating in itself, but is not my theme here.[5] I am interested rather in the three cited Pauline passages. Here they are in full (in Cyprian's sequence):[6]

> 1 Cor 7:39–40: [39]A wife is bound as long as her husband lives. But if her husband dies, she is free to be married to anyone she wishes, only in the Lord. [40]But in my judgment she is more blessed if she remains as she is. And I think that I too have the Spirit of God.
>
> 1 Cor 6:15–17: [15]Do you not know that your bodies are members of Christ? Should I therefore take the members of Christ and make them members of a prostitute? Never! [16]Do you not know that whoever is united to a prostitute becomes one body with her? For it is said, "The two shall be one flesh." [17]But anyone united to the Lord becomes one spirit with him.
>
> 2 Cor 6:14: [14]Do not be mismatched with unbelievers. For what partnership is there between righteousness and lawlessness? Or what fellowship is there between light and darkness?

Cyprian's citation of these three Pauline passages conceals two serious problems. First, it is not clear that any of these passages prohibits mixed marriage; all three are ambiguous, as we shall see. Second, Cyprian fails to cite a fourth passage, which constitutes the real challenge to those who believe that Paul prohibited mixed marriage:

> 1 Cor 7:12-14: [12]To the rest I say—I and not the Lord—that if any believer has a wife who is an unbeliever, and she consents to live with

[4] Cyprian, *Ad Quirinum* 3.62 (CCSL 3.153-154). The *Ad Quirinum* is sometimes known as *Testimonies from Scripture.*

[5] Thus e.g. Ambrose uses Genesis 24:9 as the basis for his preaching against mixed marriage between Christians and non-Christians (whether Jews, gentiles, or heretics); he does not cite any NT passage as a source of the prohibition. See Ambrose, *De Abraham* 1.9.84-85 (CSEL 32.555-557); cf. too Ambrose, Epistle 62.2 ad Vigilium (CSEL 82.121).

[6] Translation follows the NRSV with some modifications.

> him, he should not divorce her. [13]And if any woman has a husband who is an unbeliever, and he consents to live with her, she should not divorce him. [14]For the unbelieving husband is made holy through his wife, and the unbelieving wife is made holy through her husband. Otherwise, your children would be unclean, but as it is, they are holy.

No matter how we interpret "For the unbelieving husband is made holy through his wife, and the unbelieving wife is made holy through her husband" (1 Cor 7:14), one thing is clear: in these verses Paul is permitting, or at least is not opposing, the union of a believer with a nonbeliever. No prohibition here.

Augustine saw these two problems. In a tract written around 421 C.E. Augustine debates one Pollentius, otherwise unknown, about the correct interpretation of 1 Cor 7:10–11 and Matthew 19:9 concerning divorce. Along the way they also discuss 1 Cor 7:12–14. Pollentius argues that "This, therefore, is the Lord's commandment, both in the Old Testament and the New, that only spouses of the same religion and faith may remain joined to each other."[7] Pollentius buttresses this contention by appeal to Deuteronomy 7:3–4 (a passage that Cyprian had missed) and 1 Cor 7:39.[8] Augustine summarizes Pollentius' argument and then asks:[9]

---

[7] Augustinus, *De adulterinis coniugiis* 1.21 25 (CSEL 41.372): "hoc est domini praeceptum tam in veteri quam in novo testamento, ut nonnisi unius religionis et fidei coniugia sibi maneant copulata"; cf. too 1.21 25 (CSEL 41.372) "dominus iussit ne coniugia sibimet diversae religionis copularentur"; 1.21 26 (CSEL 41.374) "dominus prohibet fideles infidelibus iungi."

[8] Neither Pollentius nor Augustine cite 1 Cor 6:15–17 or 2 Cor 6:14 in this connection. Hayes (*Gentile Impurities*, 98) does not know of any church writer who cites Deut 7:3–4 as a source for a Christian prohibition of mixed marriage. Pollentius is one.

[9] Augustinus, *De adulterinis coniugiis* 1.21 25 (CSEL 41.372): "si hoc ergo est domini praeceptum tam in veteri testamento quam in novo et hoc iubet dominus, hoc docet apostolus, ut nonnisi unius religionis et fidei maneant copulata coniugia, quare contra hoc domini iussum, contra doctrinam suam, contra praeceptum testamenti veteris et novi iubet apostolus ut diversae fidei coniugia maneant copulata?" My translation is based on that of *The Works of Saint Augustine A Translation for the 21st Century: I/9 Marriage and Virginity* (tr. Ray Kearney; ed. David G. Hunter; Hyde Park, New York: New City Press, 1999).

> If this is the Lord's commandment, in both the Old Testament and the New, and this is what the Lord commands, and this is what the apostle teaches, namely, that only spouses of the same religion and faith may remain joined — why then, in opposition to the Lord's command, and in opposition to his own teaching, and in opposition to the commandment of the Old Testament and the New, does the apostle [in 1 Cor 7:12–14] order spouses of different faiths to remain joined?

After some further discussion, Augustine says "As I recall, in none of the works of the New Testament, either in the Gospel or in any of the writings of the apostles, is it clearly stated without ambiguity that the Lord has prohibited believers from being joined in marriage to unbelievers."[10] Augustine knows that most of his predecessors (he cites Cyprian by name) believe that the Church's prohibition of mixed marriage derives, at least in part, from Paul, but Augustine is not convinced. On the one hand, the utterances of Paul that are cited to support the prohibition are ambiguous and, on the other hand, 1 Cor 7:12–14 seems to deny the prohibition altogether. For Augustine the prohibition does not derive from scripture.

Augustine is right. To derive a prohibition of mixed marriage from the writings of Paul will require a great deal of exegetical work. The exegete will need to clarify the ambiguity of 1 Cor 7:39–40, 1 Cor 6:15–19, and 2 Cor 6:14–18, and, further, to show that, appearances to the contrary notwithstanding, 1 Cor 7:12–14 opposes mixed marriage, or at least does not permit it. In other words, the exegete will have to make Paul say something that he did not say. I shall now survey ancient Christian exegesis of these four Pauline passages, from Tertullian to Augustine, in order to show what a difficult challenge they presented—and present—to those who want Paul to prohibit mixed marriage.[11]

---

[10] Augustine, *De adulterinis coniugiis* 1.25 31 (CSEL 41.378): "Non enim tempore revelati testamenti novi in evangelio vel ullis apostolicis litteris sine ambiguitate declaratum esse recolo, utrum dominus prohibuerit fideles infidelibus iungi."

[11] J. M. Ford, "Saint Paul the Philogamist: 1 Cor VII in Early Patristic Exegesis," NTS 11 (1964–65) 326–348 does not discuss the verses that are central to this paper. For samples of ancient exegesis on 1 Corinthians see Judith L. Kovacs, *The Church's*

1 Cor 7:39–40

In these verses Paul returns to the theme of the inviolability of marriage which he had raised earlier in the chapter: a Christian couple may not divorce (1 Cor 7:10–11). A wife is bound to her husband as long as he lives; if she becomes a widow Paul prefers that she not remarry at all (1 Cor 7:40). Preference aside, Paul does permit the widow to remarry but "only in the Lord" (1 Cor 7:39). What does this mean?

In his treatise *To his Wife* (written ca. 200 C.E.) Tertullian argues that it means "in the name of the Lord, which without doubt means 'to a Christian'."[12] In another treatise written a few years later

Bible: 1 Corinthians Interpreted by Early Christian Commentators (Grand Rapids: Eerdmans, 2005); Gerald Bray, *Ancient Christian Commentary on Scripture New Testament vol. VII 1-2 Corinthians* (Downers Grove: InterVarsity Press 1999). On First Corinthians I have consulted four representative modern commentaries (one English, early twentieth century, Anglican; two German, mid twentieth century, Lutheran; one American, early twenty-first century, Catholic): Archibald Robertson and Alfred Plummer, *A Critical and Exegetical Commentary on the First Epistle of St Paul to the Corinthians* (ICC; New York: Scribner's, 1911); Hans Lietzmann, *An die Korinther*, vierte von Werner G. Kümmel ergänzte Auflage (HNT; Tübingen: Mohr Siebeck, 1949); Hans Conzelmann, *A Commentary on the First Epistle to the Corinthians* (Philadelphia: Fortress, 1975; Hermeneia; German original 1969); Joseph Fitzmyer, *First Corinthians* (Anchor Bible; New Haven, Conn.: Yale University Press, 2008). I note the religious orientation of the commentator because at times it is not irrelevant. E.g. Conzelmann 121 n. 24 writes as a Lutheran ("Paul's view of marriage is diametrically opposed to that of the Roman Catholic Church"); Fitzmyer 298 writes as a Catholic ("… if Paul … under inspiration could introduce … an exception [to the prohibition of divorce] on his own authority, then why cannot the Spirit-guided institutional church of a later generation make a similar exception?"). No doubt my own Judaism is somehow evident in this paper.

[12] *Ad Uxorem* 2.2.4: "tantum in Domino id est in nomine Domini quod est indubitate Christiano" (CCSL 1.385–386). See also 2.1.1 (CCSL 1.383). Latin text (and French translation): Charles Munier, *Tertullien à son épouse* (SC 273; Paris: Cerf, 1980). The same point in *De Corona* 13.4-5 (written 208 C.E.): "ideo non nubemus ethnicis, ne nos ad idololatriam usque deducant, a qua apud illos nuptiae incipiunt. Habes legem a patriarchis quidem, habes apostolum in domino nubere iubentem" (CCSL 2.1061). See Jacques Fontaine, *Tertulliani De Corona* (Collection Érasme; Paris: Presses universitaires de France, 1966), 159–160.

Tertullian cites 1 Cor 7:39 to prove the concordance of the old law with the new. The old law prohibits marriage between the people of God and idolaters, and so does the new.[13] Tertullian has no doubt that his exegesis is correct and that Paul prohibited mixed marriage. Cyprian and Jerome, among others, follow Tertullian and simply assume that "only in the Lord" means "to a Christian."[14] They in turn are followed by many modern scholars.[15]

---

[13] *Adversus Marcionem* (written 207/8) 5.7.8: "certe praescribens tantum in domino esse nubendum, ne qui fidelis ethnicum matrimonium contrahat, legem tuetur Creatoris allophylorum nuptias ubique prohibentis" (CCSL 1.683). See *Tertullien Contre Marcion Livre V*, ed. Claudio Moreschini (SC 483; Paris: Cerf, 2004), 168. Same point in *De Monogamia* (written 214) 7.5: "illa nuptura in domino habet nubere, id est non ethnico sed fratri, quia et vetus lex adimit coniugium allophylorum" (CCSL 2.1238).

[14] Cyprian (cited above); Jerome, *Adversus Jovinianum* 1.10 (PL 23.234; written in 393); Pelagius Commentary on 1 Cor 7:39 (written ca. 405): "Tantum ut infideli vel infidelium ritu non nubet" (Alexander Souter, *Pelagius's Expositions of Thirteen Epistles of St Paul* (3 vols.; Texts and Studies 9; Cambridge: Cambridge University Press, 1922–1931), 2.170); Pollentius cited by Augustine (see above). Origen too seems to understand "only in the Lord" to mean "to a fellow Christian"; see below.

[15] Three of my four sample modern commentaries explain that "only in the Lord" means "only to a Christian." Robertson and Plummer, 161: "only as a member of Christ which implies that she marries a Christian." Lietzmann, 37: "mit einem Christen." Fitzmyer, 329: "Paul prefers that she marry a Christian, which is a counsel against entering into a mixed marriage. Paul is undoubtedly extending a Jewish notion, expressed in such OT endogamic regulations as Dt 7:3, Ezra 9:2, 11 QTemple 57:19 …, to the Christians of Corinth." Conzelmann makes no clear statement. Albrecht Oepke, RAC 4 (1959) 659 s.v. Ehe, writes simply "Mischheirat schliesst Paulus aus (1 Cor 7.39)." I am astonished that none of our four representative commentaries cites a study of the Pauline phrase ἐν κυρίῳ. Is it possible that there is no such study? Cf. A. Deissman, *Die neutestamentliche Formel 'In Christo Jesu'* (Marburg, 1892) and A.J.M. Wedderburn, "Some Observations on Paul's Use of the Phrases 'In Christ" and "With Christ'," *JSNT* 25 (1985), 83–97 (with bibliography). Fitzmyer notes that Paul's "she is free to be married to anyone she wishes" seems to echo the formulary of Jewish divorce as attested in documents of the Judean desert (e.g. DJD 2:105) and the Mishnah (Gittin 9:3), but this parallel does not clarify the meaning of ἐν κυρίῳ. Had Paul wished to restrict the Christian widow to remarriage with a believer, he could have said simply "but only to a believer" (πιστῷ).

Matters are not so simple, however. Augustine remarks on the ambiguity of the phrase "only in the Lord." It might mean "to a Christian" or it might mean "as a Christian," that is, piously, with proper motivation.[16] Theodoret of Cyrrhus (b. ca. 393–d. ca. 466) tries to have it both ways in his commentary, glossing the words "only in the Lord" with "that is, to a fellow believer, to a pious person, chastely, properly."[17] Ambrosiaster (writing between 366 and 384 C.E.) writes similarly.[18] But John Chrysostom (writing probably in the 380s or 390s) saw the phrase as a demand for propriety without any reference to mixed marriage: if a widow seeks to remarry, her motives and conduct must be pure or "in the Lord." This is how the passage is construed by Epiphanius of Salamis (ca. 375) too.[19] In support of this interpretation I would adduce Ignatius' Letter to Polycarp. The letter, written in the early decades of the second century C.E., contains a paragraph about marriage, in which Ignatius writes "It is right for men and women who marry to establish their union with the approval of the bishop that the marriage may be according to the Lord and not according to lust."[20] The phrase "according to the Lord" reminds us, of course, of the Pauline

---

[16] Augustine, *De adulterinis coniugiis* 1.25 31 (CSEL 41.378): "'tantum in domino' quod duobus modis accipi potest: aut christiana permanens aut christiano nubens."

[17] Theodoret in PG 82.277 and 285.

[18] Ambrosiaster in CSEL 81,2.90: "tantum autem in domino. Hoc est ut sine suspicione turpitudinis nubat et religionis suae viro nubat."

[19] John Chrysostom, Homily 19.7 on 1 Cor 7:39 in PG 61.160; Epiphanius, Panarion 59.6 (GCS 31.371 ed. Holl) writes: τὸ δέ ἐν κυρίῳ τουτέστιν τὸ μὴ ἐν πορνείᾳ μὴ ἐν μοιχείᾳ μὴ ἐν κλεψιγαμίᾳ, ἀλλ' ἐν εὐνομίᾳ ἐν παρρησίᾳ ἐν σεμνῷ γάμῳ , ἐπι μένοντα ἐν τῇ πίστει ἐν ταῖς ἐντολαῖς ἐν εὐποιίαις ἐν εὐλαβείᾳ ἐν νηστείαις ἐν εὐνομίᾳ ἐν ἐλεημοσύναις ἐν σπουδῇ ἐν ἀγαθοεργίᾳ. ταῦτα γὰρ συνόντα καὶ παραμένοντα οὐκ ἀργοὺς οὐδὲ ἀκάρπους καθίστησιν εἰς τὴν τοῦ κυρίου παρουσίαν

[20] Ignatius To Polycarp 5.2: πρέπει δὲ τοῖς γαμοῦσι καὶ ταῖς γαμουμέναις μετὰ γνώμης τοῦ ἐπισκόπου τὴν ἕνωσιν ποιεῖσθαι, ἵνα ὁ γάμος ᾖ κατὰ κύριον καὶ μὴ κατ' ἐπιθυμίαν. Translation follows William R. Schoedel, *Ignatius of Antioch* (Hermeneia; Philadelphia: Fortress, 1985), 272.

phrase "in the Lord"—indeed, it has been suggested that Ignatius is alluding here to our Pauline passage.[21] Ignatius shows that what the phrase means to exclude is not mixed marriage but lust.

Now, of course, one could argue that even if the primary meaning of the phrase "in the Lord" is "modestly, properly, without lust," unions with non-believers would be prohibited too because by definition they are immodest, improper, and lustful. Perhaps. But if this assumption is correct, we will have to concede that the prohibition of mixed marriage retreats from the primary semantic field to the secondary. And we have the remarkable comment of the remarkable Theodore of Mopsuestia (ca. 350–428) to show that this assumption is not necessarily correct and that the verse may not be a prohibition of mixed marriage at all. Theodore writes, "'Only in the Lord': preserving her piety should she marry an unbeliever."[22]

1 Cor 6:15–17

In these verses Paul preaches against *porneia* (1 Cor 6:13,18), illicit sexual relations (usually translated "fornication"). Paul singles out for specific mention sex with a prostitute (1 Cor 6:15). We may presume that he is referring to some notorious incident in the life of the Corinthian Christian community, just as he was in 1 Cor 5:1 when he condemned the relationship of a Christian man with his stepmother. Paul's argument is that a Christian's body belongs to God. He illustrates this idea with two images: first, the bodies of Christians are "limbs" or "members" of Christ (1 Cor 6:15); second, a Christian body is "the temple of the holy spirit" (1 Cor 6:19). Hence Christians are to cling to the Lord, avoid *porneia* (1 Cor 6:18), and not sin with their bodies—that is, sexually.

---

[21] "Ignatius is apparently thinking of St Paul's words in 1 Cor vii 39," writes J. B. Lightfoot in *The Apostolic Fathers Clement Ignatius and Polycarp* (vol. 2; London: Macmillan, 1889–1890; repr. Peabody: Hendrickson, 1989), 350. Lightfoot also cites a parallel phrase in Clement of Alexandria.

[22] Karl Staab, *Pauluskommentare aus der griechischen Kirche* (Münster in Westf: Aschendorff, 1933),184: Μόνον ἐν κυρίῳ τὴν εὐσέβειαν φυλάττουσα, ἐὰν ἀπίστῳ συνοικήσῃ.

We cannot be sure exactly what other sexual sins (that is, beyond consorting with a stepmother or a prostitute) Paul meant to include under the category of *porneia*.[23] Tertullian is the first to argue that Paul meant to include mixed marriage. Tertullian has already cited 1 Cor 7:39 to prove that Paul prohibits mixed marriage (see above); he has already argued that 1 Cor 7:12–14 does not permit mixed marriage (see below). He continues as follows:[24]

> In the light of all this it is evident that believers who enter into marriage with gentiles commit a sin of fornication and are to be cut off completely from communion with the brethren, in accordance with the letter of the Apostle who says "with such a one we must not even break bread" (1 Cor 5:11). Will we make bold to present our marriage certificates on that day before the tribunal of our Lord and claim that a union which he himself forbade is a union properly contracted? Is it not adultery that he prohibits? Is it not fornication? Does not one who marries an outsider violate the temple of God and "make the limbs of Christ the limbs of an adulteress" (1 Cor 6:15)?

For Tertullian the category of *porneia* (in Tertullian's Latin, *stuprum*) includes mixed marriage. Even if such marriages are solemnized with the proper certificates, at the end of time ("on that day") they will be condemned by the Lord as adultery and *porneia*. Sexual relations

[23] Lietzmann 27 and Conzelmann 111, the latter cited with approval by Fitzmyer 267, understand *porneia* to be extramarital sexual intercourse. But *porneia* usually includes more than just adultery (Fitzmyer 265). Robertson and Plummer 95 correctly remark, "*Porneia*. Illicit sexual intercourse in general."

[24] Tertullian, *Ad Uxorem* 2.3.1 (CCSL 1.387; p. 132 ed. Munier): "Haec si ita sunt, fideles gentilium matrimonia subeuntes stupri reos constat esse et arcendos ab omni communicatione fraternitatis, ex litteris apostoli dicentis *cum eiusmodi ne cibum quidem sumendum.* Aut numquid tabulas nuptiales die illo apud tribunal Domini proferemus et matrimonium rite contractum allegabimus, quod uetuit ipse? Non adulterium est, quod prohibitum est, non stuprum est? Extranei hominis admissio minus templum Dei uiolat? minus membra Christi cum membris adulterae commiscet?" The translation is that of William Le Saint, *Tertullian Treatises on Marriage and Remarriage* (Westminster, Md.: Newman Press, 1951; ACW 13), 27–28, slightly modified.

between a Christian and a non-Christian violate the Christian body which is the temple of God (1 Cor 6:19)[25] and "make the limbs of Christ the limbs of an adulteress" (1 Cor 6:15).[26]

This reading of 1 Cor 6:15 is adopted by Cyprian, not just in the *To Quirinus* (as we have seen above) but also in his *On the Lapsed* (251 C.E.). Cyprian argues that God has let the Roman state persecute the Christians because they have been lax in their faith. He draws up a list of their sins, among them "The bond of marriage joined with nonbelievers, members of Christ given in prostitution to gentiles."[27] The reference to 1 Cor 6:15 is unmistakable. In the fourth century Zeno of Verona and Jerome similarly cite 1 Cor 6:15 in order to condemn mixed marriage.[28]

The main problem with this reading of 1 Cor 6:15 is that it is wrong; Paul does not believe that marital unions between believers and non-believers constitute *porneia*.[29] He says just the opposite in 1 Cor 7:14, which I shall discuss below.

2 Cor 6:14

The theme of 2 Cor 6:14–7:1 is that believers are to separate themselves from unbelievers, so that they may avoid pollutions of body and soul, and pursue sanctification. The vocabulary and

---

[25] In their notes ad loc both Munier and Le Saint cite 1 Cor 3:16–17; those verses indeed refer to the violation of the temple of God, but there the temple metaphor refers to the Christian community as a whole (as in 2 Cor 6:16). That the Christian individual is a temple of God is the point of 1 Cor 6:19.

[26] Our texts of 1 Cor 6:15 read *pornê* (prostitute), followed by the Vulgate (*meretrix*). Tertullian, however, says *adultera* (adulteress). This is exegesis, not a variant reading. For the same exegetical move by Chrysostom see note 51 below.

[27] Cyprian, *De Lapsis* 6 (CCSL 3.223): "iungere cum infidelibus vinculum matrimonii, prostituere gentilibus membra Christi."

[28] Zeno of Verona (between 360 and 380 CE) *Tractatus* 2.7.11-12 (CCSL 22.174); Jerome, *Adversus Jovinianum* (393 CE) 1.10 (PL 23.234): "at nunc pleraeque contemnentes apostoli iussionem iunguntur gentilibus et templa Christi idolis prostituunt."

[29] Not one of my four sample commentaries even mentions mixed marriage in connection with this passage.

world-view of this paragraph are not readily paralleled within the Pauline corpus, and the paragraph seems to disturb the connection between 6:11–13 and 7:2–3. Hence many scholars argue that it is an interpolation, but whether it is Pauline, non-Pauline, or anti-Pauline, and how it came to find itself in chapter six of 2 Corinthians, are questions that have long been debated and are far from settled.[30] For my purposes, the first question is exegetical: does 2 Cor 6:14, whatever its origin, prohibit mixed marriage?

The short answer is: it does not do so explicitly, it might do so implicitly, and it might not do so at all. The key to the verse is the unusual verb *heterozugein* (the participle of which appears here), which might mean either "pull half a yoke" (lit. "to be yoked one of two") or "to pull a yoke with an unequal partner" (lit. "to be yoked with another unequally").[31] Either way, the passage warns believers not to yoke themselves to unbelievers; the difference between the two renderings is the nuance. Does the passage treat such a junction neutrally or disparagingly? Is it a union of equals or of unequals? Virtually all modern translations and commentators take it the second way (e.g. in the NRSV "do not be mismatched with unbelievers"), because the verse seems to echo the LXX's rendering of Leviticus 19:19, "You shall keep my law. You shall not breed your animals to those of a different kind (*heterozugôi*), and you shall not sow your vineyard with something different, and you shall not put on yourself an adulterated garment woven with two materials."[32] Clearly the author of 2 Cor

---

[30] See e.g. the detailed and judicious discussion in Victor Paul Furnish, *II Corinthians* (Anchor Bible, 1984), 371–383; more recent bibliography assembled by Yonder M. Gillihan, "Jewish Laws on Illicit Marriage, the Defilement of Offspring, and the Holiness of the Temple: A New Halakic Interpretation of 1 Corinthians 7:14," *JBL* 121 (2002): 711–744, at712 n 3.

[31] These two possible meanings are presented with admirable clarity by Cornelius a Lapide (1567–1637), *Commentaria in Scripturam Sacram tomus XVIII: Divi Pauli Epistolarum* (ed. A. Crampon; Paris: L. Vivès, 1868), 460–461. A third possible meaning discussed by a Lapide is "to tilt a scale." For all these meanings see LSJ s.v.

[32] Τὸν νόμον μου φυλάξεσθε·τὰ κτήνη σου οὐ κατοχεύσεις ἑτεροζύγῳ καὶ τὸν ἀμπελῶνά σου οὐ κατασπερεῖς διάφορον καὶ ἱμάτιον ἐκ δύο ὑφασμένον κίβδηλον οὐκ ἐπιβαλεῖς σεαυτῷ.

6:14 is taking the law of mixed kinds metaphorically.[33] According to 2 Cor 6:14 a union of a believer with an unbeliever is an improper (or unequal) union, a violation of the order established by God, in which each species is to remain distinct from every other.

What unions is 2 Cor 6:14 talking about? Some ancient commentators argue that sexual unions with idolaters are the main target; the verse is a prohibition of mixed marriage.[34] In support of this interpretation is the fact that the metaphor of yoking easily lends itself to a sexual meaning and Leviticus 19:19 was understood by various ancient Jewish interpreters to refer to improper sexual unions, especially mixed marriage.[35] However, modern scholars (at least the commentaries I have sampled) argue that the 2 Cor 6:14 is a general prohibition of intimacy with unbelievers and that the specific reference of the verse—if indeed it has a specific reference—is unclear. Some commentaries suggest that a prohibition of mixed marriage is implied, others are silent on the point.[36] For a fair num-

---

Translation follows *A New English Translation of the Septuagint* (ed. Albert Pietersma and Benjamin Wright; Oxford University Press, 2007). The Göttingen edition of the LXX does not offer any variants of consequence for our purposes. The *heterozug-* root does not appear in the parallel verse in Deut 22:9–11.

[33] Similarly, the prohibition of muzzling the threshing ox (Deut 25:4) is understood metaphorically at 1 Cor 9:9 (and 1 Tim 5:17–18).

[34] Cyprian (cited above note 4); Jerome (cited above note 14); Didymus of Alexandria (ca. 313–398) apud Staab, *Paulus Kommentare* 32. Origen too refers to mixed couples as those who are "misyoked with unbelievers" (see appendix below).

[35] Philo, *Special Laws* 4.203–204 (Loeb edition 8.134–137); Josephus, AJ 4.229; MMT (4Q396); 4Q271 frag. 3 lines 9–10 with the note of the editor in DJD 18.177. Cf. Calum Carmichael, "Forbidden Mixtures," *VT* 32 (1982): 394–415 and C. Houtman, "Another Look at Forbidden Mixtures," *VT* 34 (1984): 226–228.

[36] A prohibition of mixed marriage is implied by the general prohibition: see Alfred Plummer, *Second Corinthians (*ICC; New York: Scribner's, 1915), 206; Margaret Thrall, *Second Corinthians* (ICC, 1994), 473; Furnish, *Second Corinthians* 361 and 372. Calvin eloquently defends this position; see *Ioannis Calvini Opera Omnia ... Series II Opera Exegetica volume XV Commentarii in Secundam Pauli Epistolam ad Corinthios* (ed. Helmut Feld; Genève: Librairie Droz, 1994), 114–115. In contrast other commentators do not even mention a prohibition of mixed marriage: see e.g. Hans Windisch, *Der zweite Korintherbrief* (Göttingen: Vandenhoeck & Ruprecht, 1924; Meyers Kommentar), 212 ("eine all-

ber of ancient and medieval commentators the verse warns against consorting spiritually with idolaters, heretics, or Jews; consorting carnally through mixed marriage does not make the list.[37] I conclude that if 2 Cor 6:14 prohibits mixed marriage, it does so implicitly, subtly, and indirectly—and perhaps not at all.

I return to the question of origins. If 2 Cor 6:14 is Pauline, it provides, like 1 Cor 7:39, discussed above, ambiguous evidence at best for a Pauline prohibition of mixed marriage. In the absence of solid evidence documenting such a prohibition, not much can be based on 2 Cor 6:14 (or 1 Cor 7:39, for that matter). If 2 Cor 6:14 is not Pauline, as many scholars argue, then it has nothing to tell us about Paul's attitude to mixed marriage, no matter how it is construed. One argument advanced by scholars to "prove" that 2 Cor 6:14 cannot derive from Paul is the fact that it seems to be at odds with positions that the genuine Paul takes elsewhere.[38] The author

---

gemein gehaltene, an keine lokale Situation gebundene Bekehrungsmahnung"); Lietzmann, 129 ("Worauf sich das im einzelnen bezieht, können wir wieder nicht sagen"); Rengstorf, ThDNT 2.901 s.v. *heterozugein* (no mention of marriage).

[37] In their discussions of mixed marriage, referenced above, neither Tertullian nor Pollentius nor Augustine cites 2 Cor 6:14. In their commentaries ad loc. neither Theodoret nor Pelagius nor Ambrosiaster mentions marriage. For what it is worth I note that not a single one of the excerpted commentaries on 2 Cor 6:14 presented in *Ancient Christian Commentary on Scripture* (see note 11 above) even mentions marriage. For Pelagius, as for some modern scholars, the unbelievers of the passage are heretics rather than gentiles; Pelagius (ed. Souter 266) writes: "Nolite iugum ducere cum infidelibus. Nolite illis coniungi vel aequari; quia iugum simul non trahunt nisi pares: id est, nolite iungi pseudoapostolis vel his qui in idolio recumbebant [1 Cor 8:10]." And here is Thomas Aquinas on the passage: "Hoc ergo dicit nolite iugum ducere, id est nolite communicare in operibus infidelitatis, cum infidelibus. Et hoc propter duo. Primo quia aliqui erant inter eos, qui reputabantur sapientiores, non abstinentes ab idolot[h]itis, et ex hoc scandalizabant inferiores. Alii autem erant qui communicabant cum Iudaeis in traditionibus seniorum. Unde Apostolus hortatur eos cum dicit nolite, ut non communicent cum Iudeis in traditionibus legis, neque cum gentibus in cultu idolorum. Utrique enim infideles sunt." See *Tomus Sextusdecimus D. Thomae Aquinatis ... Complectens Expositionem In Omnes D. Pauli Apostoli Epistolas* (Rome 1570), 103C-D. No reference to mixed marriage.

[38] E.g. Furnish, *Second Corinthians*, 376.

of 2 Cor 6:14 instructs his followers not to associate with idolaters, but in 1 Cor 5:9–10 Paul explicitly instructs his followers to continue associating with idolaters "else you would need to leave the world," and in 1 Cor 7:12–14 Paul explicitly tolerates mixed marriage. As we have already seen in this essay, and as Augustine well observed, any claim that Paul prohibits mixed marriage comes up against 1 Cor 7:12–14. I turn now to that passage.

1 Cor 7:12–14

In these cryptic verses, Paul addresses the situation of a Christian married to a non-Christian, and makes two main points. First, the Christian spouse does not have to separate from the non-Christian spouse; on the contrary, if the two partners agree to continue the marriage, they should remain together. Second, if the non-Christian spouse does not agree to continue the marriage, presumably because s/he objects to the Christian life of the Christian spouse, they should divorce, in which case the Christian spouse is free to re-marry. The first point is apparently directed (as many scholars have noted) at those members of the church of Corinth who were saying that the mixed couple must separate, for the sake of the spiritual health ("holiness") of either the Christian spouse or the community as a whole or both. The second point clearly shows the difference between a Christian marriage and a mixed marriage. In a Christian marriage divorce is prohibited, and if, for whatever reason, the couple separate, re-marriage is prohibited for as long as either spouse remains alive (1 Cor 7:10–11; 7:39). But in a mixed marriage divorce is possible, and remarriage after such divorce is permissible.[39]

For Tertullian these verses are a problem, for they seem to show that Paul permits, or at least tolerates, mixed marriage. In fact,

[39] Origen and Ambrosiaster, among others, deduce that a real marriage is the partnership of two believers; the union of a Christian with a non-Christian is not a marriage but something else (Ambrosiaster calls it a coniugium). See Origen, commentary on 1 Cor 7:12 (Jenkins, *JTS* 9 [1907–1908], 504–505—see note 64 below); Ambrosiaster, commentary on 1 Cor 7:15 in CSEL 81,2.77.

Tertullian reports that some Christian women, having been married to non-Christian husbands, cite these verses of Paul as proof that they have not violated any law of the church! Tertullian solves the problem posed by 1 Cor 7:12–14 by restricting the applicability of the passage. Paul indeed does permit an already existing mixed marriage to continue, but only if the marriage had originally been contracted before the conversion of the Christian spouse. Thus, two Gentiles marry; one of them converts to Christianity, while the other remains a Gentile—in this case, and in this case only, does Paul permit the couple to remain together. If a Christian were to inquire about the permissibility of joining a Gentile in marriage, surely Paul too, Tertullian says, would prohibit such a union. In other words, Paul's timeless and broadly applicable teaching about mixed marriage is contained in 1 Cor 6:15 and 7:39 (see above), while his tolerance of mixed marriage in 1 Cor 7:14 is not timeless but contingent, not broadly applicable but specific. It is not the rule but the exception.

Tertullian's narrow reading of 1 Cor 7:12–14 has found many followers, both ancient and modern.[40] In Catholic canon law, the so-called Pauline privilege (*privilegium Paulinum*), derived from this verse, obtains only in the case described by Tertullian: if one spouse of a non-Christian couple converts to Christianity, and if the other spouse objects to, or interferes with, the Christian life of the newly converted spouse, the Christian partner may divorce the non-Christian spouse and then marry a Christian—all with the blessing of the church.[41]

---

[40] Ancient: Ambrosiaster, commentary on 1 Cor 7:13 (CSEL 81,2.75-76); Theodoret, Commentary on 1 Cor 7:14 (PG 82.277); Jerome, *adversus Iovinianum* (PL 23.233-234); John Chrysostom, Homily 19 on 1 Cor 7 (PG 61.155); Augustine, *de adulterinis coniugiis* (CSEL 41.367 and 372-373); Pelagius, Commentary on 1 Cor 7:14 (vol. 2; ed. Souter, 163); Severian of Gabala (d. ca. 409) in Staab, *Paulus Kommentare* 250. Modern: Robertson and Plummer, 141; Fitzmyer, 297; Neither Lietzmann nor Conzelmann comment on this point.

[41] See e.g. ODCC (3rd edn, 1997), 1243 s.v. Pauline Privilege. The details do not concern us.

However, is it certain that 1 Cor 7:14 addresses only this one particular case? This narrow interpretation of 1 Cor 7:14 was advanced by Tertullian solely for the purpose of limiting the applicability of the verse, and thus to maintain that Paul "really" opposed mixed marriage. This is not "innocent" exegesis; this is exegesis with a point. Later in life Tertullian will adopt the same strategy in order to restrict the applicability of 1 Cor 7:39. In his *To his Wife* (written ca. 200 C.E.) Tertullian preached against the marriage of a widow; a life of continence after marriage is far superior to a life of remarriage. In the course of time Tertullian's opposition to remarriage intensifies; he finally arrives at the conclusion that marriage by a widow is prohibited. But does not Paul explicitly permit a widow to marry (if only in the Lord)? How can a prohibition of remarriage be squared with 1 Cor 7:39? In his *On Single Marriage* (written 214 C.E.) Tertullian argues that Paul's permission to remarry applies only to the widow who had been married as a Gentile to a Gentile and who, after the death of her husband, converts to Christianity. Such a widow may remarry since her new Christian husband is deemed to be not her second husband but her first; but if a Christian woman married to a Christian man becomes a widow, then Paul too, says Tertullian, would surely prohibit her remarriage.[42] Tertullian's interpretation of 1 Cor 7:39 is no less ingenious than his interpretation of 1 Cor 7:14. Each is designed to restrict the applicability of the biblical verse.[43]

Just as there is nothing in 1 Cor 7:39 to suggest that Paul is speaking only about widows once married to non-believers, there is nothing in 1 Cor 7:14 to suggest, let alone require, that Paul is speaking only of mixed marriage brought into being by the conversion of a spouse to Christianity.[44] The verse makes just as much sense if Paul

[42] Tertullian, *De Monogamia* 11; see esp. 11.10 (15): "Itaque et mulier, si nupserit, non delinquet, quia nec hic secundus maritus deputabitur, qui est a fide primus" (CCSL 2.1246). Text in *Tertullien Le mariage unique (De Monogamia)* (ed. Paul Mattei; Paris: du Cerf, 1988; SC 343).

[43] Students of rabbinic literature will be familiar with this rhetorical strategy.

[44] Several ancient scholars observe that Paul does not say "If anyone should marry a non-believer," but rather "if anyone has a non-believer," implying that

is speaking of a mixed marriage entered into by a Christian who is now troubled by his/her mixed union. If we were not convinced a priori of Paul's unconditional opposition to mixed marriage, we would have no reason to read 1 Cor 7:14 so narrowly.

Evidence for this comes from the commentary on 1 Corinthians by Origen (ca. 185–ca. 253). Alas, the commentary is extant only in fragments and as a result its argument is sometimes hard to follow.[45] If I have interpreted him correctly, Origen understands 1 Cor 7:12–14 as permission from Paul to contract a mixed marriage. Origen knows nothing of Tertullian's "narrow" reading. Paul simply is talking about the marital union of a Christian with a non-Christian. Like Tertullian, however, Origen is not happy with these verses as they stand and adopts a triple strategy by which to dilute their message. First, he argues, this ruling derives from Paul himself, not the Lord. "It is better to obey laws from God than to obey laws of Paul the apostle. For even though he is holy, his laws are much inferior to the laws of the Lord." Christians need not follow Paul when he is speaking on his own authority. Second, Origen disagrees with Paul. Origen observes that the consequences of mixed marriage are not necessarily as Paul depicts them. Paul says that the non-Christian spouse is "sanctified," that is, won over to Christ by the Christian spouse, but there can be no guarantee that this will happen (as Paul himself admits, 1 Cor 7:16). "For [the Christian spouse] will either succeed or fail, and will either destroy his [own] soul or, after much toil, scarcely be able to win over [the non-Christian spouse]." Third, Paul himself, says Origen, "has permitted us to think otherwise," for Paul has elsewhere clearly stated his preference that we not marry at all (1 Cor 7:40) or, if we do, that

---

the marriage already exists, and that 1 Cor 7:12–14 should not be taken as permission to enter into a mixed marriage. This is a good argument as far as it goes, but it does nothing to support what I have been calling the "narrow" reading of 1 Cor 7:12–14. See Tertullian, *Ad Uxorem* 2.2.2 (CCSL 1.385); and the commentaries of Theodoret, Pelagius, Chrysostom, and Jerome, referenced above note 40.

[45] See the appendix to this article for the text and translation of Origen's commentary.

we marry "in the Lord" (1 Cor 7:39). This argument strongly suggests that Origen understands 1 Cor 7:12–14 as Pauline permission to a Christian to enter into a mixed marriage, not merely permission to continue an already existing mixed marriage. 1 Cor 7:39 is an alternative to 1 Cor 7:12–14.

In sum, according to Origen, in 1 Cor 7:12–14 Paul permits mixed marriage but this is Paul's own opinion, no more. A little further along in the same chapter Paul shows that he does not fully approve of marriage at all, and reluctantly approves only of marriage "in the Lord," which Origen seems to interpret as "to a Christian." "Therefore, it is a good thing," says Origen, "that a person, before being surprised, carefully examine not only the present but also the future, and, having examined it, either not to marry or, if to marry, to marry in the Lord." In other words, according to Origen, on the subject of mixed marriage, indeed on the subject of marriage itself, Paul sends out mixed signals.

Whatever we may think of his criticism of Paul, Origen shows that Tertullian's narrow exegesis of 1 Cor 7:12–14 is neither inevitable nor necessary. Like Tertullian Origen sees 1 Cor 7:12–14 and 1 Cor 7:39 as opposed to each other; Tertullian solves that opposition through exegesis, but Origen allows it to abide in creative tension.

As I intimated above 1 Cor 7:12–14 also stands in opposition to 1 Cor 6:15–17. Tertullian and his many followers cite 1 Cor 6:15–17 as further evidence of Paul's opposition to mixed marriage, and further evidence of the need to interpret 1 Cor 7:12–14 narrowly. However, if 1 Cor 6:15–17 is speaking about mixed marriage, there is not just opposition but contradiction between those verses and 1 Cor 7:12–14. I shall now argue, aided by patristic exegesis, that 1 Cor 7:12–14 shows that 1 Cor 6:15–16 cannot be speaking about mixed marriage, because for Paul mixed marriage does not come under the prohibited category of *porneia*.

Exegetes ancient and modern agree that the key to 1 Cor 7:14 is the root *hagios* ("holy" or "sacred") which appears in the verse twice in a verbal form (variously rendered as "has been consecrated" or "has been sanctified" or "has been made holy"), with reference to the non-Christian spouse, and once as an adjective, with reference to the offspring of the mixed marriage.[46] What might these words mean in context? How is a non-Christian spouse made holy "in" or "through" a Christian spouse? And in what sense are the offspring of a mixed marriage "holy? Exegetes have long struggled with these questions but have not achieved consensus—far from it.[47] But we can make a few points with confidence.

In this verse the word *hagios* and its derivatives do not have their usual Pauline meaning. In the letters of Paul, and indeed elsewhere in the NT, "the holy ones" (or "saints," *hoi hagioi*) and "the sanctified ones" (*hoi hêgiasmenoi*) are synonyms for "the members of the holy community," people who would later come to be called "Christians."[48] Thus, for example, 1 Corinthians is addressed "to the church of God which is at Corinth, to those sanctified in Christ Jesus, called to be saints" (1 Cor 1:2). But surely that cannot be the meaning of these terms here in 1 Cor 7:14—Paul is speaking of non-believers! Further, v. 16—"Wife, for all you know, you might save your husband. Husband, for all you know, you might save your wife"—clearly implies that there is still a step that awaits the non-Christian spouse beyond "sanctification" if he or she is to be "saved." That step, of course, is to accept Christ and join the church.

Not "members," then, but "sanctified" (the spouse) and "holy" (the offspring). Many ancient exegetes thought these words meant "brought closer to Christ," that is, either the spouse or the offspring or both are candidates for conversion. A Christian spouse is in a good position to "win over" the non-Christian spouse, whether by preaching or by exemplary behavior. Many exegetes cite or allude to 1 Peter 3:1 in support of this idea: "Wives ... accept the authority

---

[46] I say "offspring," because the English word "children" invariably suggests youngsters, but the Greek term *tekna* (as many scholars have noted) can refer to people of any age, hence "offspring."

[47] Our four sample commentaries give ample bibliography; the most recent detailed discussion is perhaps Gillihan, "Jewish Laws on Illicit Marriage," who also gives (731–741) a full survey and summary of recent scholarship.

[48] See e.g. BDAG s.v. *hagiazô* 2 and s.v. *hagios* 2dβ List of passages in Gillihan, "Jewish Laws on Illicit Marriage," 715 n. 13.

of your husbands, so that, even if some of them do not obey the word, they may be won over without a word by their wives' conduct." A Christian parent can instill Christian beliefs and values in a child, even if there is a non-Christian parent in the house. The child is "a candidate for faith and salvation."[49] Most modern scholars are not convinced by this exegesis, objecting that the notion of sanctification by a spouse and holiness by birth would seem to be distinct from the process of education, but they have not been able to agree upon anything better. As a minimum we can say that the non-Christian spouse and the offspring are made sacred, to one degree or another, by one means or another, by virtue of their proximity to the Christian spouse and parent.

The "holiness" of this relationship means that *porneia* is absent. The *hagios* language of 1 Cor 7:12–14 contrasts markedly with the *porneia* language of 1 Cor 6:13–19. Marriage (1 Cor 7:2–6), even mixed marriage (1 Cor 7:12–16), provides a licit outlet for sexual desire. In contrast, sexual relations with a prostitute (1 Cor 6:15–16) exemplify *porneia* (1 Cor 6:13; 6:18–19).[50] John Chrysostom asks

---

[49] "designatos sanctitatis ac per hoc etiam salutis" is how Tertullian puts it, *De Anima* 39.4 (CCSL 2.842-843), in J. H. Waszink, *Quinti Septimi Florentis Tertulliani De Anima Edited with Introduction and Commentary* (Amsterdam: Meulenhoff, 1947), 56, paraphrase of text 440, commentary 446–447. Waszink cites Jerome's discussion of this text in his Epistula 85 (ad Paulinum).5 (PL 22.753–754) (CSEL 55.137–138): "Tertullianus ... disseruit, asserens, sanctos dici fidelium filios, quod quasi candidati [this is the text of PL; CSEL prints candidatae which I cannot construe] sint fidei, et nullis idololatriae sordibus polluantur." The phrase "candidatus fidei" also appears in Jerome, *Adversus Jovinianum* 1.10 (PL 23.234 top). Same idea in Pelagius, commentary on 1 Cor 7:14 (vol. 2; ed. Souter; 163–164), cited by Augustine, *De Peccatorum Meritis* 3.12(21) (PL 44.198–199) and *De Sermone Domini in Monte* 1.16(45) (PL 34.1252). The same idea appears in John Chrysostom (see below).

[50] *Porneia* and a *hagios*-word form a contrasting pair in 1 Thess 4:3; *porneia* and *akatharsia* (absence of cleansing) form a contrasting pair in 2 Cor 12:21, Gal 5:19, Eph 5:3, and Col 3:5. Other related passages listed by Gillihan, "Jewish Laws on Illicit Marriage," 715 n. 11. In rabbinic literature too *qadosh* frequently refers to sexual propriety; see e.g. Y. Megillah 3:2 74a (R. Judah the Patriarch is called "the holy one" because he never looks at his sexual organ).

why a (male) believer is prohibited from remaining married to his adulterous wife (his understanding of "prostitute" in 1 Cor 6:15[51]) but is permitted to remain married to his non-believing wife (1 Cor 7:14). Is not the sin of unbelief greater than the sin of illicit sex?[52] To this question John gives a series of answers which boil down to three: an adulterous marriage is no longer a marriage, while a marriage between a believer and a non-believer is still a valid union; a husband who remains with his adulterous wife sins with her (i.e. has sexual relations with her) precisely in the arena in which she herself had sinned, not so a faithful Christian married to a non-Christian; the adulterous wife is too far gone to be reclaimed for the faith, but in a mixed union there is every hope that the Christian spouse will win over the non-believing spouse.[53]

Whatever we may think of Chrysostom's answers, his excellent question highlights the difference between 1 Cor 6:15–16, a case of *porneia*, condemned and prohibited by Paul, and 1 Cor 7:12–14, a case of holiness (described with *hagios* language), tolerated, perhaps even permitted outright, by Paul. Mixed marriage for Paul is not *porneia*. We cannot be sure exactly what Paul meant when he called the spouse "sanctified" and the offspring "holy," but we can be sure that he meant as a minimum that the sexual relationship between this husband and wife is not *porneia* and that their offspring does not suffer any taint of *porneia*.[54] Hence we must conclude, against

---

[51] Cf. Tertullian (note 26 above).

[52] Several modern scholars have asked the same question: see e.g. Michael Newton *The Concept of Purity at Qumran and in the Letters of Paul* (Cambridge University Press, 1985; SNTSMS 53), 105–106; Dale Martin, *The Corinthian Body* (New Haven: Yale University Press, 1995), 250–251, as cited by Gillihan, "Jewish Laws on Illicit Marriage," 741; J. Ayodeji Adewuya, *Holiness and Community in 2 Cor 6:14-7:1* (New York: P. Lang, 2001), 145.

[53] John Chrysostom, Homily 19.2–3 on 1 Cor 7, PG 61.154–155. Apparently Chrysostom did not know the *pericope adulterae* ([John 7:53–8:11]).

[54] I do not understand Gillihan's statement "There is no hint of a moral judgment *of the children* in Paul's claim that they are holy instead of impure" ("Jewish Laws on Illicit Marriage," 715; also 737 n. 80). It seems obvious that there is a moral judgment, based not on the offspring's actions but on their origin.

Tertullian, that 1 Cor 6:15–16 has nothing to do with mixed marriage.[55]

Chrysostom argues that the *hagios* language here should be understood minimally; the spouse is not "really" sanctified, and the offspring is not "really" holy. All Paul means is that the spouse and the offspring are candidates for salvation and that the relationship is licit. Chrysostom argues as follows (I add some explanations in brackets):[56]

> Paul says (1 Cor 7:14) that "the unbelieving husband is made holy through his wife" – so great is the abundance of your purity [that you, the Christian wife, can sanctify your husband]. What then? Is the Greek [the unbelieving husband] holy [*hagios*]? Of course not. Paul said not "he is

[55] Tertullian, *Ad Uxorem* 2.2.9 (CCSL 1.387) writes of mixed marriage according to Paul (trans. Le Saint), "Whatever is unclean has no part in what is holy. It can do nothing except defile it out of its own filth and kill it" (quod immundum est cum sancto non habet partem nisi ut de suo inquinet et occidat). Similarly, Hayes, *Gentile Impurities* 98, writes, "What is strongly implied in Paul's writings – that intermarriage is *zenut* [the rabbinic Hebrew equivalent of *porneia*] which unites holy and impure persons as one flesh or body, resulting in the defilement of the holiness of the former and of Christ himself – becomes explicit in the writings of the church fathers." Hayes, misled by Tertullian, is wrong about Paul, who nowhere implies, strongly or otherwise, that mixed marriage is *porneia*; he says precisely the opposite in 1 Cor 7:14. Gillihan's critique of Hayes is too gentle; see Gillihan, "Jewish Laws on Illicit Marriage," 728 n 52.

[56] Homily 19.3 on 1 Corinthians, PG 61.155: *Ἡγίασται γὰρ*, φησὶν, *ὁ ἀνὴρ ὁ ἄπιστος ἐν τῇ γυναικί.* Τοσαύτη ἡ περιουσία τῆς σῆς καθαρότητος. Τί οὖν; ἅγιός ἐστιν ὁ Ἕλλην; Οὐδαμῶς· οὐ γὰρ εἶπεν, Ἅγιός ἐστιν, ἀλλ', Ἡγίασται ἐν τῇ γυναικί. Τοῦτο δὲ εἶπεν, οὐχ ἵνα δείξῃ ἐκεῖνον ἅγιον, ἀλλ' ἵνα ἐκ περιουσίας τὸν φόβον ἐξέλῃ τῆς γυναικός, κἀκεῖνον εἰς ἐπιθυμίαν ἀγάγῃ τῆς ἀληθείας. Οὐ γὰρ τῶν σωμάτων τὸ ἀκάθαρτον, ὧν ἐστιν ἡ κοινωνία, ἀλλὰ τῆς προαιρέσεως καὶ τῶν λογισμῶν. Εἶτα καὶ ἀπόδειξις· εἰ γὰρ ἀκάθαρτος μένουσα γεννᾷς, τὸ δὲ παιδίον οὐκ ἀπὸ σοῦ μόνης, ἀκάθαρτον ἄρα τὸ παιδίον, ἢ ἐξ ἡμισείας καθαρόν· νυνὶ δὲ οὐκ ἔστιν ἀκάθαρτον. Διὸ καὶ ἐπήγαγεν, *Ἐπεὶ τὰ τέκνα ὑμῶν ἀκάθαρτά ἐστι· νυνὶ δὲ ἅγιά ἐστι·* τουτέστιν, οὐκ ἀκάθαρτα. Αὐτὸς δὲ ἅγια ἐκάλεσε, τῇ περιουσίᾳ τῆς λέξεως πάλιν ἐκβάλλων τῆς τοιαύτης ὑποψίας τὸ δέος.

> holy" but "he is made holy through his wife." He said this not in order to show that he is holy, but in order through overstatement[57] to remove from the wife the fear [that she ought not remain with her non-Christian husband], and in order to lead him to a desire for the truth. For impurity is not of the bodies and the communion of bodies, but of the mind and the thoughts. [Consequently she may remain with her husband.] And then the proof: If you were to remain impure [because of this relationship] and bear a child, the child, not being from you alone, would be impure, or [at most] half pure. But now, [since your relationship is not impure,] the child is not impure. Therefore he added "Since [otherwise] your children would be impure, but now they are holy," that is, not impure. He called them "holy" in overstatement [lit. by the abundance of the expression], again in order to cast out the dread of such suspicion [that she might be impure through remaining with her husband].

According to Chrysostom, when Paul says that the non-Christian spouse is sanctified and the offspring is holy, he does not really mean what he says; after all, neither one is a Christian and neither one is "saved," consequently neither is really "holy" at all. In this verse "holy" means "not impure." The rhetorical function of 1 Cor 7:14 explains the overstatement: Paul said what he said solely for the purpose of reassuring the Christian wife that she may remain in her relationship with her non-Christian husband.

Chrysostom suggests that the *hagios* language in 1 Cor 7:14 should not be taken literally; Paul is deliberately overstating his case for the purpose of rhetorical effect. This suggestion was taken up by other exegetes of the Antiochene school, Theodoret of Cyrrhus and Theodore of Mopsuestia. Theodoret writes, "Paul set

---

[57] The translator in the Nicene Post-Nicene Fathers 1st series vol. 12 (available online at http://www.ccel.org/ccel/schaff/npnf112.iv.xx.html and various other sites) translates ἐκ περιουσίας "as completely as possible," but I think that the phrase looks ahead to the τῇ περιουσίᾳ τῆς λέξεως at the end of the paragraph (note the πάλιν, "again"). Chrysostom means the following: when Paul tells the wife that her non-Christian spouse "has been made holy," and, again, when he tells her that her children are "holy," in each case he is overstating the matter in order to reassure her.

these things down with some measure of hyperbole, in order to persuade [the Christian partner] not to abandon the union." The ever-remarkable Theodore says that the holiness language here is simply Paul's way of indicating approval, that is, approval of the perpetuation of the marriage. "Paul said this because [the believers] were afraid that the unbelievers would contaminate them through sexual contact."[58] If Chrysostom's influence were as strong today as it was in fifth century Antioch, modern scholarly discussions of 1 Cor 7:14 would be shorter and fewer.

Conclusions

This essay has focused on the question: does Paul prohibit mixed marriage, that is, a marriage between a believer (what we might call a Christian) and a non-believer (a non-Christian)? According to many ancient church writers, and according to many modern scholars, the answer is yes. Tertullian is the first to argue that Paul prohibited the marriage of a Christian to a non-Christian—he was also the first Christian to argue that Christians are prohibited from marrying non-Christians—and he was widely followed, especially by writers in the Latin west.[59] However, an examination of the Pauline passages cited by these writers reveals that Paul has little to say on mixed marriage and much of that is ambiguous.

---

[58] Theodoret, commentary on 1 Cor 7:14 in PG 82.277; Theodore of Mopsuestia apud Staab, *Paulus Kommentare* 182. Κατὰ τὸ ἡμέτερον δηλονότι ἀγόμενον βούλημα ἅγιον εἶναι δύναται. Ἡγίασται ἀντὶ τοῦ κεκάθαρται. ταῦτα δὲ εἶπεν, ἐπειδὴ ἀμφέβαλλον μὴ μιαίνοντες τῇ τῶν ἀπίστων κοίτῃ οἱ ἄπιστοι. (These two sentences are not a unit; each of them derives from a different catena.)

[59] Why Greek churchmen were so much less interested than their Latin brethren in documenting a prohibition of mixed marriage, I do not know. An excellent summary (to which I am much indebted) of the Western Latin tradition on the prohibition of mixed marriage is provided by Robert Bellarmine (1542–1621), *De Sacramento Matrimonii caput XXIII de cultus disparitate* in his *Opera Omnia* (vol. 5; ed. Justinus Fèvre; Paris 1873; repr. Frankfurt: Minerva, 1965), 116–120.

Tertullian and his followers, ancient and modern, cite 1 Cor 6:15–19 and 1 Cor 7:39 to prove that Paul prohibits mixed marriage. The first of these is a dramatic denunciation of illicit sexual relations (*porneia*), on the grounds that the body of a Christian is the body of Christ and the temple of the holy spirit. The second of these is a command from Paul to a Christian widow that, if she is to remarry, she is to remarry "only in the Lord." Neither of these verses unambiguously addresses mixed marriage. To argue that Paul's concept of *porneia* includes mixed marriage is to assume what needs to be demonstrated; such an argument also contradicts what Paul says in 1 Cor 7:14, according to which a non-Christian spouse is "sanctified" by his or her Christian spouse. The meaning of the command to marry only in the Lord is not at all clear. Perhaps it includes a prohibition of mixed marriage, perhaps not; many ancient commentators thought that it did not.

Some ancient writers, and their modern continuators, also cite 2 Cor 6:14 as evidence that Paul prohibited mixed marriage. This verse opens a paragraph that encourages believers in Christ to keep their distance from non-believers. Certainly marriage with a non-believer would seem to be a violation of this exhortation, but it is important to note, yet again, that marriage is not explicitly mentioned, and, if Paul (or whoever the author is) meant to include mixed marriage, he did so only obliquely. Some commentators, ancient and modern, see this verse as a prohibition of mixed marriage, others do not.

So, what are we left with? Not a single verse in the Pauline corpus explicitly and unambiguously prohibits a believer from marrying a non-believer. On the other side stands 1 Cor 7:12–14, the only passage in the Pauline corpus to talk about mixed marriage. No matter how we interpret this cryptic and enigmatic passage, one thing is certain: these verses do not prohibit anything. Just the opposite. Paul declares mixed marriage, at least after the fact and perhaps before the fact, at least in some circumstances and perhaps in all circumstances, to be licit; the believing spouse is to remain with the non-believing spouse in sanctioned wedlock. Anyone who argues that Paul prohibits mixed marriage has to come to terms with the plain meaning of 1 Cor 7:12–14. I conclude that Paul did not prohibit mixed marriage, and that such a prohibition was the work of formative Christianity only in the second century C.E.[60]

And so, at last, the question of why: why does Paul not oppose mixed marriage? We can only speculate, of course; for whatever they are worth, here are three speculations, presented in order from the less to the more plausible.

First, perhaps the reason is practical. Perhaps Paul noted the demographic realities of the early Christian communities. There were still so few believers in the world, whom else could they marry but non-believers? A shortage of eligible spouses within a community can result in marriages with outsiders. Such was the situation, for example, in Spain in the early fourth century. There was an "oversupply of (Christian) girls," with the result that they were being given in marriage to Gentile men. Canon 15 of the Council of Elvira (306 C.E.) prohibited the practice.[61] Perhaps Paul estimated that there was an undersupply of potential brides (and grooms) within the fold, but unlike the canonists of Elvira, did not try to solve the problem through legislation. He yielded

---

[60] Paul is the only Jew of antiquity who argued on principle against a prohibition of mixed marriage. In the pages of Philo, Josephus, and rabbinic literature we can occasionally hear the voices, and see the actions, of Jews who enjoyed sexual relations with gentiles, but no other Jew of antiquity said anything as radical as 1 Cor 7:12–14. (For two runners-up see: Josephus AJ 4.145–149; Y. Sanhedrin 2.4[6] 20c statement of R. Yosi on the wives of Solomon.) Hence I am not persuaded by those who want to explain the rulings of 1 Cor 7, at least 7:12–14, by appeal to halakhic (Jewish legal) reasoning and terminology. For such attempts see Gillihan, "Jewish Laws on Illicit Marriage," and Peter Tomson, "Paul's Jewish Background in View of his Law Teaching in 1 Cor 7," in *Paul and the Mosaic Law* (ed. J.D.G. Dunn; WUNT 89; Tübingen: Mohr Siebeck, 1996), 251–270.

[61] Friedrich Lauchert, *Die Kanones der wichtigsten altkirchlichen Concilien* (repr. Frankfurt: Minerva, 1961), 16: "Propter copiam puellarum gentilibus minime in matrimonium dandae sunt virgines Christianae, ne aetas in flore tumens in adulterium animae resolvatur." Was there an oversupply of brides or an undersupply of grooms?

to the inevitable and did nothing to discourage the members of his flock from seeking mates outside the fold.

Second, perhaps the reason is eschatological. Paul believes that the world is passing away, that the end time is at hand, and that as a result everyone should remain in place.[62] Those who are unmarried should remain unmarried, and those who are married should stay married. The intermarried couple too should remain as they are and, if possible, not divorce. This explanation makes all the more sense if we construe 1 Cor 7:12–14 as permission after the fact: Paul is addressing mixed couples who already are couples. Unmarried believers should not marry non-believers—they should not marry anyone. Mixed marriage is not a problem that will bother the church for long, thinks Paul.

Third, perhaps the reason is theological. Paul believes that there is no longer Jew or Greek in Christ, that ethnic distinctions no longer matter, that all people are alike the children of God. Paul believes that the old Jewish rules of table fellowship no longer obtain, and that believers may freely sup with unbelievers (1 Cor 10:27; cf. Gal 2:12–14). If Paul believes all this, surely he could believe too that the followers of Christ may freely marry non-believers. Perhaps he thought that mixed marriage was a fine way to spread the light of truth and the knowledge of Christ. The Jewish prohibition of mixed marriage was irrelevant to Paul, and the Christian prohibition was a century or more in the future.

---

[62] This point is brought out nicely by O. Larry Yarbrough, *Not Like the Gentiles: Marriage Rules in the Letters of Paul* (SBLDS 80; Atlanta: Scholars Press, 1986), 113.

APPENDIX: ORIGEN ON 1 COR 7:12–14

Fragments of Origen's commentary on 1 Corinthians (preserved in the catena tradition) were published one hundred years ago in an exemplary edition by Claude Jenkins (1877–1959; in 1934 he became Regius Professor of Ecclesiastical History and Canon of Christ Church at Oxford).[63] The text is in bad shape, and a large gap separates what Origen wrote from the fragments now extant. I translate here two paragraphs from that commentary in order to show how I understand how Origen understood 1 Cor 7:14. The logic of Origen's argument is not always clear, or at least is not always clear to me, and I have no doubt that my translation (which apparently is the first) has room for improvement.

§XXXV Τοῖς δὲ λοιποῖς λέγω ἐγώ, οὐχ ὁ κύριος. τοῖς μὲν γεγαμηκόσιν οὐκ ἐγὼ νομοθετῶ, ἀλλ' ὁ κύριος· τοῖς δὲ μὴ γεγαμηκόσιν ἀλλ' ἑτεροζυγοῦσιν ἀπίστοις οὐκ ἔχω νόμον δοῦναι ἀπὸ θεοῦ· οὐδὲ γὰρ ἄξιοί εἰσι νόμων θεοῦ· ἀλλ' ἀκουέτωσαν ἡμῶν. καὶ χρήσομαι εἰς τὸ νοηθῆναι τὰ κατὰ τὸν τόπον γεγραμμένοις ἐν τῷ νόμῳ. οἱ νόμοι οἱ κατὰ Μωσέα οἱ μὲν θεοῦ εἰσιν, οἱ δὲ Μωσέως. καὶ τοῦτο ἐπιστάμενος ὁ κύριος διαφορὰν νόμων θεοῦ καὶ νόμων Μωσέως εἶπεν ἐπὶ μὲν τῶν ὑπὸ θεοῦ νενομοθετημένων Ὁ γὰρ θεὸς εἶπεν Τίμα τὸν πατέρα καὶ τὴν μητέρα, ἐπὶ δὲ τῶν ὑπὸ Μωσέως Μωϋσῆς διὰ τὴν σκληροκαρδίαν ὑμῶν ἐπέτρεψεν ὑμῖν ἀπολῦσαι τὰς γυναῖκας. τηρήσας γοῦν τὰ τοῦ βιβλίου τοῦ ἀποστασίου εὑρήσεις οὐκ ἐκ προστάγματος κυρίου τὸν νόμον γεγραμμένον. Μωϋσῆς μὲν οὖν ὑπηρετῶν θεῷ νόμους ἔδωκεν δευτέρους παρὰ τοὺς νόμους τοῦ θεοῦ· Παῦλος δὲ ὑπηρετῶν τῷ εὐαγγελίῳ νόμους ἔδωκεν δευτέρους τοῖς ἐκκλησιαστικοῖς μετὰ τοὺς νόμους τοὺς ἀπὸ θεοῦ διὰ Ἰησοῦ Χριστοῦ. καὶ καλόν ἐστιν ἀκούειν νόμων ἀπὸ κυρίου ἢ ἀκούειν νόμων Παύλου τοῦ ἀποστόλου. κἂν γὰρ ἅγιος ᾖ, ἀλλὰ πολλῷ ὑποδεεστέρους ἔχει νόμους τῶν νόμων τοῦ κυρίου.

---

63 Claude Jenkins, "Origen on I Corinthians," *JTS* 9 (1907–1908), 231ff, 353ff, 500ff and 10 (1908–1909), 29ff. The text presented here (digitized by the TLG) was published by Jenkins in *JTS* 9 (1907–1908), 505–506 lines 57–72 and 1–20. In *JTS* 10 (1908–1909), 270 C. H. Turner wrote "I do not think that the *Journal of Theological Studies*, in the nine years of its existence, has published any contribution to theological learning more solid and more valuable than the edition of the fragments of Origen on St Paul's epistles to Ephesus and Corinth."

§XXXVI [Ἡγίασται γὰρ ὁ ἀνὴρ ὁ ἄπιστος ἐν τῇ γυναικί, καὶ ἡγίασται ἡ γυνὴ ἡ ἄπιστος ἐν τῷ ἀδελφῷ.]

Ὡς κρᾶσίς τις γίνεται τῶν δύο, ἀνδρὸς καὶ γυναικός, εἰς σάρκα μίαν ὥσπερ οἴνου καὶ ὕδατος· καὶ ὥσπερ μεταδίδωσιν ὁ πιστὸς ἁγιασμοῦ τῇ ἐθνικῇ γαμετῇ, ἢ τὸ ἐναντίον ἡ πιστὴ τῷ ἀπίστῳ ἀνδρί, οὕτω καὶ ὁ ἄπιστος μεταδίδωσι μολυσμοῦ τῇ πιστῇ γυναικὶ ἢ τῷ πιστῷ ἀνδρὶ ἡ ἄπιστος γυνή. διὰ τί γὰρ φησὶν Ἡγίασται ἡ ἄπιστος ἢ ὁ ἄπιστος τ<ῷ> λαμβάνειν τι ἀπὸ τοῦ πιστοῦ ἢ ἀπὸ τῆς πιστῆς, καὶ οὐχὶ βεβηλοῦται τ<ῷ> λαμβάνειν τι ἀπὸ τοῦ ἀπίστου μέρους; ἕκαστος γὰρ ἐκ τοῦ περισσεύματος τῆς καρδίας διαλεγόμενος τῷ ἑτέρῳ ἢ μεταδίδωσιν ἢ μεταλαμβάνει, καὶ τῷ χρόνῳ πάντως νικᾷ τὸ ἕτερον. καὶ τίς χρεία, φησί, τοιούτου ἀγῶνός τε καὶ κινδύνου; ἢ γὰρ ἐπιτεύξεται ἢ ἀποτεύξεται, καὶ ἤτοι τὴν ψυχὴν αὐτοῦ προσαπολέσει ἢ πολλὰ καμὼν μόγις κερδῆσαι δυνήσεται. διὰ τοῦτο καλόν ἐστι πρὶν προληφθῆναι ἄνθρωπον ἐπιμελῶς οὐ μόνον τοῦτο ἀλλὰ καὶ τὸ μέλλον σκοπεῖν, καὶ σκοπήσαντα ἢ μὴ γαμεῖν ἢ γαμοῦντα ἐν κυρίῳ γαμεῖν. γυνὴ γὰρ δέδεται ἐφ᾽ ὅσον χρόνον ζῇ ὁ ἀνήρ· ἐὰν δὲ ἀποθάνῃ ὁ ἀνήρ, ἐλευθέρα ἐστὶν ᾧ θέλει γαμηθῆναι, μόνον ἐν κυρίῳ. οὐκ ἀκούομεν τοῦ μόνον ἐν κυρίῳ, ἀλλὰ τὸ ἐλευθέρα ἐστὶν ᾧ θέλει γαμηθῆναι ἀναγινώσκομεν, οὐκέτι δὲ συνετάξαμεν τὸ μόνον ἐν κυρίῳ. καίτοι γε κἀκεῖ ὅτε εἶπεν μόνον ἐν κυρίῳ, πάλιν ἀνέκρουσεν τὸν λόγον εἰπὼν μακαριωτέρα δέ ἐστιν ἐὰν οὕτως μείνῃ, κατὰ τὴν ἐμὴν γνώμην. τὸ οὖν εὐφημότερον εἰπὼν ὁ ἀπόστολος, τὸ Ἁγιάζεται γάρ, ἀφῆκεν ἡμῖν τὸ ἄλλο νοεῖν.

(Section 35) *To the others I say – I, not the Lord* (1 Cor 7:12). To those who are married it is not I (Paul) who legislate, but the Lord. In contrast, to those who are not married but who are mis-yoked with non-believers (2 Cor 6:14), I do not have a law to give from God, for they are not worthy of the laws of God.[64] Let them, however, listen to us (Paul). In order to

[64] In the previous paragraphs (504–505) Origen explained that only a marriage between Christians was a real marriage, whereas the union of a Christian with a non-Christian is not deemed a marriage. See note 39 above. On 504 line 44 Origen again, as here, refers to the mixed married as those who are "misyoked."

make the contents of this passage understood I (Origen) will use what is written in the Law. The laws according to Moses—some derive from God, others from Moses. The Lord, understanding the difference between the laws of God and the laws of Moses, said concerning the laws legislated by God, *God has said, Honor your father and mother* (Matthew 15:4, citing Exodus 20:12), but about the laws set down by Moses, *Moses, on account of your hardness of heart, permitted you to divorce your wives* (Matthew 19:7–8, citing Deuteronomy 24:1–3). Considering carefully what scripture says about the *bill of divorce,* you shall find that the law was written not in accordance with a commandment of the Lord. This shows that Moses, in serving God, gave additional [lit. second] laws beside the laws of God.[65] Paul too, in serving the Gospel, gave to the people of the church additional [lit. second] laws beyond the laws from God through Jesus Christ. It is better to obey laws from the Lord than to obey laws of Paul the apostle. For even though he is holy, his laws are much inferior to the laws of the Lord.

(Section 36) *The non-believing husband is sanctified in the wife, and the non-believing wife is sanctified in the husband* (1 Cor 7:14). Like a mixture of wine and water, the two, husband and wife, become *one flesh* (Matthew 19:5 and 1 Cor 6:16, citing Genesis 2:24). And just as the male believer shares sanctification with his Gentile wife, or, in the opposite case, the female believer with her unbelieving husband, thus too the male unbeliever shares pollution with his believing wife, or the unbelieving wife with her believing husband. Why then does Paul say that the unbeliever, whether female or male, is sanctified, by taking something from the male or female believer?[66] Why is the believer not profaned by taking something from the unbelieving part? Each spouse, discussing with the other *out of the abundance of the heart* (Matthew 12:34), either gives or receives, and in time completely wins over the other. And what is the need, he (Paul) says, for such a struggle and such danger?[67] For [the Christian spouse] will either

---

[65] The idea that most of the laws of the Torah are "additional" (lit. second) laws, promulgated by Moses in order to counteract Israelite tendency to sin, and consequently not binding on Christians—this idea (summed up by the word *deuterosis*) will be much developed in the third century by the Didascalia and in the fourth century by the Apostolic Constitutions.

[66] Origen asks this question not to explain Paul but to disagree with him, or at least to limit the applicability of 1 Cor 7:14. The previous paragraph establishes the fact that Paul's own legislation is not authoritative

succeed or fail, and will either destroy his [own] soul or, after much toil, scarcely be able to make a profit [that is, win over the non-believing spouse, 1 Peter 3:1]. Therefore, it is a good thing that a person, before being surprised, carefully examine not only the present but also the future, and, having examined it, either not to marry or, if to marry, to marry *in the Lord* (1 Cor 7:39). *A wife is bound for as long as her husband lives; if the husband die, she is free to be married to whomever she wishes, only in the Lord* (1 Cor 7:39). We do not obey the verse *only in the Lord* [if we marry a non-believer]; but when we read that *she is free to be married to whomever she wishes,* we have not yet connected it with *only in the Lord.*[68] However, even there [in connection with that verse], when he (Paul) said *only in the Lord,* he then restricted that utterance by saying *she is more blessed if she remain as she is, according to my opinion* (1 Cor 7:40).[69] Therefore, although the apostle has spoken this rather well-turned phrase *The non-believing spouse is sanctified,* he has permitted us to think otherwise.

All translations are mine unless otherwise credited. For the dating and attribution of early Christian texts I follow *Dictionary of Early Christian Literature* (ed. Siegmar Döpp and Wilhelm Geerlings; New York: Crossroad, 2000). Some of the early Christian texts discussed here focus more on the marriage of a Christian woman to a non-Christian man than on the marriage of a Christian man to a non-Christian woman. This gen-

---

[67] I think this means: Paul himself in 1 Cor 7:16 implies that the outcome of the debate between the believing spouse and the non-believing spouse is in doubt. Why, then, should a Christian put himself (herself) into such a dangerous situation? Origen uses 1 Cor 7:16 as evidence against Paul's optimistic statement in 1 Cor 7:14 that the Christian spouse will win over the non-believer. Not necessarily, says Origen.

[68] The logic of the argument seems to be that the restriction of *only in the Lord* offsets both the permission of 1 Cor 7:12–14 to marry a non-believer as well as the permission of the first part of 1 Cor 7:39 that a widow may be married to anyone she pleases.

[69] The logic of the argument seems to be that the permission to marry in the Lord is offset by Paul's preference that a widow not marry at all. If I understand Origen correctly, he is arguing that Paul presents three possibilities: not to marry at all (most preferred option); to marry in the Lord (that is, to a fellow Christian); to marry a non-Christian, in the uncertain hope that the Christian

der distinction is interesting and important but is not my concern; see Margaret MacDonald, "Early Christian Women Married to Unbelievers," *SR* 19 (1990): 221–234. I would like to thank Wayne Meeks and Laura Nasrallah for their comments, criticisms, and suggestions.

Chapter 9

"Someone who considers something to be impure – for him it is impure" (Rom 14:14): Good Manners or Law?

Daniel R. Schwartz

1. Introduction

At Rom 14:14, in the course of an exhortation of the members of the Christian community to be tolerant of one another and their different practices, Paul writes as follows: "I know, and am persuaded in the Lord Jesus, that nothing is impure by itself, except for someone who considers something to be impure – for him it is impure."[1] Accordingly, he holds, members of the community must respect such differential practice—which he says is characteristic of the "weak" in the community, as opposed to the strong, whose view ("that nothing is impure...") he too adopts.

There has been a good bit of discussion about the weak and their food-restrictions, which Paul exemplifies as abstention from meat and wine (v. 21). Were they Jews or Judaizing Christians, or were they adherents of some Hellenistic cult, such as Pythagorean vegetarians? I tend to follow the many who assume that the reference is

---

[1] My translation. Syntactically, there is some room for doubt as to whether Paul means that he knows and believes only what is said in the first half of the sentence (as is usually assumed, and engenders a period [so, e.g., NIV] or semicolon [so RSV and *Einheitsübersetzung*] at its end) and admits in the latter half that others consider something else to be true and for them it is, or, rather—as is argued by O. E. Evans ("Paul's Certainties: What God Requires of Man – Romans xiv. 14," *ExpTim* 69 (1957/58): 201–202)—that Paul means that he knows and believes both parts of the statement. As he notes, the use of εἰ μή, which links the two parts of the sentence closely one to another, tends to support the latter reading. Cf. below, n. 16. Apart from syntax, however, there is not much difference between the two readings, for, as I shall emphasize below, even according to the first reading the second clause of the sentence has Paul stating what *is*, not just what others think.

to Jewish practice, similar to the Sabbath observance alluded to in the same context in v. 5;[2] as has been noted, moreover, the very word Paul uses for "impure" here, *koinon*, has that meaning only in Jewish Greek.[3] But the fact is that Paul does not specify that his argument relates only to Jewish practice, and if he didn't trouble to point that out, and so left modern scholars room to think that perhaps he was referring to Pythagorean vegetarianism or the like, or perhaps simply imagining things from which someone might possibly choose to abstain, perhaps we too should leave that open.[4]

Again, there has been much discussion of the source of Paul's position, particularly with regard to his words that he "is persuaded *in the Lord Jesus*." Does this indicate that he is alluding to some particular statement or precedent by Jesus? In particular, scholars have supposed he might be referring to Mark 7:15, the logion that it is not what goes into the body but rather that which proceeds from it that makes one unclean, which Mark 7:19 takes to mean that Jesus thus declared all foods clean. I tend to agree with Räisänen that there is not much substance to the latter hypothesis, and that instead we should take the reference to Jesus to be a reference to Paul's interpretation of the import of his own faith in Jesus.[5]

---

[2] For discussions concluding that Paul is referring to observers of Jewish dietary laws, see J. M. G. Barclay, "'Do We Undermine the Law?' A Study of Romans 14,1–15,6," *Paul and the Mosaic Law* (ed. J. D. G. Dunn; WUNT 89; Tübingen: Mohr [Siebeck], 1996), 289–293, and C. M. Pate, *The Reverse of the Curse* (WUNT 114; Tübingen: Mohr Siebeck, 2000), 271–275.

[3] See F. Hauck, "κοινός," *TDNT* 3.790–791; on Rom 14:14 see ibid. 797. See also C. House, "Defilement by Association: Some Insights from the Usage of ΚΟΙΝΌΣ/ΚΟΙΝΌΩ in Acts 10–11," *AUSS* 21 (1983): esp. 146–149.

[4] So Evans, "Paul's Certainties," 199.

[5] On these possibilities (and tending to the latter): H. Räisänen, *Paul and the Law* (WUNT 29; 2nd edn; Tübingen: Mohr [Siebeck], 1987), 245–247. Räisänen's view is approved of by H. Löhr, "Speisenfrage und Tora im Judentum des Zweiten Tempels und im entstehenden Christentum," *ZNW* 94 (2003): 27, n. 46.

2. How to Read Rom 14:14

Surprisingly, however, there has been relatively little discussion of the logic and implications of Paul's own position. How, in particular, can he both deny the validity of dietary restrictions, at the beginning of the verse, and affirm it at its end? Rather, in commentary after commentary it seems that, in fact, that problem is avoided by the avoidance of the plain sense of his words at the end of the verse, namely, that the foods in question *are* impure for those who think them so. Instead, Paul's words at the opening of the verse are usually taken to constitute such a strong denial of the validity of the dietary laws subscribed to by "the weak" that not much is left for his words at the end of the verse, which can hardly be more than a call for polite toleration of the errors of the benighted weak. That is, Paul's assertion at the beginning of the verse, about nothing being impure, is taken to be as sweeping and final as his assertions at Titus 1:15 that "to the pure all things are pure" and at 1 Cor 8:4 that "we know that there is no idol in the world." As John Barclay states this position, Rom 14:14 "constitutes nothing less than a fundamental rejection of the Jewish law in one of its most sensitive dimensions...this strong denial of the Scriptural distinction between 'clean' and 'unclean' food should not be watered down."[6]

Such a strong denial leaves, as I noted, little room for Paul's closing statement in our verse that foods are impure for those who think them so, and all we are left with is a call for Christians to be tolerant of such erroneous views, for it is not worth it to get involved in an argument about such bagatelles. Such an interpretation gibes well with v. 20, where Paul again asserts that "everything is indeed clean" but nevertheless urges his readers to let it alone: "do not, for

[6] Barclay, "'Do We Undermine,'" 300. As G. Holtz notes, in connection with Rom 14:14 "wird immer wieder die Auffassung vertreten, Paulus hebe die jüdischen Speisegebote mit ihrer Unterscheidung von rein und unrein faktisch auf;" G. Holtz, *Damit Gott sei alles in allem: Studien zum paulinischen und frühjüdischen Universalismus* (BZNW 149; Berlin and New York: De Gruyter, 2007), 247, with bibliography.

the sake of food, destroy the work of God." Christians have more important things to worry about. Thus, this is an appeal for polite coexistence among people who disagree about things; Paul's appeal comes from the stance of someone who knows the others are wrong but urges other "strong" people, like him, to follow the dictates of *noblesse oblige* and be above, or beside, all of that.[7]

In fact, however, it seems that Paul's position is significantly different. This we may see by examining six points about our verse's formulation.

1. Paul speaks in the first-person singular: "*I* know…*(I)* am persuaded." Contrast, for a few of the many examples that could be cited, Rom 3:19 and 7:14, or the above-mentioned 1 Cor 8:4: when Paul refers to what he assumes are or will be accepted by his addressees as well-known facts, he uses the first-person plural ("*We* know"). In our verse, Paul is claiming only a narrower base for his point of departure—which leaves more space for disagreement.
2. Paul qualifies his "I know" by adding "and am persuaded in the Lord Jesus." Although he connects the two with "and," the latter limits the absoluteness of the former, as if to say "I know, that is, I believe", or "I know, because I believe"[8]—and knowledge based upon *pistis*, or rather a claim to knowledge concerning which a need is felt to rephrase it as one grounded in belief, is, obviously, not as universal as unqualified knowledge.[9] Contrast, for example, Rom 2:2, 3:19; 6:6,

[7] For a formulation that moves from politeness to an obligation to "love" fellow Christians and, therefore, avoid behavior that might incense "the weak," see Evans, "Paul's Certainties," 200–201.

[8] This nuance is missed and lost by those who turn Paul's two verbs into a single statement, as in the NEB: "I am absolutely convinced."

[9] After Käsemann notes concerning this combination of knowledge and belief that "the phrase is singular," he observes, following Michel, that "absolute certainty and apostolic authority form a principle" (E. Käsemann, *Commentary on Romans* [London: SCM, 1980], 375). However, I would note that a "principle"—perhaps "doctrine" would have been a better rendering of the original *Lehrsatz* here—said to rest upon "belief" is less certainly true than one posited on the basis of something more objective. How, for example, would we react if, after an information clerk told us that a certain office will be open from 9:00 until 12:00, he or she went on to add "Yes, I fully believe that to be the case"?

9; 7:14, 18; 8:28, where Paul (alone or with his audience) simply "knows" things.[10] Thus, in this second way as well, Paul himself "waters down" (as Barclay put it) his denial of the existence of the distinction between clean and unclean.

3. Paul further "waters down" his declaration that nothing, i.e., no food, is unclean, by adding a qualification: "nothing is impure *by itself* (*di' heautou*)." To understand the import of this qualification, I would underline the fact that while the usual translations render "in itself" (so RSV, NRSV), "in" seems to refer to a state of being, making Paul claim that things *are not* impure; note, for example, the way this is made explicit in the *Einheitsübersetzung* here, which has Paul saying, à la Kant, that "an sich nichts unrein *ist*" (my italics). However, Paul does not speak of *das Ding an sich*, he does not use *en heautoi* but, rather, *di' heautou* – using the preposition which, when used as here with the genitive, points to the means or instrument or agency by which a process *occurs*, things *happen*.[11] Thus, already by his choice of preposition Paul is indicating that foods *can* become impure; the point he insists upon is only that the agent that can make that happen is not within the food itself. And that, of course, is precisely what the end of the verse says: when there is an appropriate external agent, namely, someone who considers the food to be impure, that indeed makes it impure, for such a person.
4. Note that in the preceding verse (14:13) Paul opens his appeal by underlining that one should not put a stumbling block or hindrance (πρόσκομμα...σκάνδαλον) before the weaker members of the community, and this image is resumed and, the conclusion drawn from it, a few verses later: Paul's point is that "strong" Christians should not eat

---

To make the point clear, note that one may agree with H. Schlier that the addition of "I know" to "I am persuaded" constitutes a "Steigerung" in contrast to such passages as Gal 5:10, Phil 2:24, and 2 Thess 3:4, where Paul says only that he is persuaded; see his *Der Römerbrief* (HTKNT 6; Freiburg: Herder, 1977), 413. My point, however, is the reverse: that "I know" would be stronger without the additional reference to belief.

[10] For a list of Pauline statements about what he "believes," see H. Räisänen, *Jesus, Paul and Torah: Collected Essays* (JSNTSup 43; Sheffield: Sheffield Academic, 1992), 141.

[11] Cf. for example Ep Jer 26 (Rahlfs): people can move an idol but it cannot move *di' heautou*—by itself.

what their "weak" fellows forbid lest they be guilty of causing them "to stumble" (προσκόμματος) (vv. 20– 21). This language, based upon the prohibition in Lev 19:4 about putting a stumbling block (LXX: *skandalon*) before the blind, which is typically used in forbidding enticing people to sin (see Mark 9:42–47 and parr.), indicates that if, when the weak and the strong eat together, the strong eat what the weak consider to be impure, that will somehow cause the weak to "stumble."

What does Paul mean here? Does he fear that the weak will leave the Church, or, rather, that they will violate their own dietary rules? On the one hand, the opening of v. 20, "do not, for the sake of food, destroy the work of God," which motivates the call upon the strong to avoid causing the weak to fall, seems to imply that since the weak take their prohibitions seriously it is to be feared that they will leave the community of God, i.e., the Christian community, if they are forced to choose between it and their own dietary practices. Some commentators hold that that is, indeed, Paul's point: Jewish Christians who insisted upon adherence to Jewish dietary rules might leave the Church if the other ("stronger") Christians insisted on eating what those rules forbade; the usage would be similar to that in 1 Cor 1:23 and Gal 5:11, for example, where Christian preaching might drive Jews away. Given his hope (expressed especially in chapters 9–11) that Israel will come to join the Church, Paul would be, on this interpretation, urging the "strong" Christians of Rome not to impose obstacles in the way of Jews who would indeed join them, or stay with them, if they were not put off by what is eaten at Church gatherings.

However, that interpretation is difficult, for two reasons. First, because Paul's characterization of those who adhere to those dietary rules as "weak" should lead us to believe that they will not be able to resist those who are "strong," so if they ate together it is likelier that they would be led astray by the latter and abandon their own dietary practices. And that, secondly, seems to be precisely what Paul is saying in the last verse of chapter 14: that if the "weak" are caused to abandon their own dietary practices not out of faith but only due to social pressures, that is, if they eat what the "strong" eat although they think it is forbidden, they will be sinning—"for all who have doubts and nonetheless eat are condemned, for it (their eating) does not proceed from faith, and all that is not from faith is a sin."[12] This, to my mind, is already far beyond watering down; here Paul is saying that if Jews who think certain foods are impure nonetheless eat them they will be sinning. The only way for them not to sin when they eat that which they consider impure is to accept the faith that, for them as for Paul, will bring the "knowledge" that indeed nothing is impure.

5. Note that the verb Paul uses for what the weak think is quite a respectable one—*logizomai*. This verb, characteristic of Paul,[13] need not imply any reservations or doubts on his part, such as might be implied by our "imagine" or "suppose," although it can have such a sense (as at Rom 2:2–3). Rather, just as Paul "reckons" things to be true at Rom 3:28 and 8:18 and that suffices to posit them, so too do the weak "reckon" certain foods to be unclean and that, according to Paul too, suffices for them. To again use the *Einheitsübersetzung* as a foil, note that while at 3:28 it allows Paul to proclaim "wir sind der Überzeugung," at 14:14 it allows the "weak" only "betrachten." I see no reason to think Paul would be pleased by such a distinction.
6. Finally and perhaps most simply, note that Paul does not merely say that the weak, who subscribe to dietary restrictions, should be allowed to abstain from that from which they think they ought to abstain. He does not confine himself to what should be done. Rather, he asserts that "he who considers something to be impure – for him it *is* impure." While *we* might tend—both because of the widespread tendency to take Paul's opening denial to be very complete, and because we, today, are used to thinking like Paul that really no foods are clean or unclean—to reduce that assertion to its functional implication, namely, to the statement that those others should be allowed to observe what they think obliges them, that is not what the words say. Rather, Paul says that for those who think something is impure *it is indeed impure*—and it would be, accordingly, wrong to lead them (via a "stumbling-block") to violate such prohibitions. That is, the weak are bound by rules that are based upon an assumption that is baseless, and is extraneous to their belief as Christians,

[12] For the insistence that this verse indeed refers to the weak, as we too assume, not to the strong, see among others Pate, *Reverse of the Curse*, 275, n. 130.

[13] See esp. W. H. G. Thomas, "Apostolic Arithmetic: A Pauline Word-Study," *ExpTim* 17 (1906): 211–214, also BDAG, 598.

and even raises difficulties for their life in common with other Christians—and nevertheless they are bound by those rules and it is wrong to entice them to violate or abandon them.

Thus, to summarize my analysis of Rom 14:14, it appears to bespeak the basic position that things that are indifferent from a legal point of view are endowed with a legal status by people's considerations about them. For people who consider some food unclean, it *is* unclean. This is a point of view that ascribes great legal significance to people's considerations as opposed to how things "really" are—and I would like next to show that, no matter how used we are to thinking of Paul as both antinomian and, when it nevertheless comes to law, an adherent to the principles of natural law, such a stance is indeed basic for Paul elsewhere as well. I will focus upon two Pauline examples—in Gal 3 and Rom 5.

3. COMPARE GAL 3 AND ROM 5

First, and most simply, note that recognition of this Pauline position seems to me to be fundamental for a proper understanding of Paul's discussion of faith vs. law in Gal 3. In his argument there with Galatian Christians who were tending to undertake Jewish law, Paul does not merely assert that those who undertake to fulfill the Law are wasting their time and their energy, for the route to salvation is not via law but, rather, via faith, as is indicated by the examples of Abraham and Habakkuk (vv. 6–9, 11). Rather, he also claims, in vv. 10–14, that those who undertake to observe the Law are bound by it and, accordingly, are under a curse—the curse that applies to those who do not fully fulfill the Law. That is, those who have undertaken to observe the Law are in fact bound by God to do so—just as Rom 14:14 asserts that foods a person considers to be impure *are* impure for him. Commitment to the Law does not only waste one's time and energy, and perhaps raise false hopes. Rather, Paul holds, it creates an obligation to fulfill the Law.

Second, back in Romans, we find Paul in a bind in chapter 5. It is clear that his basic point there is the comparison between Adam and Jesus: Adam engendered sin and death and Jesus abrogated them. Paul makes that point fairly fully at 5:18: "Then as one man's trespass led to condemnation for all, so too one man's act of righteousness leads to acquittal into life for all." However, it is noteworthy that this is the second time that Paul tries making that statement; he began it with very similar wording back in v. 12, but got stuck and sidetracked in the middle. Namely, after beginning there with "Therefore, just as sin came into the world through one man, and death came through sin, and so death spread to all because all have sinned," instead of continuing with what Jesus did he instead turns aside, in vs. 13, to defend the notion that sin existed before the days of Moses: "sin was indeed in the world before the law, but sin is not reckoned when there is no law."

Here, it is evident that Paul's problem is that, given the general proposition that without law there can be no sin, he cannot claim that Adam—who lived well before the days of the lawgiver, Moses—brought sin into the world. His resolution of the problem entails a distinction between sin itself, which did exist since Adam, and the "reckoning" of sin, which became possible only with the giving of the Law.

I see two possible ways of interpreting that distinction. One is a distinction between sin and penalty for sin: just as it is usual for legal systems to admit that someone cannot be punished for a crime if no law lays down the penalty, even if it would have been logical to impose a punishment (*nulla poena sine lege*; (אין עונשין מן הדין), so too Paul. However, that is not a likely interpretation of Paul's intention here, for he refers to sin, not to punishment, and to make "reckon" mean "reckon and entail punishment" is pretty wild exegesis, or eisegesis. In any case, as Lichtenberger puts it, that point would be quite "trivial";[14] far be it from Paul to think that a sin is

[14] H. Lichtenberger, *Das Ich Adams und das Ich der Menschheit: Studien zum Menschenbild in Römer 7* (WUNT 164; Tübingen: Mohr Siebeck, 2004), 129 (on Rom 7:7).

not a sin merely because, for whatever reason, it is impossible to punish the perpetrator.

Rather, Paul seems to be saying something else: that although there was sin in the world before the Law was given, it was not "reckoned" as sin because the people doing the sinning had no criteria by which they could reckon it as such. Just as, for example, Molière's *bourgeois gentilhomme* spoke prose his whole life but didn't know it until his teacher defined prose for him, so too, Paul asserts, there was sin since the days of Adam but only since Moses has man had the ability to recognize it for what it is. This is, then, another way of saying what Paul puts at 3:20: "through the Law we became conscious of our sin," and at 7:7: "I would not have known what sin was had it not been for the Law." For all practical purposes, that is, sin exists only if we are aware of it. Paul makes this claim very clear by distinguishing sin from death—for Adam introduced death too into the world, but there is no need for us to discuss awareness of it because death happens whether we are aware of it or not. Sin, in contrast, has its consequences only if we are aware of sinning. But such a view goes hand in hand with that we have found in Rom 14:14, namely, that if someone thinks ("reckons") that doing something would be a sin, for him or her it is in fact a sin. If at 14:14, with which we began, Paul was saying that for a person λογίζομένῳ something to be unclean it is unclean, at 5:13 he is asserting, similarly, that once the Law came, sin is ἐλλογεῖται against those who perform it. In both cases, it is the *logos*, not the *physis* of the matter, that constitutes the sin—and that which it constitutes really *are* sins. Just as much as they are real in chapter 5, for they serve to define Jesus' atoning function, so too are they real in chapter 14.

4. PAUL – MAN OF FAITH AND JEW OF THE DIASPORA

If we ask, now, what could have led Paul to such a position, I see two main possibilities. One of them has to do with Paul himself and is phrased quite well by Käsemann, in his commentary on

Rom 14:23, which I discussed above in my fourth point. Commenting on Paul's statement that it would be a sin to violate dietary laws contrary to one's own belief, Käsemann explains as follows: "If on Paul's view blessedness depends on faith, fall from this necessarily means condemnation."[15] That is, Paul's recognition of the importance of belief for him entails his recognition of its importance for others as well. Of course, it can entail it only if, and to the extent, that Paul realizes his own limits as an individual, which willy-nilly mean that others might hold beliefs different from his own with the same conviction. As I indicated in Section II, it seems that that is precisely what Paul does realize, and accept, in his discussion of the weak and their dietary rules. If Paul did not accept the validity of dietary rules for those who subscribe to them, he would be hard put to explain why his own faith had any valid implications for him.[16]

The other contribution to Paul's stance takes us, finally, beyond Paul himself to what this collection terms Paul's "Jewish matrix." It leads us to recognize that for many Jews, and certainly for Judaism as it was coming to be in the age of Paul, the important and binding things were those that we undertake upon ourselves in full cognizance of the fact that others do not. This point of view is expressed and embraced quite plainly, for example, by a younger Jewish contemporary of Paul in Rome: when Josephus needed to explain, in his *Antiquities*, why some Jewish teachers and their hotheaded followers risked their lives to tear down an image of an eagle that Herod had hung up over one of the gates of the Temple of Jerusalem, the phrasing he chose is that "the Law forbids those who choose to live according to it (even) to imagine setting up images and to prepare dedications of living beings" (*Ant.* 17.151). Here, then, is a plain statement, and affirmation, that the observance of Jewish law is a matter of per-

---

[15] Käsemann, *Commentary on Romans*, 379.

[16] Thus, Evans' suggestion, that our verse be construed as having Paul's belief and faith govern both statements (that nothing becomes impure in and of itself but things do become impure via someone's thought), is quite an attractive one. See above, n. 1.

sonal choice—but once that choice has been made the demands of the Law are valid and binding for those who made the choice, although of no consequence for those who did not.

To understand the full import of Josephus' statement, it is useful to compare the way he told the same story fifteen or twenty years earlier, in his *Judaean War*. There, at 1.650, Josephus had simply explained that "it was simply not done (*athemitos*) for there to be any icon or bust or any image of a living creature in the Temple." In comparing this to Josephus' parallel statement in *Antiquities*, two salient differences should be noted: in the *War* Josephus limits the prohibition to a particular *place*, and the authority for the prohibition is in the realm of *convention*—what is done or not done. People play no role in formulating the obligation; people are not mentioned and no reference is made to anything actually formulated or decided upon as a law. Rather, Josephus says that an icon in the Temple is *athemitos*—it is simply not done; the adjective "refers primarily not to what is forbidden by ordinance but to violation of tradition or common recognition of what is seemly or proper."[17] In the *Antiquities*, in contrast, Josephus speaks of the Law and it applies everywhere—but only binds such people as choose to undertake to live according to it.

The difference between Josephus of the *War* and Josephus of *Antiquities* is the difference between a Judaean priest, indeed, a Jerusalemite priest, who had just gotten off the boat in Rome, and a Jew of the Diaspora. Judaean priests, Jerusalemite priests, could take their Jewishness for granted; they were Jews due to their circumstances, it was a given, and they could easily think that the rules that obliged them were givens as well. Just as priests were priests because they *were* priests, having been born as priests, without any decision on their part, and just as the Temple in which they served was where it was because that was where it had to be, no person having been involved in that decision because, so the Bible taught, it had been chosen by God Himself, so too was it natural to assume that the rules that bound them were equally given. Jerusalemites in Jerusalem did

---

[17] BDAG, 24.

what Jerusalemites did as the default position, just as naturally and without choice as they were born and as they died. Jews in Rome, however, were living in the Diaspora, which means they were living as Jews *despite* their circumstances, not because of them; in a place where being Roman was the default, they were Jews because they chose not to do like the Romans but, rather, to be Jews. In such circumstances, it was all the more natural to assume that the rules which bound them were products of a similar, volitional, process. That is what Josephus bespoke in his account in the *Antiquities* about Herod's eagle, and that is what Paul—another Jew of the Diaspora—bespeaks in his account in Rom 14:14 of what makes unclean food unclean.

5. Diaspora Judaism and Pharisaic-Rabbinic Judaism

But there is more. For it seems that just as the major distinction, or dichotomy, between Jews of Judaea and Jerusalem, on the one hand, and Jews of the Diaspora, on the other, may be discerned here, so too may a similar distinction be observed among Jews in Judaea itself, during the latter part of the Second Temple period. Namely, if above I emphasized the priestly logic of the view that assumes that Law is embedded in and derives (just as the identity of the priesthood and the location of the Temple) from the nature of things, now I shall note that the latter half of the Second Temple period saw the development, under the impact of Hellenism, and of the loss of national sovereignty which meant basically Diaspora existence even in Judaea, a type of non-priestly Judaism which tended in the same direction as the Diaspora: a view of law as divorced from nature and deriving, instead, from the will and decisions of the individual Jew. That is, a certain diasporization, which is an artificialization, seems to have characterized non-priestly Judaism in Judaea just as much as it characterized Judaism of the Hellenistic Diaspora. Space and time do not allow me to set this thesis forth more fully here, and I have done so elsewhere,[18] but I will give a few

[18] See especially my "Law and Truth: On Qumran-Sadducean and Rabbinic

examples of that other, Pharisaic and proto-rabbinic orientation:

According to a dispute recorded in the Mishnah (*m. Ketub.* 13:2), the "sons of the high priests" held that if a man went abroad and his neighbor supported his wife in his absence, the money is considered to be the traveling husband's debt and so he must repay the neighbor upon his return. Probably that sounds fair to all of us; our stomachs, or our hearts, tell us that this is right. Any man who was so nasty as to leave his wife with no means of support and then refused to repay the generous neighbor is surely worthy of all of our contempt, and even if he thought he had left his wife enough money and she squandered it we would surely condemn him if he made such an argument to his neighbor instead of settling that dispute in private with his wife. But stomachs and hearts are natural; as Paul put it, the natural law which is written in our hearts, to which our consciences bear witness (Rom 2:15), is not the same as positive, formulated, law. Therefore, in contrast to the high priests, the rabbis—who were devotees of positive law—insisted that the returning husband could not be forced to repay the neighbor because, in the absence of a promissory note or any other formulation of the money as a loan, it was not, legally, a loan. A debt that was not called a debt is not "reckoned" a debt; *mutatis mutandis*, that is Paul's position in Rom 5 about sin not being reckoned a sin until Moses published the Law.

According to that mishnaic story, one Dosa b. Hyrcanus agreed with the "sons of the high priests." Accordingly, it is interesting to note that, according to another mishnaic story (*m. Roš.Haš.* 2:8), that same figure complained vociferously when a rabbinic court, that had erred in proclaiming the beginning of a new month a day earlier than the astronomical facts warranted, insisted on the validity of its decision. Again, according to a third mishnaic report

Views of Law," *The Dead Sea Scrolls: Forty Years of Research* (ed. D. Dimant and U. Rappaport; Leiden: Brill and Jerusalem: Yad ben Zvi, 1992), 229–240; and "Josephus on the Pharisees as Diaspora Jews," in *Josephus und das Neue Testament: Wechselseitige Wahrnehmungen* (WUNT 209; ed. C. Böttrich and J. Herzer; Tübingen: Mohr Siebeck, 2007), 137–146.

(*m. 'Ed.* 3:2) it was the same Dosa who held that an unminted flan (metal blank, "planchet") could be considered "money," according to the terms of Deut 14:25, for it had its value whether or not that fact had been stated upon it—but the other rabbis agreed that it wasn't money until it had been minted, that is, until the proper authority had called it money. In all of these cases, as others, the Mishnah deploys Dosa b. Hyrcanus as the flag-bearer of the realist view in order to point up its own position, namely, that human decisions endow things with their legal status no matter what their nature dictates.[19]

I will conclude with a case where the same point is made most demonstratively, and most similarly to Paul's case in Rom 14, namely, a case where what is law for some is not law for others:

> If someone says to a woman "I betrothed you" but she says "you did not betroth me," he is forbidden to marry her relations but she is allowed to marry his relations. If she says "you betrothed me" but he says "I did not betroth you," he is allowed to marry her relations but she is forbidden to marry his relations.
>
> (*m. Qidd.* 3:10)

That is, if Sam asserted that he had betrothed Ruth but she denied it and a court could not find evidence to uphold Sam's claim (perhaps the witnesses and documents, if there were any, had disappeared), the court is bound to enforce upon Sam the prohibitions of incest that would have ensued had his claim been true—such as the prohibition that he marry Ruth's sister or mother. And the same would be true, in reverse, had Ruth made the claim and Sam denied it. But the court will not forbid anything

[19] Note that particularly the "money" case shows how much this was a matter of principle for the rabbis, for it is unlikely that many people had flans available. For this emblematic use of Dosa in the Mishnah, see my "On Pharisees and Sadducees in the Mishnah: From Composition Criticism to History," in: *Judaistik und neutestamentliche Wissenschaft* (FRLANT 226; ed. L. Doering, F. Wilk, and H.-G. Waubke; Göttingen: Vandenhoeck & Ruprecht, 2007), 140–144.

to the denying person. Here we have, in the full sense of Paul's words, someone who thinks something is forbidden and it is, accordingly, indeed forbidden for him or her, although not for others. Indeed, it is forbidden to them even against their will (were that not the case the issue would not come to court, nor would the Mishnah have to address it), something which can be very far-reaching: if Sam claimed he had betrothed Ruth he will not be allowed to marry any of Ruth's near relations because according to his claim such a marriage would be incestuous, and if Ruth claimed Sam had betrothed her she will not only be forbidden to Sam's near relatives, as the Mishnah notes; in fact, she will not be allowed to marry anyone at all as long as Sam is alive, for according to her claim she is already married and the Torah does not allow polyandry. That is, the fact that the person thinks something is the case entails the system recognizing prohibitions for that person even when the person does not want them. That is, basically, the position espoused by Paul at Rom 14:20–23, where, as we have seen, he forbids the strong to do anything that might bring the weak to want to do something that they, the weak, think is forbidden to them—even though Paul, and the strong, believe that in fact there is no basis for the prohibition.

6. CONCLUSION

In her recent discussion of our verse, Gudrun Holtz offers four arguments in support of her assumption (contrary to a widespread claim—see above, n. 6) that Paul, in asserting in the first part of our verse that nothing is impure, did not mean to abrogate the Jewish distinction between pure and impure food and to lead the Jewish Christians of Rome ("the weak") in that direction. As she notes: (1) law-observing Jews too can express similar views about nothing being impure "by itself;" (2) Paul himself, in 1 Cor 7:17–18, expresses the conviction that Jewish in the Church should maintain their Jewish way of life; (3) the fact Paul can tolerate circumcision (Rom 4:9–12) makes it likely that he would tolerate Jewish dietary laws too; and (4) Rom 14:1–15:6 relativizes the importance of the ways of life of both parts of the Christian community, so in 14:14 too we should understand that "es Paulus nicht um die Abschaffung *einer Lebensweise*, der gesetzesobservanten, geht, sondern um die *Relativisierung beider*."[20] Basically, my reading of Rom 14:14 seconds that of Holtz by underscoring that Paul's wording in the verse itself points in the same direction, from both sides: he "waters down" his own certainty about impurity not existing (it is his private opinion, it is only belief, and it pertains only to impurity "by itself") and he says that foods considered impure by "the weak" really are impure for them and it would be sinful for them to violate such prohibitions. This Pauline stance, I have furthermore argued, reflects what was common for Diaspora Jews and Pharisaic-rabbinic Jews, who were well aware of the artificial and self-imposed nature of the rules according to which they lived—points that were certainly intensified for someone like Paul, who was intensely aware of his own beliefs and their impact upon the way he conducted his own life. This must have led Paul to realize that if what he believed was true and binding for him, what others believe must be true and binding for them. As Holtz argues, the only way to allow people of such different truths and obligations to live together in a single community is by relativizing the importance of the whole issue, and that is what Paul calls upon the Christians of Rome to do.

[20] Holtz, *Damit Gott sei alles*, 247–250; original emphases.

CHAPTER 10

PAUL AND THE JEWISH LEADERS AT ROME: ACTS 28:17–31

Justin Taylor, SM

Towards the end of the Book of Acts, Paul has arrived in Rome as a prisoner awaiting the hearing of his appeal to Caesar. The final episode (Acts 28:17–31) concerns principally his dealings with the Jewish community of the city. A few days after his arrival, he asks the leaders of the community to come and see him in the quarters where he lives under the guard of a soldier. To those who come he explains his presence in Rome. They reply that they have had no news from Judea concerning Paul himself; but, since they have heard of "this sect (*hairesis*)" and especially that "everywhere it is spoken against," they would like to hear further from Paul about his own views. A day is set, and they return to his lodging "in great numbers." Paul spends the whole day testifying and trying to convince them, with results similar to those he has met with before in arguing with his fellow Jews: some are convinced but others are not. As they depart, Paul quotes Isa 6:9–10, according to the Septuagint—a text that Jesus also quotes in the Gospels—and declares (v. 28): "Let it be known to you then that this salvation of God has been sent to the Gentiles: they will listen."[1]

---

[1] New Testament quotations are from the Revised Standard Version. On Paul's speech, see Stanley E. Porter, *Paul in Acts* (Library of Pauline Studies; Peabody, MA: Hendrickson, 2001), 162–163 (= reprint of *The Paul of Acts: Essays in Literary Criticism, Rhetoric and Theology* [WUNT 115; Tübingen: J.C.B. Mohr (Siebeck), 1999]); Marion L. Soards, *The Speeches in Acts: Their Content, Context, and Concerns* (Louisville, Kentucky: Westminster/John Knox Press, 1994), 130–133. On the Lukan Paul's quotation of Isaiah, see François Bovon, "'How Well the Holy Spirit Spoke Through the Prophet Isaiah to your Ancestors!' (Acts 28:25)," in idem, *New Testament Traditions and Apocryphal Narratives* (Princeton Theological Monograph Series 36; Allison Park, Penn.: Pickwick Publications, 1995), 42–50 (originally given in German in 1983); Craig A. Evans, *To See and*

This episode raises at least two issues that are relevant to our theme of "The Jewish Matrix of Paul." There is first the question, whether it represents, for Luke author of Acts, the definitive breach between Paul and his own people and even between the Church and the Jews. In a word, is this the moment when Paul separates himself from his Jewish matrix?

Here scholarly opinion, like that of the apostle's hearers, is divided. For some, he is declaring that it is useless to continue to preach the Gospel of Jesus to the Jews: "For — in the words he quotes from Isaiah — this people's heart has grown dull, and their ears are heavy of hearing, and their eyes they have closed; lest they should perceive with their eyes, and hear with their ears, and understand with their heart, and turn for me to heal them." So, it seems to many commentators, the Jewish people as a whole is condemned for not receiving the message of Paul. [2] By contrast, "this salvation of God has been sent to the Gentiles: they will listen." From now on, then, the Church must turn its attention exclusively to the Gentiles. The book ends on this solemn note, which must be supposed to be the last word on the subject of Luke's Paul.

Other scholars, however, do not read the text this way. [3] They

---

Not Perceive: Isaiah 6.9–10 in Early Jewish and Christian Interpretation (JSOTSup 64; Sheffield: JSOT Press, 1989), 120–127; Gert J. Steyn, *Septuagint Quotations in the Context of the Petrine and Pauline Speeches of the Acta Apostolorum* (Biblical Exegesis and Theology 12; Kampen: Kok Pharos, 1995), 213–229; David W. Pao, *Acts and the Isaianic New Exodus* (WUNT, 2. Reihe 130; Tübingen: J.C.B. Mohr [Siebeck], 2000), 101–109.

[2] See Patrick Faure, *Pentecôte et parousie, Ac 1,6-3,26. L'église et le mystère d'Israël entre les textes alexandrin et occidental des Actes des Apôtres* (*EBib*, nouvelle série 50; Paris: Gabalda, 2003), 18–24, who gives as examples of authors for whom Israel is rejected: F. Baur, J. Gnilka, E. Haenchen, G. Lohfink, A. George, H. Conzelmann, R. Maddox, J. Sanders, J. Jervel, J. Tyson.

[3] For examples of authors for whom Israel is divided rather than condemned as a whole, see Faure, *Pentecôte et parousie*, 24–33: A. Schlatter, A. Harnack, O. Bauernfeind, J. Koenig, R. Brawley, F. Bovon, D. Moessner, R. C. Tannehill, D. Tiede, V. Fusco. To this list others may be added, such as Bart-Jan Koet, "Paul in Rome (Acts 28,16–31): A Farewell to Judaism?", *Bijdr* 48 (1987): 397–415. Faure himself develops a convincing argument for this interpretation and shows that it is clear in the Western Text of Acts.

point out that this is not the first time in Acts that Paul announces to a Jewish audience that he is "turning to the Gentiles." [4] Already, at Antioch-of-Pisidia, when "the Jews ... contradicted what was spoken by Paul, and reviled him," Paul and Barnabas replied: "It was necessary that the word of God should be spoken first to you. Since you thrust it from you, and judge yourselves unworthy of eternal life, we turn to the Gentiles" (13:45–46). That declaration does not, however, prevent Paul from entering the synagogue at Iconium and there speaking with such effect "that a great company believed, both of Jews and of Greeks" (14:1). At Corinth Paul is again in the synagogue; on being "opposed and reviled," he once more declares: "From now on I will go to the Gentiles" (18:5–6); but even so, in the next chapter he is speaking boldly in the synagogue at Ephesus (19:26). So, is it necessary to take Paul's third declaration in Rome as more definitive than the other two? In any case, this is not the ending of Acts, which concludes, in verses 30–31, with Paul's preaching and teaching. [5]

The Book of Acts ends in Rome, so we cannot follow Paul any further, to see whether he continues to preach to his fellow-Jews. But can we be sure that, in the perspective of Luke, he would not have done so? Even the statement "this salvation of God has been sent to the Gentiles: they will listen," does not have to mean that divine salvation has been, as it were, transferred from the Jews to the Gentiles; rather that, in the words of Isaiah 40:5 (LXX), quoted in Luke 3:6, "all flesh shall see the salvation of God"[6]—and the Gentiles will welcome this message, just as at Antioch-of-Pisidia, the Gentiles "were glad and glorified the word of God" (Acts 13:48).

As for the Lukan Paul's quotation of Isa 6:9–10, John Kilgallen points out that such prophetic declarations were intended as

---

[4] Thus, for example, John Kilgallen, "'And I Will Heal Them' (Acts 28:27)," PIBA 23 (2005): 87–105, esp. 91–92.

[5] Kilgallen, "'And I Will Heal Them' (Acts 28:27)," 90.

[6] See the marginal references in Nestle-Aland; on the other hand, Huub Van de Sandt, "Acts 28,28: No Salvation for the People of Israel? An Answer in the Perspective of the LXX," *ETL* 70 (1994): 341–358 sees here rather an allusion to Ezek 3:6b (LXX).

admonitions, to bring about conversion—a return to God—rather than as final condemnations; he argues, quite reasonably, that in the context of Acts it has the same purpose.[7] He also draws attention to the fact that, at least in most Greek MSS, the tense and mood of the final verb, *iasomai*, are future indicative—"I will heal (them)." Even if the verb itself is subordinated grammatically to the subjunctives that follow *mêpote* ("lest"), and so is "subjunctive in meaning, we can still underline the point that the sentence, 'I will heal', as signalled by the indicative mood, contains in it the implication: if you convert I am willing to heal." [8]

I believe that these latter arguments are persuasive. They are further strengthened by two phrases that are not in the standard critical text edited by Nestle-Aland. The first is v. 29, found in the majority of Greek manuscripts, as well as in several witnesses of the so-called Western Text, notably the Old Latin; they are not, however, found in the Alexandrian witnesses, especially Sinaiticus and Vaticanus, that almost invariably determine the modern critical text. [9] This verse reads: "And when he (Paul) had said these words, the Jews departed, holding much dispute among themselves." Here, it seems, the Jewish community of Rome continues to be portrayed as divided—as in v. 24—between those who accept the Gospel and those who do not. Then, in v. 30, where we are told that Paul "lived there two whole years at his own expense, and welcomed all who came to him," some ancient authorities

[7] "'And I Will Heal Them' (Acts 28:27)," 88–89; similarly Van de Sandt, "Acts 28:28: No Salvation for the People of Israel?," 358: "The whole of vv. 25c–28, however, represents a prophetic reproof, modelled upon the passages of severe criticism in Isaiah and Ezekiel, and is intended to incite the Roman Jews to convert."

[8] "'And I Will Heal Them' (Acts 28:27)," 95, referring to R. Funk, F. Blass and A. Debrunner, *A Greek Grammar of the New Testament and Other Early Literature* (10th edn, Chicago: University of Chicago Press, 1961), 186, # 369.

[9] Compare Marie-Émile Boismard, *Le texte occidental des Actes des Apôtres, edition nouvelle entièrement refondue* (*EBib*, nouvelle série 40; Paris: Gabalda, 2000), 428. Boismard held that the Western Text corresponded to an earlier version of the Book of Acts composed by Luke.

add: "Jews and also Gentiles."[10] Is this simply a gloss, or does it represent the original text?[11] I will not try to argue the latter, but will simply point out that, at least according to one version of the story—whether it is original or represents an ancient interpretation—those who continued to frequent Paul included Jews as well as Gentiles.[12] Thus not every reader in antiquity took Paul's declaration in vv. 25–28 as constituting a definitive breach with his own people.

In any case, Paul's words and his audience's reactions concern the Jewish community of Rome, or, to be more strictly accurate, representatives of that community: have we all along been reading too much into the text to see in it the destiny of the Jewish people as such?[13] Furthermore, the text simply shows the group who heard Paul as divided: we are not even told that those who did not accept Paul's message were more numerous than those who did. Once again, we should not read too much into the text—and certainly not that for Luke, the Jewish people as a whole, with a few individual exceptions, rejected the Gospel.

The second point of interest for our topic concerns the content of Paul's teaching or preaching in Rome, both to the members of the Jewish community and also to those others who came to him in his lodging. According to Acts 28:23, on the day of his second meeting with the Jews, "Paul expounded the matter to them from morning till evening, testifying to the kingdom of God and trying to convince them about Jesus both from the law of Moses and from the prophets." The final summary of Paul's activity during

---

[10] Two Greek manuscripts, several Latin manuscripts and an asterisked reading in the Syriac version revised by Thomas of Harkel.

[11] For Boismard, *Le texte occidental*, 428, this phrase belongs to the Western Text.

[12] In any case, according to Van de Sandt, "Acts 28:28: No Salvation for the People of Israel?," 343, "most scholars — he notes as exceptions E. Haenchen, J. Gnilka, P. Zingg and S.G. Wilson — feel that Jews are included here as well," namely among the "all" to whom Paul continues to preach and teach.

[13] Compare Kilgallen, "'And I Will Heal Them' (Acts 28:27)," esp. 89, n. 7, who emphasizes that Paul's words are addressed only to "some Jews" and not to "all Jews."

the two years he lived in private lodgings (28:31) says that, to all who came to him, he was "preaching the kingdom of God and teaching about the Lord Jesus Christ quite openly and unhindered (*akôlutôs*)."[14] To these two statements, according to which Paul preached about the kingdom of God and also taught about Jesus, I would like to add his own declaration made to the Jewish leaders in his first interview with them (v. 20): "... it is because of the hope of Israel that I am bound with this chain."

With these expressions attributed to Paul at the end of Acts, we can compare similar ones attributed to Jesus at the beginning of the book. Thus, according to Acts 1:3, the risen Jesus "presented himself alive after his passion by many proofs, appearing to [the apostles] during forty days, and speaking of the kingdom of God." In the next verse (4) he tells them "not to depart from Jerusalem, but to wait for the promise of the Father"—an expression that is symmetrical with that of "the hope of Israel." Thus the words of Jesus at the beginning of the book and those of Paul at the end form a certain *inclusio*[15]—which, by the way, furnishes a literary argument for seeing the actual conclusion of Acts as its planned and proper ending, and not as some sort of truncation or unfinished breaking off.[16] Let us look more closely at these expressions.

---

[14] I.e. "unhindered" by his condition as a prisoner (vv. 16 and 20; cf. Phil 1:14 and 2 Tim 2:9), rather than "unhindered" by Jewish opponents (v. 25; cf. 1 Thess 2:16).

[15] Thus also Marie-Émile Boismard and Arnaud Lamouille, *Les Actes des deux Apôtres* (vol. 2; *EBib*, nouvelle série 13; Paris: Gabalda, 1990), 355.

[16] There is a vast literature on the ending of Acts. We mention here only some recent publications: Daniel Marguerat, "The Enigma of the Silent Closing of Acts," in David P. Moessner (ed.), *Jesus and the Heritage of Israel: Luke's Narrative Claim upon Israel's Legacy* (Luke the Interpreter of Israel 1; Harrisburg, Pa: Trinity Press International, 1999), 284–304; Heike Omerzu, "Das Schweigen des Lukas: Überlegungen zum offenen Ende der Apostelgeschichte," in *Das Ende des Paulus: Historische, theologische und literaturgeschichtliche Aspekte* (ed. Friedrich Wilhelm Horn; BZNW 106; Berlin and New York: Walter de Gruyter, 2001), 127–156; François Vouga, "La fin des Actes comme accomplissement du programme théologique de Luc," in Emmanuelle Steffek and Yvan Bourquin (eds), *Raconter, interpreter, annoncer. Parcours du Nouveau Testament. Mélanges offerts à Daniel Marguerat pour son 60e anniversaire* (Le monde de la Bible, 47; Genève: Labor et Fides, 2003), 314–323.

"The kingdom of God (*basileia tou theou*)"—an expression that occurs 32 times in the Gospel of Luke—is found only six times in Acts. Three of these occurrences we have just seen, one attributed to Jesus and two to Paul. The other three occasions are: 8:12, where Philip in Samaria has been preaching "the good news about the kingdom of God and the name of Jesus Christ"; 14:22, where Paul, retracing his steps from Derbe through Lystra, Iconium and Antioch-of-Pisidia, tells the new believers that "through many tribulations we must enter the kingdom of God"; 19:8 (a text already referred to), where Paul in Ephesus "entered the synagogue and for three months spoke boldly, arguing and pleading about the kingdom of God." To these we could add 20:25, in which Paul, bidding farewell to the elders of Ephesus and summing up his ministry, tells them: "I know that all you among whom I have gone preaching the kingdom will see my face no more." At least in terms of statistics, "the kingdom of God" does not seem to play an important role in Acts. And yet its occurrence at the beginning and at the end of the book might suggest that the expression should not be overlooked. What does it mean?

There is little doubt how Jesus' apostles at the beginning of Acts understand "the kingdom of God." After all that has happened, and after forty days in which their risen Master has been teaching them about the kingdom of God, their eager question to him on the Mount of Olives is: "Lord, will you at this time restore the kingdom (or kingship) to Israel?" (Acts 1:6). If Jesus had indeed been preaching a purely spiritual kingdom, his disciples have even yet failed to understand. The resurrection of Jesus, far from diverting their minds to an otherworldly plane, seems rather to have revived the hope that, as the two disappointed disciples on the road to Emmaus had put it, "he was the one to redeem Israel" (Luke 24:21). His death on the cross had seemed to put an end to such hopes; now he was raised up and vindicated—yes, the time had surely come. Note that Jesus does not reply directly to this question, but tells the apostles that it is not for them to know "times or seasons which the Father has fixed by his own authority" (v. 7). So the question concerning the restoration of the kingdom to Israel remains open. In the meantime, they will receive power from the Holy Spirit and will be Jesus' witnesses "in Jerusalem and in all Judea and Samaria and to the end of the earth" (v. 8)—or is it 'to the end of the *land*?"[17] I suggest that this exchange between the risen Jesus and his apostles makes it at least legitimate to think that in the further occurrences of the term "the kingdom of God," the dimension of "restoration of the kingdom to Israel" may not be entirely lacking. In other words, to the end of the Book of Acts, Luke's Paul may be "arguing and pleading" about a reign of God that included—even if it did not consist entirely of—the restitution of that reign in an Israel liberated and restored.[18] In that perspective, of course, Jesus raised from the dead, whatever else he may be, is indeed the one who is to "redeem Israel."

Now let us look at the expression "the promise of the Father – *tên epangelian tou Patros*," for which Jesus tells the apostles to wait in Jerusalem and which, he reminds them, "you heard from me" (Acts 1:4). The precise expression does not recur in Acts; but the book contains eight further uses of the Greek word *epangelia*, all but one of which (23:21) could be relevant. What is this "promise of the Father," which can also be translated, as in the New Jerusalem Bible, "what the Father has promised?" In the immediate context of Acts, it seems to be identified with the promised sending of the Holy Spirit as in Luke 24:49: "for John baptized with water, but before many days you shall be baptized with the Holy Spirit" (Acts 1:5). Two further uses of the term *epangelia*, in 2:33 and 2:39, also identify "the promise" or "what was promised" with the Holy Spirit.

On the other hand, someone familiar with the Scriptures who heard the expression "the promise of the Father," would probably have thought spontaneously of God's promise made to Abraham and his descendants, to settle them in the land that God had chosen for them. This is precisely the meaning that Stephen express-

[17] Thus Daniel R. Schwartz, "The End of the *Gê*," *JBL* 105 (1986): 669–676. On the other hand, the second occurrence in Acts 13:47 of the expression *heôs eschatou tês gês*, in a quotation of Isaiah 49:6, clearly refers to a mission to the Gentiles.

[18] Similarly Boismard and Lamouille, *Les Actes des deux Apôtres*, vol. 2, 263.

es in his speech before the Sanhedrin, when he recalls that "as the time of the promise drew near, which God had granted to Abraham, the people grew and multiplied in Egypt" (Acts 7:17). Paul, again in the synagogue of Antioch-of-Pisidia, speaks explicitly of "the promise made to our ancestors" (13:32); this promise, he declares, God has fulfilled by bringing to Israel "a saviour Jesus" (v. 23) and then by "raising Jesus" (v. 33). Finally, before governor Festus and King Agrippa II, Paul affirms that "I stand here on trial for the hope in the promise made by God to our fathers, to which our twelve tribes hope to attain, as they earnestly worship night and day. And for this hope I am accused by the Jews" (26:6–7).

This last quotation couples the "promise" with the corresponding "hope." We have already seen that Paul declares to the Jewish leaders at Rome: "it is because of the hope of Israel that I am bound with this chain" (28:20). This expression is not explained in the context. Paul has already made a similar declaration before the Sanhedrin in 23:6; seeking to introduce a division into the assembly composed of both Sadducees and Pharisees, he cries out: "Brethren, I am a Pharisee, a son of Pharisees; with respect to the hope and the resurrection of the dead I am on trial." There the "hope" is combined with "the resurrection of the dead." Speaking before governor Felix, Paul seems to identify both: "having a hope in God… that there will be a resurrection of both the just and the unjust" (24:15).

Is the "hope of Israel" meant to be fulfilled by the resurrection of the dead? And has the promise made by God "to our fathers" already been fulfilled by the gift of the Spirit at Pentecost? Was the land all along simply an allegory of the world to come? At any rate Paul ends his address to King Agrippa by declaring: "I (say) nothing but what the prophets and Moses said would come to pass: that the Christ must suffer, and that, by being the first to rise from the dead, he would proclaim light both to the people and to the Gentiles" (26:22–23). [19]

---

[19] For a detailed discussion of the expression "the hope of Israel," see Hermann J. Hauser, *Strukturen der Abschlusserzählung der Apostelgeschichte (Apg 28,16–31)* (Analecta Biblica 86; Rome: Biblical Institute Press, 1979), 88–95.

I strongly suspect that somewhere behind these passages of Acts, there is a great text of the prophet Ezekiel (37:1–14), which prophesies the resurrection of a multitude of dry bones that "are the whole house of Israel." The prophecy concludes: "And you shall know that I am the LORD, when I open your graves, and raise you from your graves, O my people. And I will put my Spirit within you, and you shall live, and I will place you in your own land" (vv. 12–13).

In the light of this text of Ezekiel, we can make a synthesis of everything we have been seeing. The resurrection of Jesus and the gift of the Holy Spirit show that God's promise, in which Israel has hoped, is in the course of being fulfilled. The final fulfilment of that promise will be the perfect realisation of Ezekiel's vision: the dry bones will come to life again, both literally in the resurrection from the dead, and figuratively in the restoration of Israel. Furthermore, according to Paul, both Jews and Gentiles will have a share in the world to come. This will be the kingdom of God, established by his Messiah Jesus.

This, I believe, is what Luke's Paul was trying to convince the Jewish leaders at Rome to accept. They were divided on the question. But, declares Paul, even if they do not receive the message, "this salvation of God" has been sent to the Gentiles—and they will hear. In mean time, Paul continues to receive all who want to come to him—both Jews and Gentiles, as we have seen, at least according to one version of the story—and to proclaim the kingdom of God and teach about the Lord Jesus Christ.

The Paul we have been dealing with up till now is, of course, the Lukan Paul, essentially a literary construct. It is always a good question to what extent this Lukan Paul corresponds to the Paul of the (undisputed) letters—also a literary construct, be it noted, even though constructed by the real Paul their author.[20] Answers on all points have differed widely.

---

[20] See the discussion by Porter, *Paul in Acts*, 187–206, who concludes that the "standard arguments marshalled in defense of the differences between the Paul of Acts and of the letters concerning his person and work, once analyzed in detail, simply do not point to significant and sustainable contradictions." He finds a similar result concerning Paul's theology (205–206).

The first position defended in this paper was that, for the author of Acts and the Paul of its conclusion, Israel as a whole has not rejected the good news of Jesus Christ and so been in its turn rejected, but remains divided. A good case can be made out for holding that the Paul who meets with representatives of the Jewish community of Rome in Acts 28 is in substantial agreement in his attitude to Israel with the Paul of Romans 9–11. For Boismard and Lamouille, Paul's speech in Acts 28:25–27 is so close to Rom 11:7–11 that it "seems to be inspired by" the latter.[21] More recently, Kenneth Litwak has argued that, "given an appropriate appreciation of each text [Acts 28:16–31 and Romans 11], Paul's views on Jewish unbelief are complementary in these two texts, and the Paul of Acts and the Paul of the Letters do not contradict each other on this subject at these points."[22] I would agree with this position and note the following examples.

In the two meetings with the Jews of Rome, the Paul of Acts generally identifies himself with the Jewish people. This is, of course, the posture of the writer in Romans 11, especially in v. 1. An important exception would appear to be Acts 28:25, where Paul introduces his quotation from Isa 6:9–10 by saying: "The Holy Spirit was right in saying to *your* (*hymôn*) fathers through Isaiah the prophet..." Earlier (v. 17) he had addressed his hearers as "Brethren." Here, in v. 25, he seems to be dissociating himself from them, and even from his own people, although no doubt one could argue that he does so for rhetor-

---

[21] Boismard and Lamouille, *Les Actes des deux Apôtres*, vol. 2, 354.

[22] Kenneth Litwak, "One or Two Views of Judaism: Paul in Acts 28 and Romans 11 on Jewish Unbelief," *TynBull* 57 (2006): 228–249, esp. 230. He points out that one should give due weight not only to the different literary genres of Acts and Romans but also to the different Roman audiences addressed by the Paul of Acts—Jews who know nothing of "this sect" except that "everywhere it is spoken against," and the Paul of Romans—Christians, and probably in majority of Gentile origin. Litwak goes on to explain that "complementary" does not necessarily mean identical, but means that the two views are not in contradiction and may be taken as pointing in the same direction.

ical effect.[23] I draw your attention, however, to the fact that, although the modern critical text (Nestle-Aland) reads *hymôn* with Papyrus 74 and Codices Alexandrinus and Vaticanus and other important witnesses, the majority of Greek manuscripts, followed by the Vulgate, read *hêmôn*, so that Paul speaks of "*our* fathers."[24] Not too much can be made of this: the Greek New Testament is full of variations between "our" and "your." On the other hand, even if not the original text, the reading *hêmôn* shows that most Greek- and Latin-speaking readers, hearers and copyists of Acts read, heard and wrote "*our* fathers"; that is to say, they understood Luke to portray a Paul who identified himself with his hearers and, by implication, with the Jewish people, even when he is quoting a prophetic text against them.

If, as we have argued, Luke does indeed portray the Jews of Rome as divided on the issue of Jesus, this converges with Paul's view in Rom 11:2–5 that, despite the failure of the majority of the Jewish people to recognize Jesus as the Messiah, "God has not rejected his people whom he foreknew" and has kept a "remnant, chosen by grace."

Although Paul in his letters never quotes Isa 6:9–10, he does, however, in Rom 11:8 cite the rather similar Deut 29:3 combined with Isa 29:10: "as it is written, 'God gave them a spirit of stupor, eyes that should not see and ears that should not hear, down to this very day'."[25] Two verses later he cites Ps 69:23: "And David says, '... let their eyes be darkened so that they cannot see, and bend their backs for ever'." In the context of Romans, of course, the severe sayings just quoted do not, however, amount to a final rejection of Israel: Paul will go on in the same chapter 11 to speak

---

[23] Thus Litwak, "One or Two Views of Judaism," 234: "... he is speaking of Israelites in the past who rejected God's message: neither all past Israelites nor even the fathers of all the Israelites present."

[24] Among the witnesses for this reading is also the Latin manuscript *Gigas*, which frequently gives readings that antedate the Vulgate; the pronoun is missing from the Syriac version of Thomas of Harkel. For Boismard, *Le texte occidental*, 427, this was the reading of the Western Text.

[25] Compare Kilgallen, "'And I Will Heal Them' (Acts 28:27)," 97.

of the future restoration of the Jews who at present reject Jesus, to affirm that they remain God's chosen people and to declare: "... a hardening has come upon part of Israel, until the full number of the Gentiles come in, and so all Israel will be saved" (v. 25 f.). This accords with the significance we have ascribed to the use of Isa 6:9–10 in Acts: as in the original context in the Book of Isaiah, it is a call to conversion rather than a declaration of rejection.

Even Paul's final declaration in Acts 28:28: "This salvation has been sent to the Gentiles; they will listen," corresponds to that in Rom 11:11: "Through their trespass salvation has come to the Gentiles, so as to make Israel jealous." This seems already to have been the view of John Chrysostom.[26] For Boismard and Lamouille, "if Paul's declaration does not arouse the 'jealousy' of the Jews, it at least invites them to reflect deeply at the moment when they leave Paul (Acts 28:29)."[27] Litwak, for his part, concludes that it "serves in Paul's rhetoric to provoke his doubting Jewish audience to come to faith, as the Gentiles will." [28]

Litwak further remarks that, as we have already seen, Acts 28:28 ("this salvation of God has been sent to the Gentiles") echoes Isa 40:5 (LXX; "All flesh will see the salvation of God"). Now the overall theme of Isa 40 is the restoration of the Jewish people after the Exile. One may reasonably infer that the same theme of restoration lies on the horizon of Paul's expressions in Acts. If so, there is convergence with the epistolary Paul: the future restoration of Israel is an explicit theme of Rom 11, especially from v. 23 on. [29]

If the expression "the kingdom of God" is rare in Acts, it is also infrequent in Paul's letters (only in Rom 14:17; 1 Cor 4:20; 1 Cor 6:9; 1 Cor 15:50; Gal 5:21; Col 4:10–11; 1 Thess 2:12; 2 Thess

[26] John Chrysostom, *In Acta Apostolorum*, Hom. 55.1 (*PG* 60.380): "Then he provokes their jealousy arising from the Gentiles, adding: (v. 28)." Chrysostom appears to read the entire passage as addressed to the Jews in general.

[27] Boismard and Lamouille, *Les Actes des deux Apôtres*, vol. 2, 355.

[28] "One or Two Views of Judaism," 240.

[29] For a more detailed study of Rom 11, including further examples of convergence with Acts 28, see Litwak, "One or Two Views of Judaism," 241–248.

1:5). We should also mention 1 Cor 15:24–25, to which we shall shortly return, where, at the end, Christ "delivers the kingdom to God the Father after destroying every rule and every authority and power. For he must reign until he has put all his enemies under his feet." It is not unreasonable to think that Paul deliberately avoided using this expression, so characteristic of Jesus' teaching, since it would mean little or nothing to "Greeks" unless initiated in the Bible,[30] and might even lead to charges of sedition against the Roman empire.[31] On the other hand, Paul's use of "the kingdom of God" deserves close study, although this is not the place for it.[32]

What does interest us now is that at least some scholars have argued that the epistolary Paul, especially in 1 Thess 4:13–18 and 1 Cor 15:22–28, expected an earthly kingdom as an element in his eschatological scenario. Here we would have an important counterpart to the views we have imputed by inference to the Paul of Acts.

The view that the epistolary Paul looked forward to a messianic kingdom on earth was not uncommon in nineteenth- and early twentieth-century scholarship, especially in Germany.[33] As the twen-

---

[30] Thus, for example, Francis W. Beare, "Jesus and Paul," *Canadian Journal of Theology* 5 (1959): 79–86, cited by George Johnston, "'Kingdom of God' Sayings in Paul's Letters," in Peter Richardson and John C. Hurd (eds), *From Jesus to Paul: Studies in Honour of Francis Wright Beare* (Waterloo, Ont.: Wilfrid Laurier University Press, 1984), 143–156, esp. 143, who remarks: "I think that Beare is basically correct in affirming Paul's usage in transposing from Hebrew, or Aramaic, modes to Greek for apologetic and missionary purposes."

[31] Compare Acts 17:6–7, where an outcry is raised is raised at Thessalonica: "These men who have turned the world upside down have come here also, and Jason has received them; and they are all acting against the decrees of Caesar, saying that there is another king, Jesus."

[32] Thus George Johnston, "'Kingdom of God' Sayings in Paul's Letters," 144: "But one really needs to examine afresh the eight kingdom-of-God texts in Paul's letters, set down in Greek and sent to congregations that contained a large element of Greek-speaking converts." Similarly Richard Bauckham, "Kingdom and Church According to Jesus and Paul," *Horizons in Biblical Theology: An International Dialogue* 18 (1996): 1–21. Both emphasize the continuities between Jesus and Paul.

[33] See Seth Turner, "The Interim, Earthly Messianic Kingdom in Paul," *JSNT* 25 (2003): 323–342, esp. 325, citing in n. 7, G. Billroth, H. Olshausen, W.M.L. de Wette, F. Godet, R. Kabisch, W. Bousset, J. Weiss, H. Lietzmann, A. Schweitzer; he remarks that the most recent defender of this view is L. J. Kreitzer.

tieth century wore on, it attracted less scholarly favor, because commentators tended to regard Paul's eschatology either as incoherent[34] or as having no place for an earthly kingdom.[35] Recently, however, there has been a revival of support for this approach, notably on the part of P. Stuhlmacher and E. P. Sanders. Heikki Räisänen compares their views, which are not identical, and also the opinion of Ben Witherington III, and notes that "we thus have three versions of the earthly kingdom to be established in the parousia: (1) a temporary kingdom on the earth, to be followed by the dissolution of the earth and final bliss in the beyond (Sanders); (2) a temporary kingdom on a transformed earth, followed by final bliss on this very earth (Stuhlmacher, implicitly at least); (3) no temporary kingdom, but the final reign of God on a transformed earth (Witherington)." [36]

Seth Turner, for his part, observes that hope for a messianic kingdom on earth is expressed in contemporary Jewish apocalyptic literature: he cites 4 Ezra 7:26–28 and 2 Bar 29:3–30:1, 40:1–4 and 72:2–74:3. Both these texts are dated later than Paul's letters, but some such idea, he suggests, may well go back earlier, for example to the *Apocalypse of Weeks* (cf. 1 En 91:12–14).[37] Now apocalyptic thought formed part of what we might call the "Jewish matrix" of Paul;[38] so he could well have been acquainted with such notions. Turner himself argues: "Taken together, 1

---

[34] Turner, "The Interim, Earthly Messianic Kingdom in Paul," 325, cites W.G. Kümmel and J. Baumgarten.

[35] Turner, "The Interim, Earthly Messianic Kingdom in Paul," 326, cites H.-A. Wilcke.

[36] See Heikki Räisänen, "Did Paul Expect an Earthly Kingdom?," in A. Christophersen et al. (eds), *Paul, Luke and the Graeco-Roman World: Essays in Honour of Alexander J.M. Wedderburn* (JSNTSup 217; London and New York: Sheffield Academic Press, 2002), 2–20, esp. 3–6, who gives the citations from Stuhlmacher, Sanders and Witherington. Räisänen's own view is that "Paul's future hopes do *not* add up to a consistent total picture" (18).

[37] "The Interim, Earthly Messianic Kingdom in Paul," 323–324.

[38] See, for example, M.C. de Boer, "Paul and the Apocalyptic Eschatology," in *Encyclopedia of Apocalypticism*, (vol. 1; ed. J. J. Collins; London: Continuum, 2000), 345–383 (cited by Turner, "The Interim, Earthly Messianic Kingdom in Paul," 323, n. 1).

Thess. 4.13–18 and 1 Cor. 15.22–28 suggest that Paul thought that there would be an interim, terrestrial messianic kingdom. 1 Thessalonians (and Romans 8.19–23) points towards an earthly kingdom without telling us if this is to be permanent or interim. 1 Corinthians indicates that this kingdom has a definite end."[39]

In Räisänen's words: "The notion that Paul is an 'apocalyptic realist' is alive and well in the scholarly world."[40] Perhaps the expression "eschatological realist" might be better chosen. In any case, it refers, of course, to the epistolary Paul; it could equally well apply, I believe, to the Paul of Acts.

---

[39] "The Interim, Earthly Messianic Kingdom in Paul," conclusion at 341. On the contrary, C.E. Hill, "Paul's Understanding of Christ's Kingdom in I Corinthians 15:20–28," *Novum Testamentum* 30 (1988): 297–320—an article that Turner seeks to counter—concludes: "It appears inescapable, therefore, that Paul understands the kingdom of Christ in I Cor. 15:24–28 to be Christ's present, cosmic lordship which he exercises from heaven."

[40] "Did Paul Expect an Earthly Kingdom?," 6.

Chapter 11
Judaizing the Nations: The Ritual Demands of Paul's Gospel

Paula Fredriksen

Memoriae Krister Stendahl sacrum

At some point between the years 410 and 415, Paulinus of Nola wrote a long letter to his friend and fellow bishop, Augustine of Hippo. Addressing Augustine as "the blessed teacher of Israel," Paulinus asked about the interpretation of a variety of verses from both testaments (ep. 121.1,2). Especially confounding, Paulinus wrote, were Paul's statements about the Jews in Romans 11. "As regards the Gospel," Paul had said about his kinsmen, "they are enemies, because of you [Gentiles]; but as regards election, they are beloved, because of the forefathers" (Romans 11:28).

What good does being "beloved of God" do for the Jews, Paulinus now asked, if they are damned outright for being the enemies of Christ? Behind this, he continued, stood a more fundamental question: Why had God configured salvation as a zero-sum competition between Gentiles and Jews in the first place? Does not Paul's statement imply that the Gentiles could not have believed unless the Jews, first, had not believed? "How was God... . . incapable of acquiring both peoples, rather than having only one or the other?" Paulinus asks. "If the Jews are beloved of God, how will they perish? And if they do not believe in Christ, how will they not perish?" (ep. 121.2,11).[1]

---

[1] *quomodo iidem et inimici propter nos qui credidimus ex gentibus, tanquam non potuerint gentes credere nisi Iudaei non credidissent; aut ipse unus omnium creator Deus. . . capax non fuerit acquisitionis utriusque nisi alterum pro altero possideret.* Paulinus' queries come at a moment in their correspondence when both he and Augustine are pondering how a just God could both harden the Jews so that they do not believe and also condemn the Jews for their unbelief. At stake is the understanding of Ps

Augustine, of course, is one of the West's most influential interpreters of Paul. He is also the author of several strong misreadings of the apostle, and especially of the letter to the Romans. The doctrine of predestination as the plumb line for understanding Romans 9–11; the "all Israel" of Romans 11:26 as an exclusively Christian eschatological society composed of both Gentiles and Jews; the doctrine of Original Sin as framed by Romans 5.12; the redemption of Jew and of Gentile as equally relying on "justification by faith"—these teachings all appear in Augustine's reading of Romans. They had evolved in response to the challenge of Manichaean Christianity, and to the formative influence of late Roman Platonism. For this reason, Augustine's Paul more readily fits the fourth and fifth-century Latin West than he does the mid-first-century Hellenistic Diaspora.[2] These teachings contoured Augustine's answer to Paulinus's questions; to varying degrees, they contour still—I think to our detriment—the interpretive work of modern New Testament scholars in search of the Paul of history.

But some of the less familiar elements of Augustine's Paul derived from a presupposition about gods and humans that spanned their two distinct historical moments. This is the idea, and the social reality, that *ethnic distinctiveness and religious distinctiveness are simple synonyms, and native to all ancient peoples*. In other words—and in common with many New Testament scholars—both Paul and Augustine held that *mos maiorum* or *religiones patriae* or παράδοσις πατρικῶν functioned both to prescribe appropriate cult and to

---

59:12 ("Slay them not, lest my people forget"), 1 Tim 2:4 ("God wants all people to be saved'), and most especially chapters nine through eleven of Paul's letter to the Romans. See discussion in P. Fredriksen, *Augustine and the Jews: A Christian Defense of Jews and Judaism* (New York: Doubleday, 2008), 324–331.

[2] For the ways that Augustine's understanding of Paul, and especially of Romans, differs from Paul's original meaning, see P. Fredriksen, "Paul and Augustine: conversion narratives, orthodox traditions, and the retrospective self," *JTS* (1986): 3–34; and P. Fredriksen, "The Philosopher's Paul and the Problem of Anachronism," in *Paul Among the Philosophers* (Bloomington: Indiana University Press, 2009), 61–73. All of my own articles cited in the current essay are available in PDF format on my web page: www.bu.edu/religion/faculty/fredriksen.

serve as ethnic boundary markers.[3] Unlike most modern NT scholars, however, Augustine held that this function of marking ethnic boundaries continued to define Israel *secundum carnem* in the first generation of the church, and *rightly* so. I think that Paul would agree. This principle also sustained Augustine's contention that the Temple in Jerusalem always stood at the heart of Paul's religious universe. I think that Paul would agree. And it supported Augustine's conviction that, in the first generation of what would eventually become the church, Jewish Christians, Paul emphatically included, continued to live according to their ancestral practices, while the apostles encouraged gentile Christians, without converting to Judaism, to Judaize. I think that Paul would agree.[4]

From this historical fact—that in Mediterranean antiquity, cult defined ethnicity and ethnicity defined cult—Augustine distilled theology: a Jewish Jesus, a Jewish Paul, and a Judaized first generation of Gentiles served his defense of the doctrines of creation and of incarnation. I want to deploy this fact historically, to use it as a cardinal point in my reconstruction of Paul and of his mid-first-century context. For historical reasons, I will end up asserting many of the same positions that Augustine, for theological reasons, also asserted. Unlike Augustine, I will conclude my reconstruction

---

[3] E.J. Christiansen, *The Covenant in Judaism and in Paul: A Study of Ritual Boundaries as Identity Markers* (Leiden: E.J. Brill, 1995). That Paul worked to overcome or dispose of such boundaries and ethnic distinctions functions for most NT scholars as the defining effort of his mission: see (for only one example) J.D.G. Dunn, *The Theology of Paul the Apostle* (Grand Rapids: William B. Eerdmans, 1998) and the essays collected by him in *Paul and the Mosaic Law* (Tübingen: Mohr [Siebeck], 1996).

[4] On the continuing Torah-observance of the apostles, and particularly of Paul, for the entirety of the first generation of the movement, *de doctrina Christiana* 3.6,10; *ep.* 40.4,6 (on Paul's Torah-observance, against Jerome); *Contra Faustum* 12.3 and passim. On the laudable and appropriate Judaizing of the first generation of Christian Gentiles, see Acts 15:29 and Eph. 2:11–22, *c. Faust.* 32.12. On the centrality of the Temple and the positive importance of blood sacrifices, *c. Faust.* 6 passim; 22.21. Discussion in P. Fredriksen, *Augustine* (2008), 235–302. The present essay argues that Paul—though for reasons different from Augustine's—also supported these positions.

of Paul's mission and message by urging that a whole host of theologically-imbued concepts and vocabulary—and especially the phrase "Law-free mission"[5]—be dropped by scholars who quest for the historical Paul.

1.

Gods and humans were the two key populations of ancient society, which could thrive only if gods were happy. Cult was the index of human loyalty, affection and respect. Cult made gods happy, and happy gods made for happy humans. The converse was also true: deprived of cult, gods grew angry. When gods were angry, people paid.[6]

---

[5] For a similar conclusion though a different argument, M. Nanos, "The Myth of the 'Law-Free' Paul Standing Between Christians and Jews," *Studies in Christian-Jewish Relations* 4 (2009), 1–21.

[6] "From Britain to Syria, pagan cults aimed to honour the gods and avert the misfortunes which might result from the gods' own anger at their neglect," notes Robin Lane Fox; "Any account of pagan worship which minimizes the gods' uncertain anger and mortals' fear of it is an empty account," *Pagans and Christians* (New York: Knopf, 1987), 39. "The best that humans could hope for was that they could keep the gods in a good mood," D. Potter writes ("Martyrdom as Spectacle," *Theatre and Society in the Classical World* (Ann Arbor: University of Michigan, 1993), 134). Roman piety combined with patriotism, since the proper execution of traditional cult "is not only of concern to religion, but also to the well-being of the state," Cicero *de legibus* 1.12.30. See B. Isaac, *The Invention of Racism in Classical Antiquity* (Princeton: Princeton University Press, 2005), 467 and nn. 121–127, for many expressions by Roman authorities of this view. Christians no less than pagans were aware that divine wrath was the consequence of neglecting cult, and they blamed these gods, qua evil δαίμονες, for inspiring persecution against them: see A. Reed, "The Trickery of the Fallen Angels and the Demonic Mimesis of the Divine: Aetiology and Polemics in the Writings of Justin Martyr," *JECS* 12 (2004): 141–171. Israel's god could be alienated by neglect of proper cult, too: Once the daily sacrifices were interrupted and the sancta polluted, Josephus reports, the divine presence quit Jerusalem's temple, *Bellum Judaicum* 5.412; 6.300 (hereafter cited as *BJ*); cf. *Antiquities of the Jews* 20.166 (hereafter cited as *AJ*).

Cult focused on actions, on showing and (no less important) on being seen to show respect for the gods. Peoples inherited their protocols for showing respect, and these protocols defined what we call "religion." At the same time, these protocols also designated ethnicity. "Different nations have different customs," remarked Athenagoras, "and no one is hindered by law or by fear of punishment from following his ancestral customs, no matter how ridiculous these may be," (*Legatio* 1). True of pagans, true of Jews, as Celsus observed: Jews "observe a worship which may be very peculiar, but it is at least traditional. In this respect they behave like the rest of mankind, because each nation follows its particular customs" (*c. Celsum* 5.25).

Note that ancient peoples, Jews included, did not "believe" or "believe in" their ancestral customs. They enacted them; they preserved them; they respected them; they trusted or trusted in them.[7] This same practical stance describes, too, how ancient peoples—again, Jews included—coped with the gods of others. That the gods of others existed was another commonsense fact, demonstrated by the existence of that god's people. The Bible, the prime textual residence of Israel's God, acknowledged the existence of these other gods, who were the deities of the nations. "All the peoples walk, each in the name of its god," says the prophet Micah, "but we will walk in the name of the Lord *our* God forever and ever" (Mic 4:5, and frequently elsewhere, especially in Psalms). "Who is like you, O Lord, among the gods?" Moses asked (Exod 15:11). The LXX subordinated these other gods to Israel's God by conjur-

[7] That is, they had confidence that the ancestral observances that they enacted were in fact pleasing to the god. To translate πιστεύω as "believe" too easily conjures for us the sentiments and psychological states of post-Romanticism (e.g., authenticity, genuine affection, individual subjectivity, self-authenticating intensity, and so on). Especially when dealing with early Christian materials, such as the gospels or Paul's letters, πιστεύω as "believe" runs head-on into the theological existentialism of Bultmannian hermeneutics, and more generally into the polemical jargon of the Reformation. For these reasons I find that the second choice given in definition 1.a. of Bauer-Gingrich-Danker—"believe in something, *be convinced of something*"—better protects against anachronism.

ing the ranked divinities of the Hellenistic universe: "The gods of the nations are δαίμονες" sang the Psalmist in Greek (95:5, LXX): a δαίμων was specifically a lower, cosmic god.[8] More concretely, and more generally, diplomatic relations between peoples in the Hellenistic and Roman periods were negotiated by generating connections of kinship, discovering an ancient family bond that had been effected by their respective gods. Since the Jewish god did not leave behind offspring as the Greek gods did, his people built kinship lines and, thus, diplomatic relations by mobilizing the progeny of the patriarchs: In this way, for example, Jews and Spartans, through a distant union between a grand-daughter of Abraham's with Heracles, became συγγενεῖς.[9]

Israel's god was famously demanding of his people, insisting that he be the sole recipient of their worship. And Jews generally do seem to have drawn the line at λατρεία, excusing themselves (to the irritation of sensitive pagans) from performing public cult

---

[8] When Ps 95:5 (LXX) hymned the gods of the nations as δαίμονες, the word seems to function in its original meaning of "lower divinity," used comfortably as such by pagan authors as well: H. Chadwick, "Oracles of the End in the Conflict of Paganism and Christianity in the Fourth Century," *Mémorial André-Jean Festugière: Antiquité paiënne et chrétienne* (Geneva: Patrick Cramer, 1984), 125–129; J. Rives, "The Decree of Decius and the religion of the empire," *JRS* 89 (1999): 135–154; J. Rives, *Religion in the Roman Empire* (Oxford: Blackwell, 2007), 20. Later Christian usage made "demons" solely evil, as they appear to be already in Paul. On the demons' status as cosmic gods, see too Augustine, *de civitate dei* 9.23.

[9] "After reading a certain document," announces a Spartan king to the Jewish high priest, "we have found that Jews and Lacedaemonians [Spartans] are of one γένος, and share a connection with Abraham" (1 Macc 12:21). This συγγένεια appears also in 2 Macc 5:9, and Josephus reports the same tradition, a Hellenistic Jewish fabrication, *AJ* 12.226; for the Abraham-Heracles connection, see 1.240–41. For discussion see C. Jones, *Kinship Diplomacy in the Ancient World* (Cambridge, Mass.: Harvard University Press, 1999), 72–80; and E. Gruen, "Jewish Perspectives on Greek Culture and Ethnicity," *Ancient Perceptions of Greek Ethnicity* (Cambridge, Mass.: Harvard University Press), 361–364. Paul of course also avails himself of this idea of Abraham as "the father of many nations," in Rom 4:11–18; more confusingly, see Gal 3:7–14; Gen 17:5. See on this last issue S. Stowers, *Rereading Romans: Justice, Jews, and Gentiles* (New Haven: Yale University, 1994), 227–250.

acts to foreign gods. But Jews of course knew that these gods existed, and that a sensible show of courtesy went far toward placating both the deity and his or her people. Moses, in Greek, had seemed to counsel handling such relations gently when he advised "Do not revile τοὺς θεούς the gods," (Exod 22:28, LXX). Commenting on this verse, Philo remarked that such sensitivity ensured peace between Israel and the nations, "for reviling each other's gods always causes war" (*Questions and Answers on Exodus* 2.5). He goes on to note that Jews should also respect pagan rulers "who are of the same seed as the gods," 2.6).[10] Despite pagan complaints about Jewish separateness and 'interfaith' insensitivity, a wealth of epigraphical evidence supports what we also know from Hellenistic Jewish texts: many Jews acknowledged the existence of foreign gods, treated them with civility (if not with public cult), and in general fitted themselves along side their pagan contemporaries in the god-congested universe of antiquity.[11]

---

[10] See P. van der Horst, "'Thou Shalt Not Revile the Gods': The LXX Translation of Exodus 22:28(27), Its Background and Influence," *Studia Philonica* 5 (1993): 1–8. Philo's politic pragmatism contrasts sharply with the tone taken in Hellenistic Jewish apocalyptic texts, Wisdom 13–15; similarly, Rom 1:18–35; 1 Cor 15:24.

[11] In the third century B.C.E., Moschos Iudaios liberated his slave at the prompting of two local gods; text and translation of Moschos' inscription available in E. Schürer and G. Vermes *et al.*, *A History of the Jewish People in the Age of Jesus Christ* (Edinburgh: T&T Clark, 1973–1987), 3:65 (hereafter cited as *HJP*). Niketas of Jerusalem contributed 100 drachmas to subvene a Dionysiac festival around 150 B.C.E.; see *HJP*, 3:25. Herod's building program of pagan (especially imperial) temples is discussed in *HJP*, 1:304–311; see Josephus, *AJ* 16.136–149, who also mentions Herod's paying for the imperial liturgies as well. On Herod's sponsorship of the Olympic games, *AJ* 16.149. "To the Most High God, the Almighty, the Blessed... Pothos, son of Strabo, dedicated in the prayer-house, according to his vow, his house-bred slave Chrysa, on condition that she be unharmed and unmolested by any of his heirs, under Zeus, Gaia, and Helios," reads a manumission inscription from the Bosporus, mid-first century C.E. The Jewish god dominates its invocation; Greek gods cluster at its close. What is the ethnicity, then, of the donor, Jewish or pagan? See I. Levenskaya, *The Book of Acts in its Diaspora Setting* (Grand Rapids: W.B. Eerdmans, 1996), 111–116 (with the full text of the inscription on p. 239); also L. Levine, *The Ancient Synagogue* (New Haven: Yale University, 2000), 113–123. M. Williams assembles transla-

Pagans returned the favor, acknowledging and showing respect for the god of the Jews. In the Temple before the year 66 C.E., they came as tourists to Jerusalem. How many? We have no way of knowing, but the lay-out of Herod's temple suggests that the numbers were high. Herod expanded the area around the old sanctuary to some thirty-five acres, enclosing it with a magnificent wall running nine-tenths of a mile along its perimeter.[12] Concentric courtyards of graduated size ringed the Temple's interior sacred space. The innermost court, closest to the sanctuary, was reserved for the priests; the next two, circumscribing the area, belonged respectively to Jewish men and to Jewish women. But the largest court of all, the one that surrounded these others, was the vast and beautiful Court of the Nations—an important architectural feature, I will argue shortly, for understanding a key element of Paul's gospel.

The Greek diaspora lacked Jewish temples, but it supported many Jewish assemblies. Whether designated as a συναγωγή, a προσευχή, a *collegium*, a πολίτευμα or a σύνοδος, such foundations have been recovered from Italy to Syria, from the Black Sea to North Africa. Wherever there were Jews, it seems, there were synagogues.[13]

---

tions of the ancient primary evidence for Jews as ephebes, citizens of pagan cities, members of town councils, officers in gentile armies, in *The Jews among the Greeks and Romans: A Diasporan Sourcebook* (Baltimore: Johns Hopkins University, 1998), 107–131. Going to the gymnasium and being a member of the ephebate meant that one was a member of the citizen body, thus with obligations to the city's gods. The first-century C.E. inscriptions listing the ephebes' names in Cyrene (Jesus son of Antiphilos and Eleazar son of Eleazar) are dedicated to the gods of the gymnasium, Hermes and Heracles, as J. Barclay notes, *Jews in the Western Mediterranean Diaspora, from Alexander to Trajan [323 BCE to 117 CE]* (Berkeley: University of California Press, 1996), 235; see too ibid. pp. 326–31 on Jewish participation in civic life.

[12] For the physical layout of the temple and the ways that it architecturally encoded Jewish purity rules, see especially E. P. Sanders, *Judaism: Practice and Belief, 63 BCE – 66 CE* (Philadelphia: Trinity Press International, 1992), 55–76.

[13] On the wide dispersion of synagogues and their archaeological remains, see Levine, *Ancient Synagogues* (exhaustively); also E. Gruen, *Diaspora: Jews amidst Greeks and Romans* (Cambridge: Harvard University Press, 2002), 105–32.

No less often, interestingly, where there were synagogues, there also seem to have been pagans. Some of these pagans were patrons of synagogues and major donors to Jewish activities: spelled out in mosaics and inscribed on donor plaques, their generosity was publicly proclaimed by Jews honoring their benefactions. Interested pagans built synagogue structures or lavishly decorated their interiors; they sponsored Jewish philanthropic initiatives; they participated in Jewish prayer and study, and took part in Jewish fasts or feasts.[14]

Scholars, repeating the language of our ancient evidence, refer to such pagans as 'god-fearers' or as 'Judaizers.' The terms are elastic, which fits the imprecision of our data. Occasional pagan involvement stands at one end of a behavioral spectrum; the explicit and voluntary assumption of some Jewish customs stands at the other. The point, for our present purposes, is that all of these pagan sympathizers, to whatever degree they chose to participate in Jewish communal life, did so *as pagans.* They also continued in their native cults. No formal constraints from the Jewish side seem to have abridged what was an ad hoc, improvised, and voluntary arrangement. And such pagan involvement in synagogue life continued well

---

[14] Julia Severa, a priestess in the imperial cult, was honored by an inscription for having built a synagogue; Capitolina, a wealthy woman and self-described god-fearer (θεοσεβής) furnished mosaics. On these and other pagan benefactors, L. Levine, *Ancient Synagogue*, 111, 121, 479–83; on god-fearers and proselytes at Aphrodisias, J. Reynolds and R. Tannenbaum, *Jews and Godfearers at Aphrodisias* (Cambridge: Cambridge Philological Society, 1987). The third-century date that the authors originally assigned to the inscription has been challenged, and scholars now contemplate dates well into the Christian period: A. Chaniotis, "The Jews of Aphrodisias: new evidence and old problems," *SCI* (2002), 209–242. A later date raises the intriguing possibility that some of the non-Jewish donors might have been Christians as well as pagans. Pagan "god-fearing" was a "wide and loose category" (Levinskaya, *Acts in its Diaspora Setting*, p. 79), not a technical designation for clearly-demarcated or defined group (such as προσήλυτος would be for 'convert'). All of these studies cite numerous pertinent collections of inscriptional materials. Acts routinely depicts gentile god-fearers together with proselytes and Jews in diaspora synagogues, 13:16, 14:1, 16:14,17:1–4, etc.; on Gentiles in Alexandria joining in Jewish celebrations, e.g., Philo, *Life of Moses* 2.41–42.

on into the Christian period: indeed, the third-century (or, perhaps, fifth-century) Christian writer Commodian complained that Jews welcomed the pagan *medius Iudaeus* into the synagogue without making the least effort to proselytize him (*Instructiones* 1.37.1–10).[15]

Refusal to worship the gods was the public behavior that pagan critics universally associated with Jews. It offended them. Nonetheless, majority culture by and large tolerated this singular aspect of Jewish behavior precisely because it was a demand of the Jewish God, and was therefore ancient and ancestral. This same ancient premium on ethnic loyalty which excused Jewish non-participation in public cult, however, also fed a special category of pagan anti-Jewish hostility. Eyeing god-fearers with mockery and distrust, fellow pagans objected to their assumption of some Jewish practices, wary of where it might lead. Again, Celsus: "If the Jews maintained their own law, we should not find fault with them, but rather with those who have abandoned *their own traditions* and professed those of the Jews" (*c. Celsum* 5.41). The father starts keeping the Sabbath and avoiding pork, grumbled Juvenal, and the next thing to happen is that the sons become circumcised, keep Moses' laws, and despise the laws of Rome (*Satires* 14.96–106).

Judaizing was a slippery slope. It could lead to Judaism. Pagans occasionally chose to affiliate themselves so extremely with Jewish ancestral practices that they became ex-pagans. In a culture where what we call 'religion' was seen as an innate, not a detachable, aspect of identity, this phenomenon scarcely made sense: it was tanta-

---

[15] '*Dicant illi tibi si iussum est deos adorare,*' *Instructiones* 1.37.10. On god-fearers, see, exhaustively, B. Wander, *Gottesfürchtige und Sympathisanten* (WUNT 104; Tübingen: Mohr-Siebeck, 1998), but cf. J. Lieu, "The Race of the God-fearers," *JTS* 46 (1995): 483–501; most recently, Terence L. Donaldson, *Judaism and the Gentiles: Jewish Patterns of Universalism (to 135 CE)* (Waco, Tex.: Baylor University Press, 2007), 467–82 ("Sympathization" [sic]). On the continuing gentile presence (both pagan and Christian) in synagogues well into the Christian period, P. Fredriksen and O. Irshai, "Christian Anti-Judaism: Polemics and Policies, from the Second to the Seventh Century," *Cambridge History of Judaism* 4 (2006): 977–1034, at 985–998.

mount to changing one's ethnicity. What we term 'conversion' was understood by ancient contemporaries as forging a political alliance, entering the Jewish πολιτεία and, as Celsus complains, assuming foreign laws and traditions.[16] (For that reason, it struck some observers as a species of treason.[17]) Worse than turning their backs on their human kin, however, was the fact that such people also turned their backs to the gods who were theirs by birth and blood. They thereby disrupted the fundamental relationship between gods and their humans. Such behavior not only insulted the pagan community: it endangered the pagan community, because it insulted that community's gods, and angry gods made for sorry humans. Remarkably, however, pagan culture by and large accommodated contemporaries who underwent such a drastic change of status, and 'converts'—προσήλυτοι—made up some of the Diaspora synagogue's population as well.[18] The greater number of non-natives in Jewish assemblies, however, most probably would have been god-fearers. And as long as these god-fearers continued to honor their

---

[16] E.g., Philo, *Special Laws* 1.9.51; see S. Cohen, *Beginnings of Jewishness* (Berkeley: University of California Press, 1999), 126; on conversion to Judaism more generally, ibid., 140–174. Cohen's "category 5" misdescribes "god venerators" (i.e., god-fearers) as "denying or ignoring all other gods," 171: on the contrary, god-fearers remained active pagans who added Israel's god to their particular pantheon. For further thoughts on the concept "conversion" when dealing with early Judaism, see P. Fredriksen, "Mandatory Retirement: Ideas in the Study of Christian Origins whose Time has Come to Go," *Studies in Religion/Sciences Religieuses*, 35/2 (2006): 231–246, at 232–37.

[17] For an analysis of Juvenal's jibe, see M. Stern, *Greek and Latin Authors on Jews and Judaism* (Jerusalem: Israel Academy of Sciences and Humanities, 1974), 2: 94–107. The emperor Domitian executed some members of the Roman aristocracy for "atheism," that is, for spurning their own gods on account of treasonable loyalty to "the customs of the Jews," (Dio, *Roman History* 67.14,1–2). Tacitus complains that such people, abandoning *religionibus patriis*, disown their own gods, country and family (*History* 5.1–2). See further the discussions in P. Schäfer, *Judeophobia* (Cambridge, Mass.: Harvard University Press, 1997) and in J. Gager, *The Origins of Anti-Semitism* (New York: Oxford University, 1983).

[18] On god-fearers and proselytes, literature cited n. 14 above; inscriptions pertaining to these two populations may be found in Williams, *Jews Among Greeks*, 163–172.

own ancestral customs and their own gods, the larger pagan urban community tolerated their honoring the Judean god, too.

With this as its context, how do we understand Paul's gospel?

2.

Modern scholars habitually describe Paul as a "monotheist," and they are right to. But Paul is an *ancient* monotheist. This means that, while Paul's allegiance is firmly fastened on the god of Israel as the highest and most powerful god, Paul is perfectly aware of other gods as well. Unlike Philo, Paul is not courteous toward or about these gods: in fact he insults them, and he wants his pagans to have nothing to do with them. These gods represent Paul's cosmic opposition, and he looks forward to the day of their defeat.[19]

Meanwhile, he complains about their effects. The θεὸς τοῦ αἰῶνος τούτου had blinded the minds of unbelievers (2 Cor 4:4; Pagans? Jews? cf. 2 Cor 3). The ἄρχοντες τοῦ αἰῶνος τούτου, if by this phrase Paul intends astral powers, have crucified the son of Paul's god (1 Cor 2:8). The divinities formerly worshiped by his congregations in Galatia, he says, are not "gods by nature" but mere cosmic lightweights, στοιχεῖα unworthy of fear or worship (Gal 4:8–9: note that Paul demeans their status, but does not deny their existence). Such gods, in fact, are mere δαίμονες, subordinate deities, "demons" (1 Cor 10:20–21). "Indeed, there are many θεοί and many lords," he tells his pagans in Corinth (1 Cor 8:5–6); but soon, these lower powers, currently worshiped through images, will themselves acknowledge the god of Israel when Christ defeats them and estab-

---

[19] In antiquity, all "monotheists" were polytheists, because all gods existed. Ancient monotheists assumed a divine architecture, where a single god stood at the pinnacle of sanctity and power. Ancient monotheism, in other words, is about the organization of the divine realm, and not about its absolute population. On the problems with using the word "monotheist" to describe ancient people (be they Jews, Christians or pagans), see Fredriksen, "Mandatory retirement," 241–43. For Paul's many references to other gods, see Dunn, *Theology*, 33–38.

lishes the kingdom of his father (1 Cor 15:24–27). In the End, these beings, wherever they are—above the earth or upon the earth or below the earth—will also bend their knees to Jesus (Phil 2:10).[20]

Paul's confidence that these gods will soon be defeated, and his efforts meanwhile to turn his pagans from them, are both aspects of his apocalyptic convictions. These were expressed in the accents peculiar to the early Jesus movement, which was itself apocalyptic. That is, the convictions and commitments of its disciples—the very way that they defined the mission and message of Jesus, made sense of his resurrection appearances, and articulated beliefs about his second coming—all drew upon larger traditions of Jewish apocalyptic eschatology.[21] Some of those traditions addressed directly the fate of non-Jews once Israel's redemption dawned. These traditions were mixed: some negative, some positive, both sometimes appearing in the same text. But the tradition that mattered to the new movement was the one that foretold the nations' inclusion, together with a reassembled Israel, once God's kingdom dawned.[22]

This inclusive eschatological Jewish tradition about receiving pagans into the kingdom might seem little different from the inclu-

---

[20] For the definition of ἄρχων as a subordinate and evil divine entity, see *A Greek-English Lexicon of the New Testament and Other Early Christian Literature* (ed. W. Bauer, with F.W. Gingrich and F.W. Danker; Chicago: University of Chicago Press, 1979). Definition 3: δύναμις; definition 6: ἐξουσία; definition 4.ß: στοιχεῖα; definitions 3 and 4.

[21] On the specifically apocalyptic linkage between the mission of Jesus and the later mission about him, see Fredriksen, *Jesus of Nazareth: King of the Jews* (New York: Knopf, 1999), 74–154 (as refracted through Paul), 261–266 (Acts).

[22] For a review of both inclusive and exclusive passages, see P. Fredriksen, "Judaism, the Circumcision of Gentiles, and Apocalyptic Hope: Another look at Galatians 1 and 2," *JTS* (1991): 543–48, with references; on the ways that this conviction about eschatological Gentiles informs the early mission, Fredriksen, *Jesus of Nazareth*, 125–37 (Paul), 261–66 (original disciples). "There simply was no unified view whatsoever on the religious status of non-Jews, either now or in the future. The range of diversity is striking," notes Donaldson, *Judaism and Gentiles*, 512. On the Gentiles' participation in Israel's eschatological salvation, see further ibid., 499–507, and the quotation in n. 25 below.

sive non-eschatological Jewish practice of receiving pagans into diaspora synagogues. But there was a crucial difference, one that throws the diaspora Jesus movement into sharper relief. The synagogue's προσήλυτοι were no longer pagans: they were Jews of a special kind. The synagogue's god-fearers or Judaizers, however, were 'active' pagans. Barring what we call conversion to Judaism, *all* sympathetic outsiders were pagans. They worshiped the gods native to them, however many other gods (including Israel's god) they might add on. *But the kingdom's pagans were a special and a purely theoretical category*: they were ex-pagan pagans or (to use the wiggle-room made available by our two English words for the single Greek ἔθνη), they were ex-pagan Gentiles.[23] When the Lord of the universe reveals himself in glory, say these Jewish apocalyptic texts, the nations will destroy their idols, repudiate their gods, and worship Israel's god together with Israel.

The anticipated destruction of their idols did not imply that, at the End, these pagans converted to Judaism. Conversion entailed the full assumption of Jewish ancestral practices and especially, for men, circumcision: apocalyptic texts fall short of claiming that. In the event, the nations do *not* convert; but they do "turn"—στρέφω—with an assortment of prefixes in the Greek texts. When God redeems Israel, the nations will *turn from* the lesser gods whose images they worship and *turn to* the god of Israel. "*Turn* to me!" cries God to the nations (Isa 45:22, LXX: ἐπιστράφητε). "All the nations *will turn* in fear to the Lord God... and bury their idols" (Tobit 14:6; ἐπιστρέψουσιν).

---

[23] Modern English uses two words, *Gentiles* and *pagans*, where the Greek only has one, τὰ ἔθνη. And the two English words have different connotations, the first connoting ethnicity (the person in question is not a Jew), the second connoting religion (the person in question is neither a Christian nor a Jew). In Paul's lifetime, however, with the exception of ex-pagan προσήλυτοι, pagans were Gentiles and Gentiles were pagans. The distinction between ethnicity and religion created by our two English words, in brief, leads to anachronism when describing the first several centuries of the spread of Christianity. For this reason, I use 'pagan' in the present essay where common usage would expect 'gentile,' in order to emphasize the bond of cult and ethnicity.

But this "turning" to Israel's god is not the same as converting to Judaism, as Paul himself insists. His pagans are not to "become" Jews. But they are to live as if they were eschatological pagans—which, by his lights, they are. During the brief wrinkle in time between the resurrection and the Parousia, Paul's pagans are to worship only Paul's god, the god of Israel, empowered to do so by that god's risen Son. "You *turned* to God from idols, to worship the true and living god," Paul tells his Gentiles in Thessalonika, "and to wait for his son from heaven," (1 Thess 1:9; ἐπιστρέψατε).[24] By being "in Christ," these pagans are spared two kinds of divine wrath: that of their own gods, infuriated by the lack of cult; and that of the god of Israel, which "is coming" (v. 10; cf. Gal 4:8–9).

Note that both in the older Jewish apocalyptic traditions and in their newer Christian refraction, the nations join *with* Israel, but they do not *join* Israel. To phrase this point in Christian theological vocabulary, you do not need to be Jewish to be saved. At the End, the human population of God's kingdom reflects quotidian demography: Israel and the nations together worship Israel's god.[25]

---

[24] 'Επιστρέφω comes into Latin as *converto* (thus, at 1 Thess 1:9 *conversi estis*), and the Latin comes into English as "conversion," completely obscuring the very important distinction between "turning" and "converting" in this context. Thus Acts 15:3 (RSV) speaks (wrongly) of the 'conversion of the Gentiles' for ἐπιστροφὴν τῶν ἐθνῶν, while translating ἐπιστρέφουσιν at 15:19 (properly) as "Gentiles who are *turning* to God." The argument in Acts 15 is precisely that Gentiles do not and should not need to "convert" to be part of the movement, as "certain individuals" urge by insisting on circumcision (15:1): the only thing to convert to at mid-first century is Judaism, since a separate "Christianity" does not yet exist. See Fredriksen, "Mandatory Retirement," 232–235.

[25] "The final pattern [of eschatological inclusion] focuses not on Gentile attitudes and activity in the present but on the possibility that a substantial number of Gentiles would turn to worship God in the eschatological future. This expectation, deeply rooted in Israel's scriptures, did not exist in isolation but was always one aspect of a larger eschatological scenario centered on Israel itself . . . Israel's self-understanding required that the final establishment of God's glory should be universal and that the nations as well should be included in God's purposes," (Donaldson, *Judaism and Gentiles*, 509). See too C. Hodge, *If Sons, Then Heirs: A Study of Kinship and Ethnicity in the Letters of Paul* (New York: Oxford University 2007), 138, on how Paul's logic in Romans 9–11 required that he keep these two groups, Jews and Gentiles, "separate but linked."

Paul also invokes the very Roman idea of adoption to express this distinct-but-together relationship of Israel and his Christian pagans. Roman adoption was both a legal and a religious act. Entering a new family entailed taking on obligations to new ancestors and new gods: adoption was superintended by a *pontifex.*[26] In this regard, adoption in Roman culture is much like 'conversion' was in Judaism: both represent the legal creation of kinship bonds and an adjusted pantheon. Paul, however, does not think that Christian pagans should convert to Judaism, and so he deploys this image carefully. Israel, adopted already as God's son, descends from "the fathers"—Abraham, Isaac, and Jacob—according to the flesh; to them God has made many promises (ἐπαγγελίαι, Rom 9:4; cf. 15:8; ἐπαγγελίαι τῶν πατέρων). Pagans-in-Christ are also from Abraham's lineage, since Abraham was the father of many nations (Gen 17:4; Rom 4:17); but they descend from Abraham *alone*, not also from Isaac and Jacob.[27] Because of the Spirit, however, these pagans too are now sons, heirs to the "promise" to Abraham; like Israel, they too can now call God "Abba, Father" (Genesis 12:3; Rom 8:15; also Gal 4:6, where the spirit of Jesus effects the adoption). [28]

---

[26] On the role of the pontifex in Roman adoption, M. Beard, "Priesthood in the Roman Republic," *Pagan Priests: Religion and Power in the Ancient World* (ed. M. Beard and J. North; Ithaca: Cornell University, 1990), 38. Marriage, for ancient women, also represents the legal creation of kinship and, at the same time, the crossing of a religious boundary: as Plutarch notes, "It is becoming for a wife to worship and to know only those gods that her husband esteems," *Moralia* 140D.

[27] But cf. Hodge, *If Sons*, 94 and passim, who reads Romans 9:7, descent through Isaac, as referring to Gentiles-in-Christ.

[28] When Paul speaks of "the promise" in the singular, he refers to God's promise to Abraham about the redemption of the Gentiles (e.g., Gen 12:3). But, as Stanley Stowers notes, "for Israel, there were many promises, not one. Because Romans is about gentiles, the promises peculiar to Jews bear only a mention [i.e., at 9:4 and at 15:8]... In 15:8, Paul speaks of the fathers (plural), who include Jacob, Joseph, Moses, and many others who are not fathers of the gentiles in the same way as Abraham. Only Abraham received the promise that in his seed the gentiles would be blessed. This promise does not lessen the significance of the other fathers for the Jews (9:5)," *A Rereading of Romans*, 133.

But this new kinship is *not* tantamount to "conversion," because these Gentiles are adopted not into Israel's family, but into God's. God, not Abraham, is their "Abba," made such not κατὰ σάρκα but κατὰ πνεῦμα. Put differently: redeemed Israel and the pagans-in-Christ together share the same heavenly father κατὰ πνεῦμα, but κατὰ σάρκα they remain distinct.[29]

3.

Paul's pagans received the divine spirit through baptism, specifically baptism into Jesus' death. The spirit also "sanctified" these pagans. These ideas correlate to others: ideas about sacrifice, about purity, and about holiness. To understand them, we have to look to their source: the rules of Leviticus, and the operation of the Temple.

All purity rules in antiquity, pagan and Jewish, describe ritual protocols which enabled the worshiper to approach and to interact with divinity.[30] The zone of this interaction was often around altars, and thus often had to do with sacrifices. Specifically biblical tradition governed the approach to divinity by two binary distinctions. One was the distinction between pure/impure or clean/unclean (טהר/טמא in Hebrew; καθαρός/ἀκάθαρτος in Greek). The other was the distinction between holy/profane or separated/common (קדש/חל in Hebrew, ἅγιος/κοινός in Greek).[31]

---

[29] "Peter" in Acts 15:8–9 (RSV) makes this same point. "God, who knows the human heart, testified to them [the Gentiles] by giving them the Holy Spirit, just as he did to us; and in cleansing their hearts by faith he has made no distinction between them and us." Κατὰ πνεῦμα, these Gentiles with their hearts cleansed stand together with the apostolic community, whose hearts have likewise been cleansed; κατὰ σάρκα, they remain distinct, and thus the apostolic assembly rejects the motion to require the circumcision (thus, conversion) of gentile members.

[30] On pagan concepts of purity/impurity, see now R. Parker, *Miasma: Pollution and Purification in Early Greek Religion* (New York: Oxford University, 1993).

[31] "Pure" (καθαρός) and "holy" (ἅγιος) are two distinct concepts, but the Greek κοινός, "common," begins to function as a synonym for ἀκάθαρτος in some Hellenistic Jewish texts. Thus, e.g., 1 Macc 1:62, where people refuse to eat

The pure/impure distinction refers first of all to Levitical or ritual impurity, a highly contagious condition arising from certain natural bodily processes, or from contact with or even proximity to certain polluting substances or objects. Such a state was virtually unavoidable, all but universal, and, finally, temporary. It implied no moral condition: the impure person was not *eo ipso* a sinful person. The remedy for this sort of impurity is purification.[32]

Another type of impurity resulted from certain sexual and/or cultic sins.[33] To distinguish it from the first kind, scholars have designated this sort of defilement as "moral" or "figurative" or "metaphorical" or "spiritual" impurity.[34] It did not regulate access to the Temple. It did articulate moral status. Such defilement was *not* contagious, it was volitional, and it was avoidable.[35] The sinner defiled not only him or herself, but also the sanctuary and the land (Lev 18:25, 20:3). The remedy for the impurity of sin is cessation of the sinful activity, repentance, and a special day of purgation with its own special sacrifices, Yom Kippur (Lev 16).

A second set of biblical categories, holy/profane or separated/common (חל/קדש; Lev 10:10), also governed proximity to the sanctuary. Something "holy" could be rendered "common" or "profane" (*pro-*

"unclean" food; Mk 7:2, 5; Acts 10:14–15; Rom 14–14. I thank my colleague Daniel Schwartz for bringing the example from 1 Macc to my attention.

[32] Biblical legislation clusters at Lev 11–15 and Num 19. E. P. Sanders provides a useful table of biblical impurities together with their means of purification and the zone of affected activity, in *Jewish Law from Jesus to the Mishnah* (Philadelphia: Trinity Press International,1990), 151.

[33] Sexual, e.g., Lev 18:1–30; 20:10–21; ritual (idolatry, cultic infanticide, magic), Lev 20:1–5; Deut 7:25 and 12:29–31 (idolatry).

[34] See especially A. Büchler, "The Levitical Impurity of the Gentile in Palestine before the year 70," *JQR* 17 (1926): 1–81. For the ways that "impurity of sin" comes to relate specifically to pagans or paganism, see J. Klawans, "Notions of Gentile Impurity in Ancient Judaism," *AJS Review* 20:2 (1995): 285–312; C. Hayes, *Gentile Impurities and Jewish Identities: Intermarriage and Conversion from the Bible to the Talmud* (New York: Oxford University Press, 2002).

[35] Some late Second Temple Jewish communities, such as those represented by Jubilees and by the Dead Sea Scrolls, do treat moral impurity as contagious: see Klawans, "Notions," 293–98 and the literature cited nn. 40–60.

before, outside; *fanes* altar). Iron tools cutting the stone of the altar, for example, would render the altar unfit (Exod 20:22). And the ordinary could be made holy, meaning "separated out" from the common and dedicated to God. When choosing a perfect animal for sacrifice, for example, the worshiper would pronounce the offering קדש, thus קרבן (cf. Mark 7:11). Similarly, a Jewish groom pronounces his wife קדש לי, "sanctified to me," set apart from all others for himself.[36]

The purity legislation of Torah was binding only on Jews. How does it help us to understand Jewish views of Gentiles in the Roman period? Ritual impurity seems an irrelevant category. Israel, not the nations, is the focus of this purity legislation, both in the Bible and in later rabbinic opinion.[37] Moral impurity presents a more complex problem. Again, the biblical legislation is directed specifically to Israel, but the warnings refer to "the nations" having committed similar sins. "Do not defile yourself with any of these things [incest, adultery, ritual infanticide, homosexual intercourse] for *by all these things the nations that I cast out before you defiled themselves, and the land became defiled... and the land vomited them out*" (Lev 18:24). The natives of Canaan, God seems to be saying here, had defiled themselves and the Land with this behavior. The same behaviors, imputed to pagans, routinely show up in the vice lists of Hellenistic Jewish writings, among which, emphatically, Paul's letters.[38] Pagans, in this view, would be not intrinsically impure, but functionally

---

[36] On the long history of this phrase, which goes back well into the period of the late Second Temple, see M. Kister, "'According to the Law of Moses and the Jews': The History of a Religious and Legal Formula," (Hebrew) *Atara l'Haim: Studies in the Talmud and Medieval Rabbinic Literature in honor of Professor Haim Zalman Dimitrovky* (Jerusalem: Magnes, 2000), 202–208. For early rabbinic comments on the biblical protocols for sanctifying an offering in Lev 1:2, see Sifra, parasha B, 4.

[37] Sanders, *Judaism*, 156; Klawans, 'Notions', 302–309 on Tannaitic literature.

[38] "The use of purity language for correct behavior and impurity terms for transgression, highly visible in Paul, is what leads so many New Testament scholars to confuse the entire issue," E.P. Sanders, personal correspondence, 29 June 2009. For Paul's lists of Gentile vices, see, e.g., Rom 1:18–31; cf. Gal 5:19–21, there as "works of the flesh"; 1 Cor 6:9–11 (personal, not abstract nouns: "idolators, adulterers, sexual perverts... and such were some of you"); cf. 1 Thess

impure, made such by their enduring attachment to idols (not to mention their habitual indulgence in the various forms of πορνεία that invariably accompany idolatry in Jewish anti-pagan rhetoric, e.g., Rom 1:18–35).

But moral defilement, even that contracted through the worship of idols, is not contagious, and the lay-out of Herod's temple underscores this fact: Jews were able to walk through the Court of the Nations on their way to their own areas without fear of defilement. (The pagan presence in the synagogue would be even less problematic, since synagogues were not sites of sacrifice, thus not regulated by purity concerns.) However, "though not inherently impure, Gentiles are inherently profane"[39]—that is, common, not separated out, when compared with Israel, the "holy" nation set apart from the other nations by God for himself. Even a (theoretical) pagan who had not defiled himself with idols would still be κοινός, thus not suitable to be brought close to the altar of Israel's god.

Paul's letters are shot through with the language of sanctuary, sacrifice, purity, and holiness. Alas, much of it is confusing. His efforts to describe Christ as a sort of sacrifice defy clarity. Paul's reference to Christ as a paschal lamb in 1 Cor 5:7 is less christological than hortatory: in this passage, he urges his pagans to cleanse themselves of the leaven of pride in view of the fact that the (metaphorical) holiday of Passover is already underway. The paschal image, in other words, refers to Jewish time-keeping, not to a sacrificial death on the part of Christ. 2 Corinthians 5:21 and Rom 8:3, Christ as חטאת/ἁμαρτία or as περὶ ἁμαρτίας also seem confusing, especially if scholars have rightly understood the Temple's own dynamics of purity: sin sacrifices cleanse the sancta, not the sinner.[40] The ἱλαστήριον of Rom 3:25, finally, is a sacrifice of expiation; but

4:4–6. For a discussion of such vice lists in Hellenistic Jewish literature, E. Käsemann, *Commentary on Romans* (Grand Rapids: Eerdmans, 1980), 49; on Paul's lists, see the chart in Dunn, *Theology of Paul*, 662–663.

[39] Klawans, 'Notions', 292, cf. 298.

[40] Thus J. Milgrom, *Leviticus 1–16* (New York: Doubleday, 1991), 254–58. J. Klawans, *Impurity and Sin in Ancient Judaism* (New York: Oxford University, 2000), 3–20 offers a succinct review of various scholarly perspectives.

again, the image is extremely confusing (and, I think, confused). In Leviticus, the sacrifice is brought by penitent humans; in Romans, it is God who brings Jesus. The closest analogy to a sacrifice in Paul's time that would bear away the sinner's sin would be the scapegoat of Yom Kippur. But Paul nowhere uses this image and, besides—a nod to the eucharistic traditions—you do not eat scapegoats.[41]

By comparison, Paul's language of ἁγιασμός with respect to his pagans-in-Christ, and his representations of his own work as priestly service, are surprisingly clear, as is his reference to the rituals of Jerusalem's temple that serve as his template. His Thessalonian pagans, for example, having turned from their idols to the living and true god, have attained ἁγιασμός: the RSV translates "sanctification," but we should equally understand "separation" or "dedication." These Christian pagans, through their cleaned up ritual and sexual behavior, are separated from or distinguished from the other pagans, the ones who do not know God (1 Thess 4:4–5). Those who *do* know God have been called 'not to impurity'—the moral consequence of idolatry and porneia—but "in holiness" (v. 7). Elsewhere, Paul simply refers to these ex-pagan pagans as "holy ones" (ἅγιοι, RSV 'saints' Rom 1:7; 1 Cor 1:2). They have been made holy—or separated, or dedicated to God—by God, through the spirit, in Christ (1 Cor 1:2).

We should hear Paul's language of purity, separation and sanctification in terms of the biblically-based binary pairs טמא/טהר and חל/קדש that govern access to the sanctuary in Jerusalem. Thanks to God's spirit (or to Jesus' spirit), these pagans have been separated out from their fellows, adopted into God's family, cleansed to participate in the eucharistic sacrifice of Christ—1 Cor 10 elaborates this whole

---

[41] Dunn, *Theology of Paul*, 212–23 labors to transform the intrinsic messiness of Paul's sacrificial references into coherence, but a confused account of Jewish blood offerings, and of Paul's metaphorical usages of them, nonetheless emerges. See, e.g., his attribution of an atoning function to the corban Pesach, 217; his imputation of 'sinlessness' to the sacrificial animal, loc. cit. and again 221, while conjuring the Yom Kippur offering as well. As J. Klawans notes, the sacrificial animal is neither sinful nor sinless, neither "innocent or guilty. The animal is food," *Purity, Sacrifice, and the Temple* (New York: Oxford University, 2006), 44.

set of ideas.[42] When speaking of God's spirit, Paul likens his pagans to the Jerusalem temple: "Don't you know that you are God's temple, for God's spirit dwells in you? . . . For God's temple is ἅγιος, as you are" (1 Cor 3:16). "Your body is a temple of the holy spirit" (6:19). "We are the temple of the living god" (2 Cor 6:16).

New Testament scholars will sometimes point to these verses by way of arguing that, for Paul, Jerusalem's temple has been superseded by this new, spiritual "temple" of the Christian community. I argue the opposite: Paul praises the new community by likening it to something that he values supremely. If he valued the temple less, he would not use it as his touchstone.[43] This is not an either/or situation: for Paul, God's spirit dwells *both* in Jerusalem's temple *and* in the "new temple" of the believer and of the community (Rom 9:4; cf. Matt 23:21).

---

[42] On Paul's analogy of eucharist to sacrifice in this passage, Klawans notes how Paul draws a contrast "between proper worship on the one hand and idolatry on the other. This contrast – which is drawn elsewhere (1 Cor 8:4–6, 13; 2 Cor 6:16) – is instructive, and it allows us to juxtapose the picture of early Christian worship in a Pauline, Diaspora community with Acts' picture of the apostles' [temple] worship in Jerusalem. In Acts 2, we are presented with a picture of early Christians performing both Eucharistic and sacrificial rituals. In 1 Corinthians 10, we are presented with a different picture: that of Gentile Christians in Corinth who do not have the option of performing sacrificial rites and Eucharistic rites. Jewish sacrificial devotion outside of Jerusalem is out of the question. Other local forms of sacrifice are equally out of the question, because they are idolatrous. And what is Paul's message? That early [Gentile] Christians must choose one or the other: it's either idolatry or the worship of God, either sacrifice or eucharist... [But] Paul himself did not articulate a broadly antisacrificial perspective. In his view, the Jewish cult is proper and effective, though it refers primarily to the people of Israel (cf. Rom 9:4). *The sacrificing that he does reject...is idolatry.* But to a Gentile in the Diaspora, rejecting all sacrifice but the Jerusalem cult is little different from rejecting all sacrifice whatsoever. The origin of the idea that the eucharist is a replacement for sacrifice is likely to be found in this kind of social reality, among those who – unlike the disciples in Jerusalem – actually had to choose between two distinct options: eucharist *or* sacrifice," *Purity*, 221.

[43] So similarly F. W. Horn, "Paulus und der Herodianische Temple," *NTS* 53 (2007): 184–203, esp. 191 and (with reference to supposed traditions emanating from Stephen and the Hellenists) 196.

The second half of Romans, I think, particularly works against an either/or view of God's in-dwelling spirit. The sanctity, dignity and probity of the Temple cult provides the inclusio that shapes the second half of the letter, from 9:4 to 15:16–27, where Paul likens his own mission to the Temple service. The RSV's famously bloodless translation of Paul's Greek terms masks Paul's Temple imagery in 9:4, where δόξα/כבוד speaks precisely of God's glorious presence in Jerusalem's sanctuary, and λατρεία/עבודה refers to the cult of offerings enacted there. Chapters 9 through 15 move from Jerusalem to Jerusalem, where Paul anticipates performing his own priestly work, "sacrificing" God's good news, presenting "the offering of [his] pagans," now acceptable because they have been set apart/made holy by the holy spirit.[44] His pagans, through Christ, have moved from wrong ritual—the worship of idols—to right ritual, the worship of the true god. They are thus fit for intimate contact with the divine.[45]

4.

What conclusions can we draw from this very quick survey of Paul's mission and message?

1. First, we should not be tricked by the pagan complaints about Jewish ἀμιξία (separateness) or μισόξενος βίος ("foreigner-hating lifestyle"). Learned Greco-Roman ethnic stereotyping routinely leveled such accusations of anti-social behavior at for-

[44] εἰς τὸ εἶναί με λειτουργὸν Χριστοῦ Ἰησοῦ εἰς τὰ ἔθνη, ἱερουργοῦντα τὸ εὐαγγέλιον τοῦ θεοῦ, ἵνα γένηται ἡ προσφορὰ τῶν ἐθνῶν εὐπρόσδεκτος, ἡγιασμένη ἐν πνεύματι ἁγίῳ (Romans 15:16). On Paul's vocabulary here see further Horn, "Paulus und der Tempel," 200–201.

[45] The Temple instantiates such intimacy. Horn, commenting on Paul's conceptual breakthrough in Romans—Paul's using priestly language to describe his mission and Temple imagery to describe pagan Christians—rightly observes, "Damit ist der Tempel wohl noch jüdischer boundary marker gegenüber den Heiden, er wächst aber doch zugleich in der Rolle eines identity marker für Juden, Judenchristen und Heidenchristen," "Paulus und der Tempel," 203; cf. also 201 n. 65.

eigners.[46] The specifically anti-Jewish material looms large in the extant evidence because the later church incorporated and amplified those traditions so much; and often, New Testament scholars repeat these accusations of clannishness and separateness to explain tensions between Christian and non-Christian Jews (with Paul serving on both sides of the fence). But as the rich and variegated literary remains of Hellenistic Jewish culture and as the plenitude of inscriptions attest, Jews vigorously participated in majority culture socially, politically, and intellectually: in many ways, *except for their general refusal to participate in public pagan cult,* Jews were *not* all that separate.[47] A high degree of social integration coexisted with religious—better, ethnic—distinctiveness.

2. We often read that, through the gospel, Paul came to see the wrong-headedness of Israel's "covenant distinctiveness." Christian Gentiles and Christian Jews, in this view, together comprise a "new Israel," where no such distinctions obtain. (Gal 3:28 is often pressed into service here.) This *vetus Israel / verus Israel* contrast is not native to Paul's thinking.[48] Paul, further, continuously draws distinctions between Israel and the nations ("the Jew first and also the Greek").[49] The divinely granted promises, privileges, and prerogatives of Israel, "the gifts and the call of God," abide forever (Rom 11:29). This distinction between Israel and the nations, and these convictions about God's constancy, shape the most programmatic discussion that we have from Paul, namely his letter to the Romans. Like other apocalyptically minded Jews of his era, Paul too held that the kingdom's demography would reflect then what

[46] Isaac, *Invention of Racism*, 324–500 provides a superb overview of ancient ethnic stereotyping; on Jews in particular, 440–491. He notes that "Christian activity is responsible for the preservation of a good deal of ancient source material on Jews that is not available for other ethnic groups in antiquity," 441.

[47] See esp. Seth Schwartz, *Imperialism and Jewish Society, 200 B.C.E. to 640 C.E.* (Princeton, NJ: Princeton University Press, 2001).

[48] Against this traditional (mis)interpretation of Paul as envisioning two Israels, one ethnic and fleshly, the other spiritual and saved, see Hodge, *If Sons*, 102.

[49] Hodge considers this motif in detail, *If Sons*, 137–53.

the world holds now: Jews and Gentiles, Israel and the nations. [50]

The "saved Israel" of Romans 11:26 came to refer exclusively to Christians only in the second century, once later theologians, re-reading the Septuagint and relinquishing Paul's vision of a fast-approaching eschatological resolution, referred the promises of Israel to their own churches.[51] But for Paul, the hardening of Israel, which enables the mission to the Gentiles, is providential and temporary (Rom 11:25–26), while for Augustine, for example, it is punitive and permanent. The bishop accordingly must re-define "Israel": "all Israel" that is saved must become *Christian* Israel, the "Israel" of the church (e.g., ep. 149.2,19). But for Paul, "Israel" always means his "kinsmen according to the flesh – they are Israel" (Rom 9:4). The distinction of the covenant, and of the promises to the forefathers, remain. Romans ends with the Gentiles rejoicing "*with* God's people" (Rom 15:10).

3. The Temple remains absolutely central, driving all of Paul's messy metaphors for Jesus' death as a sacrifice. No less importantly, it also supplies the chief terms by which Paul conceptualizes the incorporation of his pagans-in-Christ into Israel's redemption. The language of "sanctification" means that these pagans have been separated out and, through the spirit, dedicated to God. (That also means that there is nothing intrinsically problematic for Paul about distinctiveness or separateness: that is how election works.) Paul's temple imagery; his way of speaking about offerings; his distinguishing between types of Gentiles as either קדש or חל, ἅγιος or κοινός; his condemnation of pagan cult; his insistence on their worshiping Israel's god alone[52]—in and through all these ways, Paul demands that his pagans Judaize.

---

[50] For a similar conclusion based on different arguments, see M. Nanos, *The Mystery of Romans* (Minneapolis: Fortress Press, 1996).

[51] Fredriksen, *Augustine*, 41–78 traces this turn in second-century Christian rhetoric and theology with particular reference to Justin and to Tertullian. M. Simon, *Verus Israel* (London: Littman Library of Jewish Civilization, 1986; orig. pub. 1948), though now dated, remains essential.

[52] Gods too are ethnic in antiquity, and Israel's god is no exception. The scope

4. Finally, we should see clearly what Paul is asking of his pagans, and what (so far as we know) absolutely all of the apostles in the early years of this messianic movement were demanding of their gentile followers: No λατρεία to native gods.[53] This was not an ethical demand so much as a *ritual* demand. More than this—as Paul surely knew—it was specifically a *Judaizing* demand.[54] The

---

of his activities may be universal, and he interacts with whichever humans he will (see e.g., Amos 9:7 for Philistines, and Arameans; so too Rom 3:29); but he is no non-historical, universal high god such as we see in much later middle- and late Platonism (e.g., in Sallustius' Περὶ θεῶν καὶ κόσμου. Paul's god, "the god of the Gentiles also" (Rom 3:29), remains emphatically the god of the patriarchs, the promises, the prophets, and the scriptures: in brief, the god of Jewish history (Rom 15:8). In pronouncing God's oneness at Rom 3:29, Paul invokes the Shema as he recaps his mission. Precisely in and through its ineradicable Jewishness, Paul's gospel brings the good news of universal redemption.

[53] The Book of Acts, written c. 100 C.E., offers a vivid and realistic description of early responses to this socially disruptive message. Itinerant apostles were actively repudiated by synagogues, run out of town by irate gentile citizens, and occasionally punished by cautious Roman authorities attempting to keep the peace. In the thirties and forties C.E., this unprecedented and disruptive policy of separating pagans-in-Christ from their native cults gives the measure of the apocalyptic mind-set, and indeed of the time-frame, of the earliest apostles. Christ would return soon; all would be finally resolved. While, notoriously, Acts conforms to and confirms neither the chronology implicit in Paul's letters, nor indeed Paul's own view of his mission as exclusively to Gentiles, both Paul and Acts cohere in their presentation of this early urban response. Thus, Paul lists his woes, variously inflicted by Jews, by pagans, and specifically by Romans, in 2 Cor 4:8–9; 6:4–5; 11:24–26. Cf. Acts 13:50; 14:2,4–6,19; 16:20–24 (in v. 21, pagans complain to magistrates about Paul and Silas: "They are Jews and are advocating customs that are not lawful for us to adopt or observe"); 17:5–9; 18:12–17 before Gallio in Corinth; 19:23–41 the tumult in Ephesus.

[54] Paul had condemned Cephas for trying to force pagans in Antioch to Judaize (ἰουδαΐζειν, Gal 2:14), in that context meaning to assume ancestral Jewish food practices (2:12). Worshiping the god of Israel and him alone, however, while a uniquely Jewish behavior in the quotidian, was for Paul the eschatological destiny of all humanity (e.g., Rom 11:25–35): on this point, speaking to his pagans, his eschatological perspective overtakes their quotidian circumstances. Besides, using the term would have only contributed to confusion: it normally referred either to proselytism (full "conversion") or to god-fearing (adding the Jewish god to a pagan pantheon), both of which Paul not only does not endorse, but actually condemns (conversion to Judaism, Gal passim; god-fearing, e.g.,1 Cor 5:11). In brief, common usage prohibited his employing the term positively in the context of his mission.

Jesus movement, out of apocalyptic conviction, required its Gentiles to enact precisely that behavior that majority culture (and Jews as well) associated universally and exclusively with Jews: to foreswear public sacrifice. Born Jews had been the occasional object of pagan resentment because of this behavior; proselytes that much more so. But when fellow pagans also began to disrespect the gods, this went too far, and the gods' people struck back. It is from this population—the deviant pagans of the Jesus movement—that the martyrs would come.[55]

This insistence that none other than the god of Israel be worshiped ultimately came from the first table of the Law. It was defining; it was non-negotiable; it was uniquely Jewish. For all of the reasons reviewed above, then, but most especially for this one, the last way we should describe Paul's gospel to the Gentiles is to say that it was 'Law-free.'

* I wish to thank colleagues Michael McGarry of the Tantur Ecumenical Institute, Jerusalem, and Joseph Sievers of the Cardinal Bea Centre for Jewish Studies, Rome, whose invitations to speak on Paul in his Jewish matrix provided me with the opportunity to gather my thoughts on this subject; and Oded Irshai, Serge Ruzer, Ed Sanders, and Gregory

[55] On pagans-in-Christ foreswearing traditional sacrifices, see also M. Nanos, *The Irony of Galatians: Paul's Letter in First-century Context* (Minneapolis: Fortress Press, 2002), 257–71. On the persecution of pagan Christians not because they were Christian but because they were deviant pagans, thus sure to anger the gods, see T. Barnes, "Legislation against the Christians," *JRS* 58 (1968): 32-50; F. Millar, "The Imperial Cult and the Persecutions," *Le culte des souverains dans l'empire Romain* (Entretiens Hardt vol. XIX; Vandoeuvres: Geneva, 1973), 145–175; Lane Fox, *Pagans*, 419–34. Dressing pagan Christians in the arena as characters from classical mythology both amused the crowd and, perhaps, assuaged insulted gods, K. Coleman, "Fatal Charades: Roman executions staged as mythological enactments," *JRS* 80 (1990): 44–73. On the links between the synagogues' "persecution" of Christian Jews and majority culture's persecution of Christian pagans see also M. Goodman, "The Persecution of Paul by Diaspora Jews," *The Beginnings of Christianity* (Jerusalem: Yad Ben Zvi, 2005), 376–87; also Fredriksen, *Augustine*, 79–98.

Tatum, for their very helpful criticisms of an earlier version of this paper. Thanks too to my student Christopher Stroup for special assistance.

My introduction to the historical Paul came via Augustine, when I as an undergraduate first read Krister Stendahl's luminous essay, 'Paul and the Introspective Conscience of the West.' With his deep knowledge of Paul's letters and his appreciation for the patristic refractions of Pauline theology, Krister became an invaluable conversation partner in the three-plus decades since that time, as well as my much-loved mentor and friend. The present essay I offer to his memory, with deepest gratitude, respect, and love. ᾿Εν εἰρήνῃ κοιμήσις αὐτοῦ: זכרו לברכה. In peace his sleep, and may his memory be for a blessing.

Bibliography

Aageson, James W. *Written Also for Our Sake: Paul and the Art of Biblical Interpretation*. Louisville, Ky.: Westminster John Knox, 1993.

Abadie, P. and J.-P. Lémenon (eds.) *Le judaïsme à l'aube de l'ère chrétienne, XVIIIe congrès de l'ACFEB (Lyon, septembre 1999)*. Paris: Cerf, 2001.

Abegg, Martin G., Jr. "Paul, 'Works of the Law' and MMT." *Biblical Archaeology Review* 20.6 (1994): 52–61, 82.

———. "4QMMT, Paul, and 'Works of the Law'." Pages 203–16 in *The Bible at Qumran: Text, Shape, and Interpretation*. Studies in the Dead Sea Scrolls and Related Literature. Edited by P.W. Flint. Grand Rapids: Eerdmans, 2001.

Adewuya, J. Ayodeji. *Holiness and Community in 2 Cor 6:14–7:1*. New York: P. Lang, 2001.

Aletti, Jean-Noël. "Saint Paul, exégète de l'Écriture." Pages 37–59 in *L'Écriture âme de la théologie: actes du Colloque tenu à Bruxelles du 17 au 19 septembre 1989*. Edited by R. Lafontaine et al. Institut d'Études Théologique 9. Bruxelles: Institut d'Études Théologique, 1990.

———. "Romains 4 et Genèse 17: Quelle énigme et quelle solution?", *Biblica* 84 (2003): 305–325.

Arcari, Luca. "Sui rapporti tra Apocalissi 'con viaggio ulraterreno' e 'senza viaggio ultraterreno'. Indagine per una 'storia' del 'genere apocalittico'." *Henoch* 26 (2004): 64–84.

Aristarchus of Samos, *A History of Greek Astronomy to Aristarchus, Together with Aristarchus's Treatise on the Sizes and Distances of the Sun and Moon, a new Greek text with translation and notes*. Edited by Sir Thomas Heath. Oxford: Clarendon Press, 1913.

Arnim, J. von. *Stoicorum veterum Fragmenta*. 4 vols. Leipzig, Teubner, 1903–24.

Attridge, Harold W. "Greek and Latin Apocalypses." Pages 159–186 in John J. Collins, ed., *Apocalypse: The Morphology of A Genre, Semeia* 14 (1979).

Auwers, J.-M. and A. Wénin, eds., *Lectures et relectures*, FS, P.-M. Bogaert. Bibliotheca ephemeridum theologicarum lovaniensium 144. Leuven 1999: University Press.

Avemarie, Frederick. "Paul and the Claim of the Law according to the Scripture: Leviticus 18:5 in Galatians 3:12 and Romans 10:5." Pages 125–48 in *The Beginnings of Christianity: A Collection of Articles*. Edited by J. Pastor and M. Mor. Jerusalem: Yad Ben-Zvi, 2005.

Baker, William R. "Did the Glory of Moses' Face Fade? A Reexamination of καταργέω in 2 Corinthians 3:7–18." *Bulletin for Biblical Research* 10 (2000): 1–5.

Balsdon, J.P.V.D. *Life and Leisure in Ancient Rome*. London: Bodley Head, 1969. Repr., London: Phoenix Press, 2002.

Balsdon, J.P.V.D., and Barbara M. Levick. "iuvenes." Pages 791–792 in *The Oxford Classical Dictionary*. 3d ed. Edited by Simon Hornblower and Antony Spawforth. Oxford: Oxford University Press, 1999.

Barbaglio, G., *La prima lettera ai Corinzi: Introduzione, versione e commento*. Scritti delle origini cristiane 16. Bologna: EDB, 1995.

———. *Gesù di Nazaret e Paolo: Confronto storico*. Bologna: EDB, 2006.

Barclay, J. *Jews in the Western Mediterranean Diaspora, from Alexander to Trajan [323 BCE to 117 CE]*. Berkeley: University of California Press, 1996.

———. "'Do We Undermine the Law?' A Study of Romans 14:1–15, 6." Pages 289–293 in *Paul and the Mosaic Law*. Edited by J.D.G. Dunn. WUNT 89. Tübingen: Mohr [Siebeck], 1996.

Barnes, T. "Legislation against the Christians." *Journal of Roman Studies* (1968): 32–50.

Barnett, Paul. *The Second Epistle to the Corinthians.* Grand Rapids, Mich.: Eerdmans, 1984.

Basta, Pasquale. *Gezerah Shawah: storia, forme e metodi dell'analogia biblica*. Subsidia Biblica 26. Roma: Editrice Pontificio Istituto Biblico, 2006.

———. *Abramo in Romani 4: l'analogia dell'agire divino nella ricerca esegetica di Paolo.* Analecta Biblica 168. Roma: Editrice Pontificio Istituto Biblico, 2007.

Bauckham, Richard. "Kingdom and Church According to Jesus and Paul." *Horizons in Biblical Theology: An International Dialogue* 18 (1996): 1–21.

Bauer, W., ed., with F.W. Gingrich and F.W. Danker. *A Greek-English Lexicon of the New Testament and Other Early Christian Literature.* Chicago: University of Chicago Press, 1979.

Baumgarten, Albert I., "The Name of the Pharisees." *Journal of Biblical Literature* 103 (1983): 411–428.

———. "The Pharisaic Paradosis." *Harvard Theological Review* 80 (1987): 63–77.

———. "Metaphors of Memory." Pages 77–89 in *Der Odem des Menschen ist eine Leuchte des Herrn: Aharon Agus zum Gedenken.* Edited by Ronen Reichman. Heidelberg: Universitätsverlag, 2006.

Beard, M. "Priesthood in the Roman Republic." Pages 47–48 in *Pagan Priests: Religion and Power in the Ancient World.* Edited by M. Beard and J. North. Ithaca: Cornell University Press, 1990.

Beck, Norman. *Mature Christianity in the 21st Century: The Recognition and Repudiation of the Anti-Jewish Polemic of the New Testament.* New York: Crossroad, 1994.

Belleville, Linda. *Reflections of Glory: Paul's Polemical Use of the Moses-Doxa Tradition in 2 Corinthians 3.1–18.* Journal for the Study of the New Testament, Supplement Series 52. Sheffield: Journal for the Study of the Old Testament Press, 1991.

Berger, K., "Jesus als Pharisäer und frühe Christen als Pharisäer." *Novum Testamentum* 30 (1988): 231–262.

Bettiolo, Paolo, Alda Kossova, Claudio Leonardi, Enrico Norelli, and Lorenzo Perrone, eds., *Ascensio Isaiae.* 2 vols. CCSA, 7–8. Turnhout: Brepols, 1995.

Betz, Hans Dieter, *The "Mithras Liturgy": Text, Translation, and Commentary.* Studien und Texte zu Antike und Christentum, 18. Tübingen: Mohr Siebeck, 2003.

Betz, Hans-Dieter, ed. *The Greek Magical Papyri in Translation, Including the Demotic Spells.* 2d ed. Chicago: University of Chicago Press, 1992.

Bieler, Ludwig. *THEIOS ANER: Das Bild des "Göttlichen Menschen" in Spätantike und Frühchristentum.* Unveranderter reprogafischer Nachdruck der Ausgabe: Wien, 1935 (Band I) und Wien, 1936 (Band II). Repr., Darmstadt : Wissenschaftliche Buchgesellschaft, 1967.

Bieringer, Reimund. "'Come and you will see' (John 1,39): Dialogical Authority and Normativity of the Future in the Fourth Gospel and in Religious Education." Pages 179–202 in *Hermeneutics and Religious Education.* Edited by H. Lombaerts and D. Pollefeyt. Leuven: Peeters, 2004.

Bieringer, Reimund and Mary Elsbernd. *Normativity of the Future: Reading Biblical and Other Authoritative Texts in an Eschatological Perspective.* Leuven, Paris and Walpole: Peeters, 2010.

Bieringer, Reimund and Jan Lambrecht. *Studies in 2 Corinthians.* Biblioteca Ephemeridum Theologicarum Lovaniensium 112. Leuven: Leuven University Press and Peeters, 1994.

Bieringer, Reimund, Pollefeyt, D. and F. Vandecasteele-Vanneuville, eds. *Anti-Judaism and the Fourth Gospel: Papers of the Leuven Colloquium, 2000.* Assen: Van Gorcum, 2001.

Blanton, Thomas R. IV. *Constructing a New Covenant: Discursive Strategies in the Damascus Document and Second Corinthians*. Wissenschaftliche Untersuchungen zum Neuen Testament, 2. Reihe 233. Tübingen: Mohr [Siebeck], 2007.

Boccaccini, G., *Middle Judaism: Jewish Thought, 300 B.C.E. to 200 C.E.* Minneapolis: Fortress, 1991.

———. "Esiste una letteratura farisaica?" *Ricerche storico bibliche* 11/2 (1999): 23–41.

Boismard, Marie-Émile. *Le texte occidental des Actes des Apôtres, edition nouvelle entièrement refondue*. EBib, nouvelle série 40. Paris: Gabalda, 2000.

Boismard, Marie-Émile and Arnaud Lamouille, *Les Actes des deux Apôtres*, vol. II. EBib, nouvelle série 13. Paris: Gabalda, 1990.

Bonner, Stanley F. *Education in Ancient Rome from the Elder Cato to the Younger Pliny*. London: Methuen, 1977.

Bonsirven, Joseph. *Exégèse Rabbinique et Exégèse Paulinienne*. Paris: Beauchesne, 1939.

Borgen, Peder. "Heavenly Ascent in Philo: An Examination of Selected Passages." Pages 246–268 in James H. Charlesworth and Craig A. Evans, eds., *The Pseudepigrapha and Early Biblical Interpretation*. Sheffield: Sheffield Academic Press, 1993.

Bousset, Wilhelm. "Die Himmelsreise der Seele." *Archiv für Religionswissenschaft* 4 (1901): 136–169; 228–273. Repr. Darmstadt: 1960.

Bovon, François. "'How Well the Holy Spirit Spoke Through the Prophet Isaiah to your Ancestors!' (Acts 28:25)." Pages 42–50 in idem, *New Testament Traditions and Apocryphal Narratives*. Princeton Theological Monograph Series 36. Allison Park, Pa.: Pickwick Publications, 1995.

Bray, Gerald. *1–2 Corinthians*. Ancient Christian Commentary on Scripture 7. Downers Grove: InterVarsity Press, 1999.

Bruce,F. F. *1 and 2 Thessalonians*. Word Biblical Commentary 45. Waco, Tex.: Word Books, 1982.

Büchler, A. "The Levitical Impurity of the Gentile in Palestine before the year 70." *Jewish Quarterly Review* 17 (1926): 1–81.

Burkett, Delbert. *An Introduction to the New Testament and the Origins of Christianity*. Cambridge: Cambridge University Press, 2002.

Carmichael, Calum. "Forbidden Mixtures." *Vetus Testamentum* 32 (1982): 394–415.

Carras, G.P., *Paul, Josephus and Judaism: The Shared Judaism of Paul and Josephus*. Oxford: Oxford University Press.

Casey, P.M., *From Jewish Prophet to Gentile God: The Origins and Development of New Testament Christology*. Louisville: Westminster-J. Knox, 1991.

Chadwick, H. "Oracles of the End in the Conflict of Paganism and Christianity in the Fourth Century" in: *Mémorial André-Jean Festugière: Antiquité paiënne et chrétienne* (Geneva: Patrick Cramer, 1984): 125-129.

Chaniotis, A. "The Jews of Aphrodisias: New Evidence and Old Problems." *Scripta Classica Israelica* (2002): 209–242.

Charlesworth, James H. "Paradise." Pages 154–155 in *Anchor Bible Dictionary*. Vol 5. New York: Doubleday, 1992.

Chernick, Michael L. "Internal Restraints on *Gezerah Shawah*'s Application." *Jewish Quarterly Review* 80 (1990): 253–282.

Christiansen, E. J. *The Covenant in Judaism and in Paul: A Study of Ritual Boundaries as Identity Markers*. Leiden: E.J. Brill, 1995.

Cicero, *La république. Tome II. Livres II-VI*. Translated by Esther Bréguet. Paris : Les Belles Lettres, 2002.

Cohen, Shaye J.D.*The Beginnings of Jewishness: Boundaries Varieties Uncertainties*. Berkeley: University of California, 1999.

Coleman, K. "Fatal Charades: Roman executions staged as mythological enactments." *Journal of Roman Studies* 80 (1990): 44–73.

Conzelmann, Hans. *A Commentary on the First Epistle to the Corinthians*. Hermeneia. Philadelphia: Fortress, 1975.

———. *Acts of the Apostles: A Commentary on the Acts of the Apostles*. Hermeneia. Philadelphia: Fortress, 1987.

Collins, James J., ed. "Apocalypse: The Morphology of A Genre." *Semeia* 14 (1979).

Colpe, Carsten. "Die 'Himmelreise der Seele' als philosophische und religionsgeschichtliche Problem." Pages 85–104 in Erich Fries, ed., *Festschrift für Joseph Klein zum 70*. Geburtstag. Göttingen: Vandenhoeck und Ruprecht 1967.

Comfort, Philip W., and David P. Barrett, eds. *The Complete Text of the Earliest New Testament Manuscripts*. Grand Rapids, Mich.: Baker Books, 1999.

Conche, Marcel, *Parménide: Le poème*. With fragments, Greek text, translation, introduction and commentary. Paris: PUF, 2004.

Coppens, Josef. "Miscellanées bibliques LXXX: Une diatribe antijuive dans 1 Thess. 2 :13–16." *Ephemerides theologicae lovanienses* 51 (1975): 90–95.

Couloubaritis, Lambros. *La pensée de Parménide. Trosième édition modifiée et augmentée de Mythe et Philosophie chez Parménide*. Bruxelles: Ousia, 2008.

Craffert, D.F., "The Pauline Movement and the First-Century Judaism: A Framework for Transforming the Issue", *Neotestamentica* 27 (1993): 247.
Cranfield, Charles E. B. "The Works of the Law in the Epistle to the Romans." *Journal for the Study of the New Testament* 43 (1991): 89–101.
Danby, Herbert. *The Mishnah*. Oxford: Oxford University Press, 1950.
Daube, David. *The New Testament and Rabbinic Judaism*. Salem: Ayer Company, 1984.
Davies, William D. *Paul and Rabbinic Judaism: Some Rabbinic Elements in Pauline Theology*. Mifflintown, Pa.: Siglar Press, 1998.
Dean-Otting, Mary. *Heavenly Journeys: A Study of the Motif in Hellenistic Jewish Literature*. Frankfurt: Peter Lang, 1984.
De Roo, Jacqueline C. R. "The Concept of 'Works of the Law' in Jewish and Christian Literature." Pages 116–47 in *Christian-Jewish Relationships through the Centuries*. Edited by S. E. Porter and B. W. R. Pearson. Sheffield: Sheffield Academic Press, 2000.
De Vuippens, Ildephonse. *Le Paradis Terrestre au troisième ciel. Exposé historique d'une conception chrétienne des premiers siècles*. Paris: Librairie Saint-François d'Assise; Freiburg: Librairie de l'Oeuvre de S.-Paul, 1925.
Deconick, April D. *Seek to See Him: Ascent and Vision Mysticism in the Gospel of Thomas*. Supplements to *Vigiliae Christianae* 33. Leiden: Brill, 1996.
Deines, Roland and Karl-Wilhelm Niebuhr, eds., *Philo und das Neue Testament: Wechselseitige Wahrnehmungen*. Tübingen: Mohr Siebeck, 2004.
Deissman, A. *Die neutestamentliche Formel 'In Christo Jesu'*. Marburg: Elwert, 1892.
Del Agua Pérez, Augustín. *El método midrásico y la exégesis del Nuevo Testamento*. Bibliotheca Midrásica 4. Valencia: Soler, 1985.
Destro, Adriana and Mauro Pesce. "Il profetismo e la nascita di una religione: il caso del Giovannismo." Pages 87–106 in Giovanni Filoramo, ed., *Carisma profetico, fattore di innovazione religiosa*. Brescia: Morcelliana, 2003.
———. "Come è nato il cristianesimo." *Annali di Storia dell'Esegesi* 21 (2004): 533–543.
———. "Constellations of Texts in Early Christianity: The Gospel of the Savior and Johannist Writings." *Annali di storia dell'Esegesi* 22 /2 (2005): 337–353.
———. "Continuity or Discontinuity Between Jesus and Groups of his Followers? Practices of Contact with the Supernatural." *Annali di Storia dell'Esegesi* 24 (2007): 37–58.

Diels, Hermann and Walther Kranz. *I presocratici: Testimonianze e frammenti*. Vol. 1. 8th ed. Bari-Roma: Laterza, 2004.

Dieterich, Albrecht. *Eine Mithrasliturgie*. 3rd ed. Edited by Otto Weinreich. Leipzig: Teubner, 1923.

Donaldson, Terence L. *Judaism and the Gentiles: Jewish Patterns of Universalism (to 135 CE)*. Waco, Tex.: Baylor University Press, 2007.

Donfried, Karl P. "Paul and Judaism: 1 Thessalonians 2:13–16 as a Test Case." *Interpretation* 38 (1984): 242–253.

———. "1 Thessalonians, Acts and the Early Paul." Pages 3–26 in *The Thessalonian Correspondence*. Edited by R. F. Collins. Leuven: Leuven University Press, 1990.

———. "Paul the Jew - But of What Sort?" Pages 11–27 in *Testimony and Interpretation: Early Christology in Its Judeo-Hellenistic Milieu*. Edited by J. Mrazek and J. Roskovec. FS, Pokorny; Edinburgh: T & T Clark, 2004.

———. *Paul, Thessalonica and Early Christianity*. Edinburgh and Grand Rapids: T. & T. Clark and Eerdmans, 2002.

———. "Rethinking Paul: On the Way Toward a Revised Paradigm." *Biblica* 87 (2006): 582–594.

———. and Johannes Beutler. *The Thessalonians Debate: Methodological Discord or Methodological Synthesis?* Grand Rapids: Eerdmans, 2000.

Döpp, Siegmar, and Wilhelm Geerlings. *Dictionary of Early Christian Literature*. New York: Crossroad, 2000.

Dunn, James D.G., "The New Perspective on Paul." *Bulletin of the John Rylands University Library of Manchester* 65/2 (1982) 95–122.

———. "Works of the Law and the Curse of the Law (Galatians 3.10–14)." *New Testament Studies* 31.4 (1985): 523–42.

———. *The Partings of the Ways Between Christianity and Judaism and their Significance for the Character of Christianity*. London: SCM Press, 1991.

———. "Yet Once More 'The Works of the Law': A Response." *Journal for the Study of the New Testament* 46 (1992): 99–117.

———. *The Theology of Paul the Apostle*. Grand Rapids: William B. Eerdmans, 1998.

Dunn, James D. G., ed. *Jews and Christians: The Parting of the Ways, AD 70 to 135*. Cambridge: Eerdmans, 1992.

———. *Paul and the Mosaic Law*. Tübingen: J.C. B. Mohr /Paul Siebeck, 1996.

Dupont-Sommer, André and Marc Philonenko, eds., *La Bible*. Écrits Intertestamentaires I. Paris: Gallimard, 1987.

Eisenbaum, Pamela. "Is Paul the Father of Misogyny and Antisemitism?" *Cross Currents* 50:4 (Winter, 2000):506–524.

Elliott, Mark Adam. *The Survivors of Israel: A Reconsideration of the Theology of pre-Christian Judaism.* Grand Rapids, Mich: Eerdmans, 2000.

Ellis, Edward E. *Paul's Use of the Old Testament.* Twin Brooks Series. Grand Rapids, Mich.: Baker Books, 1991.

Emmel, Steven. "The 'Gospel of the Savior': A New Witness to the Strasbourg Coptic Gospel." *Bulletin de l'AELAC* 12 (2000): 10–19.

———. "The Recently Published Gospel of the Savior ("Unbekanntes Berliner Evangelium"): Righting the Order of Pages and Events." *Harvard Theological Review* 95 (2000): 45–72.

———. "Unbekanntes Berliner Evangelium = The Strasbourg Coptic Gospel: Prolegomena to a New Edition of the Strasbourg Fragments." Pages 353–374 in Hans-Gebhardt Bethge, Steven Emmel, Karen L.King, and Imke Schletterer, eds. *For the Children, Perfect Instruction: Studies in Honor of Hans-Martin Schenke on the Occasion of the Berliner Arbeitskreis für koptisch-gnostiche Schriften's Thirtieh Year.* Leiden: Brill, 2000.

———. "Preliminary Reedition and Translation of the Gospel of the Savior: New Light on the Strasbourg Coptic Gospel and the Stauros-Text from Nubia." *Apocrypha* 14 (2003): 9–53.

———. "Ein altes Evangelium der Apostel taucht in Fragmenten aus Ägypten und Nubien auf." *Zeitschrift für Antikes Christentum* 9 (2005): 85–99.

Engberg-Pedersen, Troels. *Paul and the Stoics.* Edinburgh: T&T Clark, 2000.

Evans, Craig A. *To See and Not Perceive: Isaiah 6:9–10 in Early Jewish and Christian Interpretation.* Journal for the Study of the New Testament Supplement 64; Sheffield: JSOT Press, 1989.

Evans, Craig A. and Peter W. Flint, eds. *Eschatology, Messianism, and the Dead Sea Scrolls.* Grand Rapids, Mich.: Eerdmanns, 1997.

Evans, Craig A., and James A. Sanders, eds. *Paul and the Scripture of Israel.* Journal for the Study of the New Testament Supplement 83. Sheffield: Academic Press, 1993.

Evans, O.E. "Paul's Certainties: What God Requires of Man – Romans xiv. 14," *Expository Times* 69 (1957/58): 201–202.

Exegetical Dictionary of the New Testament. Edited by H. Balz, G. Schneider. ET. Grand Rapids: Eerdmans, 1990–1993.

Fabris, Rinaldo. "La Scrittura in Paolo e nelle comunità paoline." Pages 87–103 in *La Bibbia nell'antichità cristiana.* Edited by E. Norelli. La Bibbia nella storia 15/I. Bologna: Edizione Dehoniane Bologna, 1993.

Falk, Daniel. "Prayers and Psalms." Pages 7–57 in *The Complexities of Second Temple Judaism*. Edited by D. A. Carson, Peter T. O'Brien, and Mark A. Seifrid. *Justification and Variegated Nomism*. Vol 1. Wissenschaftliche Untersuchungen zum Neuen Testament, Second Series 140. Tübingen: Mohr Siebeck, 2001.

Faure, Patrick. *Pentecôte et parousie, Ac 1:6–3:26: L'église et le mystère d'Israël entre les textes alexandrin et occidental des Actes des Apôtres*. Ebib, nouvelle série 50. Paris: Gabalda, 2003.

Fee, Gordon. *Pauline Christology: An Exegetical-Theological Study*. Peabody, Mass.: Hendrickson, 2007.

Feiler, Bruce S. *Abraham: A Journey to the Heart of Three Faiths*. New York: William Morrow and Company, 2002.

Feldman, L.H., *Jew and Gentile in the Ancient World: Attitudes and Interaction from Alexander to Justinian*. Princeton: Princeton University Press, 1993.

Fitzmyer, Joseph A. *The Biblical Commission's Document "The Interpretation of the Bible in the Church"*. Text and Commentary. Subsidia Biblica 18; Editrice Pontificio Istituto Biblico, Roma 1995.

———. *First Corinthians*. Anchor Bible. New Haven: Yale University Press, 2008.

———. "Paul's Jewish Background and the Deeds of the Law." Pages 18–35 in Joseph A. Fitzmyer, *According to Paul: Studies in the Theology of the Apostle*. Mahwah, NJ: Paulist Press, 1993.

Flusser, David. "The Dead Sea Sect and pre-Pauline Christianity." Pages 23–74 in David Flusser, *Judaism and the Origins of Christianity*. Jerusalem: Magnes, 1988.

———. *Judaism of the Second Temple Period: I. Qumran and Apocalypticism*, Grand Rapids, Mich.: Eerdmans, 2007.

Fontaine, Jacques. *Tertulliani De Corona*. Collection Érasme; Paris: Presses universitaires de France, 1966.

Ford, J. M. "Saint Paul the Philogamist: 1 Cor VII in Early Patristic Exegesis," *New Testament Studies* 11 (1964–65): 326–348.

Fox, Robin Lane. *Pagans and Christians*. New York: Knopf, 1987.

Fredriksen, Paula. "Paul and Augustine: conversion narratives, orthodox traditions, and the retrospective self," *Journal of Theological Studies* (1986): 3–34.

———. "Judaism, the Circumcision of Gentiles, and Apocalyptic Hope: Another look at Galatians 1 and 2." *Journal of Theological Studies* (1991): 543–48.

———. *Jesus of Nazareth: King of the Jews*. New York: Knopf, 1999.

———. "Paul, Purity, and the 'Ekklesia' of the Gentiles." Pages 205–17 in *The Beginnings of Christianity: A Collection of Articles*. Edited by J. Pastor and M. Mor. Jerusalem: Yad Ben-Zvi, 2005.

———. "Mandatory Retirement: Ideas in the Study of Christian Origins whose Time has Come to Go," *Studies in Religion/Sciences Religieuses*, 35/2 (2006): 231–246.

———. *Augustine and the Jews: A Christian Defense of Jews and Judaism*. New York: Doubleday: 2008.

———. "The Philosopher's Paul and the Problem of Anachronism." Pages 61–73 in *Paul Among the Philosophers*. Bloomington: Indiana University Press, 2009.

Fredriksen, Paula. and O. Irshai, "Christian Anti-Judaism: Polemics and Policies, from the Second to the Seventh Century." *Cambridge History of Judaism* 4 (2006): 977–1034.

Freudmann, Lillian C. *Antisemitism in the New Testament*. Lanham: University Press of America, 1994.

Frey, Jörg. "Leidenskampf und Himmelreise. Das Berliner Evangelienfragment (Papyrus Berolensis 22220) und die Gethsemane-Tradition." *Biblische Zeitschrift* 46 (2002): 71–96.

———. "Paul's Jewish Identity." Pages 285–321 in *Jewish Identity in the Greco-Roman World / Jüdische Identität in der griechisch-römischen Welt*. Edited by Jörg Frey, Daniel R. Schwartz and Stephanie Gripenrung. Ancient Judaism and Early Christianity / Arbeiten zur Geschichte des antiken Jüdentums und des Urchristentums 71. Leiden and Boston: Brill, 2007.

Furnish, Victor Paul. *II Corinthians*. Anchor Bible. New York: Doubleday, 1984.

Gager, J. *The Origins of Anti-Semitism*. New York: Oxford University, 1983.

———. *Reinventing Paul*. Oxford: Oxford University Press, 2000.

Gallagher, Eugene V. *Divine Man or Magician?: Celsus and Origen on Jesus*. Society of Biblical Literature Dissertation Series 64. Missoula, Mont.: Society of Biblical Literature, 1982.

García Martínez, F. (ed). *The Dead Sea Scrolls Translated*. Translated by Wilfred G. E. Watson. Leiden: Brill, 1994 (electronic version).

Gasparro Sfameni, Giulia. *Oracoli, Profeti, Sibille: Rivelazione e salvezza nel mondo antico*, Roma: Libreria Ateneo Salesiano, 2002.

______, *I misteri di Mithra*, in A. Bottini (cur.), *Il rito segreto. Misteri in Grecia e a Roma*, Milano: Electa, 2005, 97-103.

Gilliard, Frank D. "The Problem of the Antisemitic Comma between 1 Thessalonians 2.14 and 15." *New Testament Studies* 35 (1989): 481–502.

Gillihan, Yonder M. "Jewish Laws on Illicit Marriage, the Defilement of Offspring, and the Holiness of the Temple: A New Halakic Interpretation of 1 Corinthians 7:14." *Journal of Biblical Literature* 121 (2002): 711–744.

Gnilka, Joachim. *Il vangelo di Matteo: testo greco e traduzione*. Translated by S. Cavallini and V. Gatti. Commentario Teologico del Nuovo Testamento I/I. Brescia: Paideia, 1990.

Goettsberger, Johann. "Die Hülle des Moses nach Exod 34 und 2 Kor 3." *Biblische Zeitschrift* 16 (1924): 1–17.

Goodblatt, D., "The Place of Pharisees in First Century Judaism: The State of the Debate." *Journal for the Study of Judaism in the Persian, Hellenistic, and Roman Periods* 20 (1989): 12–30.

Goodenough, Erwin R., and A.T. Kraabel, "Paul and the Hellenization of Christianity." Pages 23–68 in *Religions in Antiquity: Essays in Memory of Erwin Ramsdell Goodenough*. Edited by Jacob Neusner. Leiden: E. J. Brill, 1968.

Gooder, Paula R. *Only the Third Heaven? 2 Corinthians 12:1–10 and Heavenly Ascent*. London: T&T Clark, 2006.

Goodman, M. "The Persecution of Paul by Diaspora Jews." Pages 376-387 in *The Beginnings of Christianity: A Collection of Articles*. Edited by J. Pastor and M. Mor. Jerusalem: Yad Ben Zvi, 2005).

Gorman, Michael J. *Apostle of the Crucified Lord: A Theological Introduction to Paul and His Letters*. Grand Rapids and Cambridge: Eerdmans, 2004.

Goulder, Michael D. "Visions and Revelations of the Lord (2 Corinthians 12:1–10)." Pages 303–312 in Trevor J. Burke and John K. Elliott, eds., *Paul and the Corinthians: Studies on a Community in Conflict; Essays in Honour of Margaret Thrall*. Leiden: Brill, 2003.

Gruen, E. "Jewish Perspectives on Greek Culture and Ethnicity." Pages 361–364 in *Ancient Perceptions of Greek Ethnicity* (Cambridge, Mass.: Harvard University Press).

Gruen, E. *Diaspora: Jews amidst Greeks and Romans*. Cambridge: Harvard University Press, 2002.

Gruenwald, Ithamar. *Apocalyptic and Merkavah Mysticism*. Arbeiten zur Geschichte des Spätjudentums und Urchristentums 14. Leiden: Brill, 1980.

Guijarro Oporto, S. and Miquel Pericás, E., "Il cristianesimo nascente: delimitazione cronologica, fonti e metodologia." *Annali di storia dell'Esegesi* 21/2 (2004): 469–496.

Hafemann, Scott J. "The Glory and Veil of Moses in 2 Cor 3:7–14: An Example of Paul's Contextual Exegesis of the OT–A Proposal." *Horizons in Biblical Theology* 14 (1992): 31–49.

———. *Paul, Moses, and the History of Israel: The Letter/Spirit Contrast and the Argument from Scripture in 2 Corinthians 3*. Wissenschaftliche Untersuchungen zum Neuen Testament 81. Tübingen: Mohr [Siebeck], 1995.

Hagen, Victor Wolfgang von. *Introduction to* Incidents of Travel in Egypt, Arabia Petraea, and the Holy Land, *by John Lloyd Stephens*. Norman, Okla., University of Oklahoma Press, 1970. Repr., New York: Dover Publications, 1996.

Hallowell, A. Irving. "Ojibwa Ontology, Behavior, and World View." Pages 141–179 in Dennis Tedlock and Barbara Tedlock, eds. *Teachings from the American Earth*. New York: Liveright, 1975.

Halperin, David J. *The Merkabah in Rabbinic Literature*. American Oriental Series 62. New Haven: American Oriental Society, 1980.

Hamerton Kelly, R. and Scroggs, R. (eds.), *Jews, Greek and Christians: Religious Cultures in Late Antiquity*. FS W.D. Davies. Leiden: Brill, 1976.

Hani, Jean. *Plutarque: Le Démon de socrate* ; *Moralia*. Vol. 7. Paris: Les Belles Lettres, 2003.

Hanson, Anthony T. "Paul as Exegete and Theologian." Pages 201–224 in idem., *Studies in Paul's Technique and Theology*. London: SPCK, 1974.

Harrington, Hannah K. "Holiness and Law in the Dead Sea Scrolls Author(s)." *Dead Sea Discoveries* 8 (2002): 124–135.

Harris, Murray J. *The Second Epistle to the Corinthians: A Commentary on the Greek Text*. New International Greek Testament Commentary. Grand Rapids and Milton Keynes: Eerdmans and Paternoster, 2005.

Harvey, Graham. *Shamanism: A Reader*. London: Routledge, 2003.

Hauser, Hermann J. *Strukturen der Abschlusserzählung der Apostelgeschichte (Apg 28,16-31)*. Analecta Biblica 86. Rome: Biblical Institute Press, 1979.

Hayes, Christine. *Gentile Impurities and Jewish Identities: Intermarriage and Conversion from the Bible to the Talmud*. New York: Oxford University, 2002.

Hays, Richard B. *Echoes of Scripture in the Letters of Paul*. New Haven, CT: Yale University Press, 1989.

Hedrick, Charles W. and Paul Mirecki. The *Gospel of the Savior: A New Ancient Gospel*. California Classical Library. Sonora: Polebridge Press, 1999.

———. "Caveat to a 'Righted Order' of the Gospel of the Savior." *Harvard Theological Review* 96 (2003): 229–238.

Heininger, Bernhard. *Paulus als Visionär: Eine religionsgeschichtliche Studie*. Herders Biblische Studien 9. Herder: Freiburg u.a., 1996.

———. "Paulus und Philo als Mystiker? Himmelreisen in Vergleich (2Kor 12:2–4; SpecLeg III 1–6)." Pages 189-204 in *Philo und das Neue Testament: Wechselseitige Wahrnehmungen.* Edited by Roland Deines and Karl-Wilhelm Niebuhr. Tübingen: Mohr [Siebeck], 2004.

Hengel, Martin. *The Atonement: The Origins of the Doctrine in the New Testament.* Philadelphia: Fortress, 1981.

———. *The Pre-Christian Paul.* London: Trinity Press, 1991.

———. *Paulus zwischen Damaskus und Antiochien: die Unbekannte Jahre.* Wissenschaftliche Untersuchungen zum Neuen Testament 108. Tübingen: Mohr [Siebeck], 1998.

———. "The Beginnings of Christianity as a Jewish-Messianic and Universalistic Movement." Pages 85–100 in *The Beginnings of Christianity: A Collection of Articles.* Edited by J. Pastor and M. Mor. Jerusalem: Yad Ben-Zvi, 2005.

Hengel, M. and Deines, R., "E.P. Sander's 'Common Judaism', Jews, and the Pharisees." *Journal of Theological Studies* 46 (1995): 39–40.

Himmelfarb, Martha. *Ascent to Heaven in Jewish and Christian Apocalypses.* Oxford: Oxford University Press, 1993.

Hobbel, Arne J. "Hermeneutics in Talmud, Midrash and the New Testament." *Immanuel* 24/25 (1990): 132–146.

Hock, Ronald. *The Social Context of Paul's Ministry: Tentmaking and Apostleship.* Philadelphia: Fortress, 1980.

Hodge, C. *If Sons, Then Heirs: A Study of Kinship and Ethnicity in the Letters of Paul.* New York: Oxford University Press, 2007.

Holmstrand, Jonas. *Markers and Meaning in Paul: An Analysis of 1 Thessalonians, Philippians and Galatians.* Coniectanea neotestamentica or Coniectanea biblica: New Testament Series 28. Stockholm: Almquist & Wiksell International, 1997.

Holtz, G. *Damit Gott sei alles in allem: Studien zum paulinischen und frühjüdischen Universalismus.* Beihefte zur Zeitschrift für die neutestamentliche Wissenschaft 149. Berlin: De Gruyter, 2007.

Horn, F. W. "Paulus und der Herodianische Temple," *New Testament Studies* 53 (2007): 184–203.

House, C. "Defilement by Association: Some Insights from the Usage of KOINÓΣ/KOINÓΩ in Acts 10–11," *Andrews University Seminary Studies* 21 (1983): 145-153.

Houtman, C. "Another Look at Forbidden Mixtures." *Vetus Testamentum* 34 (1984): 226–228.

Hübner, H., *Das Gesetz bei Paulus. Ein Beitrag zum Werden der paulinischen Theologie.* Göttingen: Vandenhoeck & Ruprecht, 1982.

Hughes, Philip E. *Paul's Second Epistle to the Corinthians*. London: Marshall, Morgan & Scott, 1962.

Hurd, John C. "Paul Ahead of his Time: 1 Thess 2:13–16." Pages 21–36 in *Anti-Judaism in Early Christianity*. Edited by Peter Richardson and David Granskou. Waterloo, Ont: Wilfrid Laurier University Press, 1986.

Hurtado, L.W., *Lord Jesus Christ : Devotion to Jesus in Earliest Christianity*. Grand Rapids, Mich.: Eerdmans, 2003.

Isaac, B. *The Invention of Racism in Classical Antiquity*. Princeton: Princeton University Press, 2005.

Janowitz, Naomi. *The Poetics of Ascent, Theories of Language in a Rabbinic Ascent Text*. Albany: SUNY Press, 1989.

Jegher-Bucher, Verena. "'The Thorn in the Flesh'/'Der Pfahl im Fleisch': Considerations About 2 Corinthians 12:7–10 in Connection with 12:1–3." Pages 388–397 in Stanley E. Porter and Thomas H.Olbricht, eds., *The Rhetorical Analysis of Scripture. Essays from the 1995 London Conference. Journal for the Study of the New Testament Supplement* 146. Sheffield: Sheffield Academic Press, 1996.

Jenkins, Claude. "Origen on I Corinthians." *Journal of Theological Studies* 9 (1907–1908): 505–506.

Jeremias, Alfred. *Babylonisches im Neuen Testament*. Leipzig: Hinrichs'sche Buchhandlung, 1905.

Jeremias, Joachim. "Zur Gedankenführung in den paulinischen Briefen." Pages 269–276 in *Abba: Studien zur neutestamentlichen Theologie und Zeitgeschichte*. Göttingen: Vandenhoeck & Ruprecht, 1966.

———. "Paulus als Hillelit." Pages 88–94 in E.E. Ellis and E. Wilcox, eds., *Neotestamentica et Semitica*. FS M. Black. Edinburgh: T&T Clark, 1969.

Jewett, Robert. *The Thessalonian Correspondence: Pauline Rhetoric and Millenarian Piety*. Philadelphia: Fortress, 1986.

Johnson, Luke T. "The New Testament's Anti-Jewish Slander and the Conventions of Ancient Polemic." *Journal of Biblical Literature* 108 (1989): 419–441.

Johnston, George. "'Kingdom of God' Sayings in Paul's Letters." Pages 143–156 in *From Jesus to Paul: Studies in Honour of Francis Wright Beare*. Edited by Peter Richardson and John C. Hurd. Waterloo, Ont.: Wilfrid Laurier University Press, 1984.

Jones, C. *Kinship Diplomacy in the Ancient World*. Cambridge, Mass.: Harvard University Press, 1999.

Jossa, G., *Giudeo o cristiani? I seguaci di Gesù in cerca di una propria identità*. Sources bibliques 142. Brescia: Paideia, 2004.

Käsemann, E. *"Paul and Israel," New Testament Questions of Today*. Philadelphia: Fortress, 1969.

———. *Commentary on Romans*. Grand Rapids, Mich.: Eerdmans; London: SCM, 1980.

Kasher, Rimon. "The Interpretation of Scripture in Rabbinic Literature." Pages 547–594 in *Mikra: text, translation, reading and interpretation of the Hebrew Bible in ancient judaism and early christianity*. Edited by M. J. Mulder. Compendia rerum Iudaicarum ad Novum Testamentum. Section 2, Literature of the Jewish people in the period of the second Temple and the Talmud. Assen: Van Gorcum; Philadelphia: Fortress Press, 1988.

Kilgallen, John. "'And I Will Heal Them' (Acts 28:27)." Proceedings of the Irish Biblical Association 23 (2005): 87–105.

Kister, M. "'According to the Law of Moses and the Jews': The History of a Religious and Legal Formula." (Hebrew) Pages 202–208 in *Atara l'Haim: Studies in the Talmud and Medieval Rabbinic Literature in honor of Professor Haim Zalman Dimitrovky*. Jerusalem: Magnes, 2000.

Klawans, J. "Notions of Gentile Impurity in Ancient Judaism." *Association for Jewish Studies Review* 20:2 (1995): 285–312.

———. *Impurity and Sin in Ancient Judaism*. New York: Oxford University, 2000.

———. *Purity, Sacrifice, and the Temple*. New York: Oxford University, 2006.

Knohl, Israel, "'By Three Days, Live': Messiahs, Resurrection, and Ascent to Heaven in *Hazon Gabriel*." *The Journal of Religion* 88 (2008): 147–158.

Koch, Dietrich-Alex. *Die Schrift als Zeuge des Evangeliums: Untersuchungen zur Verwendung und zum Verständnis der Schrift bei Paulus*. Beiträge zur historischen Theologie 69. Tübingen: Mohr, 1986.

Koenig, John. *Jews and Christians in Dialogue: New Testament Foundations*. Philadelphia: Westminster, 1979.

Koet, Bart-Jan. "Paul in Rome (Acts 28:16–31): A Farewell to Judaism?" *Bijdragen: Tijdschrift voor filosofie en theologie* 48 (1987): 397–415.

Köhne, J. *Die Ehen zwischen Christen und Heiden in den ersten christlichen Jahrhunderten*. Paderborn: Bonifacius, 1931.

Kovacs, Judith L. *The Church's Bible: 1 Corinthians Interpreted by Early Christian Commentators*. Grand Rapids, Mich.: Eerdmans, 2005.

Kramer, Werner. *Christ, Lord, Son of God*. Studies in Biblical Theology 50; Naperville, Ill.: Allenson; London: SCM, 1966.

Kümmel, Werner G. *Introduction to the New Testament*. Translated by H. C. Kee. Heidelberg: Quelle and Meyer, 1973.

Laato, T. *Paul and Judaism: An Anthropological Approach*. Atlanta: Scholars Press, 1995.

Lambrecht, Jan. *Second Corinthians*. Sacra Pagina 8. Collegeville: Liturgical Press, 1999.

Lampe, Jeffrey S. "Is Paul Anti-Jewish? Testament of Levi 6 in the Interpretation of 1 Thess 2:13–16." *Catholic Biblical Quarterly* 65.3 (2003): 408–427.

Lanfranchi, Pier Luigi. "Il sogno di Mosè nell'Exagoge di Ezechiele il tragico." *Materia Giudaica* 8 (2003): 103–112.

Laughery, Gregory J. "Reading Ricoeur: Authors, Readers, and Texts." *European Journal of Theology* 9.2 (2000): 159–170.

Le Saint; William. *Tertullian Treatises on Marriage and Remarriage.* Ancient Christian Writers 13. Westminster, Md.: Newman Press, 1951.

Lentz, J.C., Jr. *Luke's Portrait of Paul.* Society for New Testament Studies Monograph Series 77. Cambridge: Cambridge University Press, 1993.

Léon-Dufour, X., *Condividere il pane secondo il Nuovo Testamento.* 2d edn. Leumann: LDC, 2005.

Lerner, Michel-Pierre. *Le monde des sphères : I. Genèse et triomphe d'une représentation cosmique.* Paris: Les Belles Lettres, 2008.

Levenskaya, I. *The Book of Acts in its Diaspora Setting.* Grand Rapids, Mich.: W.B. Eerdmans, 1996.

Levine, L. *The Ancient Synagogue.* New Haven: Yale University Press, 2000.

Lichtenberger, H. *Das Ich Adams und das Ich der Menschheit: Studien zum Menschenbild in Römer 7.* Wissenschaftliche Untersuchungen zum Neuen Testament 164. Tübingen: Mohr [Siebeck], 2004.

Lieberman, Saul. *Hellenism in Jewish Palestine: Studies in the Literary Transmission, Beliefs and Manners of Palestine in the I Century B.C.E.–IV Century C.E.* New York: Jewish Theological Seminary of America, 5722/1962.

———. *Greek in Jewish Palestine.* New York: Philipp Feldheim, 1965.

Lietaert Peerbolte, L.J., *Paul the Missionary.* Leuven: Peeters, 2003.

Lietzmann, Hans. *An die Korinther.* vierte von Werner G. Kümmel ergänzte Auflage. Handbuch zum Neuen Testament. Tübingen: Mohr Siebeck, 1949.

Lieu, J. "The Race of the God-fearers." *Journal of Theological Studies* 46 (1995): 483–501

Litwak, Kenneth D. "Echoes of Scripture? A critical survey of recent works on Paul's use of the Old Testament." *Currents in Research: Biblical Studies* 6 (1998): 260–288.

———. "One or Two Views of Judaism: Paul in Acts 28 and Romans 11 on Jewish Unbelief." *Tyndale Bulletin* 57 (2006): 228–249.

Lo Russo, Giacomo. *La Seconda Lettera ai Corinzi. Introduzione, versione e commento.* Bologna: EDB, 2007.

Löhr, H. "Speisenfrage und Tora im Judentum des Zweiten Tempels und im entstehenden Christentum," *Zeitschrift für die neutestamentliche Wissenschaft und die Kunde der älteren Kirche* 94 (2003): 17-37.

Luciano di Samosata. *Icaromenippo o l'uomo sopra le nubi*. Pages 847–885 in *Dialoghi di Luciano a cura di Vincenzo Longo, Volume secondo*. Torino: UTET, 1986.

Luck, Georg. *Arcana Mundi : Magic and the Occult in the Greek and Roman Worlds; A collection of Ancient Texts*. Baltimore: John Hopkins University Press, 1985.

Luckensmeyer, David. *The Eschatology of First Thessalonians*. Göttingen: Vandenhoeck & Ruprecht, 2009.

Maccoby, H. *The Mythmaker: Paul and the Invention of Christianity*. London: Weidenfeld & Nicolson, 1986.

———. 'Paul and the Eucharist', in *New Testament Studies* 37 (1991): 262–265.

MacDonald, Margaret. "Early Christian Women Married to Unbelievers." *Studies in Religion* 19 (1990): 221–234.

Macy Lesses, Rebecca. *Ritual to Gain Power: Angels, Incantations, and Revelation in Early Jewish Mysticism*. Harvard Theological Studies. Harrisburg, Pa.: Trinity Press International, 1998.

Manns, Frédéric. *Il Giudaismo: Ambiente e memoria del Nuovo Testamento*. Bologna: EDB, 1993.

———. "Paul e la lecture juive des Écritures." Pages 29–39 in *Atti del V Simposio di Tarso su S. Paolo Apostolo*. Edited by L. Padovese. Turchia: la Chiesa e la sua storia 12. Roma: Pontificio Ateneo Antoniano. Istituto Francescano di Spiritualità, 1998.

Marguerat, Daniel. "The Enigma of the Silent Closing of Acts." Pages 284–304 in *Jesus and the Heritage of Israel: Luke's Narrative Claim upon Israel's Legacy*. Edited by David P. Moessner. Luke the Interpreter of Israel 1. Harrisburg, Pa.: Trinity Press International, 1999.

Marrou, Henri. *A History of Education in Antiquity*. Translated by George Lamb. London: Sheed and Ward, 1956. Repr., 1981.

Marshall, Howard. *1 and 2 Thessalonians*. The New Century Bible Commentary. Grand Rapids, Mich.: Eerdmans, 1983.

Martin, Brice L., *Christ and the Law in Paul*. Novum Testamentum Supplement Series 62. Leiden: Brill, 1989.

Martin, Dale. *The Corinthian Body*. New Haven: Yale University Press, 1995.

Martyn, J. Louis. *Galatians*. Anchor Bible 33A. Garden City, N.Y.: Doubleday, 1997.

———. *Theological Issues in the Letters of Paul.* Edinburgh: T&T Clark, 1997.

Mason, S., *Flavius Josephus on the* Pharisees. A Composition-Critical Study. Leiden: Brill, 1991.

———. *Josephus, Judea, and Christian Origins: Methods and Categories.* Peabody, Mass.: Hendrickson, 2009.

McCullough, David. *John Adams.* New York: Simon & Schuster, 2001.

McKinnish Bridges, Linda. *1 & 2 Thessalonians.* Smyth & Helwys Bible Commentary. Macon: Smyth & Helwys, 2008.

Menoud, Philippe H. "L'écharde et l'ange satanique (2 Cor 12,7)." Pages 163–171 in *Studia Paulina: In honorem Johannis De Zwaan Septuagenarii.* Harlem: De Erven F.Bohn, 1953.

Metzger, Bruce M. "The Formulas Introducing Quotations of Scripture in the NT and the Mishnah." *Journal of Biblical Literature* 70 (1951): 297-307.

Michel, Otto. *Paulus und seine Bibel.* Beiträge zur Förderung Christlicher Theologie 2.18; Gütersloh: Bertelsman, 1929.

Milgrom, J. *Leviticus 1–16.* New York: Doubleday, 1991.

Millar, F. "The Imperial Cult and the Persecutions." Pages 145–175 in *Le culte des souverains dans l'empire Romain.* Entretiens Hardt vol. XIX. Vandoeuvres: Geneva, 1973.

Mimouni, S.C., "Les 'origines' du mouvement chrétien entre 30 et 135: Des réflexions et des remarques." *Annali di storia dell'Esegesi* 21/2 (2004): 449–467.

Morray-Jones, Christopher R.A. "Paradise Revisited (2 Cor 12:1–12): The Jewish Mystical Background of Paul's Apostolate. Part 1: The Jewish Sources; Part 2: Paul's Heavenly Ascent and its Significance." *Harvard Theological Review* 86 (1993): 177–217; 265–292.

Morris, Leon. *The First and Second Epistles to the Thessalonians.* Grand Rapids, Mich.: Eerdmans, 1959.

Müller, K., "Beobachtungen zum verhältnis von Torah und Halaka in frühjudischen Quellen." Pages 105–155 in I. Broer, ed., *Jesus und das jüdische Gesetz.* Stuttgart: Kohlhammer, 1992.

Munck, Johannes. *Christ and Israel: An Interpretation of Rom 9–11.* Translated by I. Nixon. Philadelphia: Fortress, 1967.

Munier, Charles. *Tertullien à son épouse.* Sources chrétiennes 273. Paris: Cerf, 1980.

Murphy-O'Connor, Jerome. *Paul the Letter-Writer: His World, His Opinions, His Skills.* Good News Studies 41. Collegeville, Minn.: Liturgical Press, 1995.

Nagel, Peter, "Gespräche Jesu mit seinem Jüngern vor der Auferstehung:

Zur Herkunft und Datierung des 'Unbekannten Berliner Evangelium'." *Zeitschrift für die neutestamentliche Wissenschaft und die Kunde der älteren Kirche* 94 (2003): 215–257.

Nanos, M. *The Mystery of Romans*. Minneapolis: Fortress Press, 1996.

———. "What Was at Stake in Peter's 'Eating with Gentiles' at Antioch." Pages 282–318 in *The Galatians Debate: Contemporary Issues in Rhetorical and Historical Interpretation*. Edited by M. D. Nanos. Peabody, Mass.: Hendrickson, 2002.

———. "The Inter- and Intra-Jewish Political Context of Paul's Letter to the Galatians." Pages 396–407 in *The Galatians Debate: Contemporary Issues in Rhetorical and Historical Interpretation*. Edited by M. D. Nanos. Peabody, Mass.: Hendrickson, 2002.

———. *The Irony of Galatians: Paul's Letter in First-century Context*. Minneapolis: Fortress Press, 2002.

———. "The Myth of the 'Law-Free' Paul Standing Between Christians and Jews," *Studies in Christian-Jewish Relations* 4 (2009): 1–21.

Naude, Jacobus A. "Holiness in the Dead Sea Scrolls." Pages 171–198 in *The Dead Sea Scrolls Fifty Years After Their Discovery*. Vol. 2. Edited by Peter W. Flint and J. VanderKam; Jersusalem: Israel Exploration Society, 2000).

Neugebauer, Otto, "The 'Astronomical' Chapters of the Ethiopic Book of Henoch (72 to 82). Translation and Commentary." Pages 386–415 in Matthew Black, ed., *The Book of Enoch or I Enoch*. Leiden: Brill, 1985.

Neusner, J., *The Rabbinic Traditions About the Pharisees Before 70*. 3 vols. Leiden: Brill, 1971.

Neusner J. and B. D. Chilton, eds., *In Quest of the Historical Pharisees*. Waco, Tex.: Baylor University Press, 2007.

Newton, Michael. *The Concept of Purity at Qumran and in the Letters of Paul*. Society for New Testament Studies Monograph Series 53. Cambridge: Cambridge University Press, 1985.

Nickelsburg, George W. E. *Resurrection, Immortality and Eternal Life in Intertestamental Judaism*. Harvard Theological Studies 26. Cambridge, Mass.: Harvard University Press, 2006.

Nobile, Marco. "Le citazioni veterotestamentarie di Paolo." Pages 21–27 in *Atti del VII Simposio di Tarso su S. Paolo Apostolo*. Edited by L. Padovese. Turchia: la Chiesa e la sua storia 16. Roma: Pontificio Ateneo Antoniano. Istituto Francescano di Spiritualità, 2002.

Nock, Arthur D. and André-Jean Festugière. *Corpus Hermeticum* I–XII. Paris: Les Belles Lettres, 1945.

———. *Corpus Hermeticum* XIII–XVIII. Paris: Les Belles Lettres, 1945.

———. *Corpus Hermeticum, Edizione e commento di, edizione dei testi copti e commento di Ilaria Ramelli.* Milano: Bompiani, 2005.

Oegema, Gerbern S. *Für Israel und die Völker: Studien zum alttestamentlich-jüdischen Hintergrund der paulinischen Theologie.* Novum Testamentum Supplements 95. Leiden: Brill, 1998.

Okeke, G. E. "1 Thessalonians 2:13–16: The Fate of the Unbelieving Jews." *New Testament Studies* 27 (1981): 127–36.

Omerzu, Heike. "Das Schweigen des Lukas. Überlegungen zum offenen Ende der Apostelgeschichte." Pages 127–156 in *Das Ende des Paulus. Historische, theologische und literaturgeschichtliche Aspekte.* Edited by Friedrich Wilhelm Horn. Beihefte zur Zeitschrift für die neutestamentliche Wissenschaft und die Kunde der älteren Kirche 106; Berlin and New York: Walter de Gruyter, 2001.

O'Neill, John. "'Did You Receive the Spirit by the Works of the Law?' (Gal 3:2): The Works of the Law in Judaism and the Pauline Corpus." *Australian Biblical Review* 46 (1998): 70–84.

Origene, *Contro Celso.* Edited by Pietro Ressa. Brescia: Morcelliana, 2000.

Orlov, Andrei A., *The Enoch-Metatron Tradition.* Tübingen: Mohr, 2005.

Overman, Andrew J., "Kata Nomon Pharisaios: a Short History of Paul's Pharisaism." Pages 180-193 in *Pauline Conversations in Context: Essays in Honor of Calvin J. Roetzel.* Edited by Calvin J Roetzel, Janice Capel Anderson, Philip Harl Sellew, Claudia Setzer. London; New York: Sheffield Academic Press, 2002.

Paddison, Angus. *Theological Hermeneutics and 1 Thessalonians.* Society for New Testament Studies Monograph Series 133. Cambridge: Cambridge University Press, 2005.

Panaino, Antonio. "Uranographica Uranica 1: The Three Heavens in the Zoroastrian Tradition and the Mesopotamian Background." Pages 215–219 in R. Gyselen, ed., *Au carrefour des religions: Mélanges offerts à Philippe Gignoux*, Res Orientales VII. Leuven: Peeters, 1995.

Pao, David W. *Acts and the Isaianic New Exodus.* Wissenschaftliche Untersuchungen zum Neuen Testament 2. Reihe 130. Tübingen: Mohr [Siebeck], 2000.

Parker, R. *Miasma: Pollution and Purification in Early Greek Religion.* New York: Oxford University, 1993.

Pate, C.M. *The Reverse of the Curse.* Wissenschaftliche Untersuchungen zum Neuen Testament 114. Tübingen: Mohr [Siebeck], 2000.

Patte, Daniel. "Anti-Semitism in the New Testament: Confronting the Dark Side of Paul and Matthew's Teaching." *CTSR* 78 (1988): 31–52.

Pearson, Birger A. "1 Thessalonians 2:13–16: A Deutero-Pauline Interpolation." *Harvard Theological Review* 64 (1971): 79–94.

Penna, Romano. "Atteggiamenti di Paolo verso l'Antico Testamento." Pages 436–469 in *L'Apostolo Paolo: studi di esegesi e teologia*. Parola di Dio. Seconda Serie 12. Cinisello Balsamo: Edizioni Paoline, 1991.

———. *I ritratti originali di Gesù Cristo: Inizi e sviluppi della cristologia neotestamentaria*. II, *Gli sviluppi*. San Paolo: Cinisello Balsamo, 1999.

———. *Vangelo e inculturazione: Studi sul rapporto tra rivelazione e cultura nel Nuovo Testamento*. San Paolo: Cinisello Balsamo, 2001.

Perrot, C. *Gesù Cristo e Signore dei primi cristiani: Una cristologia esegetica*. Rome: Borla, 2000.

Perrotta, R., *Hairésis: gruppi, movimenti e fazioni del giudaismo antico e del cristianesimo (da Filone Alessandrino a Egesippo)*. Bologna: EDB, 2008.

Pesce, Mauro, "Isaia disse queste cose perché vide la sua gloria e parlò di lui (Gv 12,41): Il *Vangelo di Giovanni* e *l'Ascensione di Isaia*." *Studia Patavina* 50 (2003): 649–666.

Philonenko, Marc. "Testament des douze patriarches." Pages 811–944 in André Dupont-Sommer and M.Philonenko, eds., *La Bible: Écrits Intertestamentaires*. Vol 1. Paris: Gallimard, 1987.

Pines, Shlomo. "Metamorphoses of the Notion of Freedom." *Iyyun* 33 (1984): 247–65 (in Hebrew).

Pitta, Antonio, "Il discorso del pazzo o periautologia immoderata? Analisi retorico-letteraria di 2 Cor 11,1–12,18." *Biblica* 87 (2006): 493–510.

———. *Lettera ai Galati: Introduzione, versione e commento*. Scritti delle origini cristiane 9. 3d ed. Bologna: EDB, 2009.

———. *Lettera ai Romani: Nuova versione, introduzione e commento*. Linguistica Biblica NT 6. 3d ed. Milano: Paoline, 2009.

———. "Paolo e il giudaismo farisaico." *Ricerche storico-bibliche* 11 (1999): 89–106.

———. *Paolo: La Scrittura e la Legge*. Studi Biblici 57. Bologna: EDB, 2009.

———. *La seconda lettera ai Corinzi*. Roma: Borla, 2006.

———. "The Strong, the Weak and the Mosaic Law in the Christian Communities of Rome (Rom. 14:1–15:13." Pages 90–102 in J. Zangenberg and M. Labahn, eds., *Christians as a Religious Minority in a Multicultural City* Journal for the Study of the New Testament: Supplement Series 243. London: T&T Clark, 2004.

Plag, Christoph. "Paulus und die *Gezera schawa*: Zur Übernahme rabbinischer Auslegungskunst." *Judaica* 50 (1994): 135–140.

Plato. *La repubblica*. Edited by Giuseppe Lozza. Milano: Mondadori, 1990.

Plisch, Uwe-Karsten. *Verborgene Worte Jesu – verworfene Evangelien. Apokryphe Schriften des frühen Christentums*. Second Edtion. Berlin: Brennpunkt, 2002.

———. "Zu einigen Einleitungsfragen Berliner Evangeliums (UBE)." *Zeitschrift für Antikes Christentum* 9 (2005): 64–84.

Plummer, Alfred. *A Critical and Exegetical Commentary on the Second Epistle of St Paul to the Corinthians.* International Critical Commentary. New York: Scribner's, 1915.

Plutarch. *On the Sign of Socrates* (*De genio Socratis*). Pages 361–598 in *Plutarch's Moralia, VII.* Translated by Phillip H. De Lacy and Benedict Einarso. Loeb Classical Library. Cambridge, Mass.: Harvard University Press, 1968.

———. *Il Demone di Socrate : I ritardi della punizione divina, con un saggio di Dario del Corno.* Milano: Adelphi, 2005.

———. *Oeuvres Morales, Tome VIII.* Translated by Jean Hani. Paris: Les Belles Lettres, 2003.

Pontifical Biblical Commission. *The Jewish People and their Sacred Scriptures in the Christian Bible.* Città del Vaticano: Libreria Editrice Vaticana, 2002.

Porcher, Marie-Jo. "Quelques considérations sur l'usage du Psaume 32 dans l'Épître aux Romains (Rm 4,1-12)." *Revue des sciences religieuses* 77 (2003): 552–564.

Porfirio. *L'antro delle ninfe.* Edited by Laura Simonini. Milano: Adelphi, 1986.

Porter, Stanley E. *Paul in Acts.* Library of Pauline Studies. Peabody, Mass.: Hendrickson, 2001. Reprint of *The Paul of Acts: Essays in Literary Criticism, Rhetoric and Theology.* Wissenschaftliche Untersuchungen zum Neuen Testament 115. Tübingen: Mohr [Siebeck], 1999.

Potter, D. "Martyrdom as Spectacle." Pages 53–88 in *Theatre and Society in the Classical World.* Ann Arbor: University of Michigan Press, 1993.

Preisendanz, Karl - Diehl, Erich - Eitrem, Sam - Jacobi Aldolf (Hrsg.), *Papyri graecae magicae: Die griechischen Zauberpapyri.* Leipzig: Teubner, 1931.

Preisendanz, Karl - Henrichs Albert (Hrsg.), *Papyri graecae magicae: Die griechischen Zauberpapyri*, vol. 1. Stuttgart: Teubner, 2 Aufl. 1973.

Quispel, Gilles. "L'extase de Saint Paul." Pages 381–392 in A. A. Shismanian and D. Shismanian, eds., *Ascension et Hypostases initiatiques de l'âme: Mystique et eschatologie à travers les traditions religieuses. Tome I. Acts du Colloque internationale d'histoire des religions "Psychanodia."* Paris: Les Amis de Ioan P.Couliano, 2006.

Räisänen, H. *Paul and the Law.* Wissenschaftliche Untersuchungen zum Neuen Testament 29. 2d ed. Tübingen: Mohr [Siebeck], 1987.

———. *Römer 9–11 Analyse eines geistingen Ringen.* Aufstieg und Niedergang der römischen Welt: Geschichte und Kultur Roms im Spiegel der neueren Forschung II 25.4, 1987.

———. *Jesus, Paul and Torah: Collected Essays.* Journal for the Study of the New Testament Supplement Series 43. Sheffield: Sheffield Academic, 1992.

———. "Did Paul Expect an Earthly Kingdom?" Pages 2–20 in *Paul, Luke and the Graeco-Roman World: Essays in Honour of Alexander J.M. Wedderburn.* Edited by A. Christophersen et al. Journal for the Study of the New Testament Supplement Series 217; London: Sheffield Academic Press, 2002.

Reed, A. "The Trickery of the Fallen Angels and the Demonic Mimesis of the Divine: Aetiology and Polemics in the Writings of Justin Martyr." *Journal of Early Christian Studies* 12 (2004): 141–171.

Reitzenstein, Richard A. *Hellenistic Mystery-Religions: Their Basic Ideas and Significance.* Translated by J. E. Steely. Pittsburgh Theological Monograph Series 15. Pittsburgh: Pickwick Publications, 1978.

Reynolds, J. and R. Tannenbaum, *Jews and Godfearers at Aphrodisias.* Cambridge: Cambridge Philological Society, 1987.

Riaud, Jean, *Apocalypse grècque de Baruch,* in: André Dupont-Sommer and Marc Philonenko, eds., *La Bible: Écrits Intertestamentaires I.* Paris, Gallimard, 1987, 1141-1164.

Richard, Earl J. *First and Second Thessalonians.* Collegeville, Minn.: Liturgical Press, 1995.

Ricoeur, Paul. "Contribution d'une réflexion sur le language à une théologie de la parole." Pages 301–320 in *Exégèse et Herméneutique : Parole de Dieu.* Edited by Xavier Léon-Dufour. Paris: Seuil, 1971.

———. *Interpretation Theory: Discourse and Surplus of Meaning.* Fort Worth, Tex.: Christian University Press, 1976.

———. "Hermeneutics and the Critique of Ideology." Pages 270–307 in idem., *From Text to Action.* Translated by Kathleen Blamey and John B. Thompson. Evanston, Ill.: Northwestern University Press, 1991.

Ricoeur, P. and A. LaCoque. *Penser La Bible.* Paris: Seuil, 1998.

Rist, J. M. *Stoic Philosophy.* Cambridge: Cambridge University Press, 1969.

Rives, J. "The Decree of Decius and the religion of the empire." *Journal of Roman Studies* 89 (1999): 135–154.

———. *Religion in the Roman Empire.* Oxford: Blackwell, 2007.

Rivkin, E., "Defining the Pharisees: the Tannaitic Sources." *Hebrew Union College Annual* 40–41 (1969–1970): 205–249.

———. *The Shaping of Jewish History: A Radical New Interpretation.* New York: Scribner, 1971.

Robbins, Vernon K., "The Legacy of 2 Corinthians 12:2–4 in the Apocalyse of Paul." Pages 327–339 in Trevor J. Burke and John K. Elliott, eds., *Paul and the Corinthians: Studies on a Community in Conflict; Essays in Honour of Margaret Thrall.* Leiden: Brill, 2003.

Robertson, Archibald, and Alfred Plummer. *A Critical and Exegetical Commentary on the First Epistle of St Paul to the Corinthians.* International Critical Commentary. New York: Scribner's, 1911.

Rohde, Erwin. *Psyche: The Cult of Souls and Belief in Immortality Among the Greeks.* New York: Harper and Row, 1966.

Romanello, S., "Paolo e la Legge: Prolegomeni a una riflessione organica." *Rivista biblica italiana* 54 (2006): 321–356.

Rosner, Brian S. "'Written for Us': Paul's view of Scripture." Pages 81–105 in *A Pathway into the Holy Scripture.* Edited by P. E. Satterthwaite and D. F. Wright. Grand Rapids, Mich.: Eerdmans, 1994.

Ruiz, Jean-Pierre. "Hearing and Seeing but not Saying: A Look at Revelation 10:4 and 2 Corinthians 12:4." Pages 182–202 in *Society of Biblical Literature Seminar Papers.* Atlanta, Ga.: Scholars Press, 1994.

Ruzer, Serge. "The Death Motif in Late Antique Jewish Teshuva Narrative Patterns and in Paul's Thought." Pages 151–65 in *Transforming the Inner Self in Ancient Religions.* Edited by J. Assman and G. G. Stroumsa. Leiden: Brill, 1999.

———. "The Seat of Sin in Early Jewish and Christian Sources." Pages 367–91 in *Transforming the Inner Self in Ancient Religions.* Edited by J. Assman and G. G. Stroumsa. Leiden: Brill, 1999.

———. "Antitheses in Matthew 5: Midrashic Aspects of Exegetical Techniques." Pages 11–34 in Serge Ruzer, ed., *Mapping the New Testament: Early Christian Writings as a Witness for Jewish Biblical Exegesis.* Leiden: Brill, 2007.

———. "Crucifixion: The Search for a Meaning vis-à-vis Biblical Prophecy. From Luke to Acts." Pages 179–213 in Serge Ruzer, ed., *Mapping the New Testament: Early Christian Writings as a Witness for Jewish Biblical Exegesis.* Leiden: Brill, 2007.

———. "The New Covenant, the Reinterpretation of Scripture and Collective Messiahship." Pages 215–39 in Serge Ruzer, ed., *Mapping the New Testament: Early Christian Writings as a Witness for Jewish Biblical Exegesis.* Leiden: Brill, 2007.

Sacchi, Paolo. *Apocrifi dell'Antico Testamento.* Vol. 1. Torino : UTET, 1981.

———. *Storia del Secondo Tempio: Israele tra VI secolo a.C. e I secolo d.C.* Torino: SEI, 1994.

Saldarini, Anthony J. "Apocalypse and 'Apocalyptic' in Rabbinic Literature and Mysticism." Pages 187–205 in John J. Collins, ed., *Apocalypse: The Morphology of A Genre, Semeia* 14 (1979).
———. *Pharisees, Scribes and Sadducees in Palestinian Society: A Sociological Approach*. Edinburgh: T&T Clark, 1989.
Sanders, E. P. *Paul and Palestinian Judaism*. London and Philadelphia: SCM and Fortress, 1977.
———. *Paul, the Law, and the Jewish People*. Philadelphia: Fortress, 1983.
———. *Jewish Law from Jesus to the Mishnah*. Philadelphia: Trinity Press International, 1990.
———. *Paul*. Past Masters. Oxford: Oxford University Press, 1991; repr. 1996; *Ibid*. Very Short Introductions. OUP, 2001; *Ibid*. A Brief Insight. New York: Sterling Publishing, 2009.
———. *Judaism: Practice and Belief, 63 BC –66 CE*. Philadelphia: Trinity Press International; London: SCM, 1992.
———. "Reflections on Anti-Judaism in the New Testament and Christianity." Pages 265–286 in *Anti-Judaism and the Gospels*. Edited by William R. Farmer. Harrisburg, Pa.: Trinity Press International, 1999.
———. "God Gave the Law to Condemn: Providence in Paul and Josephus." Pages 78–97 in *The Impartial God: Essays in Biblical Studies in Honor of Jouette M. Bassler*. Edited by Calvin J. Roetzel and Robert L. Foster. Sheffield: Sheffield Phoenix Press, 2007.
———. "Paul," *Encyclopaedia Britannica*. Ultimate CD ROM, 2007, disc 2.
———. "Did Paul's Theology Develop?" Pages 325–350 in *The Word Leaps the Gap. Essays on Scripture and Theology in Honor of Richard B. Hays*. Edited by J. Ross Wagner, A. Katherine Grieb, and C. Kavin Rowe. Grand Rapids, Mich.: Eerdmans, 2008.
———. "Covenantal Nomism Revisited." *Jewish Studies Quarterly* 16 (2009): 23–55.
———. "Paul between Judaism and Hellenism." Pages 74–90 in *St. Paul Among the Philosophers*. Edited by John D. Caputo & Linda Martin Alcoff. Bloomington: Indiana University Press, 2009.
Sanders, James A. "Paul and Theological History." Pages 52–57 in *Paul and the Scripture of Israel*. Edited by C. A. Evans and J. A. Sanders. Journal for the study of the New Testament. Supplement Series 83. Sheffield: JSOT Press, 1993.
Saunders, Jason L. *Greek and Roman Philosophy after Aristotle*. London: Collier-Macmillan, 1966.
Schäfer, Peter. "New Testament and Hekhalot Literature: The Journey into Heaven in Paul and in Merkavah Mysticism." Pages 125–172 in Peter Schäfer, ed., *Hekhalot Studies*. Tübingen: Mohr, 1988.

———. "Der vorrabinische Pharisäismus." Pages 125–172 in M. Hengel and U. Heckel, eds., *Paulus und das antike Judentum.* Wissenschaftliche Untersuchungen zum Neuen Testament 58. Tübingen: Mohr [Siebeck] 1991.

Schäfer, P. *Judeophobia.* Cambridge, Mass.: Harvard University Press, 1997.

Schenke, Hans-Martin. "Das sogenannte 'Unbekannte Berliner Evangelium' (UBE)." *Zeitschrift für Antikes Christentum* 2 (1998): 27–34.

Schiffman, Lawrence H. *Reclaiming the Dead Sea Scrolls: The History of Judaism, the Background of Christianity, the Lost Library of Qumran.* Philadelphia and Jerusalem: The Jewish Publication Society, 1994.

Schlier, H. *Der Römerbrief.* Herders theologischer Kommentar zum Neuen Testament 6; Freiburg: Herder, 1977.

Schlueter, Carol J. *Filling Up the Measure: Polemical Hyperbole in 1 Thessalonians 2.14–16.* Journal for the Study of the New Testament: Supplement Series 98. Sheffield: Sheffield Academic Press, 1994.

Schmidt, Daryl. "1 Thess 2.13–16: Linguistic Evidence for an Interpolation." *Journal of Biblical Literature* 102 (1983): 269–279.

Schoeps, Hans-Joachim. *Paulus: die Theologie des Apostels im Lichte der jüdischen Religionsgeschichte.* Tübingen: Mohr, 1959.

Scholem, Gerschom. *Jewish Gnosticism, Merkabah Mysticism and the Talmudic Tradition.* 2d ed. New York: Jewish Theological Seminary of America, 1965.

Schulz, Siegfried. "Die Decke des Moses. Untersuchungen zu einer vorpaulinischen Überlieferung in II Cor 3.7–18." *Zeitschrift für die neutestamentliche Wissenschaft und die Kunde der älteren Kirche* 49 (1958): 1–30.

Schürer, E. and G. Vermes et al., *A History of the Jewish People in the Age of Jesus Christ.* 3 vols. Edinburgh: T&T Clark, 1973–1987.

Schwartz, Daniel R. "The End of the *Gê.*" *Journal of Biblical Literature* 105 (1986): 669–676.

———. "Law and Truth: On Qumran-Sadducean and Rabbinic Views of Law." Pages 229 – 40 in *The Dead Sea Scrolls: Forty Years of Research.* Edited by D. Dimant and U. Rappaport. Leiden: Brill and Jerusalem: Yad ben Zvi, 1992.

———. "Josephus on the Pharisees as Diaspora Jews," Pages 137–146 in *Josephus und das Neue Testament: Wechselseitige Wahrnehmungen.* Wissenschaftliche Untersuchungen zum Neuen Testament 209. Edited by C. Böttrich and J. Herzer. Tübingen: Mohr Siebeck, 2007.

———. "On Pharisees and Sadducees in the Mishnah: From Composition Criticism to History." Pages 140–144 in *Judaistik und Neutestamentliche Wissenschaft.* Forschungen zur Religion und Literatur des Alten und Neuen Testaments 226. Edited by L. Doering, F. Wilk, and H.-G. Waubke. Göttingen: Vandenhoeck & Ruprecht, 2007.

Schwartz, Jacques. *Biographie de Lucien de Samosate.* Collection Latomus, Vol. 83. Bruxelles: Latomus, 1965.

Schwartz, Seth. *Imperialism and Jewish Society, 200 B.C.E. to 640 C.E.* Princeton: Princeton University Press, 2001.

Schweitzer, Albert, *Die Mystik des Apostels Paulus.* Tübingen: Mohr, 1930.

———. *The Mysticism of Paul the Apostle.* Translated by William Montgomery. 2d ed. Repr., 1956. London: A. & C. Black, 1953.

Scott, James M. "For as Many as Are of Works of the Law Are under a Curse (Galatians 3.10)." Pages 187–221 in *Paul and the Scriptures of Israel.* Journal for the Study of the New Testament Supplementary Series 83. Edited by C. A. Evans and J. A. Sanders. Sheffield: Sheffield Academic, 1993.

———. "The Triumph of God in 2 Cor 2.14: Additional Evidence of Merkabah Mysticism in Paul." *New Testament Studies* 42 (1996): 260–281.

———. "Throne-Chariot Mysticism in Qumran and in Paul." Pages 101–119 in *Eschatology, Messianism, and the Dead Sea Scrolls.* Edited by Craig A. Evans and Peter W. Flint. Grand Rapids, Mich.: Eerdmanns, 1997.

Segal, Alan F. "Heavenly Ascent in Hellenistic Judaism, Early Christianity and their Environment." *Aufstieg und Niedergang der römischen Welt: Geschichte und Kultur Roms im Spiegel der neueren Forschung* II.23.2. Berlin: de Gruyter, 1980, 1333-1394.

———. "Torah and *Nomos* in Recent Scholarly Discussion." *Studies in Religion/Sciences religieuses* 13.1 (1984): 19–27.

———. *Rebecca's Children: Judaism and Christianity in the Roman World.* Cambridge, Mass.: Harvard University Press, 1986.

———. *Paul the Convert: The Apostolate and Apostasy of Saul the Pharisee.* New Haven, Conn.: Yale University Press, 1990.

———. "Paul and Ecstasy." Pages 555–580 in *Society of Bibical Literature Seminar Papers 1996.* Atlanta, Ga.: Scholars Press, 1996.

Seifrid, M.A., *Justification by Faith: The Origin and Development of a Central Pauline Theme.* Novum Testamentum Supplement 68. Leiden: Brill, 1992.

Seneca, *Consolazione a Marcia; Della vita felice; Della vita appartata; Della tranquillita dell'animo; Della brevita della vita; Consolazione a Polibio; Consolazione a Elvia.* Edited by Giovanni Viansino. Milano: Mondadori, 1990.

———. *I Dialoghi. Volume secondo.* Edited by Giovanni Viansino. Milano: Mondadori, 1993.

———. *Dialogues: Consolations.* Translation by René Waltz. Paris : Les Belles Lettres, 2003.

Sievers, J., "Who Were the Pharisees?" Pages 137–155 in J.H. Charlseworth and L.L. Johns, eds., *Hillel and Jesus: Comparative Studies of Two Major Religious Leaders*. Minneapolis: Fortress Press, 1997.

Simpson, John W. *The Future of non-Christian Jews: 1 Thessalonians 2:15–16 and Romans 9–11*. Ann Arbor, Mich.: University Microfilms International, 1990.

Simon, M. *Verus Israel*. London: Littman Library of Jewish Civilization, 1986.

Slomovic, Elieser. "Toward an Understanding of the Exegesis of the Dead Sea Scrolls." *Revue de Qumran* 7 (1969–1971): 3–15.

Smith, Morton. "Observations on Hekhalot Rabbati." Pages 142–60 in Altmann Alexander, ed. *Biblical and Other Studies*. Cambridge, MA: Cambridge University Press, 1963.

———. "Prolegomena to a Discussion of Aretologies, Divine Men, the Gospels and Jesus." *Journal of Biblical Literature* 90 (1971): 174–99.

———. "Ascent to the Heavens and the Beginning of Christianity." Pages 47–67 in Morton Smith. *Studies in the Cult of Yahweh, Volume Two: New Testament, Early Christianity, and Magic*. Edited by Shaye J.D. Cohen. Leiden: Brill, 1996.

———. "Two ascended to Heaven: Jesus and the Author of 4Q491." Pages 68–78 in Morton Smith, ed., *Studies in the Cult of Yahweh, Volume Two: New Testament, Early Christianity, and Magic*. Edited by Shaye J.D. Cohen. Leiden: Brill, 1996.

Soards, Marion L. *The Speeches in Acts: Their Content, Context, and Concerns*. Louisville, Ky.: Westminster/John Knox Press, 1994.

Söding, Thomas. "Heilige Schriften für Israel und die Kirche. Die Sicht des Alten Testaments bei Paulus." Pages 222–247 in *Das Wort vom Kreuz: Studien zur paulinischen Theologie*. Wissenschaftliche Untersuchungen zum Neuen Testament 93. Tübingen: Mohr, 1997.

Souter, Alexander. *Pelagius's Expositions of Thirteen Epistles of St Paul*. 3 vols. Texts and Studies 9; Cambridge: Cambridge University Press, 1922–1931.

Staab, Karl. *Pauluskommentare aus der griechischen Kirche*. Münster in Westf: Aschendorff, 1933.

Stanley, Christopher D. *Paul and the Language of Scripture: citation technique in the Pauline Epistles and contemporary literature*. Society for New Testament Studies Monograph Series 74. Cambridge: Cambridge University Press, 1992.

Stegemann, E.W. and W. Stegemann. *Urchristliche Sozialgeschichte. Die Anfänge im Judentum und die Christusgemeinde in der mediterranen Welt*. Stuttgart: Kohlhammer, 1995.

Stemberger, Günter. *Pharisäer, Sadduzäer, Essener*. Stuttgart: Katholisches Bibelwerk, 1993.

———. *Ermeneutica ebraica della Bibbia*. Translated by V. Gatti. Studi Biblici 127. Brescia: Paideia Editrice, 2000.

Stendhal, Krister. *Paul Among Jews and Gentiles and other Essays*. Philadelphia: Fortress Press, 1976.

———. *Final Account: Paul's Letter to the Romans*. Minneapolis: Augsburg Fortress, 1995.

Stern, Menahem. *Greek and Latin Authors on Jews and Judaism*. 3 vols. Jerusalem: Israel Academy of Sciences, 1974–1984.

Steyn, Gert J. *Septuagint Quotations in the Context of the Petrine and Pauline Speeches of the Acta Apostolorum*. Biblical Exegesis and Theology 12. Kampen: Kok Pharos, 1995.

Stockhausen, Carol Kern. *Moses' Veil and the Glory of the New Covenant: The Exegetical Substructure of II Cor. 3,1–4,6*. Analecta Biblica 116. Roma: Pontificio Istituto Biblico and Biblical Institute Press, 1989.

Stowers, Stanley. *A Rereading of Romans: Justice, Jews, and Gentiles*. New Haven & London: Yale University Press, 1994.

Tabor, James D. "Returning to the Divinity: Josephus's Portrayal of the Disappearance of Enoch, Elijah, and Moses." *Journal of Biblical Literature* 108 (1989): 225–38.

———. *Things Unutterable: Paul's Ascent to Paradise in its Greco-Roman, Judaic, and Early Christian Contexts*. Lanham, MD: University Press of America, 1986.

———. "Heaven, Ascent to." Pages 91–94 in *Anchor Bible Dictionary*. Vol. 3. Edited by D. N. Freedman. 6 vols. New York, 1992.

Talbot, Eugène. *Oeuvres complètes de Lucien de Samosate*. Translated with an introduction and notes. Paris: Hachette, 1912.

Talmon, Shemaryahu. "The Community of the Renewed Covenant." Pages 3–24 in *The Community of the Renewed Covenant: The Notre Dame Symposium on the Dead Sea Scrolls*. Edited by Eugene Ulrich and James VanderKam (Christianity and Judaism in Antiquity Series, 10; Notre Dame, Indiana: University of Notre Dame, 1994.

Tassin, C., "Paul dans le monde Juif du Ier siècle." Pages 176–181 in J. Schlosser, ed., *Paul de Tarse : Congrès de l'ACFEB (Strasbourg 1995)*. Lectio divina 165. Paris: Cerf, 1996.

Tatum, Gregory Tatum. *New Chapters in the Life of Paul: The Relative Chronology of His Career*. Catholic Biblical Quarterly Monograph Series 41. Washington DC: Catholic Biblical Association, 2006.

Theissen, Gerd "Judentum und Christentum bei Paulus. Sozialgeschichtliche Überlegungen zu einem Beginnenden Schisma." Pages 331–356 in M. Hengel and U. Heckel, eds., *Paulus und das antike Judentum*, Wissenschaftliche Untersuchungen zum Neuen Testament 58, Tübingen: Mohr [Siebeck], 1991.

Theological Dictionary of the New Testament. Edited by G. Kittel and G. Friedrich. Translated by G. W. Bromiley. 10 vols. Grand Rapids, 1964–1976.

Thomas, W.H.G. "Apostolic Arithmetic: A Pauline Word-Study," *Expository Times* 17 (1906): 211–214.

Thrall, Margaret E. *A Critical and Exegetical Commentary on The Second Epistle to the Corinthians.* 2 vols. *International Critical Commentary.* Edinburgh: T&T Clark, 1994-2000.

Thurén, L.T., *Derhetorizing Paul: A Dynamic Perspective on Paul Theology and the Law* Wissenschaftliche Untersuchungen zum Neuen Testament 124. Tübingen: Mohr [Siebeck] 2000.

Tiwald, M., *Hebräer von Hebräer: Paulus auf dem Hintergrund frühjüdischer Argumentation und biblischer Interpretation.* Herders Biblische Studien 52. Freiburg in Breisgau: Herder, 2008.

Tomson, Peter T., *Paul and the Jewish Law: Halakha in the Letters of the Apostle to the Gentiles.* Compendia rerum iudaicarum ad Novum Testamentum III/1. Assen/Maastricht: Van Gorcum; Minneapolis: Fortress Press, 1990.

———. "Paul's Jewish Background in View of his Law: Teaching in 1 Cor 7." Pages 251–270 in *Paul and the Mosaic Law.* Edited by J.D.G. Dunn. Wissenschaftliche Untersuchungen zum Neuen Testament 89. Tübingen: Mohr [Siebeck] 1996.

Towner, Waine S. "Hermeneutical Systems of Hillel and the Tannaim: A Fresh Look." *Hebrew Union College Annual* 53 (1982): 101–135.

Turner, David L. "Matthew 23 as a Prophetic Critique." *Journal of Biblical Studies* 4.1 (January 2004): 23–42.

Turner, Seth. "The Interim, Earthly Messianic Kingdom in Paul." *Journal for the Study of the New Testament* 25 (2003): 323–342.

Turner, Victor. *Anthropology of Performance.* New York: PAJ Publications, 1986.

Ulansey, David M., *Mithras and Perseus: Mithraic Astronomy and the Anatolian Perseus Cult,* Ph.D. diss., Princeton University, 1984.

Van de Sandt, Huub. "Acts 28:28: No Salvation for the People of Israel? An Answer in the Perspective of the LXX." *Ephemerides theologicae lovanienses* 70 (1994): 341–358.

Van der Horst, Peter W. "'Thou Shalt Not Revile the Gods': The LXX Translation of Exodus 22:28(27), Its Background and Influence." *Studia Philonica* 5 (1993): 1–8.

———. "Omgaan met anti-joodse teksten in het Nieuwe Testament." *Appel Kerk en Israel*: 1–13. Cited 25 August 2009. Online: http://www.appelkerkenisrael.nl/Lezingen/pvdhorst.pdf.

Verdet, Jean-Pierre. *Histoire de l'astronomie ancienne et classique.* Paris: PUF, 1998.

Vermes, Geza. *The Complete Dead Sea Scrolls in English*, New York: Penguin, 1997.

Vouga, François. "La fin des Actes comme accomplissement du programme théologique de Luc." Pages 314–323 in *Raconter, interpréter, annoncer. Parcours du Nouveau Testament. Mélanges offerts à Daniel Marguerat pour son 60e anniversaire*. Edited by Emmanuelle Steffek and Yvan Bourquin. Le monde de la Bible, 47. Genève: Labor et Fides, 2003.

Walker, William O. *Interpolation in the Pauline letters*. Journal for the Study of the New Testament Supplement Series 213. Sheffield: Sheffield Academic Press, 2001.

Wallace, Daniel B. "1 Thessalonians: Introduction, Outline, and Argument." *Bible.org*: 1–11. Cited 25 August 2009. Online: http://bible.org/series-page/1-thessalonians-introduction-outline-and-argument.

———. *Is 1 Thessalonians 2:13–16 an Interpolation? Bible.org*: 1–10. Cited 25 August 2009. Online: http://bible.org/article/1-thessalonians-213-16-interpolation.

Wallace, Mark I. *Second Naïveté: Barth, Ricoeur, and the New Yale Theology*. Studies in American Biblical Hermeneutics, 6. 2d ed. Macon, Ga.: Mercer University Press, 1995.

Wanamaker, Charles A. *The Epistles to the Thessalonians: A Commentary on the Greek Text*. Grand Rapids: Eerdmans, 1990.

Wander, B. *Gottesfürchtige und Sympathisanten*. Wissenschaftliche Untersuchungen zum Neuen Testament 104. Tübingen: Mohr [Siebeck], 1998.

Waszink, J. H. *Quinti Septimi Florentis Tertulliani De Anima Edited with Introduction and Commentary*. Amsterdam: Meulenhoff, 1947.

Watson, F., *Paul, Judaism and Gentiles: A Sociological Approach*. Society for New Testament Studies Monograph Series 56. Cambridge: Cambridge University Press, 1986.

———. "I Received from the Lord… Paul, Jesus and the Last Supper." Pages 103–124 in *Jesus and Paul Reconnected: Fresh Pathways into an Old Debate*. Edited by T.D. Still. Grand Rapids: Eerdmans, 2007.

Weatherly, Jon. "The Authenticity of 1 Thessalonians 2.13–16: Additional Evidence." *Journal for the Study of the New Testament* 42 (1991): 79–98.

Wedderburn, A.J.M. "Some Observations on Paul's Use of the Phrases 'In Christ" and "With Christ'." *Journal for the Study of the New Testament* 25 (1985): 83–97.

Weinfeld, Moshe. "Jeremiah and the Spiritual Metamorphosis of Israel." *Zeitschrift für die altestestamentliche Wissenschaft* 80 (1976): 17–56.

Wenham, David. *Paul: Follower of Jesus or Founder of Christianity?* Grand Rapids: Eerdmans, 1995.

Westerholm, S., *Israel's Law and the Church's Faith: Paul and His Recent Interpreters*. Grand Rapids: Eerdmans, 1988.

———. *Perspectives Old and New on Paul: The "Lutheran" Paul and His Critics*. Grand Rapids, Mich.; Eerdmans, 2004.

Williams, M. *The Jews among the Greeks and Romans: A Diasporan Sourcebook*. Baltimore: Johns Hopkins University, 1998.

Williamson, Clark. *Has God Rejected His People? Anti-Judaism in the Christian Church*. Nashville: Abingdon, 1982.

Wilson, Steven G. *The Gentiles and the Gentile Mission in Luke-Acts*. Cambridge: Cambridge University Press, 1973.

Windisch, Hans. *Der zweite Korintherbrief.* Meyers Kommentar. Göttingen: Vandenhoeck & Ruprecht, 1924.

Wischmeyer, Otto. "2 Korinther 12,1–10. Ein autobiographisch-theologischer Text des Paulus." Pages 277–288 in *Von Ben Sira zu Paulus: Gesammelte Aufsätze*. Edited by Eve-Marie Becker. Tübungen: Mohr [Siebeck], 2004.

Wright, J. Eduard. *The Early History of Heaven*. New York: Oxford University Press, 2000.

———. "Biblical Versus Israelite Images of the Heavenly Realm." *Journal for the Study of the Old Testament* 93 (2001): 55–71.

———. "Whither Elijah? The Ascension of Elijah in Biblical and Extrabiblical Traditions." Pages 123–147 in *Things Revealed: Studies in Early Jewish and Christian Literature in Honor of Michael E. Stone*. Edited by Esther G. Chazon, David Satran and Ruth A. Clements. Leiden: Brill, 2004.

Wright, N.T. *The New Testament and the People of God*. London: SPCK, 1992.

———. "Paul and Qumran." *Bible Review* 14.5 (1998): 18–54.

Yarbrough, O. Larry. *Not Like the Gentiles: Marriage Rules in the Letters of Paul*. Society of Biblical Literature Dissertation Series 80. Atlanta: Scholars Press, 1986.

Zeitlin, Solomon. "Hillel and the Hermeneutic Rules." *Jewish Quarterly Review* 54 (1963/1964): 161–173.

www.ingramcontent.com/pod-product-compliance
Lightning Source LLC
Chambersburg PA
CBHW031231090426
42742CB00007B/154

* 9 7 8 0 8 0 9 1 4 7 4 0 3 *